Rites of Birth, Marriage and Death Among the Semites

Rites *of* Birth, Marriage, Death *and* Kindred Occasions Among *the* Semites

by
JULIAN MORGENSTERN

HEBREW UNION COLLEGE PRESS / CINCINNATI

QUADRANGLE BOOKS / CHICAGO

1966

 For information, address: Quadrangle Books, Inc., 180 North Wacker Drive, Chicago 60606. Manufactured in the United States of America.

Library of Congress Catalog Card Number: 66-11867

To

the Memory of

Helen T. Morgenstern

Beloved Wife, Comrade, and Life Partner

and

Loving and Beloved Mother

in Answering Love and Devotion

Preface

This is the latest in a series of scholarly books published under the auspices of the Alumni Association of the Hebrew Union College–Jewish Institute of Religion. Every five years, contributions are made to the Quinquennial Fund by members of the Alumni, on the anniversary of their ordination, in order to support the publication of books of academic worth written by members of the faculty of the College–Institute and by colleagues.

It is to us a source of high gratification that this volume offers another opportunity to express our affection and esteem for the distinguished president emeritus of the Hebrew Union College, Dr. Julian Morgenstern. Almost twenty years have passed since his retirement from the heavy administrative burdens of his office. During part of that time, while he still made his home in Cincinnati, he continued to preside over research seminars in Biblical study, and to set down the results of long years of scientific investigation of Biblical history in essays and books long delayed for want of free time. Since his departure from Cincinnati to Macon, Georgia, he has maintained his habitual unflagging pace, setting a matchless example for colleagues in academic pursuits and in the rabbinate. His eye has not dimmed, and the power of his vigorous pursuit of the meaning of Scripture has not abated. Even while this book is in press, he is busily engaged in further efforts to increase our understanding of the life of our people in Biblical times.

The last time I wrote something for "Morgy," as he is affectionately known to the students of his time, was in 1942 when I wrote a rabbinical thesis on a Biblical theme under his guidance; I am not certain that I ever really expressed to him my profound pleasure at the privilege of learning from him. I am happy, therefore, that the coincidence of my election to office by my colleagues and the publication of this volume gives me the precious opportunity, on behalf of all his students and friends, to say "thank you" to him for all that he has taught us and for all that he did and wanted to do for our beloved Hebrew Union College.

BERTRAM W. KORN, *President,*
Alumni Association of the Hebrew Union College—Jewish Institute of Religion

Author's Note

This book was begun some forty-five years ago and was well under way in 1921, when the manifold duties of the newly assumed presidency of the Hebrew Union College demanded that it be put aside. Not until almost forty years later could work upon it be resumed and the book brought to completion, and this only with the devoted and invaluable assistance, in the literary revision of the original manuscript, of my beloved and loving daughter, Jean H. M. Greenebaum.

Accordingly, we must ask our readers to bear in mind that when we describe beliefs and customs current in the Near East "today," we mean those of forty or more years ago. In more recent times revolutionary changes, particularly in politics, economics, and social and communal relations, have wrought changes in some of the cultural institutions which we have considered. However, in the long view of history, over a span of several thousand years, it cannot be taken amiss if we include the last half-century in our "today."

Together we offer this work to the public in the high hope that it may have some positive value for the history of religion in general, and of Judaism, Christianity, and Islam in particular, and also for the understanding of various institutions and practices of Western social culture of the present day.

J. M.

Contents

Rites of Birth, Marriage and Death Among the Semites

I

Introduction

In the life of every human being three moments have always been critical above all others: the moments of birth, marriage, and death. Even today, civilized man still has a strong sense of their importance. But primitive man, animated almost entirely by immediate, personal considerations, felt intuitively that his own life and the lives of his clan and his tribe depended directly upon the favorable or unfavorable outcome of these three decisive moments.

The problem of self-maintenance, of existence, forced itself upon primitive man in the remotest period of history, when the human mind had just begun to rise above mere animal intuition and habit to the first, vague processes of reasoning thought and purposive action. Experience taught him that, alone, he could not measure his strength successfully with the larger, stronger, and more vicious denizens of the earth. Further experience with animals and his fellow men taught him the value of group organization in conserving and increasing his physical resources. Accordingly, the clan, and then the family, became the earliest units of human existence and social organization. The propagation of children, the consequent increase in the size and strength of the clan, and the safeguarding of the life of every member thereof thus became the primary problems of early man.

All this was still in the infancy of the human race. The concept of God or of gods had not yet evolved. However, the developing human mind vaguely sensed some powerful force beyond the immediate, visible world. Only half of man's existence was spent in the broad light of day, where his senses functioned normally and fully. The other half was passed in the veiling darkness of night, when sight was obscured, when familiar objects took on strange shapes, and mysterious, intangible powers seemed ever present and threatening. And then there was the greater darkness which came with death, when all the senses failed and the body lay still and moldering, and the size and strength of the clan were weakened by so much.

Small wonder, therefore, that the belief in spirits developed early in the mental evolution of mankind—spirits who peopled the earth thickly, unseen yet omnipresent—who caused the countless, strange, inexplicable experiences of existence. Did a leaf rustle or a branch drop from a tree untouched, did the wind blow with unusual violence or unaccustomed sound, did the body itch or a tooth ache, it was the working of some unseen spirit. And when death came through natural causes, and the body lay in lifelike form, yet with life completely gone, cold, rigid, motionless, and presently decomposition set in, again it was a spirit of the unseen world which had wrought this.

Small wonder, too, that in the main these spirits were conceived of as evil. The human mind accepts the good things of life as matters of course, as man's natural due or as his own fabrications, the fruit of the labor of his hands, as something normal, therefore easily comprehended and requiring no explanation. But the unhappy experiences of life—misfortunes, sufferings, vain struggles, and bitter disappointments—give pause and bid man seek explanation. Invariably he finds this explanation outside himself and his world. He blames luck or fate or chance or God—or the devil, perhaps, if he is a modern, an evil spirit if he is a primitive man.

Therefore, in the mind of early man evil spirits far exceeded good in both number and power. Moreover, they were particularly active and malevolent, and mere humans were susceptible to their attacks, especially at such critical moments of life as birth, marriage, childbearing, and death. Consequently, the pressing problem of primitive existence took the practical form of safeguarding human life against these evil spirits, either by placating them in order to win their favor and protection or at least to render them indifferent and harmless, or, if this was impossible, by warding off their attacks just as one would ward off the attack of an earthly enemy, whether man or beast.

This principle of placating the evil spirits or of warding off their attacks was much the same as with a human foe, but the application necessarily differed. In primitive society the principle that might is right was almost universally valid. Possession through might was therefore possession through right. Accordingly, wherever evil spirits had prevailed over a human being, he was in their possession; he was their property by right of their might, and they were free to work their malignant will upon him without restraint. His life was completely forfeit to them, and they could take it from him at whatever moment they pleased; then he would die. From this possession by evil spirits he had to be freed. A man might be redeemed from their power by the offering of gifts, which would seem to them equal in value to his life. Or a counterattack might be made on the evil spirits in order to expel them forcibly from his body, or from whatever of his it was of which they had taken possession. And once persuaded or compelled to relinquish possession, effective safeguards had to be set up to constrain these spirits thereafter.

Thus, evil spirits might be induced to relinquish their hold upon a man's life or property by means of a gift of redemption—in other words, a sacrifice. Perhaps the underlying idea was that evil spirits, much like human beings, might regard an assured sacrifice in the present as preferable to an uncertain human life in the future; for they had to face the consideration that a human life might in some unforeseen manner be snatched from their power. Occasionally, again like poor mortals, evil spirits might be tricked or deceived into relinquishing their right of possession; for, although of abundant power, evil spirits, precisely like men, were at times extraordinarily stupid or gullible. Or evil spirits might be cast out by the performance of certain rites which primitive human imagination and reason suggested and which experience seemed to have proved efficacious. Once expelled, they might be kept from regaining possession through the repetition at the proper moments of sacrifices, rites, or other safeguards.

These redemptive sacrifices usually had a fairly uniform character and manner of offering, since the resources of primitive men were necessarily limited. However, the rites of repelling or casting out evil spirits were varied and manifold. They might consist of many different ceremonies of exorcism or of the recitation of innumerable incantations of varying content and form. These ceremonies and incantations might be joined, repeated, and expanded in countless complex combinations—for, presumably, if one ceremony or incantation was effective, its repetition or its association with other similar ceremonies or incantations would be doubly so.

This might be called magic by some; by others it might be termed religion. It was magic so long as the ceremonies of exorcism and the presumptive reaction of the spirits thereto were mechanical, automatic, invariable, and impersonal. It was transformed into religion when these spirits had ceased to be conceived of as impersonal, mechanical powers, and had become personalities, mischievous and malevolent, with evil designs and individual and varying powers and impulses, beings which could be placated and rendered indifferent or even friendly by sacrifice and homage, or opposed and frustrated by incantation and exorcism.

From these primitive beginnings, in part at least, religion has evolved. Sacrifice developed, became systematized, and in time invested with new, larger, and more positive meaning. Incantation and homage grew into prayer and reverence. Many of our own cherished rites and ceremonies today had their beginnings in ancient beliefs and practices. The study of rites and ceremonies, their origin and history, is therefore of more than passing interest and significance.

Rites of birth, marriage, and death have been examined again and again, and interesting and ofttimes valid conclusions have been established. In many respects this is not a new study, as the many authoritative works by eminent scholars cited in the notes will indicate. In one essential respect, however, this study differs from its predecessors in that it confines itself strictly to a limited field, viz., the Semitic peoples and those nations and racial and religious groups which came into direct cultural contact with them or which evolved from them. This limitation of investigation is intentional. The almost countless theories in regard to the origin of circumcision, for example, each backed by the authority of some eminent scholar, is the best proof of the uncertainty and confusion resulting from extending the range of a study such as this over too wide a field. It does not follow with absolute, logical certainty, that, because circumcision was practiced by Semitic peoples and also by the aborigines of Australia, a single, common concept and purpose must constitute the origin of the practice among both groups. Such may have been the case, but logically it need not have been. The correct scientific procedure would be to investigate thoroughly the origin and history of the institution of circumcision within each group, then to compare the conclusions reached so that it may be determined what, if anything, these practices have in common, rather than to assume unquestioningly that they have everything in common, that they are in every respect one and the same ceremony, with practically identical origin and purpose and parallel historic development. In other words, an investigation such as this belongs rather to the field of ethnology than to that of anthropology. For this reason this study limits itself to the investigation of rites of birth, marriage, death, and related moments among the Semites and their immediate neighbors.

Our sources of enlightenment are rich indeed. The monuments of ancient Semitic cultures unearthed in excavations, the Bible and other ancient Semitic writings, and the records of classical and medieval authors, are supplemented by the varied and informative accounts of observant travelers and ethnologists of modern times. Hence, our knowledge from these varied sources is sufficient to permit far-reaching conclusions. In general, the method employed was to work backward from the known present to the less known or unknown past, to collate the significant material furnished by modern travelers and observers bearing upon the particular topic under consideration, and from this to trace the various ceremonies and institutions until their origins, fundamental purposes, and subsequent histories became apparent.

II

Birth Rites of the Modern Urban and Rural Semites

Practically all primitive peoples, not only in ancient times but also today, regard the period immediately following birth as critical for both mother and child, especially for the latter. They believe that evil spirits threaten the frail, little body from all sides,[1] that even the very deity who gave the child its life may, in a changed and contrary mood, seek to recall his gift. Due precautions must be taken to avert these dangers. Accordingly, many rites of varying nature are regularly performed. These may be partly magical, designed to ward off the threatening evil powers, and partly devotional, in that they imply due recognition of the prior, proprietary right of the deity or spirit which has given life, and seek to conciliate him by sacrifice, prayer, and other tokens of submission and homage. Many such ceremonies are practiced by Semitic peoples today.

In Syria every newborn child is rubbed with a piece of dough which has been kneaded with sesame oil. This is then shaped into a kind of cross and fastened, so that everyone can see it, upon the door of the room in which the child lies. The purpose of this ceremony is to avert the evil eye. Similarly, among the Moslems of Jerusalem every newborn child is received in a wooden vessel, is washed in warm water, is anointed with oil and salt, and is often rubbed with myrtle. After the midwife has placed the baby in the cradle, she takes a mortar, knocks upon it, and says, "Boys and girls are the illusions . . . of midwives."[2]

The Yezidis, living in the vicinity of Sheikh Adi, consider it of prime importance that their children be baptized immediately after birth in the holy waters of the stream which flows near their sanctuary. Those not dwelling near this sacred stream also have their children baptized in its water, which is brought in skins for this purpose by *cawwals,* a class of inferior priests.[3] Differing slightly from this account, Layard states that the Yezidis give the name immediately after birth, but that the rite of baptism is reserved for a future day, when the child can be carried to the tomb of Sheikh Adi and can bear immersion in the sacred waters.[4] Elsewhere, however, he says that, if possible, the baptism takes place within seven days after birth, and that the Yezidis circumcise their sons at the same age and in the same manner as do the Moslems.[5] Another traveler likewise states that the Yezidis baptize their children upon the seventh day after birth.[6] Our most authoritative chronicler of the beliefs and practices of this strange people records that they practice both circumcision and baptism in imitation of their Jewish and Christian neighbors, and that the rite of baptism ought to be performed before the end of the first week, but, if not done then, surely within the first two months, and under all circumstances before the completion of the first two years.[7]

In Moslem Palestine: "As soon as a child is born, it is rolled up in clothes which have been sprinkled with salt in order to harden the skin and prevent the child from being injured by the air, to which it is now exposed for the first time. The common people do not unwrap these for two or three days."[8] Elsewhere we are told: "When a baby is born, be it boy or girl, they are immediately plunged into a bath of salt brine, and, after being well massaged, are powdered again with fine salt, this being kept up until the day of weaning."[9]

Likewise: "In Syria and Palestine it is still the custom to cover new-born children with salt. A native mother can not imagine how any child is not thus favored. 'Poor thing,' she will say, 'it was not salted at all.' "[10]

An outstanding authority in the field of Palestinian folklore states: "The midwife . . . bathes the baby and anoints its body with oil in which fine powdered salt has been dissolved. This is believed to strengthen the skin and enable it to resist external forces. A common belief insists that non-salted children have a weak and silly character. Formerly the midwife used to powder the skin after, or even without, first anointing it . . . with pure, fine salt sifted through a piece of gauze, which procedure of course often resulted in breaking the skin. This again is a very ancient practice, for we read of it in Ezekiel 16 : 4, which compares the city of Jerusalem in its state of corruption to a wretched child 'that was not salted at all.' "[11] Elsewhere, interpreting from present-day practice the full import of the Ezekiel passage, the same author tells us: "The greatest disgrace for anyone is to be called an *ibn ḥaram* or *bandūq,* bastard. Only a *bandūq* is neglected and not salted after birth. In certain parts of Syria to say to a person that he was not 'salted' upon birth is to invite trouble."[12]

Again: "A newborn child undergoes the same procedure as in Ezekiel's time. It is bathed in warm water, and during the first week it is rubbed over its entire body with fine salt, is smeared with oil and wrapped in swaddling garments. Thereupon its mouth and eyes are anointed, and its eyes, forehead and sutures are bound with cotton, and the entire head is well wrapped. The washing with salt is to strengthen the child. From the fourth to the seventh day the salt is mixed with oil, and from then on to the fortieth day the child is washed in soap-water."[13]

Another observer says: "The midwife attends to the dressing of the baby. She rubs the little body with salt and oil and swaddles it tightly. This woman attendant comes every day for forty days to cleanse and wrap the child. Woe betide the mother or any other meddler who interferes with the wrapping and other peculiar functions of the midwife, who is very jealous of the dignity of her profession."[14] And, to cite one more account: "As soon as born, the child is rubbed all over with salt and oil, and wrapped in old garments; on the third day it is again rubbed with salt and oil, or very frequently with a mixture of salt and red earth instead. On the seventh day it has a bath, and from that day till the fortieth it is washed about once a week. After the fortieth day, infants are not washed again till they can talk, the only exception being that the face is sometimes cleaned with a little milk, but never with water. Such is the general practice, but it varies a good deal in different parts of the country."[15] That this custom of salting the newborn child was practiced in ancient Israel is, as we have learned, attested by Ezekiel 16 : 4.[16]

In Upper Egypt the following ceremonies attend the birth of a child: "The newly-born child is merely dried, not washed, and immediately laid upon a corn-sieve; beside its head lies the knife with which the umbilical cord has been cut, and corn is scattered round about. This procedure is intended to drive away the *karina,* that is the child's evil brother or sister from the spirit realm, that always makes its appearance and torments the poor child of humanity till it sickens and falls into convulsions, which are therefore also called *karina.* Immediately after the birth the mother receives melted butter with honey and fenugreek, and instead of fasting she must daily eat at least a fowl or a good piece of meat, which her female friends and neighbors give her. On the sixth day the mother in her turn sends these a plate of *kishk* (a decoction of wheat and sour milk) as a sign that they are invited for the following day. Above the head of the sleeping child is placed on this night a pitcher hung with gold coins and lighted with tapers, the pitcher being long-necked (*dorâk*) in the case of boys, short-necked (*kulleh*) in that of girls.

"On the morning of the seventh day (*yûm es-subû'a*) the house is filled with female visitors. The child is placed upon a sieve, tapers are fixed upon metal plates and on the point of a sword, and the child is carried in procession through the whole house, while the midwife scatters *bissle,* that is wheat, barley, peas, and salt, as provender for the wicked spirits. The child is shaken in the sieve, being thereby believed to lose fear for the rest of its life, and its eyes are held up to the sun to sharpen them. The cymbals and small drums, the singing and trilling of the women, make the outer world acquainted with the joy within the house. The guests present the mother and midwife with money and gold, for which they distribute parched chick-peas, St. John's bread, and walnuts.

"But the father must also keep the seventh day as a festival, especially if the child is a boy, though in many cases he does not dare up till this time to look upon his own child, since he might possibly, and quite against his will, do some harm to his tender offspring by a glance of his eye. He invites his friends to a feast, and entertains them with Koran reading, *zikrs,* and similar pious amusements, or sends for instrumental players, singers, and dancing girls. The son is brought in a sieve[17] and shown to the guests, who rejoice with the father, and perhaps also leave some gifts. A plate of candy-sugar is now sent to the kadi or some other theologian; he sucks it, and lets the sweet fluid trickle from the consecrated mouth into that of the child, and 'gives him the name out of his mouth.' This is accordingly a kind of baptism.

"On the fortieth day after childbirth the mother goes with the child to the bath, and gets forty dishfuls of water poured over her head if her offspring is a boy, and thirty-nine if it is a girl. The child also is now bathed for the first time, and mother and child are now clean and purified."[18]

A detailed account of similar ceremonies practiced at birth by the Moslems of Lower Egypt is given by Lane.[19] "One of the first duties is to wrap the new-born child in clean white linen, or in linen of some other color, but not yellow. After this some person (not a female) should pronounce the adán in the ear of the infant, because the Prophet did so in the ear of El-Ḥasan when Fatimeh gave birth to him; or he should pronounce the adán in the right ear, and the iḳámeh (which is nearly the same) in the left.

"It was formerly the custom of many of the Arabs, and perhaps is still among some, for the father to give a feast to his friends on seven successive days after the birth of a son; but that of a daughter was observed with less rejoicing. The general modern custom is to give an entertainment only on the seventh day, which is called Yóm es-Subooạ.

"On this occasion, in the families of the higher classes, professional female singers are hired to entertain a party of ladies, friends of the infant's mother, who visit her on this occasion, in the ḥareem; or a concert of instrumental music, or a recitation of the whole of the Ḳur-án, is performed below by men.

"The mother, attended by the midwife, being seated in a chair which is the property of the latter, the child is brought, wrapped in a handsome shawl or something costly; and, to accustom it to noise, that it may not be frightened afterwards by the music and other sounds of mirth, one of the women takes a brass mortar and strikes it repeatedly with the pestle, as if pounding. After this, the child is put into a sieve and shaken, it being supposed that this operation is beneficial to its stomach. Next, it is carried through all the apartments of the ḥareem, accompanied by several women or girls, each of whom bears a number of wax candles, sometimes of various colors, cut in two, lighted, and stuck into small lumps of paste of ḥenna, upon a small round tray. At the same time the midwife or another female sprinkles upon the floor of each room a mixture of salt with seed of the fennel-flower, or salt alone, which has been placed during the preceding night at the infant's head; saying as she does this, 'The salt be in the eye of the person who does not bless the Prophet,' or 'The foul salt be in the eyes of the envier.' This ceremony of the sprinkling of salt is considered a preservative for the child and mother from the evil eye; and each person present should say, 'O God, bless our lord Mohammed!' The child, wrapped up and placed on a fine mattress, which is sometimes laid on a silver tray, is shown to each of the women present, who looks at its face, says, 'O God, bless our lord Mohammed!' 'God give thee long life!' etc., and usually puts an embroidered handkerchief, with a gold coin (if pretty or old, the more esteemed) tied up in one of the corners, on the child's head, or by its side. This giving of handkerchiefs and gold is considered as imposing a debt, to be repaid by the mother, if the donor should give her the same occasion, or as the discharge of a debt for a similar offering. The coins are generally used for some years to decorate the head dress of the child. After these presents for the child, others are given for the midwife. During the night before the seventh-day's festivity, a water-bottle full of water (a dórak̩ in the case of a boy, and a k̩ulleh in that of a girl), with an embroidered handkerchief tied round the neck, is placed at the child's head while it sleeps. This, with the water it contains, the midwife takes and puts upon a tray and presents it to each of the women who put presents of money for her into the tray. In the evening the husband generally entertains a party of his friends.

"On this day, or on the fourteenth, twenty-first, twenty-eighth, or thirty-fifth day after birth, several religious ceremonies are required to be performed; but they are most approved if observed on the seventh day. One of these is the naming. I believe, however, that it is a more common custom to give the name almost immediately after the birth or about three hours after. No ceremony is observed on account of the naming.

"On the same day, however, two practices which I am about to mention are prescribed to be observed though, as far as my observations and inquiries allow me to judge, they are generally neglected by the modern Muslims. The first of these is a sacrifice. The victim is called ʿak̩eek̩ah. It should be a ram or goat; or two such animals should be sacrificed for a son, and one for a daughter. This rite is regarded by Ibn-Ḥambal as absolutely obligatory: he said, 'If a father sacrifice not for his son, and he (the son) die, that son will not intercede for him on the day of judgment.' The founders of the three other principal sects regard it in different and less important lights, though Moḥammed slew an ʿak̩eek̩ah for himself after his prophetic mission. The person should say, on slaying the victim, 'O God, this ʿak̩eek̩ah is a ransom for my son, such a one; its blood for his blood, and its flesh for his flesh, and its bone for his bone, and its skin for his skin, and its hair for his hair. O God, make it a ransom for my son from hell fire.' A bone of the victim should not be broken. The midwife should receive a leg of it. It should be cooked without previously cutting off any portion of it; and part of it should be given in alms.

"After this should be performed the other ceremony above alluded to, which is this: . . . It is a sunneh ordinance incumbent upon the father, to shave or cause to be shaved the head of the child, and to give in alms to the poor the weight of the hair in gold or silver. This should also be done for a proselyte. On the subsequent occasions of shaving the head of a male child (for the head of a male is frequently shaven), a tuft of hair is generally left on the crown, and commonly for several years another one also over the forehead.

"Circumcision is most approved if performed on the same day; but the observance of this rite is generally delayed until the child has attained the age of five or six years, and sometimes several years later."

At Tlemcen, in Morocco, the following birth ceremonies are generally observed: "On the seventh day the name is given to the child. For this ceremony the father assembles his friends, kills a sheep, if he is able, and makes a feast. Frequently also a cock is killed if the child be a boy and a hen if it be a girl; of this soup is made, which the mother drinks. On this day the infant is washed and clothed in new garments; the midwife anoints his hands and feet with henna, and then makes him stretch forth his hand, and the visiting women deposit in it pieces of money, destined for the mother.

"On the evening of this day the child ought not to be put into its cradle, nor on the following thirty-three nights; a small mattress, prepared by the grandmother on the mother's side or by some relative of the mother, is placed upon the ground. Before placing the child upon this, the midwife makes seven marks in a straight line with henna upon the wall by the head of the child and places at its side a lighted candle of green wax.

"The ceremonies which attend the birth conclude with a grand banquet upon the fortieth day, which is the one upon which the young infant is returned to its little cradle. If this banquet is to be upon a grand scale, it is held preferably in the country, in the garden of some friend.

"At the conclusion of this period the child is still subjected to various magical practices, which are intended not only to protect it, but also to free it from the evil spirits which, despite everything to the contrary, might still have entered into it."[20]

In Nablus the following custom is, or at least was formerly, observed in anticipation of childbirth: "The midwife or the matron who assists draws near holding in her hand a live serpent, with which she girds the loins of the patient. The serpent is for some moments wrapped like a cord about the body of the expectant mother. Then it is stretched around the *djawrah,* and finally its head is cut off. The bloody head is carried by the patient until her delivery. . . . The purpose of this practice is to protect the newly-born infant against the attacks of *qarînah,* always eager to strangle the little human being when he first comes forth into the light. . . . It is the blood of the serpent which wards off *qarînah*."[21]

Among the Moslems of Constantinople "a red handkerchief is bound round the mother's head, and a gauze veil of the same color is thrown over her temples. To the former is attached a bunch of charms similar to those which decorate the baby's cap, and a head of garlic fastened to a stick is propped up in a corner of the room. The Peres of the Moslems do not, like the Nereids and Vilas of the Christians, appear to be in the habit of carrying off new-born babes, but they are not the less to be guarded against, and the mother and child should not be left alone until after the bath ceremony has taken place, for fear of their being possessed by them. If, as among the poor, this is sometimes unavoidable, a broom is placed by the bedside as a preventive of evil consequences, and the red veil and kerchief are also calculated to drive away all uncanny visitors."[22] The bath ceremony referred to takes place at some suitable time between the third and the eighth day after birth.

Likewise, among the Moslem Albanians the father must keep away from the child and may not see it until it is eight days old. The mother and the child may not leave the house for the first forty days, nor may they after sunset leave the room, in which a fire is kept constantly burning. Whoever enters the house after nightfall must leap over a firebrand placed upon the threshold. Music and singing are also refrained from in order not to attract the powers of the air. A lock of the first hair of the child is cut ceremonially upon the seventh day after birth. This is placed, with some coins, in a purse and is kept there for three days. The money is then taken out of the purse, and the hair is burned. The Christian Albanians perform a similar ceremony when the child is a year old.[23]

"Among the Shiite Moslems of Persia the child is salted on the day of birth in accordance with an ancient custom. A talisman upon which verses from the Koran and prayers are written is fastened to the right arm,[24] or put somewhere near the body in order to preserve the infant from sickness, and especially from the evil eye. If the child be a girl, then at the end of seven days it is put in a hard cradle, wrapped tightly in swaddling clothes. . . . Girl babies are never taken out of doors until after the lapse of forty days, and boys not until three months, in order to guard them against expressions of admiration on the part of people who see them for the first time, for this might endanger them from the evil eye. Occasionally too, when a child is born they throw a man's trousers upon him so that the devils may not carry him away."[25]

All these ceremonies are magical in character. Their evident purpose is to guard the infant against the threatening dangers, and to ensure for it the blessings of health, strength of limbs, and length of life. With the dough, myrtle, red earth, henna, and similar substances, whatever dangerous pollution may have adhered to the child at birth is wiped away. Likewise, the cross-shaped piece of dough, fastened to the door of the child's room, absorbs or wards off the evil glance of all who enter or pass by. The head of garlic, the broom, the lighted candle at the baby's head, the burning brand upon the threshold, and the fire kept burning in the room are also effective safeguards against the demons. Iron, too, is effective for this purpose.[26] Above all else, salt, with which the newborn child is so commonly rubbed during the first seven days after birth, is employed to ward off the attacks of evil spirits.[27]

III

Birth Rites of the Modern Bedouin

Kindred practices among the nomadic Bedouin tribes of Arabia Petraea, living in the main upon a decidedly more primitive level of civilization than their urban or even than their rural, agrarian fellow Semites, are described in detail by Musil.[1]

Among the Ṣẖûr the newborn child is rubbed with oil and salt on the first and seventh days after birth. In exceptional cases it is washed in thin buttermilk and then rubbed with salt. No sacrifice is brought.

The ʿAmârîn wash the newborn child in lukewarm water and rub it with salt daily for an entire week. Were this not performed the child, they believe, would be very timorous.

In el-Kerak the newborn child is called by a special name or title, *Ṭwêreš;* it is smeared over its entire body with salt and olive oil, even in its mouth and ears. This is done once each day for seven days. It is then washed in cow-urine.

The practice of the Ḥwêṭât is to put clarified butter mixed with sulfur into the mouth of the child (*yuḥannikûh*); here, too, the infant is called *Ṭwêreš.*

Among the Terâbîn the child is purified with water and salt during the first seven days (called *sabaʿat el wǧûb,* i.e., "the seven days of need, danger, or death"); then it is washed in camel-urine and rubbed with salt.

Among the Terâbîn, the ʿAzâzme, and the Tijâha, on the seventh day the sacrifice, *Sabuʿ* (i.e., "the sacrifice of the seventh day"), or *Ṭulûʿ,* is offered. The sacrificer says, "This is the sacrifice (literally, 'redemption') for the face of God . . . ." The child, which up to that time is called only by the general name *Lâfi* or *Libbâd,* is then given its personal name and the bystanders congratulate the father.

Among the ʿAzâzme the sacrifice (*Mrûḳa*) is offered after seven days. The sacrificer says: "You must declare us free that we may live. I perform a holy rite and may God accept it for good."

The Ẓullâm say while sacrificing, "O Face of God, this belongs to Thee."

The Saʿîdijjîn offer the *Mrûḳa* already on the third day, and say thereupon:

"O Face of God, this belongs to Thee. What Thou hast given be not greedy for." With the blood of the sacrificed animal, they smear the forehead of the child.

According to the opinion of the ʿAmârîn, the sacrifice, called *Mrûḳa* or *Bdûl,* made on the eighth day after birth, is absolutely indispensable. It is regarded as being more important than the *Daḥîyye*-sacrifice.[2]

The Ṣẖûr give the child its personal name on the fortieth day after birth. Until this time it is called *Ḥreyyân* ("excrementer"). This naming ceremony is as follows: the family prepares a meal of bread and clarified butter, and invites the chiefs of the encampment. When the guests have assembled, the cousin, uncle, or brother of the mother takes the boy, brings him before the assembly, and lays him upon the arms of one of the most respected of those present, called *ṣâḥeb al-baẖt* ("master of the horoscope" or "of luck"), who proceeds to name the infant. Each one present then presents the child with a gift.

Among the Ḥwêṭât the father sacrifices a goat or a sheep for the boy, and sprinkles (*yumalliḥû;* literally, "salts") him with the blood of the animal. The mother cooks the flesh, puts it on a platter, then takes the boy, and, accompanied by a maiden, carries the platter into the men's part of the tent. She lays the child in the arms of a respected man (*ṣâḥeb baẖt*), puts the platter before him, and says, "We come to thee so that thou mayest name this newborn child." He thereupon takes saliva from his mouth, puts it into the child's mouth, breathes upon the infant, and says, "Receive saliva from my saliva, and go after my way, and you shall be called N.N."

In el-Kerak, if a child is born on Friday it is thought that it will be unlucky. Therefore it must be freed from misfortune. For this purpose a cock or a kid is sacrificed, the child is smeared with the blood, and the animal is then buried at the spot where the child was born.

Elsewhere,[3] Musil reports the birth practices of the Rwala Bedouin: "When a son is born, the father is congratulated by his nearest relatives but expresses no particular joy; neither does he send out invitations to a meat supper. No animal is sacrificed or slaughtered at the birth of a boy or a girl.

"For seven days after its birth the child is bathed in camel-urine and rubbed with salt. On either the tenth, twentieth, or fortieth day, wheat is gathered by the female relatives of the confined woman, shredded, and then a dinner is prepared from it in her tent, to which all the women of the camp are invited. This festivity is known as 'the examination of the child,' *ṭlâʿat alʿajjel.* The mother goes with the child on a visit to all her relatives, a custom called *taṭlîʿa.* Everybody presents the babe with something, often either a young camel or a colt, the gifts remaining its property."

Certain interesting and significant details of birth ceremonies are also recorded by Curtiss.[4] He says: "For a boy, when he is seven days old, they offer a sacrifice without breaking a bone, because they fear that if a bone of the sacrifice should be broken, the child's bones would be broken too." And again: "A man who has not had a child promises a fedou that he may receive the gift from a certain saint. If it should be born, when it is several [the German edition says "seven"; this is probably correct] days old, they put the blood of the sacrifice offered in payment of the vow on its forehead."

An emir of the Mwâli Arabs gave Curtiss the following account of ceremonies attendant upon the birth of a child: "The child must be taken on a pilgrimage to the shrine to which the sheik of the tribe belongs. The minister of the shrine sacrifices for them near the threshold. The child is anointed on his forehead or on his nose with a mark of the blood of the victim. They afterwards cook the meat and have a feast. The relatives and all who are present partake. The important thing is that the child should be present. If the shrine is too far away, they can sacrifice at their tents. The blood is important."

Likewise among the Bedouin the newborn child is washed in camel-urine "in order that his limbs may become strong."[5]

The underlying thought and purpose of all these ceremonies is readily apparent. Misfortune, danger, and even death threaten the newborn child and must be averted. Without these ceremonies the child would be unlucky or timorous, or its life might be forfeited. Not until these rites have been properly performed can it be said with assurance that the child will live. Until then, therefore, the child is called by the generic, impersonal name *Ṭwêreš, Lâfi, Libbâd,* or *Ḥreyyân.* Only after the performance of the prescribed rites is the infant ready to receive its own, proper, personal name. According to a fundamental Semitic concept, the name is an integral part of the thing or person, and therefore not until the child has received its own distinguishing name can it be considered to have its own identity. Thus it is clear that the performance of these rites marks the close of the short, impersonal, and unreal period of the child's existence and heralds his entrance into real, personal, individual life.

These ceremonies are plainly of a twofold nature, magical and devotional. The magical rites include rubbing the child with salt or oil, washing it with camel- or cow-urine, and putting some of the saliva of a highly respected man into the child's mouth and having him breathe upon the infant. The devotional procedures include the recital of the various formulas and prayers and the sacrifices and attendant rites. This sacrifice, called *fedû* or *fedw* ("ransom") or *ʿaḳîḳah,*[6] is entirely of a substitutionary character. It clearly recognizes that the deity or spirit which gave the infant life has the prior right to that life, and that consequently something of value and, in a sense, of similar character must be offered in exchange, the animal's life in redemption of the life of the child. As a token thereof the blood of the sacrifice is frequently smeared upon the head of the child.[7] The deity is thus induced to renounce his prior right. Hence the significance of the declaration of the ʿAzâzme, "You must declare us free, that we may live," and of the formula of the Saʿîdijjîn, "O Face of God, this belongs to Thee. What thou hast given be not greedy for."

IV

Evil Spirits at Birth

Further corroboration of this conclusion, that peculiar danger, particularly from evil spirits, threatens the newborn child during the first seven days after birth,[1] is to be found in the consideration of the following evidence.

Goldziher[2] repeats the tradition recorded by Buchārī, that the Arabs used to bring their newborn children to ʿAyisha, the wife of the prophet, in order to have her bless them. When she removed the pillows she found a razor laid under the head of the child. "We do this," they said, "in order to protect the child from demons."

Among the Jews of Hungary, and in fact among most Orthodox Jews, the night before the circumcision of a boy is called "watchnight." They believe that it is necessary to keep watch on this night, because the *šedîm,* the evil spirits, have power over the child so long as it is uncircumcised, and seek to use this power, particularly on the night before the circumcision, that is, the seventh night after birth.[3] Among the native Jews of Jerusalem a black line is made with a piece of charcoal on the walls of the room in which the mother of a newborn child lies. Nothing may be borrowed from the house during the first seven days after birth, least of all fire. Meanwhile, the father appoints one or two of his acquaintances, who are charged with the task of studying the sacred writings during the nights. The father also designates two women who are to sit beside the bed of the mother throughout the nights, in order to guard her from all evil.[4]

Of the Turkish Jews we are told that, "like the Greek baby before baptism, the Jewish infant must be carefully watched until this ceremony (circumcision, upon the eighth day) has been performed, and especially on the day preceding it. For Ashmedai, the chief of the *šedîm*, or demons, is believed to be lying in wait to stifle the child, if left for a moment unguarded."[5] Hanauer states that he was informed by a Spanish Jewess living in Palestine that for nine days after birth the mother and the child should not be left alone in a room, for La Broosha might come in the shape of a cat, and take away the child.[6] It is also a common superstition among Orthodox Jews, originating in the late Biblical period,[7] that Lilith has power to carry off newborn children, and that therefore both mother and child must be provided with proper amulets and charms.[8] In Palestine it is popularly believed that Lilith's power over a boy endures for eight days after birth, over a girl for twenty days.[9] Since in origin Lilith seems to be related to the Babylonian trinity, Lilū, Lilītu, and Ardat Lilī (the female servant of Lilū[10]), the concept of an evil spirit by this name may have developed primarily among Babylonian Jews. Actually, Lilith seems to have more in common with the last member of this evil trinity than with the two others. According to ancient Jewish folk tradition, the first human being, through a popular misinterpretation of Genesis 1 : 27, was regarded as having been androgynous, a composite male and female creature. When the two parts separated, the female part became the demonic being, Lilith. The Rabbis of the Talmud conceived of this demon as having the form of a woman, with flowing locks.[11] She consorts sexually with other demons, but also visits human beings in sexual dreams. She is intensely jealous of human offspring and seeks eagerly to take their lives in early infancy. When she can find no other prey, she attacks even her own children.[12]

A like role, particularly as it affects not only newborn infants but also pregnant women and recent brides, is played by Ḳarīna, or Ḳarinyeh, in the superstitions of the Moslems of Syria, Palestine, Egypt, and Northern Africa.[13] In fact, in Palestine she is actually the Moslem counterpart of the Jewish Lilith.[14] Her power over infants endures for the full seven days after birth and reaches its climax upon the night which marks the transition from the seventh to the eighth day.

Closely related to Ḳarīna, and in fact frequently identified with her in the superstitions of Palestine, Hedjaz, and Northern Africa, is the female demon, Umm-eṣ-ṣubyān.[15] Snouck Hurgronje describes the Meccan belief in this demon as follows: "Who is it that causes all these evils (for example, the death of infants in great numbers)? It is *Umm ec-cibjān,* alias *Qarīnah;* the female monsters who bear this name never allow mothers to enjoy their happiness undisturbed, but they speedily attack the children themselves, or else they take away the nourishment of the mother."[16] According to Doutté, the name Umm-eṣ-ṣubyān means "the mother of children," in the sense of "she who does harm to children."[17]

Likewise, according to Doutté,[18] in the Ethiopian apocryphal writings a demon named Ouerzelyia plays a role similar to that of Lilith and Umm-eṣ-ṣubyān. A particular, awesome Moroccan demon, more or less identical with Umm-eṣ-ṣubyān, is the Tábʿa. "She attacks both men and women, renders them sterile, causes the death of their children in early infancy, makes them wasteful or addicted to some particular vice, or kills their animals." She is invisible, and because of this is much more active, destructive, and feared than most demons.[19] Still another Moroccan demon, also closely related to Umm-eṣ-ṣubyān, "is a great danger to newborn babes. She comes in the shape of a bird, though she has breasts like those of a goat which are filled with blood, and if the child sucks her breast, it will die at once. As a protection against her a vessel filled with water is placed close to the child's head every night during the first week, and a net is generally hung at the door of the house or at the back of the tent, as it is from this side that the bird usually enters the place, and there it is left for forty days."[20]

In Palestine, too, a child is thought to be in particular danger, especially at the time of its circumcision, from the evil eye (*ʿēn*) or the evil soul (*nafs*).[21] Also: "There are several other demons who attack children. Sickly and weak infants—through their lowered vitality—are especially prone to be injured. All convulsions, palsies, tremors and epilepsy are caused by demons. The most dangerous evil spirits are those causing convulsions and epilepsy. They take the form of a 'flying bird.' "[22]

One of the demons "most dreaded by the Bedouins is a female spirit called *sarʿat aš-šíbe*. In appearance she is a tall, thin woman wearing a dress made of leather. This spirit wanders about the desert from camp to camp, looking for children. If she hears a child crying, she crawls near, gropes about for it with her hands till she finds it, then catches it and runs with it to her own kin. There the child is torn partly open, its blood sucked by all the spirits present, and its flesh devoured raw."[23]

Furthermore: "A *ḳurṭa* or *ḳârûẓ* is a spirit who destroys newly born boys, but does its work unobserved. If a Rwejli is married to a woman who has born him several sons, all of whom have died after a short time, and if the same thing happens with the second wife, then he knows for certain that it is a *ḳurṭa* who has done him this wrong. To appease the spirit he procures a cock with green feathers on its neck and waits until his wife comes to childbed again. When her time is near, with the live cock he draws in his tent seven circles, one within the other, kills the cock in the seventh in the center, buries it there, and lays his wife over that spot. She will then bear without any pain, and her son will not die, because the *ḳurṭa* has been given what belonged to it, *ḥaḳḳ al-ḳârûẓ*."[24]

Analogous beliefs and practices are to be found among most Semitic peoples. Somewhat similar to the above must have been the role of the ancient Accadian demon, Labartu.[25] The Shiite Persians regarded the demon *Al* as dangerous to both mother and child. *Al* is really a childbirth sickness, viz., fever of the milk, to which the mother is subject during the seven days after delivery, and which is usually fatal to both parent and offspring. This demon is pictured as a young woman, of pleasing form and ruddy color, and with hair the color of red tulips; the word *Al* literally means "scarlet." To guard against this demon, three onions are suspended at the head of the mother, who during the seven days after delivery is never addressed by her proper name. Moreover, during the first six days the child remains at the side of its mother and is not put into its cradle. On the seventh day the child is deposited in the cradle with appropriate ceremonies.[26]

All this evidence, and it might be multiplied extensively, establishes clearly that from the earliest stages of Semitic cultural evolution down to the present day the lives of both the mother in childbirth and the infant just born were thought to be directly threatened by evil spirits: not merely evil spirits in general, but specific demons, many of whom were so far individualized as to have their own personal names and their own traditional appearances by which they could always be recognized. Their power was usually thought to endure for the seven days immediately following birth and to culminate upon the last day, particularly during the night thereof, when accordingly the danger to both mother and child was greatest, and therefore all safeguards had to be redoubled. Not infrequently this danger was thought to persist for a full forty days after birth. From it both mother and child, particularly the latter, had to be freed by the performance of various prescribed apotropaic rites and ceremonies, the most important and effective of which were performed quite naturally upon either the seventh or the eighth day.

V

The Third, Seventh, and Fortieth Days After Birth

It is significant that, almost without exception, all the ceremonies thus far recorded are performed at one of three different moments: either immediately after birth, on the seventh or eighth day after birth, or on the fortieth day. Moreover, when we consider the rites of marriage, death, and other critical moments in human life, we find the same emphasis upon the day of the event itself and also upon the seventh and fortieth days thereafter. Many of the birth ceremonies which we have noted extend over the entire period from birth to or through the seventh or the eighth day, or even to the fortieth day after birth. The only exception thus far recorded is the practice of the Saʿîdijjîn of offering the *mrûḳa* sacrifice upon the third day.[1]

Thus, the ceremonies of receiving the newborn child in a wooden bowl, rubbing it with dough, myrtle, or red earth and oil, bathing it in the sacred waters of Sheikh Adi, and, above all, the interesting rite of *taḥnîk* are performed immediately after birth.

Ceremonies performed on the seventh or eighth day after birth include: the carrying of the child in a sieve through the house, while grain is scattered to ward off evil spirits; removing the infant from its cradle to a temporary bed, where it remains until the fortieth day; and the offering of the sacrifice, variously styled *ʿaḳîḳah, mrûḳa, ṭulû, bdûl,* or *sabûʿ*. Observed from the moment of birth through the seventh or eighth day is, as we have already learned, the widespread practice of rubbing the infant with salt or washing it in salt water or oil and salt.

In Egypt the seventh day after birth is called *Yom-es-Subooaʿ*, i.e., "the day of the (completion of the) week," or "the day of the seventh-day sacrifice." In addition to the various ceremonies described above, the Egyptians usually name the child upon this day. "The child is washed and salted, as among others, and then a copper basin is put above its head, which the midwife knocks with a stick to test whether the child is fearless. If it gets frightened, it will always be a coward; if, on the contrary, it is not afraid, the midwife asks the father, 'How will you name it?' The father then gives the name 'Mohammed' or 'Aishy,' or whatever he may choose; then the midwife, giving a knock again on the copper basin, says, 'Do you hear? Your name is Mohammed (or Aishy),' as the father has named the child."[2]

Among the Ṭerâbîn, ʿAzâzme, and Tijâha the sacrifice upon the seventh day after birth is frequently called *sabûʿ*, "the sacrifice of the seventh day." This sacrifice is offered for the redemption of the child. Moreover, the Ṭerâbîn call the seven days immediately following birth *sabaʿat el-wğûb,* "the seven days of need, danger or death."[3] In a similar manner the eighth day after birth, upon which the Jewish child is circumcised, is called in the Talmud *šᵉbûʿa haben,* "the week of the son."[4]

In Algeria, too, a festival in honor or on behalf of the newborn child is celebrated by the Moslem population on the seventh or eighth day after birth. The name is then given to the child, just as is the custom in Egypt.[5] Likewise, during the first eight days after the birth of a colt the animal is carefully massaged, while during this same period a strong girdle is kept bound around the belly of the mother.[6]

Among the Bedouin of the Sahara, "after the infant is eight days old, it receives an airing by being carried four times around the tent, and friends and relatives are invited to a feast, which continues for eight days, during which time all without distinction are welcome to the hospitality of the tent."[7]

And among the Bedouin of the Sinai Peninsula, "after childbirth the mother remains seven days in the tent, and some even prolong this period to forty days. On the seventh day her clothes are all scrupulously washed, and, if the child be a boy, a feast is made in its honor; but for a female child no festivities are held."[8]

Among the Moslem Berber tribes of Morocco, the seventh day marks a turning-point in the life of both mother and newborn child. Attendant rites and ceremonies of the various tribes differ materially, but all are manifestly based upon a common superstition and have a common purpose; therefore it is justifiable to generalize in every instance without specifying the tribe or locality in which the particular rite is practiced.[9]

During the seven days immediately following childbirth a curtain is suspended before the bed or room in which both mother and child lie, and during this time a candle is kept burning, or at least is lighted every evening before sunset, "probably as a safeguard against the *jnûn*." Throughout this entire period the room is not swept. In addition, the knife with which the navel-string was cut is put over the head of the child as a protection against the *jnûn;* but on the seventh day it is taken away by the mother, who uses it to cut up the meat of the animal sacrificed on that day. The mother's hands and feet are smeared with henna during these seven days, and at the same time antimony is smeared upon the eyes of the child. All manner of charms and amulets are attached to both mother and child, and a vessel filled with water is placed close to the head of the babe during these critical days. Quite frequently the father is not permitted to see the child during this entire period out of fear of the evil eye. On the seventh day the mother rises from her bed, and from that night on husband and wife resume sleeping together.

One particular rite, cited by Westermarck,[10] reveals clearly the concept and purpose underlying these seventh-day rites. "Among the Ait̲ Yúsi the mother is confined to her bed till the morning of the seventh day (*ssibaʿ*), when she gets up and has a bath. A sacrifice (*ṯṯḥeiṯ*) of a sheep or a goat is made in connection with the naming of the child. . . . After the dead animal has been removed, the mother, with the child on her back, walks three times round the place where it was slaughtered, holding one of her breasts and squeezing milk over the blood. While doing it she says some words like these: *Hâṭin ššärġ iḏun bûsebʿa āy iḏắmma,* 'Look here, I shared with you the breast (literally, 'that which has seven holes'), O this blood'; or, instead of *āy iḏắmma*, she may say, *āy äiṯ wänsáya,* 'O people of this place,' or *āy äiṯ räbbi*, 'O people of God.' Henceforth the *jnûn* of the place, to whom the invocation is addressed, will be on friendly terms with the child and its mother, treating the former as a brother or sister and the latter as a mother. After this the mother, still carrying the baby on her back, goes to the tent and walks three times round it, in a like manner squeezing some milk on the tent-cloth; and if she lives in a house, she squeezes it on the door-post, without walking round the house; but in neither case does she repeat her invocation." Quite plainly, the milk from the mother's breasts, and also the sacrifice itself, are offered to the *jnûn,* who are thought to be present at the spot where the sacrifice is offered, and thereby their sentiments toward both mother and child, presumably hostile originally, are turned to those of friendship and even of milk-kinship.

The question may well be asked, Why should the power of evil spirits, whether at the birth of children or, as we shall soon learn, at marriage, death, in sickness, or at similar critical moments in human life, be thought, in the vast majority of cases, to endure for just seven days? The fact itself is amply attested by the abundance of evidence which we have thus far adduced. But the question of the original motive or principle underlying it can be answered only by way of conjecture.

There is some reason for believing that among the ancient Semites, as is the case still today in certain Semitic localities, seven was regarded as an unlucky number.[11] So, we are told, in Palestine, in counting or measuring, "seven is omitted, being the number of the seven devils, which may come and work mischief. One says instead, 'in six,' or '*samḫat,*' 'pardon,' which vaguely resembles *sabʿat,* seven."[12] Another keen observer of life in Palestine records the following: "Many Mohammedans, when measuring (at harvest) say for the first one, 'God is One,' and for the next, 'He has no second,' then simply 'Three,' 'Four,' and so on. There are several unlucky numbers, the first being five,[13] and therefore, instead of saying the number, they often say 'Your hand,' five being the number of the fingers; seven is another unlucky number, strange to say, and is passed over in silence, or a word, 'A blessing,' is used instead; at nine Moslems often say, 'Pray in the name of Mohammed'; eleven also is not infrequently omitted, the measurer saying, 'There are ten,' and then passing on to twelve."[14]

In the same way in Babylonian religious literature, while the seven evil spirits were frequently spoken of as a group, no more than six were ever mentioned together by name.[15] On the other hand, the two groups of beneficent deities, the Igigi and the Anunnaki, consisted each of seven gods. In fact, the common ideogram of the Igigi, ,[16] designated them as "the Seven." Yet they were generally said to be eight in number, and the Anunnaki nine. Likewise, the various lists of the group of deities known as *ilSibittišunu,* "the Seven," or, literally, "they are Seven," always enumerate eight deities.[17] These instances show how scrupulously the Babylonians avoided direct mention of the number seven in enumerating or counting.

Apparently the same superstition existed among the Phoenicians, for Sanchuniathon[18] speaks of the Kabiroi as the seven sons of Sydyk and their eighth brother, Ešmun, whose name etymologically means "the Eighth." Here too, in this enumeration of a group of deities, the attempt to avoid direct mention of the number seven seems apparent.[19]

Similarly in the Masoretic text of the Old Testament the seven pre-Israelite nations of Palestine are frequently referred to, but, with the exception of three passages,[20] no more than six of these nations are ever mentioned together.[21]

In the same way, the people of Sermin, a town near Aleppo, we are told by Ibn Batoutah,[22] would not pronounce the number ten, but said instead, "nine and one." They had a mosque in their town with only nine minarets, because they would not permit the number ten. And Burckhardt[23] tells that he included only 999 proverbs in his great collection, although he might easily have included another one to make an even thousand. But he refrained from doing so, "adopting here a notion prevalent among Arabs, that even numbers are unlucky, and that anything perfect in its quantity is particularly affected by the evil eye." For the same reason undoubtedly, the famous collection of Arabic narratives is entitled *The Thousand and One Nights* instead of simply *The Thousand Nights.* This is further illustration of the Semitic practice of avoiding unlucky numbers by speaking of one more or one less than that number.

Accordingly, when only six of the traditional pre-Israelite nations of Palestine are, as a rule, mentioned together, when only six of the seven evil spirits of Babylonian religion are ever enumerated in a group, or when the Igigi are spoken of as eight rather than seven, as the ideogram for them indicates them to have been considered, we must infer that in each case the number seven was purposely avoided because it must have been regarded as unlucky or unpropitious.[24]

This evidence, scanty though it may seem, perhaps justifies the hypothesis that among the ancient Semites seven was originally considered an unlucky, ill-omened number, rather than lucky and holy.[25] It was definitely associated with evil spirits. Consequently, its mention, use, or association with any person or object was calculated to attract the evil spirits and commit the person or object into their power.[26]

Clearly then, this seven-day period after birth was that in which the evil spirits were believed to be powerful, active, and free to work their malicious will. As the period of their power drew near its close, and they saw their expected victim about to slip from their clutches, these spirits naturally redoubled their efforts to subjugate him completely. Consequently, the seventh day, and particularly the night thereof, in the veiling darkness of which these evil spirits were thought to be most active and powerful, was the period of greatest danger, the "watchnight," so-called, when the precautions and charms of the human guardians had to be correspondingly increased. The closing portion of this seventh and last day of danger, or the next day, the eighth, were the appropriate moments for the final ceremonies, the ritual purification of the tabooed person. This purification for the time being completely emancipated the individual from the power and claim of the evil spirits, and marked his solemn entry or re-entry into the conditions and activities of daily, profane existence.

Quite frequently the various birth rites and ceremonies are performed upon the eighth, rather than upon the seventh, day. In some localities in Morocco the naming of the child takes place upon the eighth day, while elsewhere, if the child was born during the afternoon, the naming takes place regularly upon the eighth day. In other localities it may take place upon either day, according to convenience. In addition, there are areas where the mother does not rise from her lying-in bed until the eighth day. Both the seventh and eighth days seem to be indiscriminately called, as the various rites are performed on the former or the latter, *s-sâbaʿ* or *nhâr s-sâbaʿ*, "the seven" or "the day of the seven."

It is clear from this that there is actually no distinction between the seventh and the eighth days, and that the former merely marks the closing moment of a peculiar state of being of both mother and child, while the latter is the first day of the new state for both. Logically, one day is quite as appropriate as the other for the performance of those rites which usher both mother and child from the one state into the other; in some localities these rites are performed upon the seventh day and in other localities upon the eighth day, but the underlying character and purpose of the rites are always the same.

Occasionally, as we have learned, some of these ceremonies are performed upon neither the seventh nor the eighth day, but upon the third day.[27] Even a rite so important as the naming of the child, together with the attendant sacrifice, is in some locales performed upon the third day. But here, unquestionably, the third day is not, as is the eighth day, a natural and logical alternative for the seventh day. Rather the implication is that the period of abnormal existence of the infant, which is shared by the mother, is thought to endure for only three days instead of seven, or else to endure in more intense degree for these three days than for the full seven. Obviously, however, the nature of this abnormal existence, and likewise the character and underlying purpose of the rites which mark its termination and the transition of both child and mother from the one state to the next, are in principle the same, whether linked with the third day, or with the seventh or eighth day.

Ceremonies upon the fortieth day are somewhat less frequent but quite as significant. The classic instance of such a ceremony is based on the ancient Israelite provision, recorded in Leviticus 12, that a woman was ritually unclean during the first forty days after the birth of a son and for eighty days after the birth of a daughter. During this period she apparently remained closely confined to her home; at least, she was strictly forbidden to contact the sanctuary or to touch anything sacred. At the end of this period she visited the sanctuary in order to offer there her sacrifice of purification. With this act she was restored to her normal state of existence. Today in non-Israeli sections of Palestine, a child is wrapped in swaddling clothes for the first forty days after birth.[28]

Among the Bedouin of the Arabian Desert a woman is regarded as unclean for the forty days immediately following childbirth.[29] Among the Fuqarâ Bedouin the customary sacrifice is offered and the name is given to the child upon the fortieth day after birth.[30] Similarly among the Ḥamāʿīdeh and Beni Ṣaẖer Bedouin women remain for the first forty days after childbirth without washing, because the water of the country is *maskouneh,* "inhabited by a spirit," and therefore could harm them. Nevertheless, they are able to drink the water without any ill effects. At Jerusalem, mother and child are conducted to the bath upon the fortieth day after birth.[31] Likewise among the native peasants of Palestine the mother takes her first bath upon the fortieth day after the birth of a child. If her husband has intercourse with her during these forty days, it is confidently believed that he will become leprous or that the child which might be born from this union will be a leper.[32] The implication is that during this entire period the mother is regarded as unclean and probably possessed by an evil spirit, inimical to her and even more so to her child, and also to those who might come in contact with her. The ritual bath upon the fortieth day delivers her from this condition. Also among the native population of Palestine today, a woman who has just borne a child wears a charm or amulet for the first forty days. The charm usually consists of a gold coin, with a complete human figure engraved upon it; this is called *maschas.*[33]

In Upper Egypt too, as we have learned, both mother and child are conducted to the bath for the first time upon the fortieth day after birth.[34] And among the Moslem Albanians the mother may not under any condition leave the house during this period. Maronite women also must remain at home during the first forty days after giving birth; in particular, they are forbidden to enter a church.[35] The Copts require that their women remain at home for forty days after the birth of a boy, but for only twenty-four days after that of a girl.[36]

Other, similar rites performed upon this day, some of which have already been noted, are: the return of a child from its temporary bed to its cradle at Tlemcen; the naming of a child at a specially prepared feast among the Ṣẖûr; the sacrifice of a sin-offering among the Falashas at the close of the forty-day period of uncleanness and the purification of the mother, in conformity with the Biblical ritual;[37] and the important ceremony of baptism, particularly as generally performed in the Eastern Church.[38]

Among the Shiite Moslems of Persia "when a child is born to a bride, they stick needles in her clothes, and let them remain there for forty days, so that no demons may approach or touch her. Should the child get sick or feel badly they suppose that an evil eye has beaten him. Should they suspect any person who is supposed to have an evil eye, they will secretly get a small piece from his clothing and burn it under the child. In so doing the evil eye is supposed to be put out."[39]

In Northern Africa the newborn child frequently goes by the general name *maḥǧûb* (literally, "the protected one") during the first forty days after birth. Then, in some localities, the ceremony of *tasmîyyah,* or giving of the name, as we have learned, usually performed upon the seventh day after birth, is performed upon the fortieth day, after which the child is called only by its own, individual name. In Morocco the first hair of the child is frequently cut upon this fortieth day.[40] In different localities and among the different tribes of Morocco various closely related rites are performed upon the fortieth day.[41] A mirror is placed under the head of the newborn babe and allowed to remain there for forty days to protect it against the evil eye. During the same period charms are attached to the right ankle of the mother and the right wrist of the child. People who by chance meet the mother during this period must give her a small sum of money, even though they are complete strangers to her. On the fortieth day the mother again visits the shrine which she had visited during her pregnancy, in order to enlist the aid of the descendant of a saint who resides in the immediate vicinity, and there makes a substantial gift to this holy man, who, in his turn, shaves the head of the child in his house, in conformity with the established custom. In some areas, sexual intercourse with the husband is resumed only upon the fortieth day.

Another interesting ceremony performed upon the fortieth day after birth is the following: "All the male inhabitants of Mecca, as well as those of the neighboring seaport of Djidda, are tattooed with a distinctive mark, by which they are recognized from every other class of people, the operation being performed by the parents so soon as the boy reaches the age of forty days."[42] Another observer describes the same practice thus: "One singular practice has been remarked by travelers, that all the male natives, both of Mecca and Djidda, except Bedouin, are tattooed in a peculiar way, which is performed by their parents when they are forty days old. It is called *meschâli,* and consists of three long incisions down both cheeks and two on the right temple, the scars of which remain through life. Instead of a deformity this is reckoned a beauty; and they pride themselves on a local distinction, which precludes the other inhabitants of Hejaz from claiming in foreign countries the honor of being born in the holy cities. This tattooing is very seldom inflicted upon female children."[43]

Concerning this same custom, we are told the following by our best authority on Meccan life:[44] "The mothers are so insistent that the three incisions (*meschâli*) be made in the cheeks of their children, because they are supposed to protect them against the evil eye." On this same day the mother prepares a festal meal for her female friends. Toward evening they all go with the child to the mosque, hand the child to one of the temple attendants, who lays it upon the lofty threshold of the Kaaba and prays over it and leaves it lying there for about ten minutes; then he returns it to its mother.[45]

According to two of the sources cited above, these incisions are made in order to distinguish those Moslems born in the holy cities from the other, less fortunate, inhabitants of the Hedjaz. But, according to Snouck Hurgronje, their real purpose is to guard the child against the evil eye. That Snouck Hurgronje's account is the correct explanation of the origin and purpose of this strange ceremony will be established later.[46]

Only one conclusion may be drawn from all this evidence, namely, that for a certain period after birth the child is thought to be in particular danger, either from malignant spirits or from the very deity who gave it life and can still easily reclaim his gift. Occasionally this period of danger is believed to endure for three days, though far more generally for seven days. In a somewhat diminished degree the danger is thought to persist for forty days. It is averted by the performance of various rites during the entire period, which culminate naturally upon the last day, the supremely critical moment of the entire period, whether it be of three, seven, or forty days.[47] Very frequently the ceremonies upon the fortieth day repeat or supplement in some way those of the seventh day. These rites culminate usually in the offering of a sacrifice and the cutting off of the first hair of the child upon the seventh or eighth, or the fortieth day, or in the rite of baptism on the fortieth day. Very frequently both ceremonies, sometimes accompanied by other, related rites, are performed upon either or both days. Not until these rites have been completely and punctiliously performed is the danger averted and the child freed from the power of the threatening spirits or of the deity who had bestowed the gift of life upon it.

In other words, during this entire period of danger the newborn child is actually in the power of supernatural beings, supposedly hostile. With the performance of these rites the danger, at least in its most immediate and threatening form, passes, and the child is redeemed. It may truthfully be said that only now does the child really begin to live as an ordinary mortal.[48]

VI

Taboo and Its Removal

We have shown that during the entire period of postnatal danger, whether enduring for three, seven, or forty days, the newborn child is believed to be in the power of, and therefore practically the property of, supernatural beings; he is therefore in a state of taboo.

The concept underlying taboo is that all things created by or emanating from a supernatural being are his, or at least are in his power. This power, or right of possession, he defends jealously. He relinquishes it only when he receives a sacrifice as a substitute for the tabooed person or object. This sacrifice may be something resembling the tabooed object, corresponding to it as nearly as possible in appearance, shape, and members,[1] or it may be a part, especially a vital yet easily dispensable part, of the tabooed object itself, a part substituting for the whole.[2] Such a substitute part, if it is a human being which is taboo, may be, for example, the hair,[3] the parings of the nails, a joint of a finger or toe, or a tooth.[4] Only after redemption by such a sacrifice may a tabooed person safely resume his normal function in everyday life.

We have already cited numerous rites intended to remove the taboo incident to birth, many of which are performed upon the seventh or eighth day after birth. This same principle of taboo and its removal, likewise upon the critical seventh or eighth day, was observed in ancient Israel. For example, the removal of taboo was prescribed in the case of the Nazirite who had been defiled by contact with a corpse,[5] of an ordinary person who had touched a dead body or entered a tent in which a dead body lay, and who must therefore be sprinkled with water containing the ashes of the red heifer,[6] of a menstruating woman or of a man who had had sexual intercourse with a woman in that state,[7] or of a man or woman who had had an issue.[8] Similarly, rites attendant upon the discharge of a vow and the consequent necessary purification endured for seven days.[9] Likewise, the ceremonies of purification of both altar and priests continued for seven full days, and the actual state of consecration and holy service began only upon the eighth day.[10]

These ceremonies had a twofold character, partly magical and partly religious or sacrificial.[11] Such rites as the ritual bath, the sprinkling with the ashes of the red heifer, or that of letting a bird fly away laden with the uncleanness of leprosy were obviously purificatory and magical in character. They were designed to expel the evil spirit and carry it far away, thus making any further contact with the danger practically impossible. However, the most important element of these ceremonies was the offering of a double sacrifice—a sacrifice of two animals, either sheep, lambs, or pigeons—one as a sin- or guilt-offering and one as a burnt-offering. The purpose of this double sacrifice, or at least of one of its two parts, was undoubtedly to remove taboo.

The cause of a taboo may be contact with either a consecrated or a contaminated object. Thus, the scrolls of the Torah or the phylacteries "defiled the hands" quite as much as contact with a dead body or some other ritually unclean object.[12] And the Nazirite, consecrated to the service of the Deity and therefore in a state of superprofane taboo, was debarred from participation in many of the ordinary activities of life[13] in quite the same manner as was the leper, clearly in a state of subprofane taboo.[14] Significantly, the ritual for each, at the close of the period of taboo, was practically the same.[15] Both rituals included the offering of various sacrifices, such as the sin-offering, the guilt-offering, and the shaving of the head.

Nor can it always be determined whether the taboo in question was subprofane or superprofane. Thus, for example, in the ritual of the red heifer,[16] it is by no means clear whether the participants had become too holy, by contact with the sacred object, or too unclean and impure, by contact with what was primarily a dead body, to share in the activities of ordinary existence. Nor did it matter in the least. The practical effects of subprofane and superprofane taboo were the same; both equally debarred the tabooed person from the ordinary pursuits of life. Apparently no distinction was made between them, and *ṭameʿ* could designate superprofane taboo and consequent disqualification from the functions of ordinary existence as well as it could designate subprofane taboo.[17] In both cases the principle of removal of the taboo and the ritual prescribed therefor were practically identical.

Moreover, the principle of taboo was very elastic. By a slight extension of this principle any person who found himself in a critical situation, or whose life was endangered, or who had in any way or for any cause whatsoever, even by accident, come into intimate or proprietary relation with a deity or other supernatural power, was regarded as being in a state of taboo. Priest, "man of God," Nazirite, warrior upon a campaign, leper, woman in her courses or at childbirth, a child during the period immediately following birth, a person dangerously ill, or one who had returned from a long, and therefore presumably perilous, journey—anyone whose life was thought to have been endangered and forfeited and which was therefore, strictly speaking, no longer entirely his own—was regarded as being in a more or less complete state of taboo, embracing all the activities of life. To pass from this state of taboo, the performance of certain rites and sacrifices was essential. With the performance of these rites the person in question passed from the state of taboo into the state of normal, daily, profane existence.

VII

The Rite of Taḥnîk

We turn now to consider certain ceremonies of particular significance among the birth rites of the Semitic peoples. We begin with the rite of *taḥnîk.*

The ceremony of putting some of the saliva of the *ṣâḥeb al-baḫt,* or "master of the luck" of the child, into the child's mouth and breathing upon him, which we have found practiced among the Bedouin, was taken over by Islam from "the days of ignorance." It is thus described by Wellhausen:[1] "The gums of the newborn child are smeared with some of the juice of pressed dates, or something similar; this is called *taḥnîk.* . . . Among the Hebrews the child was rubbed with salt; but the verb *ḥanak,* which has survived among them in the general connotation 'to initiate,' proves the antiquity of the Arabic rite, for it is derived from the Arabic word for 'gum' (*ḥanikun*). Whether *taḥnîk* means the acceptance of the child by the father as its supporter is doubtful, since the ceremony need not be performed by the father. The inhabitants of Medina were wont to bring their newborn children to Mohammed, in order that the holy man might perform this sacred rite over them; he would spit into their mouths, so that his saliva would be the first thing to enter their stomachs, and then he would put chewed dates into their mouths."[2]

Wellhausen adds the note that Musailima, the rival of Mohammed, attempted to imitate Mohammed in the performance of the rite of *taḥnîk,* but only with evil consequences. In other words, the children into whose mouths Musailima spat sickened and died, while those who underwent the same treatment from Mohammed lived and thrived. This must have proved convincingly to their contemporaries that Musailima did not possess the same supernatural powers as Mohammed and further served to stamp the latter as the true, and the former as the false, prophet. This circumstance, however, emphasizes the magical character of the rite of *taḥnîk.* Clearly, its primary purpose was to impart to the child something of the powers and qualities of the holy man. Only to a secondary degree was it calculated to expel or ward off threatening evil spirits.[3] We are told that in Morocco today, "There are various ways in which a person may be filled with the *baraka* of a saint. The latter may transfer *baraka* to his *ḫdîm* simply by spitting into his mouth. Or the saint may eat some food in the presence of his *ḫdîm* on the last day they spend together and then tell him to eat of what is left; when the *ḫdîm* has finished his meal, the saint says to him, . . . 'You have taken the loaf of bread,' meaning that the servant has now partaken of his *baraka*."[4]

It is significant that the Ḥwêṭat ceremony of putting clarified butter mixed with sulfur into the mouth of the infant, recorded by Musil, is still described by the ancient term *taḥnîk* (*yuḥannikûh*). But it should be noted also that this Ḥwêṭat ceremony is supplemented by the *ṣâḥeb baḫt*'s putting some of his saliva into the infant's mouth,[5] the very same rite as that performed by Mohammed of old.

A vestigial form of the ancient rite of *taḥnîk* may be seen in the practice, current in modern Palestine, of giving to newborn children as their first drink a few drops of water in which a date, if possible one which has been brought from Mecca, has been mashed.[6] Of the same origin and character is the following custom, recorded by Blackman: "On many different occasions women have brought their babies to me with the request that I would spit into their mouths, in order to give them *baraka* and make them live long."[7]

Unquestionably, Wellhausen's conclusion is correct, that the Hebrew verb *ḥanak,* in the sense of "to initiate, to dedicate," is derived from this rite of *taḥnîk* and from the primary connotation of *ḥanikun*, "gum."[8] Obviously then, *taḥnîk* was primarily a ceremony of initiation, initiation of a newborn child into a new stage of life. And since, in its earliest form, it consisted of putting some concrete substance into the mouth of the child for the very first time, this very important ceremony must originally have been performed almost immediately after birth, therefore upon the child's very first day of life.

VIII

The ʿAḳîḳah *Ceremony*

Easily identified as a taboo rite is the so-called *ʿaḳîḳah* ceremony. It is usually performed upon the seventh or eighth day after birth, although the custom seems to vary somewhat in different locales. It is frequently associated with the important rite of naming the child.

The complete *ʿaḳîḳah* ceremony consists of two rites, though occasionally one or the other is partially or entirely dispensed with. The first rite is the cutting off of the infant's first hair. The Arabic term for this is *ʿaḳîḳah.* From this the ceremony derived its name.[1] The second rite is the offering of a sacrifice, also traditionally known as *ʿaḳîḳah.* This *ʿaḳîḳah* sacrifice is unquestionably the same as that offered upon the seventh or eighth day after birth by certain Bedouin tribes, and variously called *sabuʿ, ṭulû, mrûḳa,* or *bdûl.*[2] As we have learned,[3] this sacrifice serves as redemption (*fedû*) for the child.

The ancient Arabic form of the sacrifice is described concisely by Wellhausen:[4] "For the birth of a male child a sacrifice was brought after a little time, generally seven days. It consisted usually of a sheep. Just as the hair was cut at every sacrifice, so at this sacrifice the first hair, with which the child was born, was cut off. Furthermore, the forehead was sprinkled with blood; hence the name, *ʿaḳîḳah.* The *ʿaḳîḳah* was taken over by Islam and is still, according to Doughty, one of the most frequent occasions for sacrifice in Arabia. It is practiced, however, only at the birth of a boy, and never at the birth of a girl."[5]

Robertson Smith likewise discusses the ceremony in considerable detail: "A ceremony of consecration or dedication was actually practiced on infants by the heathen Arabs in connection with a sacrifice called *ʿacîca.* . . . The animal chosen for the sacrifice was usually a sheep; at the same time the child's head was shaved and daubed with the blood of the victim . . . . The hair . . . was an offering to the deity, and, as such, was sometimes mingled with a meal offering. So it must have been also with the hair of the babe, for Mohammed's daughter Fatima gave the example of bestowing in alms the weight of the hair in silver. . . . The sacrifice is meant, as the prophet himself says, 'to avert evil from the child by shedding blood on his behalf.' This is more exactly brought out in the old usage—discontinued in Moslem times—of daubing the child's head with blood. . . . The blood, which ensures protection by the god, is, as in the ritual of blood-brotherhood, blood that unites protector and protected, and in this as in all other ancient Arabian sacrifices, was doubtless applied also to the sacred stones that represented the deity. The prophet offered a sheep indifferently for the birth of a boy or a girl, but in earlier times the sacrifice seems to have been only for a boy. Some authorities . . . say that the ceremony fell on the seventh day after birth, but this is hardly correct; for where there was no *'acîca* offered, the child was named and its gums rubbed with masticated dates on the morning after birth. I presume that in general the sacrifice, the naming and the symbolical application of the most important article of food to the child's mouth all fell together and marked his reception into partnership in the *sacra* and means of life of his father's group. At Medina, Mohammed was often called in to give the name and rub the child's gums—probably because in heathenism this was done by the priest. Such a ceremony as this would greatly facilitate the change of the child's kin; it was only necessary to dedicate it to the father's instead of the mother's god. But indeed the name *'acîca,* which is applied both to the hair cut off and to the victim, seems to imply a renunciation of the original mother-kinship, for the verb *'acca,* 'to sever,' is not the one that would naturally be used either of shaving hair or cutting the throat of the victim, while it is the verb that is used of dissolving the bond of kindred, either with or without the addition of *al-raḥîm.* If this is the meaning of the ceremony, it is noteworthy that it was not performed on girls, and of this the words of the traditions hardly admit a doubt."[6]

Quite naturally, Robertson Smith explains the *'aḳîḳah* ceremony in conformity with his theory of covenant-sacrifice and the establishment of a bond of relationship thereby between deity and worshiper as the basic institution of Semitic religious belief and practice. He further describes this ceremony as a rite of initiation into the tribe of the child's father, as opposed to the earlier concept and practice of kinship with the deity and clan of the mother. But this assumption, and in fact the majority of points in his argument and his conclusions are altogether hypothetical and groundless. We shall produce abundant and convincing evidence that the *'aḳîḳah* sacrifice and the ceremonies attendant thereon were all directed primarily to the evil spirits which were thought to threaten the child's life, and that this thought and practice still persist in very large measure in the procedures attendant upon birth among Moslem peoples everywhere.

Earlier in this study we cited several accounts of *'aḳîḳah* ceremonies among the various birth rites we recorded in order to arrive at our basic conclusions regarding evil spirits, the duration of their power, and taboo and its removal. To present a complete picture of the *'aḳîḳah* ceremony and to integrate it into our argument it is necessary to consider certain of these quotations again and more closely.

Lane's description of the ceremony was cited as follows: "The person should say on slaying the victim, 'O God, verily this *'aqîqah* is a ransom for my son, such a one; its blood for his blood, and its flesh for his flesh, and its bone for his bone, and its skin for his skin, and its hair for his hair. O God, make it a ransom (*fedû*) for my son from hell-fire.' A bone of the victim should not be broken."[7] Manifestly, the animal is the substitute-sacrifice for the redemption of the child from supposedly threatening evil. It is offered upon the seventh day after birth as a ransom, *fedû*, for the child, precisely like the sacrifices offered by the Ṭerâbîn, Tijâha, and 'Azâzme upon the same occasion.[8]

Similarly, as we have seen, Curtiss states that in Nebk they offer a sacrifice for a boy when he is seven days old, without breaking any bones, lest the child's bones also be broken.[9] And again: "A man who has not yet had a child promises a fedou that he may receive the gift of one from a certain saint. If it should be born, when it is several (the German edition says, more precisely, 'seven') days old, they put the blood of the sacrifice offered in payment of the vow on its forehead." Also, "in one of the villages of the Syrian Desert it is customary when a Moslem woman brings forth a son to sacrifice a cock, when she bears a daughter to sacrifice a hen."[10] We have already noted the observance of the same ceremony in Tlemcen in Northern Africa.[11]

Curtiss likewise describes the sacrifice for a child, as practiced by the Ismailiyeh, in the words of one of their own initiates: "When they make a sacrifice for a child, they slaughter the victim in the courtyard where he lives and put a few drops of blood on his forehead and on his nose, to indicate that the sacrifice is in his behalf. The breaking forth of the blood is fedou. It redeems the child. They vow to the saint that blood shall flow for the child, if he redeems it."[12] While the name *'aḳîḳah* is not applied, at least not by Curtiss, to these last-mentioned sacrifices, they are undoubtedly of quite the same character and serve exactly the same purpose as the *'aḳîḳah* sacrifice, as described by Lane.

Jaussen tells of the *'aḳîḳah* ceremony, as he observed it practiced in Nablus, in the following manner: "It is frequently upon the third day after birth, but more often upon the eighth day, that the *'aqîqah* is celebrated. The term *'aqîqat al-walad* is, for those whom I questioned, the equivalent of *ḏabîḥat al-walad,* 'the sacrifice for the infant.'

"The father of the family provides a victim, sheep, lamb or kid, and sacrifices it himself, or has it sacrificed by some other person 'on behalf of the infant.' A part of the flesh is eaten by the family and the remainder is distributed to the poor. A drop of the blood of the victim ought to be sprinkled upon the infant, upon the cheek, the neck or the breast. While smearing the blood the father or a relative says, 'In the name of Allah, the all-merciful; except Allah no other being can suffice for you.'

"According to Sheikh Aḥmad, who furnished me with these details, the *ʿaqîqah* or *d̠abîḥah* delivers the child from Gehenna. He told me that he had sacrificed the *ʿaqîqah* for all his children, male and female; but he added, 'This practice is optional, according to the Sunneh; it is highly regarded by true Moslems; actually, however, it is often neglected.' However, many Moslem women . . . affirmed that the *ʿaqîqah* in their eyes possesses an obligatory character. If the family is too poor to purchase and sacrifice a sheep or kid, it believes that it ought to compensate for the sacrifice by distributing some bread or other commodities to the poor, for on the day of the last judgment Allah will inquire of the parents whether they had sacrificed anything for the baby.

"In the case of an infant about to die before the performance of this rite, the father does not believe himself absolved by the death from offering the *ʿaqîqah* for the *walad*."[13] To this, Jaussen adds that the blood of the *ʿaqîqah* is one of the protections of the child against the many attacks of the *qarînah,* the evil eye, and the *našqah* (the evil breath).

To all this, Jaussen appends the following note: "According to the *Lisân al-ʿarab* . . . *ʿaqîqah* designates primarily the hair which pushes through on the head of the infant while still in its mother's womb. These hairs, regarded as impure, are cut or shaved off a week after birth, and during this operation a sheep is sacrificed which, by analogy, is also called *ʿaqîqah.*

"According to a tradition preserved in the *Lisân,* the prophet is said to have declared that so long as the hair of the infant has not been cut and the *ʿaqîqah*-sacrifice of a sheep has not been sacrificed, the infant will not be of any intercessionary value for his father.

"In the Ṣaḥîḥ of al-Bukhâry we read: Salmân, son of ʿAmir aḍ-Ḍahi, reported: 'I heard the Prophet say: With an infant the *ʿaqîqah* is indispensable; spread out the blood for him and remove the evil from him.'

"According to al-Bukhâry, the *ʿaqîqah* is necessary still today, and this despite the fact of its recognized pre-Islamic origin."

The manner of observing the *ʿaḳîḳah* sacrifice and ceremonies at Mecca is described as follows: "The first important day in the life of each person is that upon which the *tasmījah* (the giving of the name) takes place, viz., the seventh day after birth. The law recommends for this day the cutting of the hair of the head of the child and the sacrifice of one or two sheep, which sacrifice is called *ʿaqīqah.* This sacrifice may also be deferred until later in life, or may even be offered for a person after his death;[14] actually the people of Mecca give little thought in this ceremony to the principle of the *ʿaqīqah,* although they usually sacrifice the sheep in connection with the *tasmījah.*"[15]

On this day there is a festive assembly of friends and relatives at the house of the newborn child. Big drums are beaten in the street in front of the house. Unquestionably the purpose of this act is to frighten off the evil spirits by means of the loud noise.[16] "A learned friend or relative is entrusted with the *tasmījah*. The child is put in his arms. After beginning the solemn rite by calling upon the name of Allah, he whispers into the right ear of the child the formula of the *adān,* and into the left ear that of the *iqāmah,* and then delivers a brief religious address, preferably dealing with the significance of names, by means of which God distinguishes His creatures from each other, and finally he pronounces the name of the child. . . . This is always thought to have been determined beforehand by God. Therefore, at the end of his homily, the learned man recites the formula, 'I name you, as Allah has already named you, N.N.'

"It is not the regular custom, but it does happen occasionally, that the child is passed from one guest to the other as they sit along the wall, in order that each might have a part in cutting off the hair. For this purpose a large pair of scissors is lying upon the board upon which the child has been placed; each guest in turn cuts off a few hairs."

Closely related rites are performed upon the same day by the Moslems of Northern Africa. "At the end of seven days the festival of the giving of the name (*tasmîya*) takes place. On this day a sheep is killed; it is the victim called *ʿaqîqa.* Some sticks are laid in order upon the ground, to each of which a name is assigned. Above these the knife which is to be used in sacrificing the sheep is placed, and someone, with eyes bound, selects one of the sticks. Then one of the assistants, but not the father, takes the knife, applies it to the neck of the sheep and cuts its throat while saying: *El Maḥjoûb, seminâk flân,* that is to say, 'O protected one, we name you so-and-so.'

"The skin of the sheep is given to the mother. Among the Chiaḍma she receives the entrails and head. In Algeria, at least in the province of Oran, the flesh of the animal killed on this occasion may not be roasted, for this would bring misfortune to the child; and the mother receives the entrails and the right shoulder. In many Moroccan towns, Mogador for example, as a part of the ceremony of the seventh day the mother receives the skin, the head and the tripe of the slain sheep. . . . But in orthodox Islam the mother . . . may not receive any part whatsoever of the animal sacrificed. . . . Nor ought this sacrifice be used to furnish a banquet. Instead it is eaten by the family, and some of it is offered to the neighbors. . . . In any case, however, the sacrifice of a victim upon the seventh day after birth is regarded as obligatory, and there is no means to which one who is poor will not resort in order to be able to offer this sacrifice upon this day.

"Among the Reḥâmna the hair of the infant is cut upon the fourth day after birth. In Morocco this ceremony takes place preferably upon the fortieth day, but often there is no date fixed for it; it is so also throughout the Maghrib. But it happens nonetheless quite often, and we have been informed that such is the case in the vicinity of Mogador, that the cutting of the first hair takes place upon the seventh day, at the same time as the giving of the name. In any case, even though this last date may be somewhat exceptional, it is noteworthy that orthodox Islam regards it alone as being legal. The sacrifice of an animal, the giving of the name, and the cutting of the hair are for it one and the same ceremony. The Moslem today must fulfill seven obligations: to give a name to his son, to cut the hair of the newborn child, to give as alms the value of the weight of the hair in silver or gold, as his means will permit, to sacrifice an animal, called *ʿaqîqah,* to smear the baby's head with saffron, to circumcise him, and, finally, to distribute to the neighbors portions of the animal sacrificed. Without exception all of these are rites of purification. A *ḥadît* records that Abou Abdallah, having been asked about the significance of the cutting of the hair, replied, 'It is to purify the child from the uncleanness emanating from the bowels of its mother.' "[17] Elsewhere, Doutté reaffirms that the rite of cutting the child's first hair, or *ʿaḳîḳah,* is a ceremony of "purification," the release from an evil or impure state.[18]

In his long and detailed account of the *ʿaḳîḳah* ceremony as it is practiced among the different tribes and settlements of Morocco, Westermarck imparts many bits of information which illumine still further the nature and purpose of this peculiar institution. At the risk of seeming repetitious, we shall reproduce his remarks:

"At Fez the mother gets up on the seventh day, when the curtain is removed. She must have slippers on her feet and cover up her head, only leaving the eyes, nose and mouth uncovered, otherwise, it is believed, she would become ill. On this and on the following day she abstains from work, although she directs what is to be done in the house. On the eighth day, called *s-sâbaʿ* or *nhār s-sâbaʿ,* there is the feast of the *ʿaqîqa,* comprising the sacrifice of a ram and the naming of the child. On the morning of this day the male relatives and friends of the parents come to the house by invitation and are entertained with tea and food. . . . In the middle of the house 'the ram of the name-giving' . . . is slaughtered by the father of the child or, if he does not know how to do it, by his father or some person who has *baraka*—a *shereef* or a *fqī.* . . . When the animal is slaughtered a female slave or servant or some old woman puts salt into the wound as safeguard against *jnûn.* The head of the animal is skinned because the hair on it must not be scorched off; if it were, the infant would die. If the child is a boy the shoulder-blades of the animal must be left unbroken in order that he shall become vigorous and active; of a man who is lethargic and lazy it is said that his 'ram of the name-giving' had its shoulder-blade broken. But if the child is a girl no such rule is observed.

"After the male guests have left, the child is washed by the midwife and dressed in clothes sent by its mother's father if it is a first-born child, or otherwise in clothes procured by its father. The water used for the washing of the child must not be poured into the drains, which are haunted by *jnûn,* but is thrown into the garden or on the plants cultivated on the roof. . . .

"In the evening there is a feast for female relatives and friends. They are entertained in the same way as the men. . . . The women stay overnight and depart in the morning after breakfast. At both feasts music is performed by a band of musicians, consisting of men in the morning and women in the evening. If a child is a first-born the meals are largely composed of the meat of sheep and other food sent by the mother's father, and the sacrificed animal is also one of these sheep. . . .

"In the Ḥiáina a ram, which must be entirely white, is killed by the *fqī* of the village or a *shereef*, or some highly respected man, to whom the father hands a knife, telling him the name of the child and its mother's name. No other man is present at this ceremony, but there are a few women. . . . The infant is held in the arms of the mother or some near female relative. The ceremony, which takes place at mid-day, is called *s-sába*ʿ and the sacrifice itself is called *dbēḥt* ˢ*s-mîya*, 'the sacrifice of the name-giving'; the word *ʿaqêqa* is not used in the Ḥiáina. . . . On the same day a feast is given with music and powder play.

"In Andjra on the morning of the seventh day the midwife comes and removes the mother from the bed where she has been lying since the birth of the child, and puts her on the ground. She washes her, dresses her in clean clothes, and paints her hands and feet with henna. She also smears henna on the head, neck, navel, feet, and fingernails of the boy, and in its armpits and between its legs. I was told that this painting with henna, like all other henna ceremonies, is intended as a safeguard against *jnûn* and the evil eye; and in order to keep away those spirits she also burns benzoin in the room. The father comes with a sheep or goat, which must be at least a year old, and kills it in the yard of the house. This sacrifice is called *l-gézra de t-tesmîya*, 'the slaughter of the name-giving.' It is made whether the child be a boy or girl, and should it be omitted the child would be said to be a *jenn*, a Christian or a Jew. The skin of the animal must on no account be inflated; if it were the child would also later on become inflated. It is dried and then put underneath the baby in its bed. It is kept for some three or four years, and may then be thrown away, but must never be sold; if it were, the child would die.

"Among the Ait̲ Wäryâġer the mother generally gets up on the third day, but keeps to the house till the seventh day, when she washes, fumigates herself with benzoin, and paints her hands and feet with henna. . . . On this day there is the ceremony of name-giving. The father kills a sheep or a goat. . . . The meat of the animal is served at the feast which is given on this occasion. . . . I was told that if this sacrifice were not made the child would die.

"Among the Ait̲ Waráin, on the morning of *ass n ssbőʿŏ*, 'the seventh day,' which may also be the eighth, the child is named and a sheep slaughtered by the *fqī* of the village outside the door of the parents' house. . . . At the feast which is given in the evening the meat of the sacrificed animal, with *sĕ́ksŭ*, is served to the men; while the head, lungs, heart, liver and other internal parts suitable for food, which have been boiled together, are eaten by the women with bread. The liver must on no account be cut into pieces and fried into *bûlfäf*; if it were, the result would be that when the child has grown up and married and become the parent of a child, that child would die. The head is skinned, as the hair must not be singed off; the penalty for transgressing this rule would be that no hair would grow on the head of the child. The throat and the right shoulder-piece are not boiled till the following morning, when they are eaten by the parents; but they must take care not to break the gristle of the larynx or the shoulder blade. If the former were broken the child would have a distorted neck, while the latter must be left unbroken in order that the child may in the future have numerous progeny; they are in consequence put among the corn which is kept in the house, or are hung on the rafters, so that no dog or cat can get hold of them. There is *baraka* in them, and the gristle of the larynx is used as a charm against the evil eye. The other bones and those entrails which are not good for food are thrown into a river or buried in the ground; for should a cat eat them, the child would become like a cat and scratch people when they speak to it, and should a dog eat them, the child would become very disagreeable and quarrelsome. . . .

"Among the Ai<u>t</u> Sadděn the ceremony of *asěmma,* or name-giving, takes place in the forenoon of *ass n ssîbăʿ*. The *fqī* of the village slaughters a sheep or goat in front of the house or tent of the family, in the presence of the father and male relatives and others who care to come, but the mother is not among them. . . . Very frequently, however, the sacrifice of an animal is omitted when a child is named; indeed, in the case of a girl such a sacrifice is quite an exception, and there is no fear that the child will die in consequence. . . .

"Among the Ai<u>t</u> Yúsi . . . on the name-day a feast with invited guests is given on the meat of the sacrificed animal. Its throat, lungs, liver, and other internal parts are boiled together. The mother and midwife first eat the throat, and then the other women eat the rest with *sě́ksü*. Care must be taken that the gristle of the throat is not broken, lest the child should get a distorted neck . . . nor should the shoulder blade be broken.

"Among the Ulad Bûʿăzîz, contrary to the usual custom, the child is named as early as the third day after its birth, without any special ceremony. The mother, however, remains in bed till the seventh day. . . . On the seventh day she gets up. . . . The midwife makes cuts all over the body of the child to prevent its blood from killing it, and puts henna and soap-stone (*ġasûl*) into the wounds; so deep are these cuts that I saw scars due to them on the arm of a middle-aged man. On this day the father of the child kills a sheep, if he has any; and if he has a sufficient number of sheep of both sexes, he kills a ewe if the child is a boy, and a ram if it is a girl. . . . Among the Beni Ăḥsen also the child is named on the third day, but a sheep is killed at the same time."[19]

This Moroccan practice of the *ʿaḳîḳah* ceremony, despite the many variations in its details, brings forth clearly a number of matters of considerable importance. In the first place, it is noteworthy that in not a single instance was the rite of cutting off the first hair, with which the child is born, linked with the performance of this ceremony, and this despite the fact that, as we have learned, the cutting off of this first hair was one of the three basic elements of the ritual, and precisely that one which gave to the ceremony its distinctive name, *'aḳîḳah.* Instead, in Morocco, the first hair of the child is cut regularly on the fortieth day after birth.[20] The postponement of this particular rite may well account for the fact which Westermarck noted, that, at least in the Ḥiáina, the name *'aḳîḳah* is not used, and that the ceremony on the seventh day is usually designated by some other title.

However, the other two elements of the complete ceremony, namely, the offering of the sacrifice and the giving of the name to the child, are constantly present and closely linked. They are performed regularly upon the seventh or eighth day after birth, and only very rarely upon the third day.

Moreover, it is clear that among all the tribes and in all the settlements whose practices Westermarck has recorded, during the entire seven days after birth evil spirits are thought to be constantly present threatening both mother and child, but especially the latter, with the danger most intense upon the seventh and culminating day. The offering of the sacrifice and the attendant rites constitute the climactic stage, as it were, in the procedure of warding off these malicious demons and redeeming both mother and child from their dread power. With this ceremony behind them, the mother returns to the normal activities and relationships of daily existence, while the child, now endowed with his own distinctive name and, impliedly, now possessing a personality all his own, likewise enters into the conditions of normal existence.

That the *'aḳîḳah* sacrifice, particularly in its most primitive form, was actually offered to the evil spirits which threatened the existence of the child, is beyond question. Obviously this sacrifice was given as a ransom, or *fedû,* for the child; its life in exchange for his life, and even the various parts of its body for the corresponding members of the body of the child. This substitutionary character of the *'aḳîḳah* sacrifice is evidenced repeatedly.

In the first place, there is the general and seemingly widespread belief that if the sacrifice is not offered the child will surely die, which means, of course, that its life will be taken by the threatening evil spirits. True, one example is cited by Westermarck where this sacrifice is not offered, but, seemingly in its stead, incisions are made in the body of the infant and blood is drawn. Westermarck also cites Baker to the effect that among the Arabs of Upper Egypt "young infants are scored with a razor longitudinally down the back and abdomen to improve their constitution."[21] In this connection we call to mind the Meccan custom of making three incisions in the cheeks of newborn infants in order to protect them against the evil eye.[22] Despite the various explanations now given, and the effects now attributed to this ceremony of the bloodletting of newborn infants, there can scarcely be any doubt that here the letting of the child's blood conforms closely to the principle, which we have found clearly expressed in the Palestinian form of the ceremony, that blood must flow for the child. This is another and a very illuminating instance of the belief, current in early Semitic tradition and practice, that the essential life-principle resides in the blood.[23] Accordingly, the letting of the blood of the infant in this manner is in principle tantamount to giving the life of the child to the superhuman power, whether deity or evil spirit, which threatens the child at birth. Furthermore, it is an altogether reasonable assumption that the offering of the animal sacrifice evolved in time as the substitute for the more primary and quite dangerous practice of letting the child's blood, and that with but two exceptions, so far as recorded by Westermarck, the newer practice has in Morocco completely supplanted the older rite.

Even more indicative of the substitutionary character of the sacrifice is the extreme care which must be taken that the shoulder blade of the sacrificial animal be not broken, nor the larynx, or at least the gristle thereof, that the hair on the animal's head be not singed or scorched, that the skin be not inflated, the liver not cooked improperly or eaten by other than fully qualified persons, and that the entrails be properly disposed of. Regardless of the several explanations, largely rationalistic, which, in different localities, have come to be offered for these various procedures, it is clear that one basic principle underlies them all: that these various parts of the body of the sacrificial animal are so closely related to the corresponding parts of the body of the child that the latter will be affected in his members in precisely the same manner as the members of the animal are treated. If the animal's bones, and especially its shoulder blade, are broken, the corresponding bones of the child will be broken; if the gristle of the larynx is broken, the child will have a distorted neck; if the hair on the animal's head is singed away, the child will lose its hair, and so on. The import of all this is unmistakable. The animal corresponds to the child in every respect and detail. It is given to the evil spirits in lieu of the child.

Finally, the fact that the flesh of the *ʿaḳîḳah* sacrifice is distributed to the poor is culminating proof of its character as a substitute taboo-sacrifice.

The peculiar role played by the father or other relatives of the mother in connection with these seventh-day rites, particularly if the child is the first-born of the mother, should be noted. It has a significance for this study which will be determined later.

Of particular interest at this point is the *ʿaḳîḳah* rite itself, specifically, the cutting off, usually upon the seventh day after birth, of the first hair with which the child is born. Robertson Smith maintains, despite the testimony of numerous authorities, that this ceremony was not performed upon the seventh day after birth, but was deferred until later. He argues that *ʿaḳḳa* is too strong a term to designate the act of cutting off the scanty first hairs of a newborn babe, while it is quite appropriate to the sacrifice of the long locks characteristic of boyhood. However, the very fact that the word *'aḳîḳah* is used by Imru 'l Qais to designate the reddish first hair with which a child is born, is sufficient to refute Robertson Smith's entire argument.[24]

There seems reason to believe that in modern Syria and Palestine the cutting off of the first hair does not usually take place until after the completion of the first year. Eijub Abēla states[25] that "one should never cut the hair of a child that is not yet one year old; otherwise it might become an orphan." Both Curtiss[26] and Kahle[27] give numerous instances of the sacrificial cutting off of the hair between the first and the twelfth years. Curtiss says: "At the shrine of Mar Eljas in Ma'arret esch-Scham near Ssidnaja both Mohammedans and Christians offer sacrifices before the door. The latter also have a mass read for the soul of the boy and shave off his hair. With reference to the blood, the majority assert, 'Nothing is done with the blood.' On the other hand an old woman told me, 'The forehead of the boy is smeared with the blood, and frequently also the entire frame of the door; then it will go well with the boy. This is the custom of both Mohammedans and Christians.'"[28]

However, it is noteworthy that not a single case cited by Curtiss and Kahle is that of a normal *'aḳîḳah* hair-offering performed shortly after birth, but is, without exception, a special sacrifice offered in fulfillment of a vow, made, as a rule, at a time when the child was dangerously ill or when some other danger, real or imagined, threatened. In all these cases the hair is *fedû an el-weled,* "redemption for the child."[29] Between the moment when the vow is made and the later moment when the hair is cut off as a sacrifice, no razor may come upon the head of the child; in other words, judging by Biblical analogy, the child is in a state of taboo or consecration approximating that of the Nazirite. From this state he is freed and permitted to pass into the state of ordinary, profane life, by the sacrifice of his hair.[30]

However, in marked contrast to these instances of the sacrifice of the hair in payment of vows, performed only after the first year, Kahle remarks, quite incidentally:[31] "When there is deposited with the 'saint,' what often happens in the vicinity of Jerusalem, the first hair and nails of a child, cut off and tied up in some rag, it is understood that this act will secure blessing for the body to which they belonged." This seems to imply that, at least in the vicinity of Jerusalem, the custom is still quite general of offering not only the first hair, but also the first parings of the nails to the "saint" who has been instrumental in the birth of the child, soon after the child has come into the world. This approximates very closely the normal *'aḳîḳah,* and its underlying purpose is obviously the same: to avert evil from the child by redeeming it from the power of the "saint" who had given it birth, and thus to secure a blessing for it.[32]

Jaussen likewise states[33] that among the Arabs of Moab the *'aḳîḳah* consists in shaving the head of the newborn infant and smearing it with the blood of the sacrifice.[34] This accords fully with Lane's account of the various ceremonies performed upon the seventh day after birth, particularly the *ʿaḳîḳah* rite of shaving off the child's first hair, and with the other examples of this same rite which we have already cited.

All this evidence indicates that, at the most, there may be a tendency in certain localities today to defer the rite of cutting off the first hair of the child until a time later than the seventh day after birth. But even this modern tendency is by no means universal in the Moslem world. The conclusion can not be avoided that the original practice, which still persists in many localities, was to perform this ceremony of redemption of the child by means of cutting off its first hair upon the seventh day after birth, at the very moment of, and in connection with, the redemption-sacrifice of a substitute animal, called by various names. Furthermore, the practice of giving the weight of the child's hair in silver as alms to the poor indicates that the cutting off of the hair, like the sacrifice of an animal, has the fundamental purpose of redeeming the child from the state of taboo resting upon it from birth. This ceremony, whenever performed, marks the close of the first period of the child's life, when it is still under the influence of malignant powers, and its passing into the second period, when it is redeemed and therefore no longer taboo. The child then becomes qualified to receive its own name, to develop its own personality, to enter into membership in the tribe, and to begin ordinary existence.

IX

Circumcision

Closely related to the *'akîkah* ceremony of cutting off the hair of a child and offering it as a substitute sacrifice upon the seventh or eighth day is the rite of circumcision. The question of the origin and meaning of this strange rite has been discussed repeatedly by eminent scholars, and opinions and hypotheses of most surprising range have been advanced.[1] Thus, Herbert Spencer suggested that circumcision originated in the practice of cutting off the foreskins of captives taken in war as a sign of subjection; later it came to be generally regarded as a tribute offered by the common men to the chief, or the god, as a token of recognition of the latter's superiority.[2]

Westermarck[3] holds that circumcision originated, like various other bodily mutilations, as a means of attracting the other sex, and that the religious significance attached to it by some people is a secondary and later development.

Toy holds that circumcision sprang from the desire to increase sexual enjoyment, and that conservatism later sanctified it as a religious rite. There is no definite record anywhere, so he claims, of its direct connection at the moment of origin with the worship of any particular deity.[4]

Frazer suggests, though rather hesitatingly, that circumcision was originally intended to ensure rebirth at some future time, by disposing of the severed foreskin in such a way as to provide the circumcised man with a stock of energy upon which his disembodied spirit could draw when the critical moment of reincarnation came.[5] Frazer classifies other bodily mutilations, such as the knocking out of the teeth, under the same head. He states further that since these rites seem to be regularly performed at about the age of puberty, they also serve the secondary purpose of rites of initiation into manhood and into the tribe, with all consequent obligations and privileges. Frazer's hypothesis is based entirely upon observations of circumcision as practiced by the aborigines of Australia. Yet he suggests that this hypothesis may satisfactorily account for the sad lot of the uncircumcised in Sheol, as described in Ezekiel 32 : 17–32.[6]

According to Schwally, both the rite of circumcision and the concept of the sanctity of the male organ were derived from ancestor-worship.[7]

Loisy maintains that circumcision was originally a rite of initiation into the state of manhood, and presumably also into tribal membership.[8] He further suggests that the Israelite practice was probably borrowed from the Egyptians and hence was not practiced by the Israelites before their entrance into Canaan.[9] Basing his argument upon the account of the circumcision of all the males in Israel by Joshua immediately after the crossing of the Jordan,[10] Loisy further holds that circumcision was practiced by the Israelites in order to enable them lawfully to hold Palestine, the land of Yahweh, as their own. However, he seems to feel the untenability of this hypothesis. He himself suggests that the use of flint knives in performing the rite indicates an origin in remote antiquity, long before the entrance into Palestine. And it is questionable whether Palestine was regarded as Yahweh's land as early as when the tribes of Israel entered it. Rather, it would seem, this concept evolved only slowly and gradually and could hardly have become clearly defined and firmly rooted much before the establishment of the Israelite kingdom under David. But even granting Loisy's hypothesis for the moment, his argument fails entirely to support his altogether gratuitous suggestion that only by the performance of this rite could the tribes lawfully hold Yahweh's land. Certainly the Philistines were uncircumcised; and Genesis 34 : 15–24 implies that the people of Shechem, and possibly other Canaanites as well, were, normally at least, uncircumcised. Loisy's hypothesis is therefore entirely contrary to fact and consequently is completely groundless.

Barton proposes that circumcision was in origin "a sacrifice to the goddess of fertility, by which the child was placed under her protection and its reproductive powers consecrated to her service. . . . Originally, circumcision seems to have been a preparation for connubium,"[11] and the practice was probably transferred to an earlier age for humanitarian reasons. At the same time, the possibility of another explanation is suggested by Barton, namely, that it may have been a redemption-sacrifice, in conformity with the taboo-principle that the sacrifice of a part redeems the remainder.

Samter[12] holds that circumcision was originally conceived of as a means of warding off evil spirits by giving them some of both the blood and the body of the child; in other words, it was a ceremony of removal of taboo.[13] The eminent Dutch scholar Matthes also believes that the original purpose of circumcision was to promote fruitfulness, and that the rite was borrowed by the Semites from the Egyptians.[14]

However, the most frequently advanced and most generally accepted theory of the origin and meaning of circumcision, particularly as practiced by certain Semitic peoples, is that this rite was originally performed at or near the advent of puberty, and that the performance of this rite at an earlier age—

as, for example, in ancient Israel upon the eighth day after birth[15]—was a secondary development of the original practice. Circumcision at puberty, the advocates of this hypothesis maintain, was a ceremony of initiation into manhood, with its accompanying duty and privilege of marriage. It was also an initiation into the tribe, with its consequence of kinship with every member of the tribe and with the tribal deity. This kinship or bond of union was established primarily by virtue of the blood shed during the act, whereby an enduring covenant was established between the circumcised youth and the deity and his fellow tribesmen.[16] This hypothesis has been advanced and accepted by such representative and authoritative scholars as Robertson Smith,[17] Wellhausen,[18] Stade,[19] Smend,[20] Marti,[21] Baentsch,[22] Levy,[23] Doutté,[24] H. P. Smith,[25] Peters,[26] and many others.[27]

The grounds for this hypothesis of circumcision as a rite of initiation at puberty are stated most clearly and concisely by Wellhausen: "According to Genesis 17, Ishmael was thirteen years old when he was circumcised and, according to Buchârî 4, 81, a man was not circumcised until he was full-grown. [Note: "Ibn Abbas was asked how old he was at the death of the Prophet. He answered, 'I had just been circumcised.' He was then thirteen years old."] Originally circumcision was, so it seems, a kind of barbaric test of maturity which the youth had to undergo before he might marry. In the etymology of *ḥatana* a relationship between circumcision and bridegroom, respectively father-in-law, is clearly apparent; this relationship is implied in Genesis 34; and particularly in Exodus 4 : 24–26 Sippora circumcises her infant son instead of her husband, and touches with the bloody foreskin of the former the genitals of the latter . . . in order to indicate that circumcision of the child is a modified equivalent of the original circumcision of the young men before marriage. Legendary reminiscences of this original nature and significance of circumcision still obtain among the modern Bedouin."[28] Elsewhere, Wellhausen remarks: "That this [circumcision as a necessary preliminary to marriage] was actually the original practice is to be inferred from the word *chatan,* which connotes the act of circumcision as well as bridegroom [or in Arabic, son-in-law], upon which the meaning of *chatan damîn* ["bridegroom of blood"] in Exodus 4 : 25 depends. Still today the original custom is said to be practiced by some Arab tribes, just as also Shechem, in Genesis 34, had to be circumcised before marriage."[29]

This constitutes in substance the sum total of the argument for this generally accepted hypothesis that circumcision was originally practiced by the Semites at the age of puberty, as a rite of initiation into the state of manhood and membership in the tribe, and preparatory to marriage. Inasmuch as in ancient Israel the rite was performed upon infants on the eighth day after birth, and, moreover, inasmuch as in modern Moslem practice the rite is performed generally between the ages of two and seven years, and only exceptionally and in a comparatively few, isolated cases as late as the thirteenth year

—a fact that is admitted by practically all scholars who consider this phase of the question—it must be acknowledged that this is rather slender and precarious evidence upon which to base so far-reaching and positive a hypothesis.

Nor does this evidence itself stand the test of careful analysis. Wellhausen's chief, or only, source for his statement that circumcision is said to be still practiced by Bedouin tribes today at puberty and preliminary to marriage is Doughty.[30] Doughty was told by other tribesmen that among the Harb "the male is not circumcised in childhood, but when he is of age to take a wife; then his friends send for surgery and the young man is pilled from the pubis: the maiden also looking on, and if her lad shrink or cast a sigh, wellah, she will disdain him for a husband." But Doughty adds, what was overlooked by Wellhausen, that when he came among the Harb and asked them: "Is it so among you?" " 'Lord!' they answered, 'that so strange things should be reported of us poor people! But Khalîl, these things are told of el-Kahtân' . . . that is, of a further nation, and always far off."

Of this same practice one of our most authoritative observers says: "In Central Arabia there are some tribes where circumcision is performed at a mature age, and in a manner painful and not without danger, while the bride of the circumcised man stands by, in order to test his courage. And she will nullify her betrothal if he utters a single cry of pain."[31] To this, however, a note is added: "Various European travelers have mentioned these barbarous circumcision customs in the west and south of Arabia; the same thing was frequently told me in Mecca, and always in relation to the ʿAsîr-tribes and some tribes to the east and south of T̲âif. . . . But I must confess that doubts have arisen in my mind, whether this tale is not to be regarded as legendary. Despite repeated investigation, I have never succeeded in getting reliable information thereof. Our present reports come entirely or indirectly from city dwellers," and not from the tribes in question. It is difficult indeed not to share in this doubt and not to question, therefore, the evidence from which Wellhausen draws his conclusions.

But assuming for the moment the correctness of this tradition, there might have been added the following few instances of circumcision at the attainment of puberty among the Semites today. Petermann[32] states that among the Sunnites circumcision generally takes place at the age of puberty; among the Shiites, on the contrary, so soon as the child gets his first teeth. Frequently, however, among the Sunnites it takes place even later, but always before marriage. Furthermore, Burton relates[33] that while the customary age for circumcision is between five and six, among some classes it is performed ten years later. This is, however, clearly an exception to the general rule. According to G. Wad-el-Ward,[34] the Moslems of Palestine circumcise a boy between the ages of ten and fourteen years. This, however, does not accord at all with the testimony of the great majority of modern witnesses, but it may perhaps be the practice in some small, isolated locales. According to one of our most authoritative observers,[35] in Moslem Palestine today, circumcision is normally performed in early childhood. It is the parents' duty to see that their sons are circumcised at the proper age. However, the ceremony may be deferred for various reasons. But under any condition it should precede marriage. And actually it is a disgrace to a man to be full-grown and still uncircumcised.

Lane, too, relates that among the modern Egyptians, while circumcision is generally practiced at the age of about five or six years, among the peasants it is not infrequently delayed until the twelfth, thirteenth, or even the fourteenth year.[36] Elsewhere, as we have seen, Lane says even more specifically, "Circumcision is most approved if performed on the same day (i.e., the day of the *ʿaḳîḳah* ceremonies, the seventh day after birth); but the observance of this rite is generally delayed until the child has attained the age of five or six years, and sometimes several years later."[37] Obviously here, circumcision upon the seventh day and in relation to the *ʿaḳîḳah* ceremonies is the original and normal practice, and the postponement thereof is a secondary development.

Hoskins[38] likewise states that in Egypt, in contrast to the practice in Ethiopia, circumcision is frequently postponed until the child is twelve or fourteen years old. According to Klippel,[39] circumcision among the Bedouin of Egypt was in olden days performed upon a male just before marriage, but it is now performed at an early age. Among the Copts of Egypt also, circumcision was performed "at a proper time before marriage, at the age of eleven or twelve,"[40] while another source relates that circumcision among the Copts is usually performed in connection with marriage ceremonies, and upon boys between the ages of ten and thirteen years;[41] and according to Lane, the Copts circumcise between the ages of two and twenty years.[42] However, a more recent traveler states explicitly that among both the Alexandrian and Abyssinian Copts circumcision is practiced between the ages of six and eight years. It is not at all a religious rite; it may not be performed in a church, and in no case after baptism has been administered.[43] This Egyptian practice may perhaps be a survival of the ancient Egyptian mode of circumcision rather than the result of Semitic influence.

Practically every one of these instances of circumcision at or near the age of puberty is represented as an exception to the general rule of circumcision at a much earlier age. If this indicates anything at all, it is only that the age of puberty, or possibly the period immediately preceding marriage, was the latest possible moment at which circumcision might be performed. In other words, among those Semites who practiced circumcision a man had to be circumcised before he might marry. But it does not follow at all from this that circumcision might not have been regularly performed much earlier.

Nor does this imply that there is any direct or essential connection between circumcision and marriage. The connection may well have been altogether incidental. It may have meant no more than that, just as a male must have passed out of the state of infancy and of childhood into manhood in order to be qualified to marry, so also he must have been circumcised in order to be regarded as being in a marriageable state.[44] But marriage did not necessarily follow immediately and consequently upon circumcision any more than it followed immediately and consequently upon the attainment of puberty.

In significant contrast to all these obviously exceptional instances of circumcision at or near the age of puberty, or even later, practically all authorities agree that normally circumcision is performed much earlier. Among the Bedouin, Musil states, the third year is regarded as the time least dangerous for circumcision, and accordingly the rite is as a rule performed then.[45] Doughty says: "The nomad son is circumcised being come to the strength of three full years; and then as the season may serve without any superstition of days, and as the mother shall be able to provide corn or rice enough for her guests' supper. They sometimes put off the surgery till the morrow, in any rough, windy weather, or because of the Arabs' ráhla."[46] Jaussen writes: "No age is especially appointed for the performance of the rite. Among the Ṣeẖour they wait until the child is in his fourth or fifth year; a similar practice obtains at Maʿan; among the Belqāwīeh the rite is performed from the age of one year onward; the Šarārāt, who are poor, wait until they chance to have a sheep, in order to be able to celebrate the festival properly. In the Neǧeb it seems that the child ought to be at least two years old. Actually the operation is performed by a specialist from Gaza, who is brought for this purpose when the child is close to his second birthday, and when there is a sufficient number of children to be circumcised; and the reason for this arrangement is economy. Many families unite to pay the costs."[47] According to Burckhardt[48] and Millard,[49] the Bedouin usually circumcise the child when he is six or seven years old; according to Dickson, circumcision is performed between the ages of three and a half and seven years.[50]

In direct contradiction of the statement of Wad-el-Ward, cited above, Pierotti reports that the Moslems of Palestine generally circumcise a child upon the eighth day after birth.[51] This agrees with the tradition that Mohammed "followed the Jews in selecting the eighth (or, as the Muslims call it, the seventh . . . the day of birth not being included) day for the circumcision of his grandsons, and this day is recommended by many jurists, though there is some difficulty about the propriety of imitating the Jews."[52] Bliss, too, records that circumcision may be performed at any time between the ages of ten days and seven years, and is occasionally deferred until even later, but must under all conditions be performed before marriage.[53] Dalman states that in Palestine the circumcision of boys is regularly performed between the second and sixth years.[54] Curtiss likewise notes that in Palestine children are usually circumcised when five or six years old, though occasionally somewhat later.[55] The ceremony usually takes place at a *maqâm* or shrine, and is accompanied by a sacrifice. The blood of the sacrifice is placed upon the threshold of the sanctuary. The practice of the fellahin of Palestine is described in these words: "All Moslems are expected to be circumcised, but there is no limit of age. As festivals always accompany circumcision, the poorer classes put it off, and should death come before it is performed, the circumcision is made on the corpse. Generally the fellahin of Philistia perform the ceremony at the feast of Rubin, in the court of the mosque at Rubin. All friends and relatives go there and assist the traditional sacrifice which accompanies it."[56]

Among practically all the Arab tribes of Yemen children are invariably circumcised upon the seventh day after birth.[57] In Abyssinia circumcision regularly takes place upon the eighth day after birth.[58] Immediately after birth, however, a fowl is killed by having its throat cut in the presence of the child.[59] This is undoubtedly a preliminary substitution-sacrifice on behalf of the child. Among the Falashas water is poured upon the child immediately after birth. Circumcision is performed by women upon the eighth day, unless this happens to be a Sabbath, in which case it is performed upon the ninth day.[60] Not improbably, in both Yemen and Abyssinia Jewish influence is responsible for the very early performance of this ceremony. Among the Persian Shiites, also, according to the statement of a competent authority, circumcision is regularly performed upon the eighth day after birth, although not infrequently it is delayed for some years.[61] Among the Yezidis, according to one account, circumcision is a religious rite, but not obligatory or strictly enforced.[62] But, according to a seemingly more reliable authority, circumcision is a religious obligation among the Yezidis, and is performed one week after the baptism of the child.[63] This should take place before the end of the first week after birth, but if not then, certainly within the first two months, and absolutely before the close of the first two years.[64] The ceremony of circumcision among the Yezidis is practiced in imitation of the Jews and Christians.[65] It is followed by a feast which continues for seven days.

Somewhat in contradiction of the evidence already presented with regard to the customary age at which in Egypt the rite of circumcision is performed, is the statement of Ali Bey[66] that children there may be circumcised at all ages under twelve; however, the ceremony is most commonly performed in early childhood. According to another authority, the thirteenth year is the lastest possible age for the performance of the rite, while circumcision between the ages of four and six is quite common.[67] According to Klunzinger, the rite is performed in Upper Egypt when the children are from five to ten years old.[68]

In Northern Africa also, children are generally circumcised when about six to eight years old[69] and only occasionally is the rite deferred until the twelfth or fourteenth year.[70] More specific information with regard to the practice in Northern Africa is given by Doutté.[71] He states that among the Doukkâla "circumcision is performed ordinarily seven or eight days after birth. This is the most general custom; but one may see those who wait much longer; and there are even some young people who reach the age of twelve or thirteen years without being circumcised." Elsewhere he writes: "The Reḥâmna circumcise their children between the ages of two and five years. It is well known that the age at which this ceremony is performed varies greatly throughout all the Magrib. We have seen that among the Doukkâla this age varies from seven days to twelve or thirteen years. At Fez circumcision is performed between the second and the tenth year; at Tangiers at about the eighth year; among the Jbâla between the fifth and the tenth year; in the vicinity of Mogador between the second and the fourth year. In Algeria this operation is generally performed upon children at about the age of seven or eight years. Orthodox Islam recommends that circumcision be practiced upon the same day as the *'aqîqa,* that is, upon the seventh day after birth."[72]

This evidence bears out completely our contention that the age of puberty merely marks, as a rule, the latest possible date for the performance of the rite of circumcision, and that in the vast majority of cases the rite is performed much earlier and entirely without direct relationship either to the attainment of puberty or to marriage. This effectually disposes of the first point of Wellhausen's argument. We may now consider the remaining evidence of his "puberty-marriage" hypothesis.

The second point of his argument is likewise unconvincing. It is true that the Bible states that Ishmael was thirteen years old when circumcised.[73] But it states also that Isaac was circumcised upon the eighth day after birth,[74] and that Abraham was ninety-nine years old when he was circumcised.[75] Certainly it was the Israelite practice at the time of the composition of the Priestly Code, and probably already at a much earlier time, to circumcise boys upon the eighth day after birth. The author of Genesis 21 : 2b-5 undoubtedly meant to represent this practice as having been instituted by Abraham at the circumcision of Isaac. But it does not necessarily follow from the P Code statement, that Ishmael was thirteen years old when he was circumcised, that the traditional descendants of Ishmael were accustomed to practice circumcision at the age of thirteen years. Were this a logical conclusion, then we could equally logically assume that other traditional descendants of Abraham, the Midianites or Sabaeans,[76] for example, circumcised their male offspring only when they had attained the respectable age of ninety-nine years, the age of Abraham when he circumcised himself. In all likelihood the author meant to tell no more than that Abraham happened to be ninety-nine years old and Ishmael thirteen at the time, just prior to the birth of Isaac, of the establishment of the covenant between the Deity and Abraham,[77] of which circumcision is represented as the seal. The author cites this fact for the same reason that he tells that Abraham was seventy-five years old when he came to Canaan[78] and eighty-six years old when Ishmael was born,[79] merely because of his characteristic interest in the pedantic detail of numbers, ages, and dates, and by no means intending to imply that the Ishmaelites were circumcised at the age of thirteen years. Had this been his purpose, he would certainly have stated the fact plainly.

Nor is the conclusion which Wellhausen draws from Genesis 34 at all justified. True, the sons of Jacob demand that before Shechem may marry their sister he must be circumcised like themselves, for it would be a disgrace were their sister given to one uncircumcised.[80] Accordingly, in the J version of the story Shechem is circumcised alone, or together with the male members of his father's house; and in the E version[81] he is circumcised together with all the males of the city, apparently both married and unmarried, child as well as adult, and not merely the men of marriageable age. Thus, neither version conveys anything of the thought which Wellhausen reads into it, namely, that circumcision was essentially a marriage rite. Had this been the case, Shechem alone should have been circumcised at this time, and each of the other males only upon the occasion of his own marriage. But instead of this the J version says no more than that for an Israelite maiden to marry an uncircumcised man would be a disgrace. This merely implies the old Israelite practice of the circumcision of males in early childhood, and by no means that it was an attendant marriage rite; since Shechem had not been circumcised as a child, he naturally had to be circumcised now, before marriage.

Moreover, the E version relates that the people of Shechem adopted the Israelite rite of circumcision; and, as all the evidence indicates, this was performed very early in childhood, and never as a rite immediately preliminary to marriage. Accordingly, all the males of the city—young and old, apparently, and by no means only those who were married or on the point of marriage—were circumcised, to conform with the principles of circumcision as practiced in Israel. In other words, the tradition in Genesis 34, in either version, does not evidence any connection at all between the rite of circumcision and marriage, other than that marriage was certainly, according to ancient Israelite practice, the latest possible moment in a man's life at which circumcision might be performed, and that, accordingly, an uncircumcised person was not qualified to marry. The only conclusion which can possibly be drawn from all the evidence which has thus far been presented is that in ancient Israel, and therefore as borrowed by the Shechemites also, circumcision was a rite performed normally upon little children.

The third passage, upon which Wellhausen lays chief stress and from which he endeavors to draw the strongest support of his hypothesis, is Exodus 4 : 24–26. He and many eminent scholars after him interpret this passage as implying that in Israel circumcision was originally a ceremony of initiation into the tribe, performed at puberty, and incidentally, therefore, a rite preliminary to and attendant upon marriage.[82] The narrative here recorded is a tiny fragment which stands completely by itself, with no immediate, visible connection with any other Biblical incident or any other account of the relations between Yahweh and Moses. Undoubtedly it was once a part of a larger tradition or document. That this original tradition, even in its present literary form, was of great antiquity is proved by the unmistakably archaic character of the details of the incident, as, for example, the picture of Yahweh, apparently in human form, seeking to take the life of the child, the natural use of a flint for the operation, the obviously redemptive character of the circumcision, the formula recited by the mother during the ceremony, and the unquestionably *beena* marriage[83] background of the narrative.

On the basis of these and other cogent considerations I have proposed that this passage, actually only two and one-half verses in extent,[84] is a fragment of the Kenite Code (K), the oldest document of the Hexateuch,[85] and that it has no actual narrative connection with the passages which immediately precede and follow it in the Biblical text. Certainly, had it not been interpolated into its present position in the Biblical text, it would never have been missed.

The passage, largely because of its brief, fragmentary condition, but for other reasons as well, is extremely difficult to interpret with assurance. Therefore, probably no other Biblical passage has experienced so wide a range of translation and exposition, not only in the various ancient versions of the Biblical text but also by many authoritative Biblical scholars of recent times, of whom Wellhausen is one.

I myself have treated this passage and its many different interpretations in detail and have demonstrated convincingly, so I believe, that Wellhausen's interpretation of the passage and likewise the interpretations of almost all other scholars are incorrect and misleading in practically every respect.[86] I have shown that, contrary to the interpretation of the large majority of modern Biblical scholars, the child was not circumcised as the substitute for his father, Moses, who should have been circumcised prior to his marriage with Zipporah, of the Kenite clan, whose god Yahweh was. But Moses, for some unknown and unsurmisable reason, had not undergone this redemption rite, and his life Yahweh was now seeking to take as His due. Nor yet was it Moses at whose feet the child's severed foreskin was cast, or whose genital organ was touched by the severed foreskin in Zipporah's hand, as Wellhausen and other scholars maintain. In fact, in the narrative proper, recorded in verses 24–26, the name Moses does not occur even once, and impliedly in this particular episode Moses plays at the most only a completely passive and meaningless role. Rather it is the child, obviously born quite recently, whose life Yahweh has given and now endeavors to take, and who is redeemed from death by the prompt action of his mother, Zipporah, in thus, at the critical moment, severing her son's foreskin and presenting it to Yahweh by casting it at His feet, as the proper redemption-sacrifice for the infant. And having thus received His due, Yahweh must, of course, relinquish all further claim upon the child's life, in conformity with the basic principle of taboo-sacrifice.

Obviously, too, the child would normally have been circumcised by his mother's oldest brother, Hobab, the recognized head of the Kenite clan, but since he was not present at this critical moment, in sheer desperation the mother acted in his stead and thus saved the life of her babe. She acted as the *ḥôtenet,* the "female circumciser," in place of her oldest brother, the normal *ḥôten,* the "male circumciser." Moreover, she performed the act by means of a sharp flint stone, the most primitive cutting instrument known to man. A further implication of the passage is that among the Kenites, who were at the time of Moses still practicing *beena* marriage, and therefore reflecting a very early stage of the evolution of Semitic culture and religious principle and practice, circumcision was normally performed upon infants, presumably upon the eighth day after birth.

Having thus established the incorrectness of Wellhausen's interpretation of Genesis 17 and 34 and Exodus 4 : 24–26, and the untenability of the hypothesis which in large measure he based upon this incorrect interpretation—that circumcision was originally a rite of initiation into the tribe and preliminary to marriage, performed upon youths at the attainment of puberty—we may now take up anew the question of the true origin and nature of this rite.

In ancient Israel, circumcision was generally, though, as we shall see, not invariably, performed upon the eighth day after birth.[87] This custom is still observed by Jews today. It is significant that this ceremony is practiced upon the very same day as are, in the Arab world, the *ʿaḳîḳah* rites of the sacrifice of a substitute animal and the cutting off of the child's first hair. It is significant, too, that the day of the circumcision of a Jewish child, and of the holding of the accompanying feast, was called in rabbinic literature *šabûʿa habben,* literally, "the week of the son,"[88] just as among the present-day Bedouin the day of the offering of the redemption-sacrifice for the child is called *yôm sabuʿa,* "the day of the week," or, "the day which completes the week." It seems, moreover, that the *ʿaḳîḳah* rites are performed upon the eighth day only by people who practice circumcision later in life, but that where circumcision is performed upon the eighth day, as among the Jews, or, what amounts to the same thing, upon the seventh day, as among the tribes of Southern Arabia and in Abyssinia, the *ʿaḳîḳah* rites are not performed.

These facts can indicate but one thing: that circumcision and the *ʿaḳîḳah* are closely related ceremonies, both serving exactly the same fundamental purpose, and, moreover, that the performance of some such rite as this was imperative upon the seventh or the eighth day after birth. As we have already shown, the power of evil spirits was thought to reach its climax upon this seventh or "unlucky" day. The night before the circumcision of a boy is today still called by Orthodox Jews "watchnight." Since it is the moment of greatest danger for the child, some one must remain in the room with him and must keep awake throughout the night, to guard the infant against the evil spirits.

In addition to the instances of this "watchnight" cited above,[89] the following cases are interesting and significant in this particular connection. On this "watchnight" among the native Jews of Jerusalem, friends send lighted lamps to the house of the mother of the newly born child. In addition, a thin metal cup, holding twelve lighted wax candles as a symbol of the luck-star, is swung around on high on behalf of the child by those present, who sing during this act.[90] The purpose of this ceremony is unmistakable. Moreover, no one may enter the house of the father on any of the eight nights following the birth, and particularly on the last night, the night immediately preceding the circumcision, known as the "night of the spirits." The only exceptions are such relatives as live within the same courtyard, and learned men who are invited.[91] These last, quite obviously, are regarded as immune to the attacks of the evil spirits, and as perhaps even able in some measure to drive these spirits away.

Likewise among the Jews of the Barbary Coast, "at the birth of a boy the following customs are observed; from the day of birth until that of circumcision an entertainment is given each evening in the house, to which acquaintances and relatives are invited. That on the first night is called *Seudat Eliahu* (repast of Elijah); that on the last night before the circumcision is called *Bilada;* and all the relations and friends assemble. The Chachamim read for about two hours, after which the entertainment commences, from the conclusion of which till toward morning the time is spent in reading, chanting, etc. On the morning of the eighth day the circumcision takes place in the synagogue with great solemnities."[92]

For this same purpose of warding off the evil spirits, which are most threatening at, or just prior to, circumcision, the Moslems of Egypt, upon returning from the mosque to the house after the circumcision, sprinkle salt behind the circumcised child and upon the bystanders, "to guard against the evil eye."[93] Similarly, the peasants of Palestine hang a piece of gilded garlic upon the bed of a boy who is about to be circumcised.[94]

The account of the ceremonies attendant upon a circumcision among the Bedouin of the Sinaitic Peninsula, recorded by Palmer,[95] is in this connection most illuminating. He says: "The rite of circumcision, as practiced among the Bedawin, is attended with great festivities and rejoicing.

"On the eve of the appointed day they erect a tent, which is decorated and carpeted in readiness for the morrow's ceremony. When the morning comes, all who can afford it bring a lamb or some other contribution toward the feast, and proceedings are commenced with a public breakfast. At noon another sheep, called *'aġireh,* is sacrificed. . . . The children to be operated upon are then seated in a circle upon the carpet within the tent, and a curtain is hung before the door. They are next ceremoniously washed by their mothers, care being taken that their feet shall not touch the bare ground until the operation is complete. Each child is then decked out in all its mother's beads and ornaments, a knife is placed in one hand and a wooden cross decorated with colored rags in the other, and in this condition they are carried out and placed upon the shoulders of the men. A procession is thus formed, headed by men holding pans of burning incense, firing off pistols and beating sticks together, and makes the circuit of the tent three times.

"The mothers of the children, before leaving the tent, proceed to wash their feet in the large bowl previously made use of for the children, each holding a hand-mill balanced on her head all the time, after which they may join the procession. When these preliminaries are concluded, and the children rearranged around the tent, the operator proceeds with his duties, first asking permission of the father of each child in turn, and demanding exemption from all penalties in case of a dangerous or fatal result. He then receives a small fee for each of the children operated on. After circumcision the boy is not allowed again to enter the women's apartments. The day's festivities conclude with a grand *fantasia,* and a goat's head is generally set up as a mark for the young hunters of the tribe to shoot at, a leg or shoulder of the animal being given to the successful competitor."

Certain details of these ceremonies clearly evidence the belief in the threatening presence of evil spirits upon this occasion and the necessity of warding them off, particularly the ceremonial washing of the boys to be circumcised as well as the subsequent washing of their own feet by the mothers, the care taken that the feet of the children shall not touch the ground until the completion of the operation, the decking of the boys with their mothers' beads and ornaments, the carrying by them of the knife in one hand and the gaudily adorned wooden cross in the other, and, above all else, the procession of the men three times about the circumcision tent, accompanied by the burning of incense and the attendant loud noise. It is quite significant also that with the completion of the operation the boy is not allowed again to enter the women's apartment; in other words, circumcision clearly marks the passing of the boy from one stage of life, that of innocent childhood, with free ingress into and sojourn in the women's apartment, to that of full tribal life and theoretical maturity, when the former unrestricted association with women is forbidden. Palmer does not here give the age of the boys when circumcised, but from his statement that the boys are first washed by their mothers and are then carried in procession upon the shoulders of the men, as well as from the testimony of other travelers among the Sinaitic Bedouin, we may safely infer that they had not yet reached the age of puberty but were still quite young, probably between the ages of three and seven years.

The origin and meaning of the strange rite of the mothers balancing the hand-mills upon their heads are not at all clear. Musil makes mention of this same rite in his description of the circumcision ceremony. He says: "Circumcision is performed preferably on a Monday toward evening. But this Monday may not fall upon the 6th or 16th, 7th or 17th, 9th or 19th, or the 21st of the month. It is best when the Monday falls upon the 1st or the 15th; Wednesday and Thursday are regarded as days unlucky for the ceremony.

"In the evening a father, whose boy is to be circumcised, invites the guests to a meal. The young people gather before the tent and dance the *daḥa* dances,[96] which they accompany by the singing of little songs oft-repeated.... On the following evenings, other fathers whose boys are to be circumcised play the role of hosts.

"Meanwhile in a prominent place, preferably in the center of the camp, a large tent is erected.... On Monday the children are washed clean, and white shirts, long red cloaks and red turbans are put on them.

"Among the Ḥwêṭât just before the circumcision, the boy takes a sword, runs to the animal designated as the *'aḳîḳe*-sacrifice, and cuts the tendons on the hind legs, whereupon the animal is immediately slaughtered. Only men may eat of its flesh.

"Then the boys are brought into the tent, their feet are washed, and each is made to sit upon a large stone or upon the hand-mill. Then the tent is closed. In it are the circumciser and the immediate female relatives of the boys. All must be clean, i.e., they must not have had sexual intercourse during the preceding night, nor be menstruating, nor have given birth within the last forty days....

"During the circumcision the related women and girls stand behind the closed tent, beat upon the tent cover with their crooked knives, and let their shrill cries resound, in order to protect the circumcised boys from the evil eye. For this they receive a small present from the fathers of the boys.

"The foreskin of each boy is cut off and the blood flows upon the stone. Then the women take the boy together with the stone or the hand-mill, carry them about the tent three times and cry *lu-lu-lu-li-a* . . . while the blood drops down. Then the mother or the nearest female relative lays the heavy stone upon her head, and holds it there until the circumcised boy gives her a present of something of his father's property."[97] Here, too, the meaning of this last ceremony is not clear, although numerous hypotheses to account for it might be offered.[98] But again, the fear of evil spirits is clearly manifested upon this occasion.

In this connection, other of the various connotations of the Arabic term *'aḳîḳah* become meaningful: "(a) the prepuce of a boy when he is circumcised; (b) the wool of a *ġaḏa'* (or sheep in or before its second year); that of a *ṯanîjjah* (or sheep in its third year) is called *ġanîbah;* (c) the hair of a young one recently born, that comes forth upon its head in its mother's belly, because it is cut off on his seventh day, and of others, of beasts likewise; and (d) the sheep or goat (generally the latter) that is slaughtered as a sacrifice for the recently born infant on the seventh day after his birth, and of which the limbs are divided and cooked with water and salt, and given as food to the poor."[99] We have also found the word used occasionally with the connotation "purification,"[100] a usage not recorded by Lane.

Of the term *ġaḏa'*, used in connotation (b) above, Lane states: "Said of an offspring of a sheep or goat, 'he became in his second year,' of that of a cow and of a solid-hoofed beast, 'he became in his third year,' and of that of a camel, 'he became in his fifth year'; but sometimes, when said of the offspring of a ewe, it means 'he became six months old,' or 'nine months old,' and such is allowable as a victim for sacrifice."[101] However, a goat or a bull or a camel does not become acceptable for sacrifice until it has passed out of the state of a *ġaḏaʿ* into that of a *ṯanîy*. According to Burckhardt,[102] a camel is already called *ġaḏaʿ* in its fourth year, at which age it begins to breed.

The implication of all this is unmistakable. Like the newborn babe, the young animal for a certain period after birth, varying from six months to five years according to the physical development of the different species, is strictly taboo. It may not be used for any purpose whatsoever, either sacred or profane, not even for ordinary sacrifice. The close of this taboo period is generally marked by the loss of the animal's first teeth. At this time it is regarded as having reached maturity; also—at least in some instances—as having become able to reproduce. With the sacrifice of its wool or hair, *ʿaḳîḳah,* the animal, like the infant after the *ʿaḳîḳah* sacrifice of its hair, enters the second period of its existence. It now becomes fit for sacrifice and may be ridden, sheared, and, presumably, used for other profane purposes.[103] And the term *ġaḏaʿ,* whether applied to sheep, goats, horses, or camels, implies the passage from this first, taboo stage of existence into the second, that of ordinary life. Now a new and distinctive name is applied to the animal.

The same principle is basic to the Biblical prohibition of using, for any purpose whatsoever, any animal during the first seven days after its birth, and the fruit of a tree during its first three years.[104] During this taboo-period the tree was regarded as being *ʿarel,* "uncircumcised," and its fruit was therefore called *ʿorlah,* literally, "foreskin" (which was cut off at circumcision); similarly, the wool of a sheep, while taboo during the animal's first year, is also called *ʿaḳîḳah,* "foreskin." In other words, *ʿorlah* in the Biblical practice[105] partook of precisely the same nature and purpose as the Arabic *ʿaḳîḳah.* Both terms clearly imply that the act of removal of the natural taboo thought to rest upon animals and children during the first period of life, and upon fruit trees during the first three years of growth, and which is designated in both Hebrew and Arabic as removal or sacrifice of the "foreskin," is, broadly speaking, "circumcision."

This is final proof that the sacrifice of the foreskin, whether of children, animals, or trees, redeemed the object from the taboo thought naturally to rest upon it during the first period of its life, and marked thereby its entrance into the second period, that of profane existence. This is confirmed by the common, modern Arabic terms, *ṭahhara,* "to circumcise" (literally, "to purify, to render clean, to remove the taboo"),[106] and *muṭahher,* "circumciser."[107] In other words, circumcision is clearly recognized as, in principle, a rite of ceremonial purification and removal of taboo. The Christian Arabs of Palestine employ the same technical term, *ṭahhara* (literally, "to purify"), in the connotation "to baptize," just as the Moslems use it in the meaning "to circumcise."

We may here very properly sum up our conclusions with regard to the origin and nature of the rite of circumcision among the Semites. First, circumcision was in origin a rite of removal of taboo thought to rest upon every newborn child during at least the first seven days after birth, and continuously thereafter until redeemed. The underlying principle in the removal of all taboo was that the sacrifice of a part of the tabooed person or object redeemed the whole. By the performance of this rite the child was redeemed from the power of threatening evil spirits, or of some evilly disposed deity, and thereby entered upon the second period of his existence, that of non-tabooed, ordinary, profane life. Thus far, circumcision was in every way of common origin and purpose with the various *ʿaḳîḳah* rites, whether applied to human beings, animals, or fruit trees. Moreover, in fundamental principle and character it was identical with other rites for the removal of taboo, such as the sacrifice of the hair, particularly the first hair with which a child was born, which was as a rule cut as a part of this *ʿaḳîḳah* ceremony.

Secondly, circumcision marked the entrance of the child into ordinary, profane existence and consequent tribal membership. It served, therefore, as a rite of initiation into the tribe. But this was only of secondary import, a consequence of its primary character and purpose as a taboo-rite, and in no way accounts for its origin.

Because of its primary character, circumcision might be performed appropriately at any time between the seventh day after birth and the attainment of puberty. But until it was performed the original taboo state continued, at least in theory. By the attainment of puberty, however, circumcision must under all conditions have been performed, for the condition of childhood, or even of infancy, implied by the uncircumcised state, was not at all consonant with the condition of maturity which followed immediately upon the attainment of puberty, nor with the various duties, obligations, and privileges of maturity. Puberty was, in principle at least, the *terminus ad quem* for circumcision; but in themselves neither puberty nor marriage had for the Semites, so far as the evidence indicates, the slightest direct or primary connection with circumcision.[108]

One further aspect of circumcision must be considered here. Exodus 22 : 28 f. enjoins that upon the eighth day after birth both human and animal first-born must be given to the Deity. This can only mean sacrifice. Despite the opinions of almost all Biblical scholars, the conclusion cannot be avoided that in Israel at one time the sacrifice of first-born children was a quite common, if not the regular, practice.[109] Genesis 22 is in itself ample proof of this, and further corroboration is to be found in additional Biblical evidence. Scholars have not denied this fact; they have only maintained that human sacrifice was altogether incongruous with pure and original Yahweh-worship, and that therefore its practice in Israel must have been due entirely to foreign, non-

Yahwistic influences.[110] This argument is based largely upon two quite unscientific misconceptions: (1) that Yahweh-ritual and Yahweh-concept and religion were complete and final already at the time of Moses and the Exodus; and (2) that the moral or religious character of human sacrifice must be measured by our own modern standards, which condemn the practice as unnatural, repellent, and immoral, rather than by the standards of the period in which the ceremony was practiced.[111]

We are coming to realize, however, practically as well as theoretically, that Moses could only have laid the foundations of Yahweh-religion and no more, and that the religion of Israel is the product of natural, historic evolution, with its usual waves of progress and retrogression—from the remote desert period to the present day.[112] Moreover, if we judge the practice of first-born sacrifice from the standpoint of the early period in which it flourished, and in the light of the principles of taboo and its removal which we have established, we can understand that the sacrifice of first-born children must have seemed to the ancient Semites quite reasonable and natural. The life of the child belonged to the deity who had created it. It was therefore taboo, forfeit; consequently, it could easily be reclaimed by the deity whenever he wished. If not given this sacrifice, which was his due, the deity not only would almost surely reclaim the child nonetheless, but would also probably be angered against the family or clan, and might well be expected to visit his wrath upon them. Thus, if the first-born was not sacrificed, it would be futile to expect other and healthy children later. Just as with animals, so also the sacrifice of first-born children was a taboo-sacrifice for all future offspring, an application of the general principle that the sacrifice of a part—and that the first, and therefore presumably the best, part—redeems the remainder and renders it fit for ordinary life and use. Consequently, in the early stages of Israelite civilization in particular, as well as of Semitic civilization in general, first-born children were, beyond all question, regularly sacrificed to the proper deity or spirit as the natural and proper taboo-sacrifice.

As Israelite civilization developed, however, this old concept and practice were gradually outgrown. In all likelihood this change came about through the transition from *beena* to *baʿal* marriage, with the consequent establishment of fatherhood and the permanent presence and authority of the father within the family, and the attendant complete reorganization of family life and principles. So long as the mother's oldest brother was the head of the family or clan, parental affection could not assert itself fully. The interests of the clan transcended all considerations of parental love; and the interests of the family or clan required that first-born children be sacrificed in order that the deity might receive his due, and therefore continue to bestow his favor upon his worshipers and grant them numerous future offspring as well as other blessings. But under the conditions of *baʿal* marriage, parental affection on the part of both mother and father would have full opportunity to assert itself.

Thus, it was but a question of time and brief cultural progress until this later practice would prove stronger than the ancient beliefs, practices, and superstitious fears of a deity, the concept of whom had itself undergone considerable change and growth. Then the urge to terminate the old, cruel sacrifice would assert itself, and in time a way to attain this end would be found.

So, just as among other Semitic peoples passing through a like stage of cultural evolution, in ancient Israel, too, in time the actual sacrifice of the first-born child came to be withheld, and a supposedly fitting substitute was offered. At first this substitute was offered with hesitation, and with the thought that, should the deity ever manifest his disapproval and displeasure by sending misfortune, the original sacrifice could be promptly offered and the deity thus appeased. This would account for the frequent revival of the practice in late, pre-exilic times, at moments of national calamity and depression.[113] Eventually, however, with the advance in the level of civilization the belief became general that human sacrifice of any sort was unacceptable to Yahweh, and that He had actually commanded the substitution of a lamb for the first-born child.

In the South, in Judah, this stage of religious belief and practice was apparently reached earlier than in the North, in Israel, due to the fact that the ritual practice of the South was to a far less degree subject to the disturbing—and in many respects unspiritual and retrogressive—influence of Canaanite and foreign religious practice, and was therefore more free to develop spontaneously and in a straightforward direction. Therefore, it is not at all surprising to find that in Exodus 34 : 20 one law, of a covenant code formulated in the year 899 B.C., in the Southern Kingdom, expressly commands the substitution of a lamb for the human first-born, while in Exodus 22 : 28 f. the parallel law of a related covenant code formulated about 842 B.C. in the Northern Kingdom,[114] still explicitly commands the sacrifice to Yahweh of first-born children in precisely the same manner as firstlings of domestic animals were sacrificed to Him, that is, upon the eighth day after birth, the first day upon which, in accordance with the old, established principle, they became fit for sacrifice. This shows, as is in fact fully borne out by the historical background and purpose of the tradition in Genesis 22,[115] that in the Northern Kingdom the advance to something higher than actual first-born sacrifice came only after 842 B.C. In other words, the evidence seems ample that in the Northern Kingdom first-born sacrifice was regularly practiced in the worship of Yahweh as late as the middle of the ninth century B.C.

This is not the place to enter into an extensive discussion of this interesting and important subject of the taboo-sacrifice of firstlings and first-born. It suffices to say that the sacrifice of first-born children or, later, their redemption, either through the sacrifice of an animal substitute[116] or, eventually, by the payment of a stipulated sum of money,[117] was a taboo-offering designed to redeem all future offspring of the same mother. And this, by no means contradicts, but rather supports, our thesis that the sacrifice of the foreskin at circumcision, or of the first hair in the *'aḳîḳah* ceremony, constituted taboo-rites to redeem the very same children whom the sacrifice of the first-born child was intended to redeem. It was merely a different application of the principle that the sacrifice of a part redeems the remainder. Earlier, it was the sacrifice of the first child to redeem all future offspring of the same mother; later, it was the sacrifice of a part of the body of each child to redeem that particular child alone. Nor is there anything inconsistent or disturbing in the fact that both rites of removing the taboo upon offspring—the sacrifice of first-born children, or of animals substituted for them, and circumcision—should have been practiced simultaneously and in the same areas. It is merely another, and a very characteristic, instance of seemingly illogical duplication of rites and ceremonies in order to safeguard human life.

X

Circumcision Festivals

One further matter of importance concerning circumcision remains to be considered. It has been frequently noted by the most competent observers that the customary, although, as we have seen, by no means universal, practice today is to circumcise boys, not upon the seventh or eighth day after birth, but later in life and as a part—and as a rule apparently as the most important part—of the celebration of a festival.[1] Among the Bedouin this festival is usually celebrated at the tribal sanctuary, and among the fellahin at some important local shrine.[2]

Zwemer describes the circumcision festival in the following manner: "Bedouin children, male and female, go unclad and play together until their sixth year. The first child's festival is that of circumcision. At the age of seven years the day is fixed, sheep are killed, and a large dish of food is cooked. Women accompany the operation with a loud song and afterwards there is dancing and horseback riding and encounters with lances. The girls adorn themselves with cheap jewelry, and tent-poles are decorated with ostrich feathers. Altogether it is a gala day."[3]

Burckhardt's description of such a festival is more detailed and vivid: "It is generally arranged by those who have families in a camp, that all the young boys should be circumcised on the same day. Every man then kills at least one sheep in honor of his son—sometimes three or four—and all the members of the tribe, besides the strangers who come for the purpose, feast together during a whole day. On the festival of Ramadhan and of the sacrifice of Arafat those Arabs who have no horses run races upon their camels, while the women amuse themselves by singing loudly. Among the Sinai Arabs the girls are permitted on those occasions to let their faces be seen by the young men of the tribe,[4] who ride by swiftly on their camels, the girls at that moment raising their veils, so as to allow a hasty glance. It has been remarked that immediately after these feasts the girls are demanded in marriage from their fathers. The most prudish or coy among the girls do not join their companions in this raising of the veil, but remain in the interior of their tents."[5]

Another writer describes the same occasion as follows: "The greatest festival of the Arabs is that celebrated on the occasion of circumcision, for it is a universal custom, having more of a national than a religious character, to have this operation performed whenever the boys reach the age of six or seven years. On the morning of the day appointed for this purpose a sheep is killed in the tent by the father, and the uncle or nearest relation contributes a whole mutton ready to be boiled, or a large dish of cooked food for the entertainment of the guests. While the men are feasting in the tent the women of the encampment gather round the ornamented camel's saddle, placed in front of the entrance, and sing, in chorus, their favorite national songs in honor of the young candidate who is to be initiated, by a ceremonial rite, into the full fellowship with the older members of the tribe. As soon as the dinner is completed, the usual arrangements are made for the performance of the rite; the women standing around cheering the boy by their presence, and raising their voices in loud songs and characteristic cries of applause. The men, with lance in hand, and mounted on their mares, ride three times around the camel's saddle, and then, ranging themselves in two lines at some distance along the sides of the tent, they execute their warlike evolutions. The horsemen of the two opposing lines gallop up to an adversary, who, on being challenged, attempts to pass the challenger's mare, and if he succeeds to reach the opposite side, he, in turn, bids defiance to the opposing horsemen. This equestrian sport continues for more than an hour, while the women are singing the *assámer* and are lavishing their praises upon the best horseman and the owner of the swiftest mare."[6] Nothing is said here of the wooing of the youths and maidens and the ensuing marriages. But on the other hand, more emphasis is laid in this description upon the singing and crying of the attendant women. The significance of this procedure will be discussed later.

A similar account is given by Jennings-Bramley: "Circumcision is enjoined, and every man is circumcised; but no religious ceremony can be said to sanction the day on which this is done. In the desert they may have no one capable of safely performing the operation. A man—generally a barber—has to be brought from some way off; perhaps it may be a five days' journey. Supposing there are several boys in an encampment of the usual age—generally from five to seven—some Bedouin, going into one or other of the towns, is told to bring back with him a man who can circumcise. This settled, the news that a circumcision is to take place at such and such an encampment on such a day is sent far and wide, and all the boys are collected; the families come with all their friends, these latter bringing presents according to their means, be it a sheep or simply a bowl of rice; but never without something. A great festival is held, consisting of a great deal of galloping about and gunfiring. The boys who are to be circumcised are in a tent by themselves; the women collect around it and drown their cries by their own shrill voices. In this tent the boys remain, looked after by their mothers, for a week after the operation. During this week, while all are together, there is no end of feasting. There is dancing at night, and all that a Bedouin can desire to amuse himself is done."[7]

The account of this same occasion given by Palmer has already been quoted.[8]

The most minutely detailed account of these circumcision festivals is given by Doughty: "Now in the mild summer is the season of *muzayyins,* the nomad children's circumcision feasts; the mother's booth is set out with beggarly fringes of scarlet shreds, tufts of mewed ostrich feathers, and such gay gauds as they may borrow or find. Hither a chorus assembles of slender daughters of their neighbours, that should chant at this festival in their best array. A fresh kerchief binds about every damsel's forehead with a feather; she has earrings great as bracelets, and wears today her nose-ring, *zmèyem;* they are jewels in silver, and a few, as said, from old time are fine gold metal, *thahab el-asfr.* These are ornaments of the Bedouin women, hardly seen at other times (in the pierced nostril they wear for every day a head of cloves), and she has bracelets of beads and metal finger-rings. The thin black tresses, loosed today and not long, hang down upon their slight shoulders, and shine in the sun, freshly combed with camel urine. The lasses have borrowed new cloaks, which are the same for man or woman. Making a fairy ring apart, they begin, clapping the palms of their little hands, to trip it round together, chanting ever the same cadence of few words, which is a single verse. Hungered young faces, you might take them for some gipsy daughters; wayward not seldom in their mother's households, now they go playing before men's eyes, with downcast looks and a virginal timidity. But the Aarab raillery is never long silent, and often the young men, in this daylight feast, stand jesting about them. Some even pluck roughly at the feathers of the lasses, their own near cousins, in the dance, which durst answer them nothing, but only with reproachful eyes; or laughing loud the weleds have bye and bye divided this gentle bevy among them for wives; and if a stranger be there, they will bid him choose which one he would marry among them. 'Heigh-ho! what thinkest thou of these maidens of ours, and her, and her, be they not fair-faced?' But the virgins smile not, and if any look up, their wild eyes are seen estranged and pensive. They are like children under the rod, they should keep here a studied demeanor; but for all this they are not sirens. In that male tyranny of the Mohammedan religion regard is had to a distant maidenly behavior of the young daughters; and here they dance as the tender candidates for happy marriage, and the blessed motherhood of sons. May their morrow approach! which shall be as this joyful day, whose hap they now sing, wherein a manchild is joined to the religion of Islam; it is better than the day of his birth. The nomad son is circumcised come to the strength of three full years; and then as the season may serve without any superstition of days, and as the mother shall be able to provide corn or rice enough for her guests' supper. They sometimes put off the surgery till the morrow, in any rough windy weather, or because of the Aarab's rahla.

"The friends of the father will come in to be his guests; some of them have adorned themselves with the gunner's belt and gay baldric, rattling with the many little steel chains and brass powder-cases; and they bear upon their shoulders the long matchlocks. Therewith they would prove their hand to shoot, at the sheep's skull, which the child's *babbu* has sacrificed to 'the hospitality.' Every man kills his sacrifice, as in the ancient world, with his own hands, and the carcase is flayed and brittled with the Aarab's expedition. Nomads are all expert fleshers; the quarters hang now upon some bush or boughs, which, wandering in an open wilderness, they have sought perhaps upon a far mountain side. As the sun goes low the meat is cast into the cauldron, jidda. The great inwards remain suspended upon their trophy bush. After the flesh, a mess is cooked in the broth of such grain as they have. The sun setting, the maidens of the ring-dance disperse: the men now draw apart to their prayers, and in this time the cattle of every household are driven in. The men risen from their prayers, the supper is served in the tent; often thirty men's meat is in that shield-wide wooden platter which is set before them. A little later some will come hither of the young herdsmen returning boisterous from the field; they draw to the merry noise of the muzayyin that feel a lightness in their knees to dance. A-row, every one his arm upon the next one's shoulder, these laughing weleds stand full of good humour; and with a shout they foot it forth, reeling and wavering, advancing, recoiling in their chorus together; the while they hoarsely chant the ballad of a single verse. The housewives at the booth clap their hands, and one rising with a rod in her hand, as the dancing men advance, she dances out to meet them; it is the mother by likelihood, and joyously she answers them in her song: whilst they come on bending and tottering a-row together, with their perpetual refrain. They advancing upon her, she dances backward, feinting defense with the rod; her face is turned toward them, who maintain themselves, with that chanted verse of their manly throats, as it were pursuing and pressing upon her."[9]

Elsewhere, Doughty describes the same ceremonies, observed in another encampment, as follows: "I saw more muzayyins in the camp of the Sehamma; it was early in the morning when the children would be 'purified.' As I came by the first tent the child a moment before had been made a Moslem; but so rude was the surgery that he of the knife must be called back again. The child lamented for himself; *weyley!* woe is me. Thereby lay a ewe, for the guest meal, gurgling in her blood with the throat cut; and now the child's father severed the sheep's head from the body. I came to a second muzayyin tent; here a sâny was the surgeon. I saw him whetting his blade, and one held a sheep ready to be slaughtered. The father, encouraging his little son, set up the child and held him to ride on the sacrificial sheep's back; then he seated him again in his place, so drawing his cutlass and with a back stroke houghing him, he cut down the mutton; he cut also the throats of a goat and a kid. They now seated the child upon a vast metal charger reversed, which at other times is for the large nomad hospitality, 'the table of God in the wilderness,' some horse dung being powdered under him. This smith stood still striking a rude razor blade to a fair edge, upon his sinewed arm. He drew then the foreskin through a pierced stone shard, and there tied with a thread. 'Look thou cut not overmuch,' said the mother. Holding her child, with the other hand she blinded his eyes, and encouraged him with the mother's voice and promises of sweet milk and fat things. The sâny, with a light stroke, severed the skin at the knot: then he powdered the wound with charcoal, and gave up the child, which had not felt a pain, to his mother; and she comforting him in her bosom, bade him be glad that he was now entered in the religion of Islam. Their boiled rice and mutton were largely distributed before midday, and portions were borne through the camp, to the friends who were not present. I saw the maidens and young married women caroling in the next hours before the muzayyins."[10]

These circumcision festivals were observed by Doughty at about the middle of April. The Blunts similarly found a circumcision festival celebrated among the Ruala, a subdivision of the Aeneze group of tribes, on April 14th. It, too, was attended by singing and dancing.[11]

Curtiss says: "The festivities at marriage-festivals or at 'purification'-festivals, which may in Arabic signify both circumcision and baptism, are very primitive. At daybreak a white flag is hoisted over the festal tent; thereby all the members of the camp are invited. Soon after midday the men and women leave their work and assemble. The full-grown maidens and the young women wear only a silken garment open at the breast. Their hair hangs down loose about their shoulders and flutters about their faces during the dance. On all other occasions the dancing of the two sexes together is almost entirely unknown. But here the men and women whirl about together without restraint; the man may hug and kiss his partner, whom he has chosen according to his taste, as much as he pleases, without any objection on her part. Were a woman left without a partner she would think that she must die."[12]

Jaussen, too, says: "Circumcision is always the occasion of a festival; a solemn meal brings together relatives and friends; games are played before the tent; songs, commenced by a group of men, are carried on by the women, only to be taken up again by the men; alternating thus, they continue well into the night."[13] Elsewhere, Jaussen describes from a somewhat different standpoint the circumcision festival at the tomb of Sheikh Ġannâm: "According to an ancient practice it is about this *wely* that the circumcision of children takes place. When they have reached the age of two or three years, they are brought to the *mazâr*. The assistants form a kind of procession about the tomb. The children who are to be circumcised, mounted on mares or carried by their parents, form the center of this solemn procession, which winds slowly onward to the sound of the tambourines, mingled with the joyous shouts of the multitude; the women, advancing in separate groups, let their shrill cries be heard, which the echoes of the neighboring valleys repeat. When this procession has encompassed the tomb of Sheikh Ġannâm three times, the children are brought behind the little edifice. An expert, brought from Jerusalem, performs the rite of circumcision."[14] Obviously, this takes place on the occasion of the annual pilgrimage to the tomb of Sheikh Ġannâm and as a part of the celebration of the annual festival there.[15]

Among the fellahin and in the cities the customs are quite similar. Le Strange quotes the medieval Persian traveler, Nâsir-i-Khusrau, who visited Jerusalem in 1047, to the effect that "there are years when as many as twenty thousand people will be present at Jerusalem during the first days of the pilgrimage month Dhû-l-Hiğğeh; for they bring their children also with them in order to celebrate their circumcision."[16]

Kahle found the circumcision of children in large groups performed as a part of the great annual festival at the shrine of Nebi Mūsa, celebrated each year in the spring during the week immediately preceding Easter.[17] The children were from three to seven years old. During the ceremony a loud noise was made by the dervishes and the women to ward off the evil spirits.[18]

Similarly, Curtiss too says: "It is also customary to offer sacrifices in connection with the circumcision of boys. This may not take place until they are five or six years of age, or even later, when they are often brought to such shrines as Nebi Mūsa or Nebi Rubin, at the great annual festivals, and sacrifices of sheep are offered before the door of the makam, the blood of the victim being placed on the threshold."[19] Canaan, too, records the fact that a great blessing, *baraka,* is thought to ensue if a child is circumcised upon the festival of a prophet, as, for example, the festival of Nebi Mūsa, or upon some other important festival, particularly the *ḍaḥîyyeh*-festival.[20]

In Tangiers, according to Ali Bey,[21] the circumcision of children constitutes an important part of the celebration of the festival of the Birth of the Prophet; while in Tlemcen[22] the favorite occasion for the performance of this rite is the Ashoura-day, the tenth of Moḥarram.[23]

Several interesting and significant details of these circumcision ceremonies and festivals merit further consideration. In the first place, it is to be noted that while among certain tribes and in certain districts these circumcision festivals are held at almost any time of the year that is convenient and when the opportunity presents itself, among other tribes and in other districts they constitute, as has been said, a seemingly important part of the celebration of some great, annual festival. In the main, too, these festivals seem to be held in the early spring. Sacrifices are offered at these festivals, usually one sheep for every child circumcised. The substitutionary character of this sacrifice is unmistakable. The sheep is in almost all cases the gift of the father—although not infrequently a sheep is also given by the child's uncle—to the deity or the wely, obviously as the ransom for the child's life. Occasionally, this substitutionary character of the sheep sacrifice is emphasized by bringing the child into physical contact with the animal, usually by having him ride upon the back of the animal, either to, or around, the sanctuary.[24] Moreover, there can be little doubt that the singing, shouting, and general noise on these occasions, particularly while the circumcision is being performed, whatever may be considered their present import, were originally designed to frighten off the evil spirits, especially threatening at just that moment. In fact, this is explicitly stated by Kahle and Musil. This, too, is undoubtedly the import of the fact that, in preparation for the actual circumcision among the Bedouin, the boy is clothed in red garments.[25]

Of greater interest and significance are the dances of the maidens and the attendant selection of wives by the young men, which, according to the accounts of Burckhardt, Doughty, and especially Curtiss, play such a conspicuous role in the celebration of these circumcision festivals by the nomads. I have shown elsewhere that the chanting and dancing of the maidens in the vineyards—in the midst of the young men, who stood about and selected wives from among the dancers—were also a regular and indispensable part of the celebration of the ancient Semitic annual agricultural festivals, at least among the Canaanites and in pre-Exilic Israel.[26] So important were these dances that apparently they gave to these festivals the generic name *ḥag* (literally, "dance"). That these dances and the attendant wooing of brides play a similar role in the nomad circumcision festivals[27] would tend to indicate that in origin these circumcision festivals, with the various accompanying ceremonies, were a part of the ritual observance of the great annual festival, celebrated by the nomads in the early spring, just after their animals have cast their young, the forerunner of the Biblical Passover.[28]

Finally, attention should be called to Doughty's statement that the outer garments which the maidens wear while participating in the dances at the circumcision festivals are borrowed for these occasions. It is significant that the Mishna specifically prescribes that the maidens of Jerusalem, participating in the festival dances in the vineyards on the 15th of Ab and the 10th of Tishri, had to wear white garments which had been borrowed for the occasion.[29] Under no condition were they permitted to wear their own garments. Obviously, the use of borrowed garments was an essential festival rite.[30]

Now, in the Bible circumcision is enjoined by the Priestly Code for the eighth day after birth.[31] Undoubtedly, like so much of the ritual of the Priestly Code, this practice is of pre-Exilic origin. But it is by no means certain that circumcision upon the eighth day after birth was the universal practice in ancient Israel. Joshua 5 : 2–12 relates that Joshua circumcised the Israelites at Gilgal in connection with, and apparently preparatory to, the celebration of the Passover. It is true, as all Biblical scholars have agreed, that this chapter is composite. Verses 10–12, which alone describe the celebration of the Passover, but make no mention of the circumcision, come from P, while the remaining verses, which speak of the circumcision alone, without any specific reference to the celebration of the festival, come partly from JE and partly from D. Yet the immediate juxtaposition of these two traditions by the final redactors cannot be altogether accidental. They must have recognized some close connection between the circumcision and the observance of the festival.

This conclusion is borne out by abundant evidence. Verse 2 states explicitly that this was the second time that circumcision had been practiced in Israel. This implies, indirectly, that the custom of circumcising children upon the eighth day after birth had not yet been instituted, or at least was not known to the author of verse 2; for in such case every child born in the wilderness would have been circumcised upon the eighth day after birth, and there would then have been no occasion for this general circumcision. This suggests a question: If this was, in the opinion of the author of this verse, only the second occasion upon which circumcision had been practiced in Israel, when and what was the first occasion?

Verses 4–5 furnish the direct answer to this question. All the males who had come forth from Egypt were circumcised. In other words, the first occasion for circumcision in Israel, according to this tradition, had been at the time of the Exodus. It is immaterial whether these particular verses come from JE or D. Even if they are the product of the latter, they nonetheless voice a theory of the beginning of circumcision in Israel, based undoubtedly upon the older source, JE, or, probably more correctly, upon J alone, and certainly antedating the theory of the Priestly Code, that circumcision began with Abraham.[32]

This conclusion is amply confirmed by a careful consideration of the Biblical account of the first Passover and the tradition of the Exodus. According to Exodus 11, it would seem that only the first-born of the Egyptians were endangered by the last plague. But Exodus 12 : 21–23 makes the original basis of the tradition much clearer. On the particular night of the festival, Yahweh, or, in the original form of the tradition, the *mašḥît* (the "destroyer"), was abroad in the land, working his destructive will. All first-born, both of men and animals, were on this night subject to his power, and unless proper precautions were taken and proper rites performed, as set forth in verses 21–23, they were certain to forfeit their lives. Israel, under Yahweh's protection, observed these precautions and performed these rites, and so the lives of its first-born were saved. But Egypt, uninformed and the object of Yahweh's wrath, went ignorantly on its way, and in consequence its first-born perished.

Exodus 13 : 2, 12 f. then goes on to legislate that inasmuch as Yahweh had thus spared or saved the lives of Israel's first-born sons and cattle on the occasion of this Passover night, they must in the future belong to Him.[33] The manifest implication is that before this they had not belonged to Yahweh in the strict sense of the word, but rather, in the original form of the tradition, had been forfeit to the evil spirit, the *mašḥît,* at least for this one night in each year. Because of this deliverance by Yahweh, they were henceforth to belong to Him. The first-born males of all domestic animals were to be sacrificed; all human first-born were to be redeemed, naturally by the substitution of a lamb, just as on the occasion of that first Passover night. This was, of course, to be an annual procedure. On each recurring Passover all firstling male animals born during the year had to be sacrificed, and a lamb had to be offered to redeem each first-born child of that year. This provision is repeated in Exodus 34 : 19 f., where likewise, as we have seen, the immediate juxtaposition of this law to that providing for the celebration of the *Maṣṣôt* festival implies that these firstling sacrifices were offered upon this festival.[34]

But these are not the only Biblical provisions for participation in the celebration of the Passover. Exodus 12 : 43–50 provides specifically that no one who was uncircumcised might partake of the Paschal lamb; even the stranger or the slave who would share in the celebration of this festival had first to be circumcised.[35] Circumcision was, in other words, a *sine qua non* of the celebration of the festival, just as Joshua 5 : 2–12, despite its composite authorship, likewise implies. Unquestionably, therefore, the first occasion when circumcision was performed in Israel, according to the original J tradition, must have been precisely this first Passover. In addition to the sacrifice of the Paschal lamb, the original tradition must have told of the circumcision of all males as a festal rite.

It may seem at first thought that one consideration would make this conclusion impossible. For the tradition in its present form tells that, immediately after the sacrifice of the Paschal lamb and the accompanying ceremonies, the people set forth upon their journey out of Egypt into the desert. And it might well be asked: If the Israelites had been circumcised on the day before the Passover night, how could they commence their journey immediately thereafter? Would it not have been extremely difficult, if not altogether impossible, for them to march so soon after this painful operation? The tradition in Genesis 34 implies that circumcision of adults forbids physical exertion immediately thereafter. The answer to this question is not only not difficult but it is also of great significance.

Eduard Meyer has shown conclusively that in the J account of the Exodus from Egypt two originally totally independent, and even incongruous, traditions have become interwoven. The one dealt with the slaying of the first-born of Egypt, the making of the *maṣṣôt,* the departure from Egypt in haste at the bidding of the Pharaoh, without any further pursuit or annoyance by the Egyptians, and with the subsequent institution of the *Maṣṣôt* festival.[36]

The other account told that the occasion of Israel's desire to leave Egypt was the celebration of a festival at a place in the wilderness three-days' journey distant; in other words, this festival was to be celebrated, not in Egypt and preliminary to their departure thence, but only after they had gone forth from Egypt and had penetrated into the desert to a certain sacred place suitable for this particular purpose, three-days' journey distant from their present Egyptian home. Moreover, this festival was not something new, occasioned by the Exodus, but an old, established institution, presumably of desert, nomadic, pastoral origin and character, since it could be celebrated only in the desert. The Exodus took place immediately after and in consequence of the terrible plague of locusts, but entirely without the Pharaoh's permission. He therefore mustered his army and pursued the Israelites, but was overwhelmed by Yahweh. Israel, thus delivered, proceeded onward toward the goal of its journey, where, so the narrative in its original, unabridged form told, the festival in the desert was celebrated in the old, established manner. There and then, in the original form of the tradition, this first circumcision of all the males of Israel must have been performed. And thereafter, on the annual recurrence of this festival, all male children who were at least eight days old, and who for any reason had not yet been circumcised, underwent this rite. But the tradition in Joshua 5 implies that the male children who had been born in the desert had not been submitted to this operation. Consequently, upon the first Passover festival after entering the Promised Land, all the males who had been born in the desert were circumcised. This was therefore, as the tradition states, the second time that this ceremony was performed in this manner in Israel.[37]

One important detail of this desert festival celebration has survived in the Biblical tradition, namely, the dances of Miriam and the women of Israel, with their repeated chanting of their single-verse song.[38] But whereas the present composite text relates that this was only an incidental occasion for the dance, flowing spontaneously out of the general exultation over the overthrow of the Pharaoh, the deliverance of Israel, and the triumph of Yahweh, the original tradition must have told that these dances by the women, under the leadership of Miriam (who here plays exactly the role of the Bedouin *haši*) were an integral part of the celebration of this festival. In fact, this is implied in rabbinic tradition, which represents these dances of Miriam and the Israelite maidens as having been performed upon the seventh and last day of the Passover festival. In this connection, it is perhaps significant that Exodus 13 : 6, which, according to the J Code, records the oldest manner of celebrating the Passover festival, prescribes that upon the seventh and last day of the festival the *ḥag,* or sacred dance, shall be celebrated.[39]

Moreover, the hitherto strange and inexplicable element of the tradition, that the Israelite women were bidden to borrow garments and jewelry from their Egyptian neighbors, now becomes perfectly intelligible in this new light. These garments and jewelry, the original tradition must have told, or at least implied, were borrowed in order to be worn by the women who were to participate in the dances in their celebration of the festival in the desert, just as is the practice still today in the dances of the Arab maidens at the circumcision festivals, as described by Doughty, and as was also the practice in ancient Israel at the festival dances of the maidens of Jerusalem in the vineyards on the 15th of Ab and the 10th of Tishri, and as was also a not uncommon rite in the celebration of certain festivals in early Semitic religion.[40] Manifestly, this mention of the borrowing of these garments by the women of Israel anticipates the celebration of the festival in the desert as the aftermath of the Exodus. This accords perfectly with the original tradition of the Exodus and the ensuing celebration of the Passover, as reconstructed by Eduard Meyer. And these considerations lead to the incontrovertible conclusion that the original tradition must further have told, or implied, that these dances of the women—clad in borrowed garments and jewelry, under the leadership of a *haši,* or chief dancer, and with the repetition of a single, chanted verse—were an established and constant ritual procedure of this desert festival which the Israelites in Egypt were planning to celebrate;[41] hence, probably, the original name of this desert festival, *Pesaḥ* (literally, "a dance with a peculiar, limping step").[42]

Other details of the original tradition of the celebration of the festival in the desert have been reinterpreted, antedated by a few days, and applied by the editors of the Biblical text to the preparations in Egypt for the Exodus; thus, the motifs that the *mašḥît* was abroad in the land during that night, that in consequence the lives of all first-born were endangered, that therefore this night had to be observed as a "watchnight," that a lamb had to be sacrificed for each household and the blood sprinkled upon the doorpost and lintel of each house in order to redeem the inmates from the demon's dread power. In the original tradition, all these beliefs and rites must have been associated, not with the preparations in Egypt *before* the Exodus, but rather with the celebration of the festival in the desert *after* the Exodus.[43]

And undoubtedly the original tradition told likewise that as an integral part of the celebration of this festival in the desert all the boys, and probably all the men also, were circumcised, since it seems to have told, or implied, further that at this festival a covenant relationship of worship and protection was established between Yahweh and Israel, just as is also implied in the narrative in Joshua 5 : 12. The further implication is plain that Joshua's circumcision of the male Israelites at Gilgal was the second occasion for the performance of this rite in Israel. At the original desert festival, the boys at least, if not all the males, had been circumcised in order to guard them against the evil spirit, the *mašḥît.* Thus, this ancient desert festival, celebrated in the early spring as are many of the nomad festivals today, was, in part at least, a circumcision festival. It is significant indeed, that the details of the celebration of this ancient desert festival, the *Pesaḥ,* as we have thus established them, are identical in practically every essential detail with those of the Bedouin festivals of today.[44]

In this connection, it is important to note that later Jewish tradition very definitely associated the beginning of the rite of circumcision in Israel with the celebration of the first Passover. *Šᵉmôt rabba,* XIX (to Exodus 12 : 50) records the tradition that the Israelites in Egypt, with the exception of the tribe of Levi, were unwilling to circumcise themselves at God's bidding in preparation for the celebration of the Passover until God caused the fragrant odors of Eden to be mingled by the winds with the fragrant odors of the Paschal lamb. Then the people immediately performed the rite of circumcision in order that they might partake of the Paschal lamb. Moreover, the blood upon the lintels and doorposts was this blood of the covenant of circumcision.[45] In connection with this tradition, the twofold reference to blood in Ezekiel 16 : 6 was interpreted by the rabbis to refer to the blood of this general circumcision and to the blood of the Paschal lamb.[46]

Furthermore, according to a tradition recorded in *Babba Mᵉṣîʿa* 86b and *Bᵉrēʾšît rabba,* XLVIII (to Genesis 18 : 6) and L (to Genesis 19 : 22),[47] Abraham had circumcised Ishmael and himself just at the Passover.[48] These traditions undoubtedly preserve a reminiscence of the original close connection of circumcision with the celebration of the Passover.

In the light of all this evidence and in view of the obvious similarity of many of the details of the nomad circumcision festivals as celebrated today—usually in the early spring—to the details of the annual Passover festival in ancient Israel, we may infer that, in addition to whatever other nomad characteristics it may have possessed, the Passover was likewise originally an annual circumcision festival, at which male children were circumcised in precisely the same manner as at the nomad circumcision festivals today.[49]

Furthermore, from the fact that the K decalogue in Exodus 34 : 18–20 provides for the sacrifice of firstlings and the redemption of first-born in close connection with the command for the celebration of the *Maṣṣôt*—or, to use the unmistakably original, Israelite nomadic term, the *Pesaḥ* festival—we may draw the same inference: that circumcision, the primary rite of redemption of human offspring, was likewise practiced upon this occasion.[50] And since, as we maintain, the K document is in all likelihood the product of the reactionary, pastoral religious reformation in the Southern Kingdom in 899 B.C., the further inference is justifiable that in the Southern Kingdom, or at least in certain predominantly pastoral sections of the population thereof (the Rechabites, for example), in which the old nomadic practices and standards were zealously preserved for many generations, circumcision was regularly practiced, not upon the eighth day after birth, but rather in connection with the annual celebration of the Passover festival.[51] This practice probably continued until as late as the beginning of the eighth century B.C. In all likelihood, however, this practice was supplemented, just as among the Bedouin today, by certain kindred ceremonies befitting the critical seventh or eighth day after birth, such as cutting off the first hair of the child, and probably also giving it its name; in other words the present-day *'aḳîḳah* and *tasmîyya,* and probably also, since the verb-stem *ḥanak* has obviously gone through a long, cultural evolution in Hebrew, the rite of *taḥnîk.*

In the Northern Kingdom, however, owing to the topographical character of the country, agriculture was, as we have noted, the dominant occupation, and the raising of sheep and cattle was of only secondary importance. Consequently, the old, nomadic *Pesaḥ* gradually gave way to, was merged with, and ultimately almost completely absorbed by, the agricultural *Maṣṣôt* festival.[52] In consequence, the sacrifice of firstlings became a matter of relative unimportance, and the old, peculiar *Pesaḥ* customs and ceremonies fell correspondingly into desuetude, or were greatly modified. Accordingly, it seems that the custom naturally arose of circumcising all males, no longer upon the Passover—since as a distinct festival, not absorbed into the *Maṣṣôt* festival, this was hardly observed any more—but upon the eighth day after birth, probably in conjunction with the other rites of redemption of children performed on this day. And as the custom of the sacrifice of first-born became more and more infrequent in the Northern Kingdom as well as in the Southern Kingdom, these first-born, too, would be circumcised upon the eighth day after birth, the very day upon which, in accordance with the earlier practice, they would have been sacrificed. And finally, as the culture of Israel advanced further and further from the old desert standards and practices, the custom became general in the South as well as in the North of circumcising all males on the eighth day after birth, just as is prescribed in the Priestly Code.

Thus, the evidence seems to indicate that the practice in Israel of circumcision upon the eighth day after birth was a secondary development. And since the similar practice in southern Arabia and Abyssinia was undoubtedly based upon the older Israelite practice, it follows that everywhere in the Semitic world circumcision upon the eighth day after birth was a secondary development from the older practice of circumcising male children as a regular part of the ritual celebration of a great, annual, nomadic spring festival, when also the firstlings of animals—and originally the first-born of men as well—were sacrificed to the deity or spirit who was thought to have given them life.

However, this does not affect in the least the conclusions to which we have come with regard to the peculiar nature of the first seven days after birth, and particularly with regard to the critical character of the final day of this period. The Bedouin of today, as in so many other instances, preserve the original practice in a form but little modified from that of the Biblical, or even pre-Biblical, times. Upon the seventh or eighth day after birth an animal was sacrificed as the substitute for the child, to redeem him from the power of the threatening deity or spirit. Other cognate rites were in all probability performed, the forerunners of the modern *ʿaḳîḳah, tasmîyya,* and *taḥnîk.* At a later moment in the child's life—at the first Passover after birth, and as one of the important rites of this annual spring festival—the child was circumcised. These ceremonies marked the transition of the child from the first stage of existence, that of taboo, into which he had been born, into the second stage of existence, daily, profane life, in which he was free to participate in all the activities of his family, clan, and tribe. Accordingly, therefore, as a secondary development, these rites came to partake somewhat of the character of ceremonies of initiation.

Such, we believe, is the origin and history of circumcision and similar birth rites among the Semites in general, and in Israel in particular.[53]

XI

Baptism

Finally, the ceremony of baptism, particularly the baptism of infants, is closely related to the ceremonies of circumcision, cutting off of the first hair, and other similar rites of expulsion of evil spirits, removal of taboo, and redemption. This rite is observed chiefly in the Christian Church, although, as we have already learned, it is today practiced likewise by the Yezidis and other non-Christian sects, and was practiced by various Semitic peoples or groups in ancient times. In the Christian Church it plays exactly the same role as do circumcision among the Jews and circumcision and the various *ʿaḳîḳah* rites among the Moslems.[1]

Among many, if not most, primitive peoples water was thought to possess certain magical powers, analogous to washing away physical uncleanness, specifically to cleanse from ritual impurity and defilement, to drive out evil spirits, and to purge from sin.[2] Just this was the fundamental purpose of baptism, whether of infants or of adults;[3] in other words, it performed originally, as we have said, exactly the same functions as did circumcision and the *ʿaḳîḳah* ceremonies.

Usually in the Christian Church children are baptized upon the fortieth day after birth.[4] In Abyssinia, however, where both circumcision and infant baptism are practiced, the former takes place upon the eighth day after birth and the latter, if the child is a boy, upon the fortieth day after birth, and if a girl upon the eightieth day.[5] As has been said, Jewish influence is apparent here.[6]

Among the Copts, too, boys are baptized upon the fortieth, and girls upon the eightieth, day after birth.[7] The purpose of the ceremony, it is expressly stated, is to drive out the devil from the child.[8] Circumcision, although not mandatory, is, as we have noted, nevertheless generally practiced by the Copts, and for precisely the same purpose.[9] But the name is given to the child upon the eighth day after birth.[10] In other words, the Copts recognize in their ceremonies with newborn children the peculiar taboo character of both the seventh or eighth and the fortieth days, as well as the redemptive effect of both circumcision and baptism.

The reason why baptism of infants was fixed as a rule for the fortieth day after birth is not far to seek. We have learned that in primitive Semitic belief the fortieth day marked the close of the second[11] stage of the power of evil spirits; for this reason it was appropriate for the performance of ceremonies for their expulsion. Accordingly, Adam is represented as fasting and standing immersed to his neck in the waters of the Jordan for forty days, in order that the evil of his former acts might be washed from him.[12] And for the same reason, undoubtedly, the New Testament represents the period of the temptation of Jesus as enduring for forty days, implying thereby that with the end of the fortieth day the power of the devil ceased automatically.[13]

We have already considered in some detail a great variety of ceremonies performed upon the fortieth day after birth upon both mother and newborn child, all for the expressed or else plainly implicit purpose of freeing them from the ritual uncleanness and possession by evil spirits attendant upon this important occasion. We have noted in particular that a very common ceremony upon this day and in this connection is the first ritual bath, either by the mother alone or by both mother and child. Obviously, this ritual bath is one form of baptism.

However, baptism was and is not universally practiced upon the fortieth day after birth. Among the Mandaeans, with whom baptism plays a larger role than with almost any other group or sect, baptism of infants is prescribed normally for the seventh day after birth, but if the child be not strong enough to endure the rite without harm, or if the weather be inclement, it may be postponed for one or two months, or until the summer, or even for a year, if necessary. But it is advisable to perform the rite as early as possible, for children not yet baptized are not regarded as Mandaeans; their parents may not kiss them, and, in case of death, they are not buried with religious rites, and their souls go at once into the devouring jaws of Ur.[14] Among the Mandaeans children may be baptized only in "living," i.e., running, water, and a ring of myrtle is placed, first upon the finger and then upon the head of the child.[15] The Yezidis too, as we have seen, in addition to practicing circumcision also baptize their children upon the seventh day after birth,[16] if at all possible. In case of necessity, however, this rite may be performed at any suitable time within the first two months. Under every condition it must be performed before the close of the second year; otherwise, presumably, there is no hope for the child.[17]

On the other hand, it is interesting and significant to note that in the early Christian Church, or at least in certain sections of it, baptism of infants was practiced regularly, not upon the fortieth day after birth, but at Easter, i.e., at the time of the early Israelite circumcision festival of Passover. In Thessaly, we are told, "they baptise on the days of Easter only; in consequence of which a very great number of them die without having received baptism."[18] At Alexandria, also, children were brought in great numbers to Timothy the

Great at Easter to be baptized.[19] Elsewhere we are told that in the early Church during the second century Easter and Pentecost were set apart for the administration of holy baptism. At both these festivals, in connection with the baptism ceremony, vigils were observed.[20] These last correspond, of course, to the "watchnight" at the ancient Passover and at Jewish circumcision ceremonies.

But baptism was practiced not only upon infants but also in a great variety of cases in which, as we shall see, among the early Semites the rite of cutting off the hair was also practiced. Thus, the Bible prescribes that the man with a running sore or one who has come into contact with him,[21] the man who has had an involuntary emission,[22] a man and woman after sexual intercourse,[23] a woman after the close of her monthly periods,[24] the man who has led away the goat of Azazel, he who burns the bullock outside the camp,[25] those who participate in the preparation of and ceremonies with the ashes of the red heifer,[26] the warrior who has slain an enemy in battle,[27] and anyone who eats anything unclean and forbidden[28] are regarded as ritually unclean. From this state of taboo, complete washing of themselves and their garments in "living water," frequently accompanied by other, kindred ceremonies, frees them.[29] The Gentiles, too, were bidden, among other acts of expiation, to bathe in ever-flowing water.[30] And, as we have seen, the proselyte to Judaism[31] or Islam[32] was required to be baptized, as well as to submit to circumcision and other rites for the removal of taboo. Among the Mandaeans, too, baptism is mandatory after all acts of sexual intercourse, for a woman after the cessation of menstruation, for persons who have come into contact with an unclean person or a corpse or a stranger, or who have eaten unclean food, and for priests at consecration and on Sundays and holy days.[33]

Likewise for the expulsion of evil spirits from a sick person bathing in "pure water" was practiced by the Babylonians.[34] For the same reason, undoubtedly, Naaman, the Syrian leper, was charged by Elisha to dip himself seven times in the Jordan.[35] The symbolic or magical character of this rite is evident from its sevenfold repetition.

These facts reveal the unmistakable original character of baptism as a rite for the expulsion of evil spirits, the removal of taboo, and the admission into what is henceforth to be the normal state of existence of the person in question. They establish beyond all possibility of doubt the close relationship of the rite of infant baptism to circumcision, the *'akîkah* ceremonies, and other rites of removal of taboo. With the performance of these various rites, either singly or in combination, this first period of danger and taboo comes to an end, and the person who has undergone these rites, whether child or adult, is initiated into a new, profane period of existence, with its privilege of full participation in the daily life of the family, clan, tribe, nation, or religious sect.

XII

The Sacrifice of the Hair

1 The Sacrifice of the Hair

Among many primitive peoples the hair is regarded as the particular seat of life, vitality, and strength,[1] and, in consequence, as possessing a positive character of sanctity. For this reason, the ancient Arabs quite commonly swore by it.[2] Therefore also it was a part of the body particularly fitted to serve as the substitute sacrifice for a life, forfeit and taboo. We have seen that this was the significance of the cutting of the infant's first hair in the *'aḳîḳah* ceremony. There is much evidence also that the same rite of cutting off the hair and, frequently, of giving it to a deity, a "saint," or some other supernatural being or power was performed as a substitute- or taboo-sacrifice at other critical moments in life.

2 The Sacrifice of the Hair in Reconciliation Ceremonies

This substitutionary character of the rite of cutting off the hair is most directly apparent in the ceremony of reconciliation between a murderer and the avenger of the blood of the murdered person among the Arabs today. Curtiss has described this ceremony in detail and with numerous illustrations.[3] The life of the murderer should be taken in exchange for that of the murdered man. But with the consent of the blood-avenger this may be avoided by the performance of certain appropriate rites. Most frequently, the blood-avenger simulates the slaying of the murderer by passing a razor across his neck. A sheep is then slaughtered by cutting its throat and letting the blood gush forth. It is *fedû,* or redemption, for the murderer. Its substitutionary character is thus readily manifest. Its blood, given instead of that of the murderer, and brought forth in precisely the same manner as that in which the blood of the murderer is symbolically brought forth, compensates for, or "covers," the blood of the murdered man. Frequently, however, instead of, or, more commonly, in addition to, the sacrifice of this substitute sheep, the blood-avenger cuts off either the whole or a part of the hair of the murderer. Generally these ceremonies are accompanied by a meal, partaken of by both blood-avenger and murderer. Thereby a normal, friendly covenant-relationship is established or re-established between them. Not infrequently a payment of money or cattle is accepted in lieu of other ceremonies.

A few examples cited by Curtiss are particularly illuminating for our purpose. He says: "When the family of the murdered man . . . have guaranteed peace to the murderer, the family of the latter bring one or more sheep to the tent of the blood-avenger, while the murderer himself remains at a distance. According to the common Arabic custom, the blood-avenger first prepares coffee. However, before this is poured out, one or two of the guests ask the 'possessor of the blood,' the father or brother of the murdered man, if they may bring the murderer to him. If this is allowed, they drink coffee. Then the murderer appears and kneels down before the blood-avenger, who then cuts off some of the hair of the murderer's head, whereupon one of the women immediately breaks forth in the cry of joy (*zaghârît*). Then the relatives of the 'possessor of the blood' slaughter the sheep that had been brought by the relatives of the murderer."

Later, Curtiss relates that "the sheikh of Burme in Adjlun, a Moslem, indicated three ways in which to appease the blood-avenger: (1) the avenger accepts payment of money or the security of a reliable man; (2) he cuts off some of the hair of the murderer and says, 'I let you go free in the presence of God; let God demand blood if He will; He is the avenger'; (3) he demands no blood, but has the right to take all the property of the murderer."

Again, Curtiss was told by a Bedouin wanderer: "There is such a thing as the reconciliation-sacrifice. The murderer brings the sacrifice for the sake of peace. The avenger shaves off some of his beard. As a sign of reconciliation they kiss each other on the head and beard. If the avenger refuses to claim damage from the murderer, he shaves off the lock of hair on his forehead and lets him go."

Another traveler[4] records an instance of a man who "in a forgiving mood . . . shaves off a bit of his brother-in-law's beard (because the latter had killed the sheikh of his wife's tribe) in token of the fact that he might have taken his life but did not, after which the murderer returned to the tribe and was absolved."

Niebuhr[5] describes the same ceremony as practiced by the Druses as follows: "If a murderer believes that he and his family are too weak to defend themselves against the family of the murdered man, he goes to the nearest relative of the latter with a cord or a cloth about his neck. He excuses himself by pleading that since he is a man of honor, he could not avoid committing the murder, since the other had applied a dishonorable epithet to him. He now gives the blood-avenger, amid compliments, full freedom to take his life. Then the relative of the murdered man is obliged to forgive him. Nevertheless, this does not proceed quite so inconsequentially. The wronged man has a barber brought to shave off the beard of the murderer."

Jaussen[6] tells of the same practice among the Bedouin. He says: "When, after a murder, the guilty party has been captured and put in chains, he is not always killed, in order not to perpetuate the enmity, and also to prove his (the blood-avenger's) generosity. 'I pardon you,' says the blood-avenger. But before dismissing him, he cuts off his hair and shaves him around the head, and also both temples and chin. Then he gives him his liberty.[7]

"Among the Tiāhā a parallel practice is found. When a prisoner is taken in war, and they do not wish to put him to death, he is led to the encampment, where a corner of his head below the temples is shaved, and he is let go free."[8]

Further: "When a traitor has betrayed to the enemy the plan of a campaign, the Bedouin shave his head completely on one side and his mustache on the other, and then let him go away free."

In all these cases it is readily apparent that the shorn hair is the sufficient and legitimate substitute and redemption for the life of the murderer, criminal, captive, or traitor. This is shown even more positively by the following instance, also cited by Jaussen:[9] "Nimr ibn ʿAdwān had in a poem derided Salāmeh er-Remeïfy of the ʿAmer. Having read his satire, Salāmeh replied: 'May I divorce my wife,[10] if I do not cut off your head, when I shall have captured you.' A long time thereafter Salāmeh, passing near Ḥesbān, finds upon his way the house of Nimr. He enters and says to him, 'I have sworn to cut off your head if I meet you.' 'Do what you will,' says his adversary, seeing himself defenseless. Salāmeh took his (Nimr's) two braids of hair and cut them off, saying, 'This takes the place of your head.' And he believed that he had discharged his vow."[11]

3 The Sacrifice of the Hair in the Redemption of Vows

While in all these cases the substitutionary character of the shorn hair is readily apparent, its sacrificial character is not so manifest. However, in the following instances the sacrificial as well as the substitutionary character of the rite of cutting off the hair may be easily recognized.

Curtiss relates[12] that "a Greek-Catholic Syrian woman was in the throes of her first childbirth. Her sister stood anxiously at her bedside. When all hope had practically disappeared, she vowed to Mâr Djirdjis that, if properly born, the child should belong to him. When the child was finally born, the happy parents and the whole family acknowledged the oath. They often said to the child, 'You belong to Mâr Djirdjis!' When he was twelve years old, the entire family, including the grandmother, brought the lad to the shrine of Mâr Djirdjis near Kal'at el-Hosn in northern Syria, six miles away, four days before the annual festival, on April 23rd. On this day he appeared with many other children before the abbot, in order to have his hair cut off. This custom of cutting off the hair of consecrated boys is widespread and very old. . . . Often a present of money is made to the saint, by weighing the hair with money."

Similarly, Kahle reports:[13] "In central and northern Syria, associated with the practice of bringing to the sanctuary boys who have been consecrated by a vow, together with the accompanying sacrifice, is the custom of cutting off their hair, or a few locks thereof, and consecrating the weight of this hair in silver and gold to the sanctuary. This custom is correlated in official Islam with the *'aqîqa*-sacrifice, and in tradition is traced back to the fact that the Prophet recommended it to his daughter *Fāṭimah* at the birth of her son *Husên*. . . . The custom of cutting off the child's hair is not practiced on this occasion but only later, when the child is over a year old. Just as in Syria it is considered unlucky to cut off the hair of a child before the completion of the first year, so also in Palestine. Apparently the custom of ceremonially cutting off the hair at the sanctuary is limited to those cases where the child has been vowed to the saint; it is then practiced when the child has reached the age of eight or ten years, or even older.[14] A very old custom, it seems, has survived in this. The specific details of this custom may be established from the following instances:

"At the *Chaḍr* sanctuary at Carmel it is customary that the lad who has been vowed to the sanctuary is brought thither in ceremonial procession (called *zeffet el-'arīs,* i.e., 'procession of the bridegroom'), beautifully dressed and on horseback. His hair is then cut off on both the right and the left sides of his head. The hair is then usually weighed with gold and silver; this money is consecrated to the sanctuary, while the hair is deposited in a little niche, which is to the left of the large niche.

"In the neighborhood of Rās En Nakūra I was told that a lad of about a year old was vowed to *Nebi Schem'a,* whose sanctuary is not far from there, with these words—'O my lord, *Nebi Schem'a,* God grant that this boy grow up; in which case I will take him, cut off his hair and let him make a ceremonial visit (to the sanctuary),' or 'I will take him and have his hair cut off, and give the weight of his hair in money, and also offer a sacrifice (of an animal).' When the lad has reached the age of eight to ten years, he is brought to the prophet, and that which has been promised is performed.

"In Tibnīn a woman of the *Metāwele* told me that when her boy was two months old she had vowed him to *Nebi Yūscha'* with the words, 'O Joshua, a vow is incumbent upon me; if God—praised and exalted be He—preserves this child alive for me, I will cut his hair and give the weight of his hair in money.' When the child was ten years old she had the sheikh of the *Metāwele* in Tibnīn cut off his hair and weigh it with money. It weighed as much as twelve *bischlik*. This money was entrusted to the sheikh, who brought it to

Nebi Yūscha'. The weight of the hair in money was *fidû an el-weled,* i.e., the 'substitute for the child,' so she said.

"The attendant of the sanctuary in Safed, called by the name *Banāt Ya'kûb,* said that in such a case the following is pronounced,—'O you daughters of our lord Jacob, O our God, if you will keep this child alive for me, I will cut off his hair for you, and I will offer a sacrifice "into the face of God" for the poor and the needy.' After some years, when the child is ten or twelve years old (one may quietly wait even longer, until he has collected the necessary money), the child is brought to the sanctuary in order to cut off his hair and to bring the sacrifice. It is understood in all these instances that during the entire period in which the oath continues in effect, no scissors may come upon the child's head."

Among the native Jews of Palestine, when a boy has completed his fourth year, and his parents wish to cut his hair for the first time, they invite all their relatives and acquaintances and give each of those assembled the honor of cutting off a few hairs from the child's head, until all the hairs are removed except the earlocks; then a small banquet is made for the guests. This custom is generally performed upon Lag b^{e}'omer;[15] but many of the Sephardic Jews shave their children on the intervening days of the Passover[16] in the synagogue, and hold a feast in connection therewith. The inhabitants of Safed and Tiberias observe this same custom in the court of the tomb of Rabbi Simon b. Yochai and in the village of Meirun on Lag b^{e}'omer in connection with the celebration of the *Ḥilûlah,* or annual commemoration on this day of Rabbi Simon. The boys thus shaved are clad in garments of unusual richness, and are carried in on the shoulders of their relatives and acquaintances. There is much pomp in this celebration, and it is accompanied by dancing and singing. Many Sephardic Jews dwelling outside of Palestine in the Levant bring their little sons with them to Safed for the performance of this rite. This ceremony is called by the Arabic name *ḥalaka,* which means "cutting."[17] Among the Beni-Israel,[18] if it is thought that the child has been born in consequence of a vow, its hair is not cut until its sixth or seventh year. It is usual in all these cases to weigh the hair cut off against coins, which are given by the parents to charitable purposes.

All these instances evidence the substitutionary and sacrificial character of cutting off the child's first hair and also the close relationship of this entire ceremony to the *'aḳîḳah* ceremony, as is correctly pointed out by Kahle. Actually, throughout the entire period during which the vow is in effect, lasting until the eighth, tenth, or even twelfth year, until which time the child is considered as being preserved in life by the "saint," he is in a very real state of consecration or taboo, approximating very closely that of the Biblical Nazirite. From this state of taboo the cutting off of the hair and the offering of the sacrifice free him. The hair is given to the "saint" as substitution or redemption for the life of the lad, or, instead of this, and frequently in addition thereto, the weight of the hair in money is given either to the sanctuary of the "saint" or to the poor, who are thought to stand under the "saint's" protection.[19]

4 The Sacrifice of the Hair of Boys at Arrival at Puberty

In the light of this evidence, Lucian's account of the practice at the temple of the Syrian goddess at Hierapolis becomes significant. He says: "The hair of all boys is suffered to grow, and they consider it as somewhat sacred, that no razor may touch; when, however, they have attained the age of maturity, one lock from over the temple is cut off, and this is then, together with the first beard, generally hung up in the temple, enclosed in a silver, and sometimes in a golden, vase, on which the name of the donor is engraved. I likewise adopted this ceremony in my youth; and my lock with my name must still be seen at this day in the temple of the Syrian goddess."[20] This is in principle obviously the selfsame rite as the present-day practice reported in detail by Kahle.

In a number of very essential respects, however, this practice, as described by Lucian, seems to differ from that of today. According to the modern practice, only in the case of vows is the first hair of boys cut off at the age of from eight to twelve years; normally, so it seems, it is cut off much earlier. Thus, in addition to the instances already noted, among the Samaritans, we are told by one of our most reliable observers,[21] the hair is first cut when the child is from two to two and a half years of age, and at just about the time when it is weaned. This occasion is always celebrated with a festival, and presents are given to the child. Among the native Jews of Palestine, as we have just learned, this ceremony takes place at the close of the child's fourth year. Elsewhere, as has been noted, the first hair is cut off at the time of the *'aḳîḳah* sacrifice and ceremony, i.e., upon the seventh day after birth, under normal conditions.

But, according to Lucian, in more ancient times this rite was not performed until the lad had attained the age of puberty, and the cutting off of the first hair of his head was associated with the cutting off of the first beard. Until that time the hair was regarded as something sacred, which no razor might touch; in other words, it was under a taboo. This sacred hair, when cut off, was deposited in the temple at Hierapolis in much the same manner as, according to Kahle's account, boys' hair, cut off in fulfillment of a vow, is today deposited in a little niche at the *Chaḍr* sanctuary at Carmel; in other words, this hair was given to the deity.[22]

According to Jaussen,[23] what is undoubtedly the same ceremony is practiced by some Bedouin tribes still today. He says: "Among the Tiāhā in the Negeb all the boys wear their hair long. But when they are grown and have reached the age when the beard begins to show, a relative of the boy's father cuts off his beautiful locks, which are then speedily buried." To this, Jaussen adds a note:

"At a camp of the ʿAġarmeh a boy had his father cut off his hair, which he then quickly collected in order to bury it with care in the ground." Quite clearly, this hair is buried thus carefully and speedily because it is thought to be taboo, or even doubly taboo; because, in other words, the taboo which was thought to rest previously upon the boy was now concentrated in the hair, which had just been cut off as the taboo-sacrifice to redeem the boy. Probably, too, there is associated with this principle the idea that if an enemy or an evil spirit should gain possession of this hair, or of any portion thereof, he might well be able to work harm to the boy; but if so, this idea is certainly secondary to the concept of taboo.

Obviously, since from ancient times this rite seems to have been performed only, or at least chiefly, at the attainment of maturity, it marked the solemn passing from the state of childhood into that of manhood, with its privilege of full participation in daily, profane life, and particularly of marriage. But of equal or even greater importance than the state into which the persons pass by the performance of rites such as these is the state out of which they pass. And from all the evidence gathered thus far we may infer with comparative certainty that this period of childhood, now brought to an end, was regarded as an unbroken period of taboo, in which the child was thought to stand in the immediate possession or power of a deity. In this state, therefore, as Lucian says, the first hair of the boy, destined to be sacrificed at the proper moment as the taboo-sacrifice for him, was sacred. From this state of taboo the sacrifice of the sacred hair redeemed him. And since the goddess of the Hierapolitan sanctuary, to whom this hair was sacrificed, was unquestionably a form of the universal Semitic mother-goddess, we may safely infer that the ground of her claim, or taboo, upon all youths was that, in the final analysis, she had given them birth, or had at least played an important part therein.

The following is undoubtedly a cognate rite.[24] Among the Jews of Northern Africa the friends of the family and the schoolmates of the boy are invited to a feast on the Sunday afternoon before the Barmitzvah.[25] "When all are assembled, the barber is sent for, and he shaves the head of the boy to be confirmed, as well as the heads of his schoolmates, and every guest at the feast contributes a piece of money, which is given to the barber. After this a merry meal takes place, which often lasts until morning."

Furthermore, it appears from Lucian that it was a lock from just above the temple which was thus cut off. Accordingly, the absence of this lock of hair above the temple distinguished the man from the child and constituted a distinct and characteristic manner of wearing the hair. We can accordingly understand the references in Jeremiah 9 : 25; 25 : 23; 49 : 32 to the inhabitants of Qedar and other desert tribes, who had the temple lock cut off, and also the statement of Herodotus[26] that the Arabs were accustomed to wear their hair cut off around the temples, because they imagined that Dionysos, whom they called Orotalt, wore his hair in that manner.[27] The Tôsefta[28] relates that the heathen custom of allowing the locks above the temple to grow, impliedly in order that they might be cut off at the proper time as a ritual act, was a rite of Emorite, or idolatrous worship. Moreover, the Mishnah[29] states that the days when the heathen shaved off their beards and cut off their temple locks[30] were regarded as festivals, while in the Talmud[31] we read that he who cuts off his hair[32] is following the heathen practice of the Emorites. This last is the same practice as that recorded for modern times by Conder.[33] He says: "Last of all the *shûsheh* should be mentioned, the one long tuft of hair left at the back of the shaven head, (i.e., therefore, with the temples and the forepart of the head shaved), by which, the Moslems believe, the angel Gabriel will bear them to heaven. This fashion of wearing the hair is traced back to primitive times, and is thought to be connected with the worship of Thammuz." Quite similarly, we are told,[34] Amru ben Jahja introduced the worship of Manat, a form of the Semitic mother-goddess, into Arabia, and with it the custom of shaving the head in her honor.

These references show how widespread was the custom of cutting off the lock of hair above the temple in ancient times. Presumably among all the peoples it was shorn at the attainment of puberty, just as among Lucian's Syrians, and was ever thereafter kept closely cropped. Otherwise it could hardly have constituted a distinguishing manner of wearing the hair. Among the Arabs today the wearing of the locks of hair above the temple is regarded as the sign of the vanity of youth, with which maturity has little sympathy. Thus Doughty relates: "I enquired, 'Wherefore he wore not the horns (the locks of hair above the temples)? . . . the Bedouin lovelocks should well become his manly Annezy beauty.' *Eyad,* 'I have done with such young man's vanities, since my horn upon this side was shot away, and a second ball cropped the horn on my other.' "[35]

Musil[36] likewise states that among the Bedouin "all the young men wear braids, and the vain among them never cut them off; otherwise they are cut off, usually at about the age of thirty-five." Musil relates further[37] that "when a youth has taken his first camel as booty, he sacrifices his own hairs, in that he cuts off some of his forelocks, *kidle,* and strews it over the camel, in order that Allah may send him as many camels as there were hairs." Burckhardt[38] records a similar practice: "Among the *Maazy* Arabs, who occupy the mountains between the Nile and the Red Sea, as far as the latitude of Cosseir (and who have come within the last century, from Arabia, their mother country), it is an established and remarkable custom, that those young men only are allowed to shave the hair of the head, who have brought home some booty from an enemy. It becomes then a festival in the family, whenever one of the sons for the first time has his head shaved; while young men are sometimes met among them, whose hair still covers their heads."

In its present form, the ceremony described by Musil seems largely magical, designed to increase the number of camels the youth is destined to capture.[39]

But in the light of what we have established as the true nature and purpose of the rite of cutting off the hair, and in the light also of the parallel *Maazy* rite, cited by Burckhardt, this practice in all likelihood indicated originally that the capture of the first camel marked the transition in the life of the young man from the state of immaturity to that of manhood and warriorship; accordingly, it was marked by the taboo-sacrifice of the hair. So interpreted, this rite may be identified with that described by Lucian.[40]

These considerations seem to shed light upon the origin and purpose of an important Biblical institution. Probably as a conscious and deliberate prohibition of what was clearly recognized as a non-Yahwistic rite undoubtedly at one time observed in Israel, the law was promulgated in the Holiness Code, not to cut off the *pe'ôt,* i.e., the locks of hair above the temples and at the edge of the beard.[41] The custom thus prohibited must have been the very one described by Lucian. On the other hand, it may be inferred from Numbers 24 : 17 and Jeremiah 48 : 25, 45 that from a still earlier period the Moabites had been accustomed not to cut off the temple locks, and that these therefore served to distinguish the Moabites in appearance from the surrounding Semitic peoples. Why the Moabites may not have observed this practice is of course impossible to determine for lack of sufficient evidence. But the fact that the wearing of these temple locks distinguished the Moabites from the neighboring peoples shows conclusively that the practice of cutting off these temple locks was widespread among the ancient Semites.

But if at the time of the composition of Numbers 24 : 17 and Jeremiah 48 : 45 the wearing of the temple locks distinguished the Moabites from all peoples round about, Israel undoubtedly included, it follows that still in the days of Jeremiah the Israelites must have regularly cut off their temple locks, presumably at the attainment of puberty. Therefore, the law promulgated in the Holiness Code forbidding the cutting off of the *pe'ôt,* i.e., the locks of hair above the temples and at the edge of the beard, must be later than Jeremiah, must be an innovation by the authors of the Holiness Code, and must have been instituted by them deliberately in order to abrogate what they knew to be in origin a heathen, non-Yahwistic rite.

On the other hand, the Samson story seems to indicate that from ancient times the Nazirite, or at least he who was vowed to a perpetual nazirate, wore his hair in seven locks or braids.[42] Therefore, the innovation of the authors of the Holiness Code may have had the twofold purpose, not only of abrogating a heathen rite, but also of signifying by means of the uncut locks Israel's perpetual holiness and consecration to Yahweh as His Nazirites or devotees, or, as the Priestly Code puts it,[43] His "kingdom of priests and holy people."

It is significant that Judges 16 : 19 states explicitly that the shaving of the seven locks of Samson's hair caused his strength to depart from him completely; that is to say, his strength and vitality are represented as dwelling in these locks of hair. From this it may be inferred that the sacrifice of the temple locks by the Syrian youths, as described by Lucian, represented in the most literal sense the sacrifice to the goddess of their first strength and virility.

5 The Sacrifice of the Hair of Maidens at the Attainment of Puberty

But it was not alone the youths who, according to Lucian, thus sacrificed their hair. Once a year at Byblos, apparently at an annual Adonis festival, the women were required to cut off their hair, or, failing in this, to submit themselves for one day to sexual intercourse with strangers.[44] Lucian's language is ambiguous in the extreme. It is not definitely stated whether all women participated in this rite each year; in other words, whether upon one day in each year every woman was required to submit herself, if married, to a man not her husband, or, if unmarried, to a man who might not become her husband, or whether every woman performed this ceremony only once in her life—that is, at or shortly after the attainment of puberty, and presumably therefore as an indispensable preliminary to and preparation for marriage. The first alternative would not be altogether without analogy in the practice of peoples living at a comparable stage of civilization.[45]

But in the light of abundant evidence the second alternative seems far more probable and reasonable. Sozomen[46] undoubtedly had in mind just this rite of prostitution once in the life of each woman when he stated that Constantine destroyed the old sanctuary at Heliopolis and prohibited the ancient custom of yielding up virgins to prostitution with any chance comer before being united in marriage to their betrothed. Similarly, we read in The Testament of the Twelve Patriarchs, Judah 12, that it was "a custom of the Emorites that she who has (just) married offer herself for prostitution for seven days at the gate of the city." Ephraim Syrus,[47] too, speaks of the prostitution of the Chaldaean maidens at the behest of their parents. His words are not without import: "Who did away with the feast of the raging[48] idol, on whose festal day women prostituted themselves? Did then some star rise on those virgins that forthwith they vowed their virginity to prostitution?" Obviously this passage deals with the ceremonial prostitution of virgins in the worship of the goddess and seems to show a close affinity with the Babylonian institution described by Herodotus.

According to Schwally,[49] an undoubtedly related practice is observed in Egypt still today, for, he says, it is customary that Moslem maidens in Egypt be deflowered at the close of the marriage ceremony and seven nights before the first actual copulation. He very correctly correlates this ceremony with the widespread practice of defloration of maidens, either by artificial means or through cohabitation with some man other than the future husband, as an indispensable preliminary to marriage. Likewise among the Ghowazys, who furnish the famous dancing girls of Egypt and who boast of their pure descent from Bedouin ancestors, every maiden, so soon as she is marriageable, is required "to yield to the embraces of a stranger, and soon after to be married to a young man of her own tribe. Thus, the husband is never permitted to receive his bride in the state of virgin purity; but the Ghowazy father sells the first favors of his daughter to a stranger, making a bargain with the highest bidder."[50] Also at Mecca, we are told,[51] "a female slave, whom the master has not himself brought up from childhood, he never buys as a virgin. . . . Her owner, or, if the latter be a woman, a relative, takes her virginity when she has reached the proper age (twelve to fourteen years). Her purchaser would regard it with suspicion if this had not already taken place." There is no need to investigate this particular subject further. These instances suffice to prove the prevalence in the Semitic world of the practice of maidens submitting themselves once in their lives to some stranger as a rite prerequisite to marriage.[52]

Returning now to Lucian, the practice which he describes is undoubtedly related to the oft-discussed Babylonian practice first recorded by Herodotus,[53] and reattested by Strabo[54] and the Epistle of Jeremiah, 43, that once in her life every native woman had to go to the sanctuary of Aphrodite, or Mylitta, there to submit herself to a stranger.[55] None of these three sources states that the occasion for this ceremony was an annual festival; in fact, the language of Herodotus seems to imply that this ceremony might have been performed upon any day of the year that the woman chose. Yet his statement that the women came to the sanctuary in such numbers that aisles, marked off by ropes, had to be drawn among them to facilitate the examination of them by the visiting strangers, and the leading off of the women thus selected to places outside the sanctuary boundaries certainly implies that very many, if not all, of the women must have assembled at one and the same time, and also that men in corresponding numbers were likewise present; and this, in turn, undoubtedly implies that the occasion was the celebration of some important festival in honor of the goddess.

Nor do any of the three sources say a word about the cutting off of the hair of the women, as a rite either attendant upon or alternative to the sacrifice of their virginity. But both Herodotus and Strabo state explicitly that the heads of the women were crowned with cords,[56] while the Epistle of Jeremiah, 43, tells that the women had a cord about them, without, however, mentioning which part of the body; but it adds the significant note that at the conclusion of the act of sexual intercourse the cord was broken. From this it would seem that when the women came to the sanctuary of the goddess, their hair was bound up by a cord around the head, and that this was cut at the conclusion of the rite, and the hair was then permitted to hang down loose. So much seems certain. From this it is apparent that in the Babylonian form of the ceremony the hair played some role, though just what it may have been cannot be adequately determined. Possibly it was cut off at the conclusion of the ceremony, or, what seems more likely, the fact that during the ceremony itself the hair was bound closely to the head of the woman by the crown of cord may have represented symbolically an older form of the rite, whereby the hair of the virgin was actually cut off preparatory to and as testimony of the sacrifice of her virginity, and therefore as evidence of her fitness to be married.[57]

Justin[58] reports that "it was the Cypriote custom to send maidens before their marriage on certain days to seek their dowry by prostitution on the seashore, and to pay the offerings to Venus for their future chastity. Dido, on her way to Carthage, touched at the island at the very time and took on board her fleet eighty of these damsels to be wives to her followers and assist in peopling the city she was going to found."

It is not clear just what the words "to seek their dowry by prostitution on the seashore, and to pay the offerings to Venus for their future chastity" may mean. Possibly by the time of Pompeius Trogus the practice had been so modified that only a part of the money given to the maiden was made over to the goddess, and the rest was retained by the maiden for her dowry in a manner similar to the practice of the Lydian maidens, as recorded by Herodotus.[59] In the oldest form of the ceremony, however, all the money thus received was, in all likelihood, regarded as the property of the goddess, just as in the Babylonian form of the ceremony.[60] Moreover, since the passage from Justin states explicitly that this rite was not performed upon every day of the year, but only upon certain days, we may draw the same inference here which we have already drawn for the parallel Syrian rite described by Lucian and the Babylonian rite described by Herodotus, that in Cyprus likewise the occasion for the sacrifice of virginity was some great, annual festival, celebrated undoubtedly in honor of the Semitic mother-goddess and her offspring and paramour, Adonis Tammuz.

We may probably infer, too, that, just as in the case of the Babylonian custom, it was not the native Cypriote youths, the future husbands of these maidens, who thus consorted with them in honor of the goddess, but passing strangers—in the one particular case here recorded, the followers of Dido, who must have touched at Cyprus on her way to Carthage opportunely, just when one such festival was being celebrated.

Athanasius[61] likewise states that "the women formerly used to seat themselves in the Phoenician temples, and there offer to their gods as a 'first-fruit' sacrifice the wages of their bodies, believing that by means of this prostitution they appeased the goddess and won her favor." Were we better informed of the details of this practice, we would undoubtedly find it agreeing in most essentials with the Babylonian practice described by Herodotus. Certainly from the use of the technical term *'απαρχόμεναι* we may infer that this was a sacrifice of virginity and not prostitution on the part of all women.

The complete rite is thus amply attested. Undoubtedly, in an earlier form of the ceremony women at the attainment of the age of puberty, or shortly thereafter, and as an indispensable preliminary to marriage, had, at a festival of Adonis and the mother-goddess, to sacrifice their virginity to some stranger, and likewise, as an accompanying and not as an alternative rite, to have their hair cut off. Later, by the time of Lucian, these two rites, as was but natural and as can be paralleled by numerous rites and ceremonies of other peoples, had become alternative instead of complementary as at first. It is interesting and significant to find that Herodotus adds the note that the same ceremony was observed by the women of Cyprus, a well-known center of the worship of Adonis and the mother-goddess. This would indicate that this ceremony was common and widespread in the Semitic world. This is borne out by what we have already noted with regard to Cypriote practice.

Two additional instances of this same practice are recorded in the Bible itself. Numbers 25 : 1–9 tells that the men of Israel, invited by the Moabite maidens to participate with them in the worship of the Moabite deity, join in their sacrifices and have sexual intercourse with them. The procedure with regard to the latter act is described indirectly in an addendum to the passage by some Priestly writer. It is no public nor promiscuous cohabitation, but each man and maiden go aside to a separate booth or tent erected for this purpose, apparently just outside the precincts of the sanctuary.[62] Just this is the procedure described by Herodotus. The facts that this is a service in the worship of a particular deity and at a particular shrine, that sacrifices are offered, apparently in great quantities, and that maidens are gathered here and participate in the rites in large numbers, indicate without doubt that the tradition in its original form told of the celebration by the Moabites of some important festival, presumably held annually, at which, among other ceremonies, their maidens sacrificed their virginity. At the particular celebration referred to here, the Israelite men played the role of the passing stranger with whom this cohabitation was regularly practiced.

And again: I Samuel 2 : 22 tells that one of the sins of the sons of Eli was that they used to cohabit with the women who . . . at the door of the sanctuary. Exodus 38 : 8 states that the brazen laver in the tabernacle in the wilderness was made from the mirrors of the women who used to . . . at the door of the sanctuary. Both passages have been recognized by Biblical scholars, from the days of Ralbag on, upon ample grounds to be out of accord with the context, and therefore to be late insertions.[63]

The word *haṣôbeʾôt* occasions a slight difficulty in both passages, due undoubtedly to the wide range of connotation which it possesses. *G* renders Exodus 38 : 8b "from the mirrors of the fasting women, who were fasting at the door of the Tent of Testimony upon the day upon which he set it up." In other words, *G* sought to relieve the historical anachronism of the fact that until the tabernacle had been erected the women could not throng about its doors by inserting the final clause, "upon the day upon which it had been set up." And it attempted to relieve the difficulty created by the seemingly inexplicable *haṣôb*^{e}*'ôt* by substituting *haṣamôt '*^{a}*šer ṣamû,* "the fasting women who were fasting." *Targum Onkelos* renders *haṣôb*^{e}*'ôt* by *d*^{e} *'atîn l*^{e}*ṣala'ah,* "who came to pray," and *Targum Pseudo-Jonathan* and the medieval Jewish commentators held that it referred to women who came to the sanctuary after childbirth to purify themselves by means of sacrifices. Modern exegetes content themselves with the perfectly justifiable, but absolutely colorless, "who ministered."

I Samuel 2 : 22 is missing in all *G* manuscripts except *A*. There it is rendered: "and how they consorted with the women who stood about the door of the Tent of Testimony." Two facts stand out here: (a) these women at the door of the tabernacle were, according to this version of the text, free for sexual intercourse, and (b) undoubtedly, among other toilet articles, they were equipped with copper hand mirrors. These last were unmistakably for purposes of personal adornment,[64] naturally to make their bearers more attractive to the men who might happen to be present. The Babylonian women, described by Herodotus, Strabo, and the Epistle of Jeremiah, waiting to be chosen as soon as possible by some stranger, would naturally have sought to make their persons as enticing as possible. Particularly those who, according to Herodotus, had by reason of insufficient attractiveness to wait for a long time, and who, according to the Epistle of Jeremiah, were not deemed worthy to have their cords broken, would naturally provide themselves with all manner of toilet articles with which to heighten their charms. Among these, hand mirrors would be practically indispensable.[65] Unquestionably, therefore, these women, stationed, according to both Biblical passages, at the entrance to the sanctuary, and equipped in particular with copper hand mirrors and ready for sexual intercourse with men other than their future husbands, could only have been women gathered there for the very purpose described by Herodotus.

That both passages are late interpolations into their respective contexts is immaterial. They evidence acquaintance with the old Babylonian rite, or one strikingly similar and closely related thereto, in quite the same manner as does the passage in the Epistle of Jeremiah. Moreover, they indicate that this practice had at one time been current in Israel—to some extent, at least. This is readily comprehensible in view of the almost constant Phoenician influence upon Israelite culture and religious practice from the days of David on, and of the growing Babylonian cultural influence beginning with, or even shortly before, the reign of Ahab. Certainly the numerous references in the prophetic writings to the prostitution of the maidens of Israel[66] show that sacred prostitution, such as this was—although recognized and denounced by the prophets and their followers, as non-Yahwistic, and therefore as foreign, non-Israelite in origin and character—was common in the practice of the agricultural Baʿal religion of Israel during the greater part of the pre-Exilic period.[67]

Now it must be admitted that in none of these ceremonies of the sacrifice of virginity just discussed does, so far as can be seen, the rite of cutting off the maiden's hair play any role, either as an alternative to, or the accompaniment of, the sacrifice of virginity. Yet this by no means precludes the possibility that such may have been the case, and that the sacrifice of the maiden's hair may have played a role of some kind in these various ceremonies, just as it did in the form of the ceremony described by Lucian, and also apparently in the form of the ceremony observed at Babylon.[68]

In the same manner, the hierodules of Melcarth had their hair cut off.[69] The parallelism between this ceremony of cutting off the hair of these devotees of the deity and that of cutting off the hair of the virgins of Byblos and, as we have surmised, probably those of Babylon and Cyprus also, is further corroborated by the fact that, just as, according to Herodotus, the stranger had to cast a coin into the lap of the maiden at Babylon for the privilege of consorting with her, so, too, those who sought the favors of a hierodule had to give her a coin. In both cases the coin belonged not to the woman but to the goddess.

It is clear that the twofold ceremony of the sacrifice of virginity and the cutting off of the hair marked a transition in the life of a woman, the passing from one stage of life into another. Usually it is said that by these rites the woman devoted herself to the service of the mother-goddess, and at first glance this does seem to be the natural and obvious conclusion. But this conclusion is more seeming than real. In the first place, as we have shown, and as abundant evidence, still to be adduced, will amply corroborate, the cutting off of the hair is never a rite of consecration but, just the opposite, it marks the passage from a state of consecration, or at least of taboo, whether sub- or superprofane, into a state of ordinary, daily, profane existence. In the second place, the one fact cannot be ignored or denied, that the sacrifice of the woman's hair and the accompanying sacrifice of her virginity caused her to pass, never into a state of consecration to a deity, but into the condition of ordinary, profane life, whereby she became ready for wedlock. Later, in discussing marriage rites, we shall show that the Semitic peoples believed, in a relatively early stage of their cultural evolution, that a deity or spirit had the right of claiming a maiden's virginity. She was therefore in a state of taboo, from which she had to be redeemed before her marriage could be consummated. Therefore, we may conclude with certainty that the sacrifice of her hair and her virginity were the rites by which a maiden passed, not into a state of consecration to a deity, but, on the contrary, out of a state of consecration or taboo into that of everyday life, and specifically of readiness for marriage.

That such was the effect of the sacrifice of the hair is made particularly clear by a statement of Curtiss.[70] After discussing the redemption by means of the sacrifice of the hair of males who had been for one reason or another vowed to a deity or a sanctuary, he says: "The locks of maidens are cut much less often; but instead thereof their dowry, i.e., the purchase price which the bridegroom pays to the parents of the bride, and through which he acquires the right of possession over her, must be paid, either entirely or in part, to the weli. Thereby the father acknowledges that his daughter really belonged to him [i.e., to the weli]."

And finally, this conclusion finds support in one very significant Biblical expression: Leviticus 21 : 7, 14 forbids a priest in general and the high priest in particular to marry a *ḥ^a^lalah*. From its correlation in the text with the words for harlot, divorcee, and widow, it is clear that the word designates a woman who has had sexual relations. This term is usually derived[71] from *ḥalal* II, "to pierce," rather than from *ḥalal* I in the *pi'el*, "to profane"; in support of this derivation is cited the Arabic designation of a virgin as an "unpierced pearl." But, as I have shown elsewhere,[72] this distinction between *ḥalal* I and II, even despite the seeming support which it receives from the Arabic, is artificial and unjustified. There is in Hebrew but one root, *ḥll*, derived from an original *ḥûl*, "to be round," and with a great range of at first seemingly unrelated connotations, yet all easily traceable back to this common source. And inasmuch as quite a number of derivatives of this root, particularly in Arabic and Syriac, referring to various conditions and facts of wedlock, are evolved from the connotation "to profane," it may be safely inferred that this word also has evolved in the same manner.

This is proved definitively by the parallel expression in Leviticus 19 : 29: "Do not profane (*t^e^ḥallel*) thy daughter by making her a harlot"; in other words, the *ḥ^a^lalah* was a woman of the same class and discharged much the same function as the *zônah*, the "harlot." But etymologically, and probably literally also, the term *ḥ^a^lalah* designated this woman as "one profaned," i.e., no longer a virgin and therefore in a state of taboo, but now free for sexual enjoyment by any man who desired her. In other words, the state of free, unrestricted sexual intercourse, whether after wedlock or on the part of a harlot, and even a sacred harlot or hierodule, was one of profanity, and not of taboo or consecration.[73] The entrance of the maiden into this state was, as we have shown, frequently, if not generally, marked by the sacrifice of her hair.

6 The Sacrifice of the Hair by Women at Marriage

It is perfectly obvious that closely related to this rite of virgins cutting off their hair is the custom, frequently met with among Semitic as well as other peoples,[74] of women cutting off their hair at or just prior to marriage. In fact, these are unquestionably but two phases of one and the same rite.

Thus we are told that among the heathen Harranians some sects did not leave their houses, and that they shaved their heads with razors or with a powder, while their wives shaved their heads at marriage.[75] In Mecca "the hair dresser cuts off the hair of the bride just above the forehead and shortens her eyebrows a bit and arranges the remainder of the hair in eight braids just before the wedding."[76] Among the Bedouin in the vicinity of Maʿan, at Iraq and in the Negeb, the hair of the bride is cut short at the level of the eyes.[77] Petermann states[78] that the native Jewish women of Palestine have both hair and eyebrows shaved off just before marriage. Among the Orthodox Jews in the Middle Ages, and not infrequently still today, women cut off their hair at marriage and ever thereafter concealed it from sight by the *sheitel,* or wig of false hair, or by a handkerchief.[79] That this last custom is quite old is attested by numerous references in Talmudic literature.[80] Thus Qimhith, the mother of two high priests, accounted for her good fortune by saying that the beams of her house had never looked upon her bare head.[81] Quite probably this custom of married women concealing their hair is a substitute for an earlier custom of cutting it off at marriage.[82]

Attested by even older evidence is the practice of brides and married women covering the head with a veil, to remove which and disclose the hair was an extreme disgrace.[83] The alternative for women to not keeping the head covered or veiled was to have the hair cut off. Among the ancient Arabs, too, for a married woman to be seen with hair uncovered was a greater disgrace than to be seen naked.[84] Presumably for this reason, the hair of a woman suspected of adultery was in ancient Israel let hang loose, as of one potentially disgraced.[85] On the other hand, according to Talmudic practice, just as among many other peoples, the hair of the bride was let hang loose as a sign of her virginity.[86] These examples make it clear that the cutting off of a woman's hair coincident with the loss of virginity, and the covering of the hair ever thereafter as a sign of marriage, were widely diffused practices among the Semites. They round out our conclusion that the cutting off of the hair and the sacrifice of virginity were in origin redemptive taboo-rites, marking the passage of the woman from a consecrated or taboo state to a profane state, that they were performed in historic times in honor of the Semitic mother-goddess and were at all times preliminary to, and preparation for, marriage.

7 The Sacrifice of the Hair at the Removal of Taboo

In other rites and ceremonies the principle is even more apparent, that the cutting off of the hair enables the person in question to pass from a state of taboo, whether subprofane or superprofane, into a state of normal, profane existence. Thus, a convert to Islam from an unsanctioned religion was frequently required, in addition to being washed or anointed with water, to have his hair cut off.[87] Goldziher has interpreted this ceremony as primarily designed to expel or ward off evil spirits, and in the narrow sense this is undoubtedly correct. But in the larger sense it marks the passing from a state of ritual uncleanness, taboo, and subjection to evil spirits into the profane state of ordinary Moslem life.[88]

Quite parallel with this was the Biblical prescription that the leper when purified of his uncleanness must shave off his locks, eyebrows, and all the hair on his body.[89] By this act he passed from a state of subprofane taboo, in which evil spirits had power over him and caused his disease, into a state of ordinary, ritual profanity.

A similar occasion for the cutting off of the hair, at least in ancient times, was the return of a traveler from a journey, upon which, theoretically, he had been in such danger that his life had become forfeit to some deity or evil spirit and therefore had to be redeemed in the usual manner.[90] Wellhausen tells that the Thaqif, after having completed a journey and before they entered their homes, would visit the shrine of their goddess, Al-lat, and there cut off their hair.[91]

The same rite was likewise observed in ancient Israel. While the first and last days of the Passover and Sukkoth festivals were most sacred, the intervening or middle days also possessed a semi-sanctity. Yet the Mishnah[92] states that permission to cut off the hair on these middle days of the festivals is given to one who comes from a foreign country, or one who returns from captivity, or one who has just been released from prison, or one who has been freed from the ban by the sages, or one who has been absolved from a vow, or a Nazirite, or a leper purified from his uncleanness.[93] Here a twofold implication is unmistakable: first, that under normal conditions a person was forbidden to cut his hair during these festivals; and, second, for a person in any of the taboo states which the Mishnah lists, the urgency of the hair-cutting rite outweighed the semi-sanctity of the middle days.

Moreover, according to ancient Jewish law, one who was a leper or under a ban was prohibited from cutting his hair or changing his garments during the period that the leprosy or the ban endured, i.e., during the period of taboo.[94] Obviously the cutting off of the hair both marked the close of the period of taboo and was also the cause or means of its removal.[95] It may be added that it was a general principle in Rabbinic Judaism that one who had in any way become ritually unclean was obligated, among other rites of purification, to cut off his hair.[96] Similarly among the Falashas a person who becomes unclean in any way whatsoever must pass seven days in an isolated hut at the edge of the village, especially provided for this purpose. There his head is shaved and he is compelled to undergo ritual washings. During this period he may eat only uncooked beans.[97]

In all these cases, whether of subprofane taboo, as the leper, or of superprofane taboo, as the Nazirite or one under a vow,[98] the ritual procedure is exactly the same, and the effect thereof is also exactly the same, viz., the passing from a state of taboo into that of ordinary, profane life.

In the modern practice the custom of cutting off the hair of a person returning from a journey or of a returning prisoner of war seems to have fallen into disuse, but the taboo character of the state out of which such a person passes is amply attested by the fact that a sacrifice of manifestly substitutionary character, the so-called "sacrifice between the feet," is regularly offered. Curtiss describes this as follows: "There is the sacrifice between the feet. This is made in behalf of a pilgrim on his return from Jerusalem or from Mecca, or in behalf of someone who has been long away from home, as a soldier or a prisoner. The ceremony consists in a sheep or goat being slaughtered for the one who returns. Just before he enters the door of the house he stands with his legs spread out so that there is room for the victim to be placed between them. It is then thrown on its left side, with its head toward the south, or Mecca, if he is a Moslem, and toward the east, or Jerusalem, if he is a Christian. Its throat is then cut, sometimes just before the threshold, sometimes upon it. Some of the blood is placed upon his forehead, if he is a Christian, in the sign of the cross. He then steps over the victim and the blood into the house, though it is not considered good usage to step over the blood among strict Moslems. If he is a Christian, he then takes the bundle of clothes which he is to wear to the church. These are blessed by the priest. After he returns home he puts them on. Sometimes the priest comes to the house and blesses them."[99] To this the following note is added in the German edition of the work: "This particular sacrifice is not limited only to pilgrims, soldiers, and prisoners. When the already mentioned Hanna Chabba returned home after the fulfillment of his vow, before his entrance into the house a 'sacrifice between the feet' was offered."[100] The details of the ritual of this "sacrifice between the feet" show beyond all doubt its pre-Moslem and pre-Christian origin and character, and prove its close relationship to the various ceremonies for the removal of taboo which root themselves in the primitive religious concept and practice, as we have depicted these. Particularly close is the relationship of this "sacrifice between the feet" to the sacrifice of the hair.

8 The Sacrifice of the Hair at the Close of the Nazirate

In the case of the Nazirite in particular, the character of the rite of cutting off the hair as a means of removing taboo, and of passing thereby into the state of profane existence, is most readily perceived. Numbers 6 : 1–21 states that normally a person became a Nazirite through having taken upon himself an unusually exacting vow.[101] During his entire period of Nazirate he was *ḳadôš leYahweh,* "holy or taboo to Yahweh." During this time no razor might come upon his head, nor might he partake of anything made from grapes, nor might he touch a dead body. If he accidentally came into contact with a dead body, naturally he became unclean, and his Nazirate was thereby defiled and rendered invalid; in other words, he passed automatically from a state of superprofane taboo, or holiness, to a state of subprofane taboo, or ritual uncleanness. From this he had to be purified in the customary manner. These purification ceremonies endured for seven days. On the seventh day, when the purification ceremonies were completed and he reverted to the condition, not of the holiness of a Nazirite, of course, but to that of profane existence, he shaved his head. Or when there had been no interruption to his condition of nazirateship by reason of such an accident, and the entire period of his consecration had been successfully brought to a close, in addition to offering the prescribed purificatory or taboo sacrifices, the Nazirite also ceremonially shaved his head. This hair was burned upon the altar of the "peace-offering." This indicates its sacrificial character; it was given to Yahweh as a taboo-sacrifice to redeem the Nazirite from his state of holiness, or consecration to Yahweh, and to enable him to return to the state of ordinary, profane life.

In this connection we may again quote from Curtiss: "We may speak of those who correspond somewhat to the ancient Nazirites, who are vowed to God by some doting mother, as Samuel by Hannah. The hair remains uncut until they arrive at a certain age, is weighed when cut, and money is paid in proportion to its weight. One thus consecrated becomes a dervish, if a Moslem, and a monk, if a Christian."[102] Curtiss is unquestionably correct in thus correlating this practice with the consecration of the ancient Nazirite. But its relation to the practice of vowing boys to saints or welys at birth and later redeeming them by the offering of a sacrifice and the cutting off of the first hair, discussed in detail above,[103] is equally apparent. In all cases the cutting off of the hair serves the same purpose of removing, and thereby redeeming from, the consecration or taboo of being vowed to a deity.

Practically paralleling this procedure with the Nazirite is the statement of Lucian[104] that if one of the Galli, the male devotees of the goddess, at Hierapolis saw the corpse of a relative he was unclean for thirty days, during which time he was not permitted to enter the sanctuary. At the end of this period he shaved his head and thereafter was again granted access to the sacred precincts. Here, quite obviously, the shaving of the head is not at all a rite of consecration but rather, just as elsewhere, a rite of removal of ritual uncleanness and subprofane taboo, which the sight of the corpse had brought upon the man; the sacrifice of the hair enables him to return to his former, normal state of devotion to the goddess.

Altogether parallel with this rite, as is indicated by the quotation from the

Mishnah cited above,[105] is the ancient Jewish practice of adults shaving their heads at the conclusion of a period of abstinence or of performance of a vow. This practice is referred to specifically in Acts 18 : 18; 21 : 23 f. and in Josephus, *Wars,* II, 15, 1.

9 The Sacrifice of the Hair at the Conclusion of a Festival

A further, illuminating instance of the practice of cutting off the hair, with its underlying purpose of removal of a previously existing taboo, is found in the frequently attested practice of participants in the *ḥagg,* or pilgrimage to Mecca, or in any important religious festival not to shave their heads until the festival is concluded. The practice at Mecca has been described by many competent authorities.[106] Wellhausen remarks very correctly: "The custom of letting the hair grow during the Iḥram (the period of festal consecration or taboo) seems to be misunderstood. The hair was let grow not in order to take upon oneself a taboo (literally, 'an abstinence') but in order to sacrifice it. And the cutting off of the hair was originally not merely a sign that a sacrifice had been completely and properly offered, but was itself a sacrifice. This is indicated by the fact that at the sanctuary of Uqaiçir every tuft of hair cut off was cast into a pit, together with a handful of meal. The meal indicates unmistakably the sacrificial character of the rite, while the pit reminds us of the Ghabghab (the sacred pit or cave beside or beneath an altar or idol), into which the sacrificial blood was allowed to flow. Moreover, the practice may be cited of casting, after the slaughter of a sacrificial animal, the hair that had been cut off as something taboo ('anathema') into a sacred tree, a practice to which even Mohammed is said to have accommodated himself at Hudaibia."[107] Manifestly, the hair thus cut off was actually given to the deity. Similarly, it seems to have been the custom in the early, pre-Moslem centuries for Christian pilgrims to Mount Sinai to cut off their hair there as an act of devotion at the close of their pilgrimage.[108]

The same practice of allowing the hair to grow during the entire period of the celebration of a festival, with its obvious implication that the hair was to be cut off at the conclusion of the festival, thereby enabling the celebrant to pass in the usual manner from the state of festal consecration or superprofane taboo, was undoubtedly practiced in ancient Israel. We have already noted,[109] from the fact that under certain specific conditions people were permitted to cut off their hair during the semi-sacred middle days of the Passover and Sukkoth festivals, the implication that, normally, people were forbidden to do so during the entire period of the festival. And this is, in fact, stated explicitly in *Yer. Môʿed Ḳaṭôn* III, 81c. The reason for this prohibition given there is that the festival should not be celebrated in improper or unbecoming manner.

But that can scarcely have been the primary motive. Far more likely, all the participants in the celebration of the festival were regarded as being in a state of consecration or superprofane taboo, from which they emerged only at the very close of the festival by means of the customary rite of cutting off the hair.[110] To have cut off the hair during the course of the festival would have meant a too early termination of the period and condition of consecration.

Possibly with this ceremonial cutting off of the hair as a festival rite should be correlated the custom recorded by Thomson,[111] to which we have already referred, that on *Lag bᵉʿÔmer,* i.e., the thirty-third day after the first day of the Passover festival, the native Jews of Jerusalem make a pilgrimage to the tomb of Simon the Just, in the vicinity, and there observe a festival in the open air, at which, among other ceremonies, they cut off the first hair of their children. This is confirmed by the fuller account of another writer:[112] "The Jews come here [to the tomb of Simon the Just] very frequently on Friday and at the new moon, and, moreover, they celebrate each year on the twenty-third[113] day after Easter a festival at this grave in honor of Simon the Just. They bring their little boys with them, and here they cut off their hair for the first time. According to the weight of this hair they vow to give a sum of money to the poor." Manifestly, this ceremony has a twofold character: it partakes in part of the nature of a festival rite and in part of a rite of redemption of sons by the sacrifice of the first hair at the proper age and occasion.[114]

10 The Sacrifice of the Hair as a Mourning Rite

Finally, the hair was cut off regularly as a rite of mourning among the ancient Arabs[115] and Syrians[116] as well as in modern practice.[117] The observance of this custom by ancient Israel is attested by numerous Biblical passages.[118]

We have had ample proof that the sacrifice of the hair is in every case thus far considered a characteristic taboo-sacrifice, conforming to the general principle that the sacrifice of a part of the tabooed object redeems the remainder. There can be neither need nor reason for assuming a different origin or explanation of the sacrifice of the hair as a rite of mourning.

It is a well-established fact that most primitive peoples regard the ghost of a deceased relative or friend as a very dangerous being. Frequently, instead of striving to maintain their bond of union with him after death and burial, as Robertson Smith holds,[119] the living seem rather to fear him and seek to placate him by various rites and sacrifices or to free themselves from his power in every way possible, either by returning from the grave by a route different from that traversed thither, or by sprinkling water behind them, or by employing some other, similar agency or charm against evil spirits, or by not immediately entering the house in which the dead person had dwelt, or by entering through some opening other than the regular door.[120] Usually the malignant power of the ghost is thought to continue unimpaired for a certain period immediately following death and burial, generally seven days. During this time the mourning rites are carried out with zealous care. Thereafter, the power of the ghost gradually wanes, and accordingly the intensity of the rites of mourning may be correspondingly abated, until finally, usually at the end of a year, the power of the ghost is thought to have ceased completely and the rites of mourning may therefore be discontinued altogether.

That such concepts and practices existed among the ancient Semites is proved by ample evidence. This important question will be dealt with in detail in its proper place in this investigation.[121] Here, however, we are justified in drawing the conclusion, with Oort,[122] Samter,[123] and Elhorst,[124] and against Schwally,[125] that originally the hair, cut off as a mourning rite, was a sacrifice to the ghost of the deceased designed to redeem the surviving relatives from his dread power, to which they were subject because of his former association or relationship with them. The cutting off of the hair both marked and facilitated the passage of these persons from under the taboo, or power, of the hostile ghost.[126] For this cogent reason, Deuteronomy 14:1 prohibits the shaving of the eyebrows on the ground that this is a sacrifice to the dead, i.e., to his ghost, and therefore not to Yahweh.

11 The Taboo Character of the Hair Sacrifice

In all these instances of the cutting off of the hair as a ritual act the taboo character of the rite is self-evident. It is a redemptory sacrifice to a deity or spirit, the part substituting for the whole.[127] And throughout a man's entire life, whenever danger seemed near and his life appeared forfeit to some maleficent, supermundane power, the repeated performance of the ceremony of cutting the hair[128] and sacrificing an animal would be certain to redeem him from the taboo which had mysteriously come upon him.

XIII

Evil Spirits and Marriage Rites

Rites and practices closely related to those of birth in origin and purpose are observed throughout the Semitic world in connection with marriages. Such ceremonies, too, usually endure for a period of seven days, or, occasionally, for multiples of seven days. In fact, the ancient Arabs called the marriage celebration *sabâʿ*, "seven," because it extended regularly over seven days.[1] The original purpose of these marriage rites, the evidence will show, was likewise to ward off the attacks of evil spirits, which were thought to threaten both bride and groom, but more particularly the bride, during this period.

Thus we are told that among the Bedouin the marriage tent is pitched a long way from the camp. There the newly married couple are shut up for eight days, and no one is supposed to see them. Food is placed outside the tent door by their friends. The bride especially must not be seen for some time after the marriage.[2] Not infrequently the young couple go off by themselves to the mountains and remain there for a month, or even for two months, before they venture to return to camp.[3]

Occasionally it is only the bride who is thus secluded. So Jaussen tells[4] that "in the camps a special corner in the tents, called *ḥullah*,[5] is designed for the bride. There she spends eight days (immediately following the marriage ceremony) counting as the first the 'evening of the entrance' (i.e., of the consummation of the marriage)."

Musil likewise states[6] that among the fellahin of Palestine and the vicinity, for the first seven days after marriage the young couple may not do any work; neither may the bride leave the house, nor may the house be cleaned during this period, for this would disturb the evil spirits and cause the sudden death of both bride and groom.[7] After the close of this seven-day period the bride leaves the house in order to bathe, and during her absence the house is cleaned. Throughout these first seven days after marriage the young couple are called by a particular name, *ʿorsân;* the groom is called *ʿâris* and the bride *ʿarûs*. After these seven days they resume the titles *ḫaṭîb* and *ḫaṭîbe,* which they retain until the birth of their first child, whereupon the man is called *ǧôz* and the woman *mara*. This change of names probably indicates that during the first seven days after marriage both bride and groom are regarded as being in a state or condition differing radically from that of every other period of their life. Of such importance is the custom that the groom must remain constantly with the bride during the first seven days after marriage that "the young husband in el-Kerak who has not yet completed the first seven days with his bride is exempt from all military service."[8] The observance of precisely this same custom in ancient Israel[9] proves its great antiquity, and with it the antiquity of the principle or superstition underlying it.

Among the Bedouin, also, the bride may not be seen by anyone except the groom during the first seven days after marriage. According to Burckhardt,[10] among the Aeneze Bedouin "it is thought decent, that on the nuptials of a virgin she should remain at least one fortnight in the interior of the tent, leaving it only at night. If her husband absent himself on a journey before the expiration of that time, she may abridge the period of her confinement."[11]

Generally the bride flees to some deserted spot, known only to the groom, where she is visited by him daily, and remains there until the seventh day. During this time the young couple may cover themselves at night only with the skins of animals. At the expiration of the seven days the bride may again associate with the members of her tribe. This seventh day after marriage is called among the Ṣẖûr *yowm as-sâbeʿ*, literally, "the day of the seven," or "of the week," just as the seventh day after birth, as we have learned, is also called *yowm es-sabûʿ*. To this Musil adds that the bride who did not flee from her husband upon this occasion would bring dishonor upon herself and would bear cowardly children. Such a woman is generally addressed as *yâ rabûḥ*, "O shameless one!" Among the Ḥeǧâja the young bride flees away every evening for at least half a year; among the Ḥâmâjde, for at least a month; among the Salâjṭa and some tribes of the Ṣẖûr, likewise for half a year. Among the Ṭerâbîn and ʿAmârîn the bride does not flee away, but she may not be seen, except by the groom, for seven days. The groom, however, may leave the bridal tent, and every day of the seven he is invited to eat with some neighbor. On the seventh day the bride goes with her companions to the water in order to wash the bridegroom's clothes. After her return to the camp she is invited by neighbors to eat with them. Four days later, i.e., four days after the completion of the marriage week, she goes to visit her parents. Among the Ṣẖûr, on the seventh day the bride visits her relatives. She takes food with her, preferably a sheep, which is eaten by them. During the course of the meal she receives from her relatives all manner of gifts. These belong to her alone; she has absolute control of them, and no one may take them from her.

This flight of the bride upon her marriage night is a strange rite indeed. It is amply attested by other reliable witnesses. Jaussen,[12] too, tells that among the majority of the Bedouin tribes the bride escapes on the marriage night, flees to the mountains, and the bridegroom must pursue and search for her.

"Among the Šarârât in the evening, during the celebration by the entire clan, and while the bridegroom is participating in the festivities or in the dances of the young people of his own age, the bride takes advantage of the propitious moment to disrobe and flee away. The groom, not finding her under the tent, even though this has been well guarded, is compelled to search for her during a part of the night. During my sojourn at Mādabā it happened that a maiden succeeded in hiding herself so well that she was not found until the following morning at about ten o'clock. Her husband then brought her back to the tent, but in the evening the young woman again succeeded in escaping, and fled away for the entire night. She continued this for the following seven days. . . . If it happens that through weakness or shame she does not run away, she is blamed and is called *rabouġ*—'She who loves the easy life.'

"Among the Beni Ṣaḫer, likewise, the woman flees away on the first night after the marriage. The custom is found also among the Arabs of Sinai. But at Kerak and in Irak the practice is not established.

"It is difficult to account for this fact by the assumption of a sentiment of antipathy to marriage; for the woman hardly conceives of any vocation other than this."

Among the Mezeyne, a tribe of the Sinaitic peninsula, the bride is furnished with provisions by her female friends and is encouraged by them to run away to the neighboring mountains. If the bridegroom succeeds in finding her, he is obliged to consummate the marriage immediately and on the spot, and to pass the night with her in the open country. He then brings the bride home to her father's tent, but she escapes repeatedly and finally consents to remain in her husband's tent only after she is far advanced in pregnancy.[13] Similarly in southern Arabia the bride flees to a cave in company with her girl friends, who defend her with stones. They are driven away by the groom and his friends. The groom thereupon immediately consummates the marriage with the bride in the cave.[14]

Certainly the bride is not thus expressing any real reluctance to the consummation of the marriage, and not only to the consummation of the marriage itself but also to all successive acts of intercourse until pregnancy becomes manifest. But it is certain that what intercourse does take place during this period, and particularly the first act thereof, must be away from the home of the bride's parents and the tribal encampment. The substitute for this among some tribes is that the young couple, or at least the bride, must not be seen by anyone, and least of all by her parents and relatives, during the seven days of the marriage festivities.

Not improbably, in this practice of the flight of the bride, her pursuit by the groom, and the consummation of the marriage in some secret place, away from the home or encampment of the parents and relatives, we have the origin of the modern institution of the wedding journey. And perhaps, too, in the fear of the bride and the danger resulting from beholding her, and especially her face, we have one motive at least which gave rise to the institution of the bridal veil.[15]

An additional superstitious belief is recorded by Wilson: "In some parts of the country neither bride nor bridegroom may cross a stream for a period of seven days after the wedding, as this would be most unlucky, and would mean the cutting off of the succession, the Arabic idiom for crossing a stream being that of cutting it."[16] Another authority upon Oriental life describes the same practice in slightly varying terms.[17] He says that "the bride remains for seven days in the marriage tent and may not pass over running water, for this would carry away her progeny, if ever she has any."

Likewise among the native Jews of Jerusalem and the Jews of eastern Europe, during the seven days of the marriage festivities the groom is not permitted to leave the house.[18] Presumably the bride, too, is similarly restricted in her movements, although this is not explicitly stated in our sources. Also among the Jews of northern Africa the marriage ceremonies continue for seven days, from Sabbath to Sabbath. During this entire week the young couple remain in the house of the bride's parents and entertainments are given each evening, continuing until daybreak. The marriage is consummated upon the first night.[19]

In Mecca the law requires a man to pass the first three days after marriage with his new wife if she is a widow or a divorcee, but if she is a virgin, he must remain with her for seven days.[20] Precisely the same custom obtains also in Algeria.[21] Moreover, in this same country during the first complete month after the consummation of the marriage, a husband and wife address each other only in the lowest tones and observe many precautions not to let themselves be seen, especially at night; and in particular they carefully avoid meeting their parents.[22] In Morocco the groom is confined to the house for eight days and the bride for a period of eight to twelve months after marriage.[23] According to another source, in Morocco the bride remains secluded until the sixth or seventh day after her arrival at the house of the bridegroom.[24]

Even more explicit is the information given by Doutté concerning the marriage rites observed by the native tribes of northern Africa. Among the Doukkâla the marriage festivities continue for seven days, with a particular celebration upon the first day and another upon the seventh day. During this period the married couple remain in the marriage tent, nor can any cause, no matter how important, induce them to leave it.[25] Among the Reḥâmna the marriage is consummated in a little chamber attached to the house of the father of the groom. In this the groom takes up his abode some days before the marriage in order that he may not have to see his father and his mother. The marriage is consummated upon the first night.[26] On the following morning the groom gives his young bride a coin, undoubtedly as payment for the privilege of having consorted with her. During these seven days the bride does not wear her girdle. Only upon the seventh day does she resume it. Furthermore, during these seven days the husband may not see his relatives. The bride may see her mother upon the morning following the consummation of her marriage, but a whole year should pass before she sees her father again, unless, in case the latter has some particularly cogent reason for seeing her, he is willing to run the risk thereof; but even then this should not happen until after three or four months.[27]

Among the Copts the bride does not leave the house until after the birth of her first child or the end of the first year.[28]

Moreover, among the Egyptian Arabs "it is customary for a young husband to refrain from the exercise of his conjugal rights for a week after the marriage, and the termination of this period is considered a due cause for rejoicing."[29] According to Burckhardt[30] and Schwally,[31] it is a common practice to deflower Moslem maidens at the conclusion of the marriage service and seven nights before the first actual copulation.

Moreover, Burckhardt relates that while the young woman is being deflowered by her husband—not, however, in actual copulation—"many women assemble before the door, striking drums, singing and shouting loudly, to prevent from being heard any conversation that might pass between the newly married couple." This cannot, however, have been the real or original purpose of this peculiar ceremony, for this end could have been attained more simply and easily by causing every one to remove to some distance from the chamber. Undoubtedly, the original purpose of this practice was to frighten away by means of the loud noise the evil spirits, thought to be particularly threatening at just this moment.[32]

In southern Arabia the marriage is not consummated until the fourth night after the wedding ceremony.[33] In Abyssinia, too, the wedding festivities continue for seven days, and the marriage is consummated only at the close of the festivities.[34] And we are told that in Fez, among the Jews, the groom casts a dish of fish at the feet of the bride upon the seventh day after the marriage, in order to make her fruitful.[35] Presumably this act is preliminary to the consummation of the marriage. Among the Egyptian Jews at marriage the bride and groom exchange their garments, each for those of the opposite sex. This is done in order to deceive the demons, who are so dangerous at weddings.[36]

The significance of all these rites and ceremonies can be easily determined. We have already discussed the belief of practically all primitive peoples that virgins are in the power of evil spirits, who claim especially the right of first intercourse with them and possession of their virginal blood. Therefore both bride and groom are thought to be in extreme danger, and there is danger also for anyone who comes into contact with them or catches sight of them or is seen by them during the period when they are still subject to the evil spirits. Due precaution must be taken to protect not only both bride and groom, but also their parents, relatives, friends, and guests; hence the customs of deflowering the bride artificially, or through intercourse with a stranger or a slave[37] preliminary to the first copulation at the close of the seven-day wedding period; or of secluding the bride, or both bride and groom, in a special place for the consummation of the marriage, or even, not infrequently, for the entire period during which the power of the evil spirits was thought to be dominant; or of compelling the bride to flee away for a time or to cover her face with a veil;[38] or of performing various rites, among other marriage ceremonies, to guard against or to expel the evil spirit or spirits from the bride, or from both bride and groom, as, for example, cutting off the hair of the bride,[39] a ritual bath,[40] and, frequently, of deferring the actual consummation of the marriage until the time when the power of the evil spirits was thought to be exhausted and the consequent danger to have passed.

Of particular significance in this connection are the *ḥelîyye*-sacrifice, offered by the groom as an important and even indispensable part of the marriage ceremony, and the ritual thereof. Of this, Curtiss says: "The following account was given of the marriage customs of Mehardeh, which are common among the Greeks and Protestants. In that town they have all the weddings on a given day in the year when the harvest is over. In connection with the marriage ceremony: 'They slaughter a sheep outside the door of the house; while the blood is still flowing, the bride steps over the blood . . . the pastor thinks there is much the same idea underlying this custom as in building a new house; that unless they sacrifice an animal there will be some misfortune.' "[41]

In almost identical language, Burckhardt describes the use of blood among the Copts in Egypt. He says: "They kill a sheep as soon as the bride enters the bridegroom's house, and she is obliged to step over the blood flowing upon the threshold."[42]

There is doubtless a similar, though a somewhat different, meaning and purpose to another custom which Burckhardt describes in connection with marriage customs among the Aeneze, a Bedouin tribe: "The marriage day being appointed . . . the bridegroom comes with a lamb in his arms to the tent of the girl's father, and there cuts the lamb's throat before witnesses. As soon as the blood falls upon the ground the marriage ceremony is regarded as complete." It is also interesting to note that among the Beni Harb, in Hedjaz, it is deemed necessary to the completion of the marriage that the blood of a sheep flow upon the ground.[43] Palmer mentions another significant use of blood at a marriage among the Bedouin of the Sinaitic peninsula. After all the preliminaries have been carried through, and her future husband's abba has been thrown over the prospective bride, who with shrieks and cries has attempted to escape, the women take her in charge. "A tent is next erected for her in front of her father's habitation, to which she is conducted, and then sprinkled with the blood of a sheep sacrificed for the occasion."[44]

Musil describes the same ceremony with greater precision.[45] The details vary slightly between the Bedouin and fellahin manners of offering this sacrifice. The Bedouin manner is simpler and, for our purpose, more significant. This sacrifice is called *ḥelîyye*. When the bride is brought to the tent of the groom, the *wekîl,* or agent of the groom, offers the sacrifice and says, "This is the *ḥelîyye*-sacrifice of N (the bridegroom) for N (the bride)." Both bride and groom are then sprinkled with the blood while this formula is recited: *ḥellî ḥallki 'allâh,* "Be redeemed (from the bann); God has redeemed you." This is the custom among the Ḥêwât. "Among other tribes the bridegroom himself offers the *ḥelîyye*-sacrifice, then approaches the bride, wipes the blood from the slaughtering knife upon her sleeve and says, 'Be redeemed (from the bann); God has redeemed you.'" The flight of the bride into the desert, the pursuit by the groom, and the consummation of the marriage follow immediately after this.

Musil describes the procedure with this sacrifice among the fellahin as follows: "When it grows dark the maidens come (to the house where the bridegroom is waiting) with their oil lamps filled, and sit down and sing. Late at night they accompany the bridegroom to his house or tent, where the bride is waiting. A goat or a sheep stands there ready for the *ḥelîjje*-sacrifice. The *ḥelîjje*-sacrifice is absolutely indispensable, if the marriage rites are to be fully carried out. The animal for sacrifice must always be a female; it may not be one-eyed, sickly . . . ; it may not be a sheep or a goat which has borne young within the last seven days. The bridegroom himself offers the *ḥelîjje*-sacrifice upon the roof above the door, or in the door, or in the room where the marriage is to be consummated, and sprinkles the bride with the blood. Then he seats himself in the bride's place, and she must bring him his supper. . . . After he has eaten he gives the bride one *meǧîdi* and then with his knife cuts the ostrich-feathers from her head-dress and casts them before his feet."[46] Thereupon the marriage is consummated.

Jaussen, too, describes this sacrifice as follows: "When the night is quite advanced and the participants (in the marriage festivities) begin to tire, the friends of the groom bring him the victim, designated by the name *dabīḥet ḥullīeh*. He kills it himself as the definitive seal of the marriage. In the vicinity of Maʿān, not only the bride but also the groom are marked with the blood; while among the other Arabs it is the groom himself who puts the blood upon the forehead and breast of the bride. At Kerak the blood is not put upon the bride."[47] To this, Jaussen adds the note: "Among some Christian Bedouin the groom takes into his house the blood, while still quite warm, and with it anoints the lintel and the doorposts of the house. In order to render this anointing more perfect, the victim is frequently slaughtered upon the terrace in such a manner that the blood flows down the door. . . . Beneath the tent the blood of the victim is sprinkled about the entrance."

Elsewhere,[48] Jaussen says: "Towards evening the groom, who had been invited by his friends, returns to his house, where he receives visits and gifts according to custom. At the end of this indispensable ceremony a sheep is brought to him. Then, seizing the knife, which one of the attendants hands to him, he plunges it into the neck of the victim and says to his bride, 'Be redeemed; Allah has redeemed thee.' Among the non-Christian Arabs the groom takes in his hand some of the blood, still warm, which flows from the wound, and sprinkles his bride with it, while saying these words. This sacrifice, called *dabīḥet el-ḥullīeh,* is the final seal of the marriage contract, the act which, from both the legal and the religious standpoints, gives the bride over into the power of the groom."

The outstanding fact here, as both Musil and Jaussen testify, is that this sacrifice redeems the bride. The formula regularly recited by the groom in connection with this sacrifice, *ḥellî ḥallki 'allâh,* "Be redeemed; Allah has redeemed thee," indicates this. In the first place, it should be noted that this formula is addressed to the bride, for both verb and pronominal suffix are feminine. In the second place, the verb used here—undoubtedly in a fixed, formulistic, or technical sense—*ḥalala,* is identical with the Hebrew verb *ḥalal,* which, in the intensive, *pi'el* conjugation, *ḥillel,* means regularly "to profane," i.e., "to remove from the condition of taboo," and from which the adjective *ḥôl,* "profane," is derived.[49] Accordingly, Musil and Jaussen have correctly rendered this formula, "Be redeemed; Allah has redeemed thee."[50] With the offering of this sacrifice and the recital of this formula, the bride and, with her, the bridegroom are redeemed from taboo. Now, both bride and groom enter upon a state, not of consecration or sanctity, but of profane existence (*ḥôl*), wherein they may practice marital intercourse freely and participate in all activities of daily, profane, married life with impunity. Hence the technical name of this sacrifice, *dabîḥet ḥelîyye* or *ḥullîyye* (literally, "the sacrifice of profanation" or "the sacrifice of removal of taboo").

There can be no question, therefore, that this sacrifice of redemption is offered primarily on behalf of the bride, since the formula accompanying the sacrifice is addressed to her. The formula does not state from what the bride is redeemed, and apparently there is no longer any clear consciousness of what this is or may have been originally. Nevertheless, a number of considerations reveal this clearly. In the first place, there is the fact cited by Curtiss, that unless this sacrifice be offered and its blood be made to flow, misfortune will befall the marriage. Likewise, the facts that this sacrifice is the indispensable precursor of the consummation of the marriage, and that the blood is sprinkled, not only upon the doorposts and lintel and occasionally also upon the threshold of the house, tent, or room in which the marriage is to be consummated, but likewise, and almost invariably, upon the bride, and not infrequently upon the groom as well, and not only upon the forehead of the bride but likewise upon her breast, are convincing indications that this redemption-sacrifice is intimately associated with this first act of intercourse by the young married couple. Therefore it is a typical taboo-sacrifice, intended to free the bride from the possessive power of evil spirits. It has the same purpose as the various marriage customs and ceremonies already described. Not impossibly the blood upon the bride may have been thought in early times to symbolize the hymeneal blood, shed by the virgin upon this occasion, and may have been intended to deceive the gullible spirit into believing that he had already received that which was his due. Perhaps, too, the fact that the animal offered as the *ḥelîyye*-sacrifice must always be a female may indicate its original character as the substitute for the bride.[51]

That such concepts of the power of evil spirits over the bride, or over both bride and groom, and similar practices of redemption from their power obtained among ancient Semitic peoples is amply attested.[52] The best-known and perhaps the most convincing illustration of this is, of course, the story of Tobit. Sarah had been married to seven husbands in succession, but each had been killed by Ashmodai, the evil spirit which possessed Sarah, just when the marriage was about to be consummated. This evil spirit was, however, exorcised from Sarah by the burning of the liver of a fish, and thereafter the marriage of Tobit and Sarah was consummated without mishap.[53] In the Testament of Solomon, an early pseudepigraphic work, Asmodeus says to Solomon: "My business is to plot against the newly wedded, so that they may not know one another. And I sever them utterly by many calamities; and I waste away the beauty of virgins and estrange their hearts. . . . I transport men into fits of madness and desire when they have wives of their own, so that they leave them and go off by night and day to others that belong to other men; with the result that they commit sin and fall into murderous deeds."[54]

Similarly, the Rabbis told that three classes of people must be carefully watched in order to guard them against evil spirits: the sick, the bridegroom, and the bride. To these three classes other authorities added the following: a woman in childbirth, mourners, and the pupils of the sages.[55]

It is a superstition among the Christians of Palestine that a newly married couple should return from the church in which the marriage has been solemnized by a route different from that by which they came thither, for otherwise the man would die soon.[56] Here, the fear of evil spirits endangering the lives of the newly married couple, and particularly the life of the groom, is readily apparent. Returning from a cemetery, following a burial there, by a route other than that taken thither is a common method of eluding the ghost of the deceased. Similarly in southern Arabia, the bridegroom wears a bouquet of garlic on the marriage day as a protection against the evil eye.[57] And among the Moslems of Lifta, a village near Jerusalem, before the solemnization of a marriage the women dress a wooden pitchfork in the house of the bridegroom in the clothes of the bride, adorn it with the gold and silver ornaments of the bride, and arrange it so as to resemble a human figure. The sister of the bride takes this and dances with it before the bridegroom.[58] The purpose of this strange ceremony can only be to protect the bride from the danger supposed to threaten her at marriage and to make it come upon the puppet which represents her, and by means of which, presumably, the evil spirit is thought to be deceived.[59]

Among the Jews of Baghdad the night before the wedding is called *Lel-el-Chana,* "the night of the red stain," because it is customary on this night to stain the hands, nails, and soles of the feet of the bride and her attendants and of the groom and his companions with *chana,* henna, a kind of red stain. This is washed off the next morning, but the reddish stain remains for several weeks.[60] Moreover, in the houses of both bride and groom "the night is spent in singing and music, as it is considered injurious for the bride or the bridegroom to sleep the night before the wedding."[61] The same practice is observed by the Moslems of Moab[62] and of Egypt.[63] Here, too, the fear that evil spirits may attack both bride and groom is readily apparent. And here, too, just as in ancient Israel, the marriage festivities endure for a full seven days.

As we have seen, the power of evil spirits, conforming to the belief that seven is an unlucky number, was thought to endure for seven days. Therefore, like other important rites, the wedding ceremonies usually continued for seven days, particularly those rites intended to exorcise the evil spirit or spirits, or at least to afford some protection to the bridal couple, their families, and friends. At the close of this period the various exercises came to a natural end, since the period during which the power of the evil spirit was effective had terminated. Thereafter the couple were fully married and free to consort at will and to go about the activities of ordinary, profane life without fear of the demon which had threatened them.[64]

However, even here one restriction had to be carefully observed. Under no condition might the husband have intercourse with his wife during the seven days following the beginning for her of each monthly period. During these days she was thought to be again in a state of dangerous impurity, i.e., possessed by or under the control of evil spirits. Hence, during these seven days her husband and all men had to scrupulously refrain from associating with her.[65] From this state of uncleanness she purified herself by a ritual bath at the termination of the seven days.[66] Still today in Palestine the belief is current among the former natives of the land that if a man has intercourse with a woman before the completion of the eighth day after the commencement of her monthly period, he will be stricken with leprosy; hence the application of the proverb, *jôm ittâmin la tâmin,* "the eighth day, do not trust it."[67]

XIV

Evil Spirits and Death Rites

I Introduction

The same superstitious belief in the maleficent working of evil spirits and the duration of their power for a period of seven days, and the same or parallel practices to ward them off or expel them, manifest themselves among the Semitic peoples in ceremonies of burial and mourning for the dead.[1] The hypothesis has been frequently advanced that rites of mourning are designed primarily to effect or maintain a bond of union with the deceased.[2] This may be true in certain more advanced and enlightened circles, where broad experience and deeper thinking have overcome the original superstitious fear. But more and more scholars are inclining to the view that the origin of practically all ancient and long-persistent burial and mourning rites lies in the superstitious fear of the ghosts of the dead, conceived of as maleficent spirits, and especially inimical to surviving relatives, friends, and associates with whom they had been in intimate contact during life.[3]

Regarding this fear of the ghosts of the dead on the part of the modern native inhabitants of Palestine, Curtiss says:[4] "They have the custom, also, of slaying to benefit the souls of the departed. When anyone dies his relatives are supposed to kill one or more animals within a few days. They call this *fedou,* or redemption, although they do not seem to have any conception of the meaning of this term. They consider that in some way it benefits the dead, but it is rather the public feast to the poor that follows which is reckoned a good deed on the deceased's account. Even the most intelligent, however, believe that if they omit the ceremony some harm will befall them, apparently owing to the wrath of the departed spirit.

"The Arabs and Syrians are very sensitive on this point. They consider it necessary that a man should not neglect to perform his obligations to the departed, and they have many stories to tell of the way in which such neglected ones have appeared to them in dreams at night, reproaching them for not performing their duty in this regard."

The fact that this sacrifice is called explicitly *fedû,* "redemption," and that, apparently, it redeems the living from the wrath of the ghost of the dead, and the additional fact that the flesh is given to the poor for a public feast stamp this as a typical taboo-sacrifice. This leads to the interesting and important question of sacrifice on behalf of the dead, and particularly to the much mooted point, whether these sacrifices are offered *to,* or merely *for,* the dead. But before this question can be discussed profitably, it is necessary first to consider briefly the natural and normal concepts of existence after death which seem general and basic in Semitic belief and practice.

2 Existence of the Soul After Death

It must be borne steadily in mind that the doctrine of immortality of the soul, in the modern sense, and of reward and punishment in a life beyond the grave, are not at all primitive concepts. They are largely of speculative, theological origin, and they entered into Judaism only some time after the Babylonian Exile, and from Judaism passed in turn to Christianity and Islam. We know that, especially with regard to matters connected with death and reverence for the dead, the human mind is surprisingly conservative and tenacious of old forms and ceremonies long after it has, in theory at least, advanced to higher stages of philosophy and theology. Innumerable rites of primitive origin and significance persist in the doctrines and practices of peoples dwelling upon various planes of cultural evolution, even though their first meaning and purpose have long been completely forgotten. We have already noted significant instances of this in our consideration of rites attendant upon other critical moments of life. We shall find this evidence even more striking in rites and practices connected with death.

The opinion more or less generally and officially current in Islam with regard to the departure of the soul from the body and its fate thereafter are stated most clearly and fully by Sale:[5] "As to the soul they hold that when it is separated from the body by the angel of death, who performs this office with ease and gentleness towards the good, and with violence towards the wicked, it enters into that state which they call el-Berzakh, or the interval between death and resurrection. If the departed person was a believer, they say two angels meet it, who convoy it to heaven, that its place there may be assigned, according to its merit and degree. For they distinguish the souls of the faithful into three classes: the first of prophets, whose souls are admitted into paradise immediately; the second of martyrs, whose spirits, according to a tradition of Mohammed, rest in the crops of green birds which eat of the fruits and drink of the river of paradise; and the third of other believers, concerning the state of whose souls before the resurrection there are various opinions. (1) Some say they stay near the sepulchres, with liberty however of going wherever they please; which they confirm from Mohammed's manner of saluting them at their graves, and his affirming that the dead heard these salutations as well as the living, though they could not answer. Whence perhaps proceeded the custom of visiting the tombs of relations, so common among the Mohammedans. (2) Others imagine they are with Adam, in the lowest heaven; and also support their opinion by the authority of their prophet, who gave out that in his return from the upper heavens in his pretended night journey, he saw there the souls of those who were destined to paradise on the right hand of Adam, and those who were condemned to hell on his left. (3) Others fancy the souls of believers remain in the well Zemzen, and those of infidels in a certain well in the province of Hadramaut, called Borbût;[6] but this opinion is branded as heretical. (4) Others say they stay near the graves for seven days; but that whither they go afterwards is uncertain. (5) Others, that they are all in the trumpet whose sound is to raise the dead. (6) Others, that the souls of the good dwell in the forms of white birds, under the throne of God. As to the condition of the souls of the wicked, besides the opinions that have already been mentioned, the more orthodox hold that they are offered by the angels to heaven, from whence being repulsed as stinking and filthy, they are offered to the earth, and also being refused a place there, are carried down to the seventh earth, and thrown into a dungeon, which they call Sajîn, under a green rock, or, according to a tradition of Mohammed, under the devil's jaw, to be there tormented, until they are called up to be joined again to their bodies."

It is perfectly clear that we have to do here with many unrelated and even contradictory beliefs, which derive from various sources. Probably, as Sale pointed out, the majority of these beliefs and doctrines have their origin in Jewish traditions, writings, and teachings, which were but half understood by Mohammed and other transmitters. But certainly some of these doctrines originated in primitive Semitic belief and superstition. Among these may be cited in particular the doctrine that the souls remain in the vicinity of the graves for seven days after death, and that they can hear and understand what the living say to and about them. The primitive Semitic character of these particular beliefs will become manifest in the course of this study.

As is to be expected, the modern Bedouin retain the old, primitive beliefs to a very marked degree. Jaussen tells:[7] " 'Where does the spirit go after death?' I once asked a Bedouin. 'Into the earth,' he replied; 'near Allah,' another told me; 'into the Well of the Souls at Jerusalem,' said a third. At Maʿān I was told one day that for seven days the spirit of the dead person roams about the tomb, especially the spirits of children, but also those of adults. It returns likewise to disport itself about the tomb whenever a sacrifice is offered there. The spirit often returns to the dwelling which it inhabited; it does not harm its relatives,[8] but frequently it displays a prejudice against strangers. Others, however, contended that on the very evening of burial the spirit is judged in the tomb, and, according to its deeds, it is sent either to the place of righteousness or to the fire."

Musil is even more explicit in regard to this matter:[9] "A person's soul still lives, even after it has passed out from the body through the nostrils. As soon as the body is buried, the spirit flies to Jerusalem and through the mouth of the Well of Spirits (in the Temple area in Jerusalem) into the nether world. What it does there no one knows. Many say that it eats and works, but others deny this; 'only God knows, but not we.' Beneath Jerusalem is the assembly place of the spirits. There they wait until God shall judge mankind.[10]

"The Ḥêwât say, 'The souls betake themselves to Jerusalem and through the opening into the nether world. There they must work. Whoever has lived well, so that Allah was satisfied with him, lives the life of a rich man; but he with whom Allah was not satisfied lives a miserable existence. Both must eat and drink, just as the living eat and drink.' The Sa'îdijjîn and the Ẓullâm say the same.

"In eš-Šôbak it is said, 'The soul continues to live after a person's death. If he was righteous he enters paradise; otherwise he goes to hell. Paradise and hell lie side by side underneath Jerusalem.'

"According to the belief of the Ṣḫûr the souls of all people, Jews, Christians, Mohammedans, and Bedouin, go to one and the same place, beneath the earth and unknown. Many locate it near Jerusalem. There in the Temple area is said to be a deep cistern, through which the entrance into the nether world leads. Hither come the souls in the form of flies.

"As has been said already, both Paradise and Hell lie beneath the earth, close beside each other, are more dark than light, just as at twilight; but in Hell there is much dust and sand, but no water. In Paradise there is water, but no one knows whether anything grows there.[11]

"According to the opinion of the 'Azâzme, the souls of murdered people go to a different place.

"The dead person, whose corpse has been consumed by birds or beasts of prey, also suffers after death. His soul flies about the skeleton in the form of a fly, buzzes sadly, and begs for help. As soon as the remains are buried, it enters the nether world.

"According to the belief of the 'Amârîn, the dead reappear, especially in dreams. The soul of the sleeping person leaves its body and betakes itself to the dead, whom it sees again in the old form. But it is also possible to summon the dead. Certain persons do this, and the dead follow them.

"In the opinion of the Ṣḫûr, the murdered man appears each night and calls out the words which he spoke last before his death. . . .

"The Ḥêwât also know that the dead can be summoned. When he appears it is in his own former body, but variously clad. If he wears a beautiful garment, that is a sign that he is dwelling in Paradise, but if he appears poorly clad, this is a sign that he is suffering."

The grave is never maltreated; and in passing by it the Bedouin addresses its inmate, particularly if he is a relative or fellow tribesman, as if the dead could hear, with words of honor and affection.

"The ʿAzâzmi curses his enemy, when he passes by his grave, and says, 'May God not pity you, nor a single one of your bones.'[12]

"He fears the dead, for he can harm him even out of the grave."

Musil also records the fact that the dead person is supposed to hear the wailings which are made for him immediately after his demise.[13]

Such in brief is the concept among the modern Bedouin of the existence of the soul after death.

Naturally, the concept of the present-day urban Semites is practically the same. Canaan states[14] that "the belief is general throughout the Orient that the soul even after death is attached to the body, or to certain parts thereof. The spirits of those who have died an unnatural death remain permanently at the spot where the corpse, or parts thereof, lie. For this reason cemeteries are avoided. . . . In consequence, the spirits of persons who have been murdered—called *rassad* or *malak*—are regarded as dangerous spirits.

"In some parts of Palestine the belief is general that the souls of such as lived an evil, godless life in this world become terror-bringing demons.[15]

"The ancient Arabs, in much the same manner, conceived of the soul of the dead as having the form of a bird, usually an owl."[16]

Lyall says:[17] "The pagan Arabs had a strange and gloomy superstition that the spirits of dead men became owls, which dwelt in the graves where their bodies were laid. *Ṣadâ* and *hâmah,* the words for *owl,* thus came to mean the ghost of a dead man, and are often used where there does not appear to be any idea that the speaker is likely to die unavenged. But some say that the superstition was that only the souls of those slain without vengeance became owls, and that they flew at night above the grave, crying *isḳûnî, isḳûnî*—'Give me to drink, give me to drink.' When the blood of vengeance was shed, the thirst of the owl was quenched and he ceased to cry."[18]

Wellhausen describes the belief of the ancient Arabs with regard to the existence of the soul after death even more specifically:[19] "We come finally to the question of how the heathen Arabs conceived of the state that followed death. In the old songs the thought is expressed with all manner of variations that with death everything is ended. The 'be mindful of life' is used as the motive of the charge to enjoy this little bit of existence. No gleam of hope shines for the despairing mortal beyond this world. The general consolation is that death is universal, and that even the fleetest and most cunning wild animals cannot escape this hunter. The cry 'Be not far!' helps naught; it is an unavailing form of speech, just like other wishes. But manifestly this is only the opposition voiced from an advanced standpoint to the original implication of this cry. While both the pre-Islamic Arabs and the Koran reveal no belief in resurrection and regard the idea of a real, second life as a pure fallacy, nonetheless they hold fast in every way to the old feeling of association with the dead. They equip him for the journey into the unknown country, provide him with a portion of the means of existence, greet him, visit him, and swear by him. In other words, he is thought to still continue to exist in some manner or other; he experiences all kinds of sensations and is subject to all physical needs, such as thirst. The souls of the dead appear as birds, namely, as owls, and in this form upon the gravestones bewail their lot to each other. In the form of *ğinn* they inhabit cemeteries and waste places. Islam has retained this conception of the continued existence of the soul after death and developed it further under Jewish influence. While the dead person is being borne to the grave, he utters words which all animals comprehend, but not mortals. He hears the tapping of the shoes of those who follow his bier and understands what is called out to him. He suffers from the lamentations of his relatives. When the funeral cortege has departed, two angels come and examine him. Very much depends upon their decision; if it be unfavorable, he is immediately punished in the grave. These are all ideas which have naught to do with resurrection, and which even, in a sense, anticipate it, and must therefore be correlated with the ancient folk-conceptions."

Undoubtedly, it is just because of their concept of life after death and of the particular need of the spirits of the dead for water that many of the Bedouin tribes prefer to bury their dead near water. Burckhardt says:[20] "Arrived at the wells of Nedeym; in approaching which we passed, long after sunset, by several tombstones, called Gobour Adjouad el Are-ab; 'the bravest men of Are-ab lie buried here,' said one of our chiefs; 'their companions carry them from many-days' journey to this spot, that they may repose in the cool neighborhood of the wells, and their deeds be remembered by those who pass by here.' The Are-ab are a tribe of the Bisharein."

Doughty, too, found the regular tribal burial-place located in the vicinity of water.[21] A later observer records the fact that the Bedouin always bury their dead near water, so that the soul may drink its fill with ease.[22] And Jaussen tells[23] that the Tiaha bury their dead at Moueïloh, near the wely Eimour. They bring the corpse thither from a distance of two- or three-days' journey because there is water there, so they told him. Jaussen conjectures that this was because of the need of washing the corpse in water before burying it; but he adds that some Bedouin told him that it was because the dead are in a much happier situation in the vicinity of water. This last is more likely the true reason.

Musil, too, records that the most desirable burial places are located in the vicinity of water.[24] He also adds that wherever possible water is poured over the grave by those who have dug it, and who wash their hands over it.[25] Moreover, the 'Azâzme and Ẓullâm fill a small vessel with water and place it at the head of the corpse.[26] This is undoubtedly intended to serve the dead person in the after life. For the same reason the Ḥêwât put some meal in the grave of a man, and some paint in that of a woman. The Ṭerâbîn strew two or three measures of dried figs upon the grave. The children then gather and eat these.[27]

3 Death Sacrifices Among Modern Semitic Peoples

From this it is, of course, but a short step to actual sacrifices for the dead.[28] Of these, Curtiss says:[29] "In all parts of Syria, Palestine, and Arabia there are sacrifices for the dead. The evidence for this is derived from many personal interviews, as well as from the testimony of Doughty. I reproduce some of the testimonies received on my travels. The following is from the minister of the kursi: 'They kill animals for the dead in behalf of his spirit; they call them *fedou*. They go before him as a light, serve him in the next life as he approaches God. They become a *keffareh* for his sins. Some people have all this done before they die, in order to cover their sins.'

"Ahmed Ghazzaleh, a peasant at Nebk, said, when questioned with respect to sacrifices for the dead: 'When a man comes to die he appoints someone as executor to sacrifice some animal. It is preferable for a man to offer the sacrifice during his life. . . . He rides the animal across the narrow way on the day of judgment. Because of his obedience to God in offering the sacrifice, the victim serves him in the day of judgment, as Abraham was saved by obedience (in offering up Ishmael).'

"The minister of a Moslem shrine in Homs, who became very friendly when he was told that I was a teacher of the Torah and a friend of Abraham, affirmed that 'only the Arabs offer sacrifice for the dead.' This does not seem to be correct, as it is spoken of as a universal custom. Another testifies: 'The relatives of the dead man make someone an executor, who is to see to the sacrifice. He must not partake of it, but it must be given to the poor.' The particular time of such sacrifice undoubtedly varies. Among a tribe of Arabs in northern Syria they sacrifice three days after the death a goat or sheep, which must be a perfect animal and may be male or female. They are ashamed not to sacrifice for the dead."

Elsewhere[30] Curtiss describes the sacrifice for the dead among the Nosairis as follows: "They sacrifice for the dead before they put him in the grave. On the evening of the sixth day after the funeral there is a feast, and the next morning they have a sacrifice in the house of the dead. . . . They say, 'In the name of the saint,' and pray that God may forgive him his sins. After the sacrifices have been presented the soul may pass out of an opening over the door of the house into the body of a male child that is to be born. . . . The sacrifices cause the forgiveness of certain sins committed by the deceased.

The more food is furnished, the greater the efficacy of the sacrifice. A parent may say, 'Redeem soul by soul'; that is, redeem the soul of the man who is dead by the soul of the animal who is to be killed as the victim. 'The animal is a spirit and the sick person is a spirit. The saint accepts one in place of the other'; that is, the soul of the animal in the place of the soul of the man."

In the German edition of the same work, Curtiss says:[31] "The Sslêb sacrifice to the dead, just as other Arabs sacrifice to the welis, with the words, 'This is thy sacrifice (thy supper), O Ahmed!' When on the *Daḥîje*-festival they slaughter a camel for a dead person, they say, after calling the name of the dead person three times, 'Accept thy sacrifice.' It is offered in his name. In answer to the question, 'To whom is it offered?', I received the reply, 'To the dead.' "

Jaussen describes the sacrifices for the dead in the following, systematic manner:[32] "At the moment when an Arab is about to expire, amid the cries and lamentations of the women who have gathered in the house of death, the final preparations for the burial are quickly made. This is soon ended. Then provisions are brought beneath the tent and sheep are killed. This continues for at least seven days, sometimes even for fifteen; but in principle an entire year ought to be devoted to these marks of grief. Actually at the end of a week the nearest relative of the deceased prepares to terminate these expressions of grief. He brings, with a certain ostentation, one or several sheep, which he sacrifices in the house or under the tent; he cuts them into pieces, which he distributes to the mourners, who eat and then return to their homes. This is called in the desert the *ḍabîḥet el-ʿazā,* 'the sacrifice of consolation,' because it terminates the regular mourning. Among the Latins of Mādaba the practice is invariable, even among the Christians, and especially among the Belqāwīeh and the Ṣeẖour."[33]

Jaussen also describes another sacrifice for the dead in these words: "Among these last Arabs[34] on the very day of death a sheep is sacrificed (beneath the tent of the deceased, but not at the tomb).[35] The relative who slaughters the victim says, 'This is the supper for our dead.' Every one eats, and says, 'May Allah have pity upon our dead!' Among the Ḥamāʾīdeh one leads to the tomb a female sheep or goat, which is sacrificed upon the tomb or in the immediate vicinity. It is cooked on the spot and the participants eat it. But this does not constitute the real 'supper'; this takes place in the house of the deceased on the very same night. No one neglects to say, 'This is the supper for our dead.' "

The same sacrifices are described by Musil:[36] "The dead person is memorialized in the camp. Among the Ṣẖûr, on the very first night that the dead man lies in the grave the sacrifice *awnâse* is offered, for which only a goat may be used; if no goat is to be had, the sacrifice is postponed. Thirty days later the sacrifice *ʿaša'-l-majet* is offered; for this a sheep is always employed. On every eighth night during the first month after death the name of the dead person is always pronounced at the evening meal, and the nearest relative pours out some drops or casts some crumbs before the tent as a sacrifice for the dead man.

"The ʿAmârîn call the sacrifice offered on the first day *wanîse.* A goat or sheep may be used for it. While they slaughter it they say, 'Your value and your worth belong to God and to N (the deceased).'

"The sacrifice must be offered before sunset, for in the night angels come to the dead in order to test his conscience; for this he must be strengthened.

"Among the Ḥêwât during the first night after the death the mourners sacrifice the victim *sdâdet el-ḳabr* (among the ʿAzâzme it is called *hbûṭa*) with the words, 'This is thy supper, O N.'

"Only women and children eat the flesh of this sacrifice.

"Among the Šarârât the sacrifice for the dead on the day of burial is called *rutbe ʿan rûḥ.*

"Among the Ẓullâm, if the men who have prepared the grave meet a sheep or goat on their return home, they take the animal without asking to whom it belongs (the mourners must pay for it), and sacrifice it after the funeral with the words, 'This is thy supper, O N; we give it to you.'

"This is called *ʿaša'-l-majet,* and the Saʿîdijjîn say that thereby they feed the dead person.

"Later they memorialize the dead person on the evening of every Wednesday or Thursday; they take some sour milk or bread, cast it into the fire, and say, 'This is thy supper, O N; this is for the soul of N!'

"After the first month, on the memorial day of the deceased, they sacrifice a sheep with the words, 'This is the *ʿaza'*-sacrifice of N!'

"The Tijâha sacrifice the *ʿaza'*-offering on the tenth and thirtieth days, with the words, 'May God have pity upon him whom he comforted, and forgive him whom he created!'

"Among the ʿAzâzme the mourners offer upon the fortieth day the sacrifice *raḥma,* with the words, 'Here is the redemption-sacrifice *(fedw)* for God; its value and its worth belong to N!'"

Schumacher gives an interesting and significant account of the sacrifice offered at the death of a Bedouin woman.[37] "After a goat had been sacrificed upon the grave, and had been prepared for the mourners to eat, a second goat was sacrificed on the second evening, and was eaten by the husband and the children; this was called *wanîseh,* 'association'; this implied continued, intimate association with the ghost of the departed. Finally after seven days a third goat was slain and was eaten by the friends of the deceased; this was called *fakḳu-'l-waḥdati,* 'the redemption of isolation'; the deceased, it implied, was henceforth to forget completely her house, husband, and children; they themselves desired release from the ghost of the deceased."

Another observer relates[38] that among the Otäbe tribe of Bedouin on the seventh day after death "an old, toothless sheep or goat is sacrificed in order to avert evil. The relatives and all present eat the sacrifice. The bones may not be broken, but are laid whole in the grave, or, if this be too distant, are hidden under a stone, in order that the deceased may ride upon the animal."

One other sacrifice, regularly offered for the dead, is of particular significance. It is the so-called *ḍaḥîyyeh*-sacrifice. It is closely related to and goes by the same name as the *ḍaḥîyyeh*-sacrifice offered by pilgrims to Mecca during the great annual pilgrimage, on the tenth of the month *Dhû-l-Ḥiğğah,* in the valley of Mina, near Mecca, and by pious Moslems in other localities on the same day. In honor of the dead this sacrifice is regularly offered either on the annual anniversary of the death or else in the spring. The importance and persistence of this sacrifice is attested by Doughty.[39] He says: "There is a sacrifice for the dead, which I have seen continued to the third generation. I have seen a sheykh come with devout remembrance, to slaughter his sacrifice and to pray at the heap where his father or his father's father lies buried; and I have seen such to kiss his hand, in passing any time by the place where his sire is sleeping, and breathe out, with almost womanly tenderness, words of blessing and prayer; . . . and this is surely comfort in one's dying, that he will be long-time so kindly had in his children's mind."

We have already seen that, in his account of the *ḍaḥîyyeh*-sacrifice among the Ss̱lêb, Curtiss tells that they believe that the sacrifice is offered directly to the dead person, whose death is commemorated and whose name is called out three times.[40] Curtiss records likewise the words of an Ismailiyeh:[41] "The *ḍaḥîyyeh* may be for a man's father or mother who is dead. It is a vow to God. It is a universal custom long prevailing. It is for the breaking forth of blood to the face of God, on behalf of the dead. Usually before a man dies, he requires his relatives to take a solemn oath, that they will make annual sacrifices on his behalf. They are afraid of God if they are unfaithful. They never neglect such sacrifices. . . . No use is made of the blood. The bursting forth of blood is absolutely indispensable.

"A Moslem, speaking with reference to the *ḍaḥîyyeh*-sacrifice, observed: 'The bursting forth of the blood is the most important thing.' The Mawali Arabs hold the same view: 'The vow is presented to the face of God. Anyone who is washed and is ceremonially clean may kill the victim. They take its blood and make a stripe on the back of the animal. It is a mark of the good one; that is, of the weli. It indicates that the sacrifice has been presented to him. They cook the victim and eat it, and share its flesh with the poor. The sacrifice is not complete without the shedding of blood. It would not do to get a certain quantity of meat and eat it in their houses; without the bursting forth of the blood, there is no fulfillment of the vow. . . . They never use the term fedou—but they employ the verb from which fedou comes.' "

Before describing the *ḍaḥîyyeh* proper, Jaussen narrates an interesting and significant incident with regard to it.[42] "A Ṣaḫary, well known at Mādabā, one certain year offered the *ḍaḥīeh* for his deceased father in the customary manner. When the camel had been cut in pieces and was about to be put in the cauldron in order to be boiled, he perceived that he had no more water; so he asked one of his assistants, a Šarāry, to go and bring some from a neighboring spring. In payment for his trouble this one demanded one of the feet of the camel, which he carried away with him without having first passed it through the fire. The following night the dead man appeared to the Ṣaḫary quite irritated and said to him, 'You have sent me a camel which has only three feet; the Šarāry has carried away the one that is missing; how do you want me to complete my pilgrimage?' The poor Bedouin was compelled to offer another *ḍaḥīeh,* according to all rules." To this, Jaussen adds the note that in the Neğeb the *ḍaḥīeh* is called *fedū,* and the *fedū* is offered for the family and its property into the face of Allah.

Elsewhere[43] Jaussen speaks of the *ḍaḥîyyeh*-festival and sacrifice in the following terms: "The day of the festival having arrived, a camel is procured, free from every blemish or deformity; it may not be one-eyed, nor deprived of an ear, nor marked with a burn; it ought to be three years old, and consequently capable of carrying a burden, whether it has already done so or not. Upon its back is put all that constitutes a complete equipment: breeches, tunic, mantle, girdle, handkerchief, cord of the *kefīeh* and an empty water bottle. The camel is set at liberty; the poor of the tribe dart in pursuit, and each one endeavors to lay hold of what he can during the flight. The camel is then led before the door of the tent. If anyone has died recently, a relative of the deceased draws near, seizes his knife, and plunges it into the neck of the animal, while calling the dead man by his name, 'So and so, take thy *ḍaḥīeh.*' The blood ought to be sprinkled upon the ground. The camel is then flayed, cut into pieces and put in the cauldrons in order to be cooked and eaten by the participants. If anyone wishes to take a piece and carry it away, this is permitted, provided that everything has been placed for a few moments upon the fire. All this ought to be done outside the tent. The entrails of the victim are cast away; only the Šarārat, because of their great poverty, gather and eat them.

"The Bedouin do not explain their customs, but content themselves with preserving them. However, in the present case they have explained to me that, in their opinion, the garments placed upon the camel are destined for the dead man, who is naked and needs clothing; the camel is intended to serve him in performing his pilgrimage to Mecca. The *ḍaḥīeh*-festival therefore has a twofold aspect: a sacrifice for the dead, for, while sacrificing the victim, the sacrificer says, 'O so and so, take thy victim; there is no blindness in it nor any heaving (a certain sickness that causes it to shake its head), and by God, I am telling the truth!'

"According to Ibrahim aṭ-Ṭouāl, the *ḍaḥīeh* among the Arabs is also occasionally intended to expiate sins. The sacrificer then says, 'O God, accept my sacrifice!' Everything ought to pass through the fire, even the feet and the entrails, which are cast away.

"Among certain Arabs, the Rualah, for example, the camel which is to be sacrificed is led before the tent near some flat stones, which are placed upon the ground like flag-stones and are intended to receive the blood. The stone which has been anointed with this blood will be put by Allah in the scales on the day of judgment. The sins of the dead man will be put in the opposite scale, and if the stone outweighs them, the sins will be forgiven. According to Mohammed eḏ-Ḏiab, among the Eben Rašīd the sacrificer pierces the neck of the victim, which is then led immediately around the house; in falling to the earth the blood traces a kind of circle, which will protect the house.

"Among some Arabs, when the victim has breathed its last, the skin of the camel is torn just above the hump, and a little salt is poured into a gash made in the flesh.

"The importance which certain Arabs attach to the *ḍaḥīeh* as a sacrifice is clear from the custom which Ibrahim aṭ-Ṭouāl described to me in his house in the presence of a certain Zeben and an Abou'l-Ġanam. When an Arab fears that his *ḍaḥīeh* might not be offered after his death, because there is no one in his family to perform this service, he offers it himself during his lifetime: seven sheep or an ox or camel. After his death he will derive the same benefit from this, as if it had been offered for him by someone else at the regular time, i.e., at the great *ḍaḥīeh*-festival which follows immediately after his demise.

"Furthermore, in the opinion of the people of Maʿān, it is not only the dead man who will suffer, if he does not receive his *ḍaḥīeh,* but even more the neglect will affect his family. For this sacrifice a camel is required, for which, however, during seven successive years a sheep may be offered as the substitute sacrifice.[44]

"In case a dead person has not received his *ḍaḥīeh,* he frequently appears to a member of his family, who then makes haste to prepare the funeral meal for him.

"Invariably at Maʿān the *ḥawly,* the yearling lamb, is considered improper for the *ḍaḥīeh*-sacrifice. Sāleḥ, my interpreter, pretended that the *ḍaḥīeh* is sacrificed, not for the dead, but only for the living."

Musil's account of the *ḍaḥîyyeh*-sacrifice and festival corroborates that of Jaussen and adds a few significant details.[45] He says: "Every year the people of Arabia Petraea visit the graves of their ancestors, about which other graves may lie. Almost every family brings a goat, sheep, or camel, healthy and without blemish, and sacrifices it upon the grave; or if not upon the grave, then close beside it. The blood is either made to flow immediately upon the grave, or else it is caught and the grave and all near-by graves are sprinkled with it. Meanwhile the sacrificers say, 'Here is your supper, O our dead!' The flesh of the animal is cooked and eaten immediately. In the evening they pour some oil upon the *naṣaba*-stone.

"When a Ṣaḫary comes to the grave of a relative or an ancestor and brings milk with him, he pours a bit upon the grave and says, 'For the soul of my father!' or 'For the soul of my dead relative!'

"The ʿAmârîn make a pilgrimage every spring with their sheep to the graves of their ancestors. There they encamp for a considerable time. They offer sacrifices as food to their ancestors and give them milk to drink. When the blood of the sacrifice or the milk flows upon the graves they say, 'This is a sacrifice for the soul of N!' They likewise lay upon the grave as gifts empty cartridges, buttons, bright threads, pieces of salt, and the like.

"Among the Ṣḫûr on the *ḍaḥijje*-festival the nearest relative takes a perfect camel, puts upon it a saddle, sack and water-bottle, and, if the dead man has smoked, his pipe and tobacco, in short everything that one might need for a long journey, and leads the loaded camel through the entire camp. He holds in his hand a curved knife. And he calls out as loudly as possible, 'O N, O N, O N, here is your *ḍaḥijje*-sacrifice; I give it to you as a gift of duty!' Now and then he turns to those present and says to them, 'O N, you are witness; this is the *ḍaḥijje*-sacrifice of N!' When he has returned to his tent, he makes the camel kneel down, slaughters it, while he continues to repeat the above formula, and gives it, with all that it carries, to his poor fellow-tribesmen.

"Among the Šarârât, on the *ḍaḥijje*-festival they load upon the camel the saddle-bag, shirt, mantle, headdress, cord, girdle, shoes or sandals, the *ḳadḥa*-plant for making a fire, a flint, material for the fire, a sack, a water-bottle, a cup, a pipe, a full tobacco-pouch, a staff, a comb, a full bag of meal, dates, curds, and salt. Frequently miserly sons take the camel of the widow, their mother. Thereupon she mounts upon it and cries out, 'I will not dismount until you give me the camel N!' Before sacrificing the camel is examined by strangers, to make sure that it has no blemish. The sacrificer says, 'O my father, here you have your *ḍaḥijje*. It is neither concealed from nor begrudged to you, and, by God, I speak the truth!' The flesh may not be cooked beneath the tent, but only behind the tent in the sun, for the camel is sacrificed for the soul of the dead.

"On the *ḍaḥijje*-festival the Ẓullâm offer a camel, a sheep or a goat, accordingly as they are able. The flesh of this sacrifice is cooked and eaten.

"The Christians of El-Kerak designate on the eighth day before the beginning of the forty-days' fast an animal, which they slaughter on the following Saturday evening, with the words, 'This is your supper, O our dead!'

"Among the Ḥwêṭât the dying man designates the female camel which is to be offered for him on the *ḍaḥijje*-festival (usually it is the animal upon which he has made the most plundering expeditions) with the words, 'O my son, offer for me the camel N!' "[46]

4 The Taboo Character of Death Sacrifices

An analysis of these beliefs and ceremonies of the Bedouin and their present-day urban kindred with regard to death, burial, and existence after death is most illuminating. It forms the natural approach to the study of similar beliefs and customs among the ancient Semitic peoples. For, especially among the modern Bedouin, many beliefs and ceremonies of the most primitive character and purpose have persisted in fairly unmodified form down to the present day. Certainly it cannot be gainsaid that in innumerable respects the Semitic nomad of today is far more primitive, and preserves primitive Semitic habits of thought and practice to a more pronounced degree, than the Babylonians of four thousand or the Israelites and Phoenicians of twenty-five hundred years ago.

Now it is noteworthy that in the beliefs and practices of these modern Semites, which we have just collated, a marked variation, confusion, and even contradiction occur. Occasionally the sacrifice offered after death is spoken of as *fedû*, or *fedw*, "redemption." Nevertheless, there seems to be a noticeable tendency not to apply this term to this sacrifice; and we have noted one particular case where the funeral-sacrifice is never called by this name. However, in describing this sacrifice and the manner of its offering and its purpose, the verb *fdw* is used more or less unconsciously.

Furthermore, the offering frequently manifests significant characteristics of the taboo-sacrifice. In very many cases, perhaps even the majority, the sacrifice may under no condition be eaten by the sacrificer himself, but must be given to the poor, the women or the children of the tribe, or to other tribesmen, particularly if they are poor.[47] Moreover, not infrequently, as we have seen, before the sacrifice may be thus eaten by the poor, it must be passed through the fire,[48] precisely as was done in ancient Israel with certain forms of the taboo-sacrifice. This passing of the sacrifice through the fire is tantamount to actually giving it to the dead. To eat of it before it has been passed through the fire means to deprive the dead person of his sacrifice. Furthermore, this sacrifice very frequently is thought to have expiatory force, to ransom the dead man from the consequences of his sins. It is particularly in this connection that this sacrifice is often designated as a *fedû*, or taboo-sacrifice. These facts tend to show that the attempt to divest this sacrifice of its *fedû*, or taboo, character is probably the expression of a progressive religious tendency, and that in its original form its taboo character was much more pronounced.

Likewise, considerable confusion exists in the present-day concept of the existence of the soul after death. Practically all the opinions recorded agree that after death the soul descends into the nether world, a place beneath the surface of the earth. The entrance to this nether world is through a well or spring or cistern, located by many near Jerusalem, usually in the Temple area.

But beyond this, opinions differ materially as to the final destination of the souls of the dead. Many hold that a man's deeds during life are weighed, and according to their merit or demerit the soul receives reward or punishment. The concept of this reward or punishment is seldom as lively as it is in official Islamic theology or general popular belief. There is no mention of a beautiful heavenly abode, with trees and fountains and gardens and entrancing maidens. At the most there is only the simple concept that the nether world consists of two compartments, Paradise and Hell. In the former there is water, but in the latter there is no water at all, but only sand. But beyond this no one knows what Paradise is like nor whether, even though there is water, anything grows there. This is a typical Bedouin concept, based upon the Bedouin's daily experience with life. Hell is an endless stretch of sand, with no water, and where, of course, nothing grows; it is a translated, absolutely waterless desert, the Nefoud of his own wanderings, where existence at its very best is most difficult and miserable. And Paradise is, *per contra,* a place where there is water, and where at least the pangs of thirst may be escaped.

But there is abundant proof that this concept of Paradise and Hell, even though characteristically Bedouin, is by no means primitive, but is rather the product of vaguely understood Moslem theological doctrine reacting upon the simple, inexperienced Bedouin mind. The Bedouin has heard something of reward and punishment, of sin and atonement, of Paradise and Hell; so naturally he pictures these in terms of his own daily experience, and conceives of Paradise as a place of water and Hell as a place of sand. And for the same reason he affirms now and then that the sacrifice offered after death is designed to expiate the dead man's sins or to serve as a *keffareh,* or atonement, for his soul; or perhaps the dead man rides the animal sacrificed upon the pilgrimage which after death he must undertake to Mecca; or perhaps by riding upon the back of the animal he may be enabled to pass over the hair-fine bridge which spans the chasm of Hell, and so find entry into Paradise.

But opposed to these doctrines of sin and expiation, of reward and punishment, and of Paradise and Hell, are certain altogether incongruous beliefs and practices, the truly primitive character of which is unmistakable. Thus, the idea that the soul of a person whose body is as yet unburied cannot find entrance into the nether world, but is in a most pitiable plight, presupposes the concept, not of a two-compartment nether world, with its Paradise for the righteous and its Hell for sinners, but a nether world with only one, single compartment, into which enter the souls of all dead who have been properly buried, regardless of the kind of lives, righteous or unrighteous, which they may have led on earth. The antithesis of existence in this nether world is denial of entrance thereto, and the consequent compulsion to roam without aimlessly and endlessly, or at least until the proper burial rites shall have been performed. This nether world is scarcely conceived of as a place of joy or reward. But neither is it a place of suffering and punishment. Rather it is negative, neither good nor bad; or perhaps good or bad accordingly as the surviving relatives of the dead man make proper provision for the welfare of his soul in its nether world existence. But the true misfortune is to be unable to enter this nether world; the fate of such a soul is miserable indeed. And this condition of the soul is determined, not at all by the considerations of the kind of life the man may have lived on earth, but solely by conditions attendant upon his death, his funeral rites, and the care for the welfare of his soul manifested by living relatives in succeeding years. For this reason, the lot of the soul of the person who leaves behind no relatives to perform the proper burial rites and to make proper provision for his soul through the long-continuing future, or of the person whose body for any reason lies unburied, or one who has been murdered and remains unavenged by his kindred, is sad indeed.

Similarly, the practices of putting food and water, particularly the latter, on or near the grave, and of burial wherever possible in the vicinity of water, presupposes that after death the soul goes to a place where food and water, and more especially water, are lacking, or at least are not plentiful. Nonetheless, the soul requires these in its shadowy existence and if they are not furnished by the surviving relatives its lot in the nether world must again be hard. Likewise, the custom of loading upon a camel, upon the annual *ḍaḥîyyeh* festival, garments, tobacco, pipe and pouch, saddle, water-bottle—in short, all that constitutes a complete equipment for an ordinary Bedouin, implies that in the nether world the soul will need these things, and that unless they are provided by the living relatives, the soul in the nether world must want for them, and perhaps must suffer through this want. It may even imply that without them the soul in the nether world must go naked and cold and miserable, just as it would under similar conditions in this life.[49] This, too, is the implication of the custom that before death the dying person designates the animal he desires to have sacrificed for him, or that the animal upon which he was accustomed to ride during his lifetime is sacrificed for him after his death. If his relatives discharge their full duty to him at and after death, then he may live in the nether world an existence quite similar to that which he had lived here on earth; and this is good, and the best that can be expected in the nether world. But if the surviving relatives are remiss in the discharge of this duty, the soul must suffer in the nether world. The character of its existence and the degree of its suffering will depend upon the degree of faithfulness and devotion with which the relatives perform their duty to it. It may be denied entrance entirely into the nether world, or else, admitted there, it may nonetheless suffer hunger, thirst, and want and go naked and cold, or have no camel to ride upon; or it may enjoy all the good things to which even the most ambitious soul might aspire. Everything depends upon the relatives.

Obviously, this is the real belief and the ancient and primitive practice of these Bedouin; and the ideas of sin and expiation, reward and punishment, Paradise and Hell, are innovations in their belief and practice.[50]

There is also, as has been said, more or less confusion and uncertainty as to whether the sacrifices are offered directly *to* the dead or merely *for* them, on their behalf. It was Curtiss who felt this uncertainty most keenly. And this was but natural; for Curtiss' contact was chiefly with the Arabs of Palestine and Syria, who are closest to civilization and whose religious beliefs and practices are therefore the most directly influenced by modern theological concepts and tendencies. Among them, the furthest departure from primitive beliefs and practices would naturally be found. The higher the plane of religious evolution to which these people have attained, the more we may expect to find among them the thought that all sacrifices are offered only to Allah.[51] Nonetheless, when Curtiss put the question directly, "To whom are these sacrifices offered?" he received the simple and unequivocal answer, "To the dead."

Among the Bedouin this thought is more general and more apparent. Here too, occasionally, the idea seems to find expression that the sacrifice is offered to Allah, or at least to a wely; but more frequently it is self-understood and beyond all question that the sacrifice is offered directly to the dead. This is particularly evident in the various formulas which are recited in connection with the sacrifice, particularly in the most common formula, "This is thy supper, O N!" or, "Here is your supper, O our dead!"[52] This is especially manifest in the thrice-repeated formula of the Ṣẖûr, "O N, O N, O N, here is your *ḍaḥijje*-sacrifice; I give it to you as a gift of duty!" coupled with the adjuration to the bystanders to bear witness to the truth of what he is saying. The same is the implication of the Šarâry formula: "O my father, here you have your *ḍaḥijje*. It is neither concealed from nor begrudged to you. I give it to you, and, by God, I speak the truth!"

Moreover, the thought is expressed repeatedly that this sacrifice is actually the food of the dead person, given to him that he may eat it. This is the further implication, too, of the usual formula, "This is thy supper, O N!" This is also the implication of the fact that among the Ẓullâm, if the men who have dug the grave meet any animal while returning from the grave, they must sacrifice it to the dead man, and the relatives of the deceased must then recompense the owner of the animal for it. Obviously, the thought here is that the dead man himself has selected the very animal which he desires, and which must therefore, regardless of cost or other circumstances, be given to him.

And this is also the implication of the absolute necessity of the *ḍaḥîyyeh*-sacrifice. So necessary is it that, if the dying man has no relative to offer this sacrifice on his behalf, he makes provision for it during his own lifetime. Obviously, without this sacrifice his existence in the nether world would be miserable indeed. And if the dead man leaves behind relatives who should offer this sacrifice on his behalf but are remiss in discharging this duty, he appears to them and demands his due. Above all, it must be an absolutely perfect animal, with no injury or blemish. Nothing else will satisfy the insistent dead.

And this, in turn, leads to another necessary inference. The dead have power to enforce their demands; and the living recognize and fear this power, and are punctilious therefore in discharging this obligation. If the living relatives should persist in neglecting this duty, the presumption undoubtedly is that the spirit of the dead will be angered thereby and will vent its wrath upon them. In other words, throughout this entire ceremonial of the dead, as we find it among the Bedouin and the lower classes of the urban or village inhabitants of Palestine and Syria, the underlying belief is unmistakably that the dead have a very insistent and indisputable claim upon their living relatives for those things which will render their existence in the nether world easier and pleasanter. If these duties are performed and these things are given to them, well and good; the living then have nothing to fear from the dead; and so far as in their power lies, the spirits of the dead may even be kindly disposed and helpful to them. But if these things are withheld, and the duties to their dead are not performed, then woe betide the living; for the dead man will undoubtedly seek to wreak his wrath upon the living for their neglect of him, and to take for himself those things which he needs in the after life and which are rightfully his.[53] Therefore the living always have, in theory at least, something to fear from the dead.

For spirits need not be always subject to reason and rule; and, as in the case of the Ṣahary and his *ḍaḥîyyeh*-sacrifice which Jaussen describes, it is so easy for a poor mortal to make a mistake, even though his intentions are the best in the world, and all unconsciously to irritate or enrage the spirit of his departed ancestor. Then woe betide him! The ghost must therefore always be kept placated and well disposed; its needs must be provided for, and its wishes—fortunately, usually simple and easily satisfied—must be anticipated. The best is not too good for it. It will accept only animals perfect in every respect. And if it indicates in any way its preference for certain particular sacrifices, these must be given to it unhesitatingly and regardless of cost. Above all else, those sacrifices which are its recognized due must be offered to it without fail and at the proper moment and with the proper ritual.

Hence the idea that the offering of these prescribed sacrifices and the performance of all other duties pleases and placates the dead, keeps them well disposed to the living, and, viewed from the opposite angle, protects the living against the dead.

And here we have the key to the right understanding of these sacrifices for the dead. They serve the purpose of *fedû,* or redemption. But instead of redeeming the soul of the dead man from the consequences of his sins, as the modern doctrine has it, and so being offered to Allah or a wely on behalf of the dead man, they were originally offered directly to the spirit or ghost of the dead man. And just as Jaussen heard from his interpreter, Sāleḥ, they are offered truly in one sense on behalf of the living. They work *fedû* for the living. They redeem the living from the dread power of the ghost of the dead.

For manifestly, since the ghost of the dead man has a claim for certain sacrifices and gifts and the performance of certain duties upon his surviving relatives, they are in his power and subject to any whims or fits of passion which may possess him. These sacrifices are therefore in origin taboo-sacrifices in the strictest sense of the term, offered to the ghosts of the dead in order to redeem the living from their dread power.[54]

This accounts for the importance of the role played by the blood in these sacrifices. As Curtiss was told, "The bursting forth of the blood is the most important thing." "Without the bursting forth of the blood there is no fulfillment of the vow." The blood must be poured out upon the ground or upon flat stones spread upon the ground for this purpose. Musil says:[55] "In front of the grave there stands a long, thin stone (stone slab; the Ẓullam call these stones *Naṣâjeb,* the Sa'îdijjîn, *Anṣâb*), which must be smeared with the blood of the sacrificial animal at every sacrifice to the dead. Preferably they sacrifice the animal in such manner that they lay it upon the stone, so that its blood shall flow from the stone down upon the grave." As Frazer has shown,[56] blood is regarded as a sacrifice peculiarly appropriate for and pleasing to the ghosts of the dead in all parts of the world. But among the Arabs, and in fact among all the Semites, the sacrifice of this blood must have had an added significance. For inasmuch as the life or the soul was thought to reside in the blood,[57] the sacrifice of this blood was the symbol that a life had been given to the dead, given to them as a redemption-sacrifice, on the principle that the life of the animal redeems the life of the sacrificer.

Probably in this same idea may be found the secret of the practice of body mutilations in honor of the dead, common in ancient Israel and among its neighbors, as well as among the present-day Bedouin,[58] as Frazer suggests. The blood which flowed from the wounds was the taboo-sacrifice, the part given for the whole, which redeemed the life of the bleeding relative from the power of the ghost of his deceased kinsman.[59] As we have seen, the sacrifice of the hair as a mourning rite had the same character and purpose, a taboo-sacrifice to redeem the surviving relatives; and, as is now clear, it must, originally at least, have been offered to the ghost of the dead person.

But one other purpose this blood served. Once offered to the ghost, it was the symbol that he had received, and presumably accepted, all that was due him, and that his claim upon the living was now fully satisfied. Therefore, the proper use or display of this blood served to ward him off and to prevent his attacking further. Hence, as we have seen, among the Eben Rašîd the sacrificer pierces the neck of the victim, which is then led immediately around the house, while the blood trickles to the ground. Manifestly the house is protected by this bloody circle because, so they believe, the ghost cannot cross it.

Reverence and the memory of former happy associations with the dead and the sense of filial affection and obligation naturally prompt the desire to maintain a certain persistent relationship with the departed. Probably even in the most primitive state of society something of this sentiment existed. With the progress of civilization it naturally evolved into our present-day concepts of enduring love for and pious duty to the dead. But in primitive society the fear of the spirits of the dead must undoubtedly have far outweighed these kindlier sentiments. Obviously, these spirits of the dead were, and in some measure still are, a power to be reckoned with.

All the more must this condition have obtained in early Semitic society as we have pictured it, where fatherhood was still an unknown, or at best a little known or valued consideration, and a man's nearest relatives were his mother and her brothers. These maternal uncles, and particularly the senior among them, a primitive Semite's most immediate relatives, exerted the most direct influence upon his life. Yet the sentiments which bound him to these uncles, who were themselves away from their clan and kinsmen much of the time, consorting with women of other clans and begetting children by them, members of their mothers' clans, could scarcely have been the same as the filial affection which binds a man to his father of flesh and blood, and which endures long after death has parted them. It may be that the impulse to foster this latent sentiment of reciprocal paternal and filial affection, and the larger assurance which it offered that there would be a close relative surviving after death to discharge all the duties to the spirit of the dead father that would render his existence in the nether world easier and happier, was a potent factor in the transition from *beena* to *ba'al* marriage among the early Semites. For surely there was a stronger and more comforting certainty that one's own sons would perform these duties for their dead father than that the sons of one's sisters would assume and faithfully discharge these obligations all their days.[60]

However, be this as it may, this much is certain, that among the early Semites the fear of the dead, and especially of dead relatives and associates, was a paramount consideration. And the necessity of the living to redeem themselves from the power of the ghosts and to guard themselves against their attacks lay at the bottom of these sacrifices and other kindred ceremonies of mourning.[61]

5 Ceremonies of Death, Burial, and Mourning and Their Underlying Purpose

These conclusions, that the souls of the dead were regarded by the primitive Semites as at least potential evil spirits which must be placated in every way possible, and that in this consideration we have the key to the original meaning and purpose of very many of their rites of burial and mourning, are borne out by abundant additional evidence.

Occasionally the fear of the ghost of the dead is manifested in ceremonies preliminary to and attendant upon burial. Oesterley suggests that the dances, which seem to play quite an important role in the rites of burial and mourning among Semitic peoples, just as they do also in their marriage rites, were intended primarily to ward off threatening evil spirits.[62]

In Damascus and among the Arabs of Moab, when a corpse is being carried to the cemetery, water is sprinkled behind it in order "to cut off the evil."[63] Among the Mandaeans, when a corpse is being carried from the house of death to the cemetery, three bundles of reeds are stuck in the earth in the courtyard, over which the bearers of the corpse are obliged to step. Then the oldest of the bearers remains behind, crouches down behind these bundles, utters a brief prayer for forgiveness of the sins of the deceased, and then presses the sacred iron seal upon the ground three times. Thereupon the corpse is carried with all speed to the cemetery.[64]

Among the Jews of Turkey and other eastern lands mourners recite Psalm 91 during the funeral in order to drive away evil spirits.[65] According to *Bammidbar rabba,*[66] this psalm was composed by Moses on one occasion when he stood in fear of evil spirits; consequently, its recital at a funeral has the force of an incantation to ward off the threatening evil spirit or spirits.[67] And in present-day Palestine, as we have seen, one of the three things which are thought to shorten life is walking behind funerals.[68]

Likewise, fear of the ghost is probably the ultimate reason for the widespread custom that the relatives of the deceased, who have dwelt in the same house with him, do not re-enter the house until a certain time has elapsed after the funeral. Jaussen tells[69] that among the inhabitants of Maʿān it is customary to invite the father or the son of the deceased under some other tent when he returns from the cemetery. He ought not to re-enter his own home immediately. It is the chief, or a friend or a neighbor, who finally conducts him to his own tent. Among the Arabs of Sinai, during the three days following the burial the members of the mourning family do not return to their own home. They remain with strangers, where they receive visits of condolence. Musil, too, relates[70] that among the ʿAmârîn Bedouin the relatives eat nothing in the evening following the burial, but on the next day they are invited to some other encampment, and there they break their fast. And among the fellahin of Syria and Palestine the custom seems to be not unknown of deserting completely a house in which a death has occurred.[71]

Probably for the same reason, funerals are never held at night unless this is absolutely unavoidable.[72] Evil spirits are generally thought by the Semites, both ancient and modern, to be especially dangerous at night.[73] With the rising of the sun their power wanes or departs completely.[74] For this reason, in Israel it was regarded as dangerous to remain in a cemetery overnight.[75] And in some villages of Palestine today on the Thursday of the Dead the women go before sunrise to the cemetery, believing that a visit later in the day is not so profitable, probably because they cannot then so readily communicate with the dead. Soon after sunrise they return home.[76]

Likewise in Aleppo "on the eve of the festival of Ramadan the women are very busy preparing the viands for the next day. The men resort to the mosque fifteen or twenty minutes after sunrise, make their prayer, and then go straight to the cemetery in order to discharge the traditional duty of visiting the dead on the occasion of important solemnities. But they always take care not to return from the cemetery by the same road by which they went."[77]

A custom in many respects the reverse of the above is observed by the Copts three times in the year, on the nights preceding their three great annual festivals, the *'Eed el-Meelád,* the *'Eed el-Gheetás,* and the *'Eed el-Kiyámeh.* Lane relates[78] that both men and women "go to the burial ground on the eve of each of these *'eeds* and there pass the night, having houses belonging to them in the cemeteries for their reception on these occasions; the women spend the nights in the upper apartments and the men below. In the morning following, they kill a buffalo, or a sheep, if they can afford either, and give its flesh, with bread, to the poor who assemble there, or they give the bread alone. This ceremony, which resembles the 'kaffarah' performed by the Muslims on the burial of their dead, is not considered as an expiation of the sins of the deceased, but probably originates from an ancient expiatory sacrifice: it is only regarded as an alms. As soon as it is done, the mourners return home. They say that they visit the tombs merely for the sake of religious reflection. In doing so, they perpetuate an ancient custom, which they find difficult to relinquish, though they can give no good reason for observing it with such ceremonies." Obviously, the underlying, ancient thought, which Lane sensed clearly even though he did not define it, was that on the eves of these three festivals the ghosts of the dead returned to their tombs in such manner that it was possible for the living to associate with them for the brief moment. In its origin the sacrifice offered upon this occasion, the primary expiatory character of which was perfectly clear to Lane, must have been offered to these spirits of the dead and have been designed to redeem the living from their dread power.

In all these instances the thought is perfectly apparent, that the closest contact with the ghosts of the dead can be obtained during the night, or, at the latest, but a few minutes after sunrise, just before these ghosts take their departure to the realm of darkness.

These considerations also account for the fact recorded by Musil, as we have seen, that "the sacrifice must be offered before sunset, for in the night angels come to the dead in order to test his conscience; for this he must be strengthened." This sacrifice is usually called "the supper of the dead." And, as we have also seen, very many of the ceremonies memorializing the dead are performed at night. The presumption here is, quite obviously, that the ghosts of the dead are present and hear and understand what is said and see what is done in their honor, and are thus pleased and appeased.[79] But it is also clear that the living do not feel altogether comfortable and at ease in the presence of these ghosts of the dead. Therefore, they take certain precautions against them and are relieved when at last these ghosts have departed to their proper abode.

Probably, too, the custom of casting stones upon graves, particularly upon the graves of those who were either powerful or wicked during life, had, as Bertholet suggests,[80] its origin in fear of the ghost. The thought underlying the practice would be that the weight of the stones upon the grave holds down the ghost of the deceased and prevents his coming forth and working mischief. This conclusion is borne out by the contrary custom of the Ṣaḫary Bedouin, recorded by Musil:[81] "If a Ṣaḫary passes by the grave of a relative, he takes a pebble off of it and says, 'We have lightened thy burden, O dead one; forget us not before thy Master.' "

This mass of evidence, with its far-reaching ramifications, shows to what extent the spirits or ghosts of deceased relatives, friends, or associates are conceived of as evil powers by the Arabs, and by other, present-day Semitic peoples. As may be expected, the same concept was current among ancient Semitic peoples also. The belief is especially well attested in Babylonian and Jewish literature.

Among the Babylonians in particular, the *ekimmu*, or ghost of the dead, was one of the seven dread evil spirits whose mischievous pranks and machinations were the basic cause of all the misfortunes and sufferings to which the living are heir.[82] One particular, oft-cited passage is especially illuminating in this connection:[83]

Whether thou art a ghost that hath come from the earth,
Or a phantom of the night that hath no couch,
Or a woman (that hath died) a virgin,
Or a man (that hath died) unmarried,
Or one that lieth dead in the desert,
Or one that in the desert . . . .
Or one that . . . .
[some lines lost]
Or one that hath been torn from a date-palm,
Or one in a boat that hath sunk in the waters,
Or a ghost unburied,
Or a ghost that none careth for,
Or a ghost with none to make offerings,
Or a ghost with none to pour libations,
Or a ghost that hath no posterity,
Or a hag-demon,
Or a ghoul,
Or a robber sprite,
(Or a harlot that hath died, whose body is sick),
(Or a woman that hath died in travail),
Or a woman that hath died with a babe at the breast,

Or a weeping woman that hath died with a babe at the breast,
Or an evil man that hath died,
Or an evil spirit,
Or one that haunteth (the neighbourhood),
Or one that haunteth the vicinity,
Or whether thou be one with whom on a day I have eaten,
Or with whom on a day I have drunk,
Or with whom on a day I have anointed myself,
Or with whom I have entered and clothed myself,
Or whether thou be one with whom I have eaten food when I was hungry,
Or with whom I have drunk when I was thirsty,
Or with whom I have anointed myself when I was sore,
Or with whom when I was cold I have clothed myself with the garment from his body;
Whatever thou be, until thou art removed,
Until thou departest from the body of the man, the son of his god,
Thou shalt have no food to eat,
Thou shalt have no water to drink,
Thou shalt not stretch forth thy hand
Unto the table of father En-lil, thy creator;
Neither with sea water, nor with sweet water,
Nor with bad water, nor with Tigris water,
Nor with Euphrates water, nor with pond water,
Nor with river water shalt thou be covered.

This passage states explicitly that all those who have been associated with a man in any way during his lifetime, even if only accidentally and momentarily, are subject to the evil machinations of his ghost. This dangerous spirit must be appeased by the performance of proper rites of burial and mourning, and food and drink must thereafter be offered to him on certain occasions; otherwise he might seize upon surviving relatives or associates and work his evil upon them. In such case he could be exorcised only with difficulty, or perhaps not at all.[84] Nonetheless, we see that the more cultured Babylonians had advanced to an attitude toward these evil ghosts somewhat in advance of the present-day Arabs, for they did not hesitate to threaten the ghost that unless he does depart from the body of his victim and cease to torment him, he will certainly not receive from the living the attention which he needs and craves; he will not receive water to drink, nor will water, even the least desirable, be poured upon his grave. Obviously, fear of the ghost was still vividly present in the mind of the ancient Babylonian; yet he had this fear, and with it the object thereof, viz., the ghost, somewhat under control. It represents some slight advance over what must have been the belief with regard to the spirits of the dead of the remote, primitive ancestors of the Babylonians of historic times. This, it is clear, must have been practically the same as that of the present-day Bedouin.

In the twelfth tablet of the Gilgamesh-epic the ghost of the dead Engidu reveals to the hero, Gilgamesh, the lot of the spirits of the dead in the nether world. The passage is fragmentary, but this much is clear, that the lot of the dead is anything but happy. The best that they may hope for seems to be to rest upon a bed, drink pure water, and have one's father, mother, and wife near. The lot of him whose corpse has been cast away unburied is that his ghost may not rest in the earth. And the ghost of him who has no living relative to show it the proper attention and to perform for it the customary rites is unfortunate indeed. It must wander about, consuming only the poor fragments of food left uneaten in the pot or cast out into the street.[85]

For this reason Ashurbanipal told with considerable self-satisfaction that after he had conquered and devastated Elam he opened the graves of the Elamite kings who had fought against his ancestors, and carried their bones away with him to Assyria, thereby imposing upon them the horrible fate of restlessness in the nether world; and he caused all food-sacrifices and water-libations to be withheld from them.[86] And elsewhere he tells that on the spot where his grandfather, Sennacherib, had been murdered, he caused a great number of Babylonians to be slaughtered as a death-sacrifice to his grandfather's ghost.[87] Zimmern, *Ritualtafeln,* p. 52, prescribes for a case where a person has been singled out and attacked by a ghost. This text, too, is fragmentary, but enough remains to show that the ritual procedure was quite complicated. Among other procedures, ceremonies were performed in honor of, and sacrifices were offered to, the spirits of the family ghosts of the man possessed.[88]

That practically the same concepts existed in ancient Israel and its neighboring nations is clear from abundant evidence. Still, in the early Rabbinic period the souls of the *r^{e}fa'im,* i.e., the ghosts of the dead, were regarded as evil spirits which worked harm to the living.[89] Particularly at funerals and immediately thereafter their malignant powers had to be feared and guarded against. The Talmud[90] records the tradition that the angel of death charged Rabbi Joshua ben Levi never to stand in the presence of women returning from a funeral, "because I go ahead of them dancing, with my sword in my hand, and I have permission to kill." For the same reason, no doubt, it was customary among Orthodox Jews upon leaving the cemetery after a funeral to draw off a shoe or sandal and cast it some distance away, and likewise to take a handful of dust or of grass and cast it behind one's back, after which the hands were washed in water. Furthermore, in some Orthodox Jewish circles the mourners, upon returning from the cemetery after a funeral, would sit down either three or seven times at brief intervals and recite certain Biblical passages.[91] The express purpose of these strange ceremonies was to ward off the evil spirits which attach themselves to mourners and which might otherwise return with them for no good purpose. While the mourners were seated, so the thought undoubtedly was, the unsuspecting evil spirits presumably went on ahead and lost their connection with the living. Probably, too, this fear of the ghost was one underlying and potent reason for the seemingly almost universal Semitic practice of burying the dead upon the very day of death; the corpse must be put out of the way as soon as possible, and particularly must not be allowed to remain overnight in the house, for then the ghost would have full and unrestricted opportunity to work mischief.[92]

In ancient Israel too, just as in Assyria, the ghost of him who had not been properly buried, or of him whose last resting place was disturbed, could not dwell quietly in the nether world. For this reason, the Bible describes the care with which the bones of Joseph were brought from Egypt to Canaan and given proper burial there,[93] and the same care with which the bones of Saul, Jonathan, and the seven sacrificed members of Saul's family were buried.[94] For a comparable reason, no doubt, the king of Moab burned the bones of his enemy, the king of Edom,[95] and Josiah exhumed the bones of the idolatrous inhabitants of Jerusalem and burned them upon the altar. Thereby he not only defiled the false altars, but he also procured the eternal restlessness of the spirits of these sinful dead.[96] The same fate is threatened by the prophets for the later, idolatrous inhabitants of Jerusalem.[97] Even worse is the fate predicted for the faithless of Israel in Deuteronomy 28 : 26, that their corpses shall be cast out to be eaten by the birds and beasts of prey; for in this case their bones will be crushed and consumed, and no possibility whatsoever of burial and of rest in the nether world will remain for them.

6 The Ceremonies of the Two Heifers

We have learned that the ancient Babylonians conceived of the ghost of a murdered man as an evil spirit greatly to be feared, and also that among the ancient Arabs[98] "the superstition prevailed that the souls of those slain without vengeance became owls, and that they flew at night about the grave crying *isḳûni, isḳûni,* 'Give me to drink, give me to drink.' When the blood of vengeance was shed, the thirst of the owl was quenched and he ceased to cry." Among the Arabs today the belief exists that, despite the lapse of time, the blood of the murdered man cries from the ground, and cries unceasingly until the blood of the murderer is shed.[99] The natives of Palestine likewise believe that on the spot where the blood of a murdered man has been shed a ghost or spirit appears every night, which constantly calls out the last words or cry of the deceased.[100] Such spirits are called *ṭauâghîṯ*. They "are to be found wherever human blood has been shed. Scarcely has the first drop of blood touched the earth when, quick as lightning, these evil spirits manifest themselves, in order to conceal themselves there so that they may terrify human beings. Frequently they take the form of the slain person or of an animal. One can hear them every evening just at nightfall unceasingly repeating the last words of the dead person, until they have been avenged upon the murderer (cf. Genesis 4 : 10)."[101]

Even if its blood cannot be avenged, the soul of a murdered man cries constantly for decent burial, so that its restlessness and suffering may be allayed, at least in part. Buckingham[102] cites the following illuminating illustration of this belief: "The Fakeer deposited in two newly made graves, which we had passed on the high road between Kalajek and Kerdakhourd, a few rags from off his clothes, to allay the spirit of the enemy who was thought to persecute us. On enquiring whose ashes these graves contained, we were told that a pious and upright Moslem of Hamadan had lately seen the shade of a former friend in a dream, who had desired of him, if he feared God, and wished to be esteemed by men, to go to the lonely spot which he named, and erect there two decent tombs, as the bodies of two devout men lay murdered there, and their souls could not have rest until the rites of sepulture were given them." Among the ʿAzâzme, as we have learned,[103] the belief is that the dead person whose corpse has been consumed by birds or beasts of prey—who, in other words, has been left unburied or has not received proper burial—suffers after death. His soul flies about the skeleton in the form of a fly, buzzes sadly, and begs for help. So soon as the remains are buried it enters the nether world.

Undoubtedly, superstitions closely akin to these underlie the peculiar ceremony recorded in Deuteronomy 21 : 1–9. If a man's corpse was found in the open country, and it was not known who had slain him, so that, quite obviously, his murder could not be avenged, it followed that his ghost had to suffer a very unhappy fate. It had to hover about the corpse, crying for burial, and haunt and torment all persons whom it could contact in any way. Very clearly, the inhabitants of the nearest village or town had most to fear from such a ghost. Regardless, therefore, of any responsibility on their part for the death of the man, it behooved them to see that he was given proper burial in order that his ghost might be laid, and they be freed from danger from it. The text does not state that the corpse was eventually buried, but undoubtedly this was a *sine qua non* of these rites, and so did not need particular mention. Moreover, the issue here was not only of burial, but also of vengeance. Since it was not known who the murderer was, the presumption was that the residents of the nearest town were in some way involved, and unless they could absolve themselves,[104] they would very probably be held responsible by the unburied ghost, who would seek to avenge himself upon them; therefore the ceremonial procedure prescribed in Deuteronomy 21 : 1–9. The elders of the town nearest to the spot where the corpse of the murdered man was found would take a heifer which had never been used for any human service, and in a valley through which flowed a perennial stream slay the animal by breaking its neck. Over the body of the slain animal they would then wash their hands and solemnly affirm their innocence of the crime. Impliedly the flowing stream carried away the water with which they had washed their hands, and with it whatever measure of guilt might for any reason have attached to them. Certainly both the place where the animal was killed and the manner of its killing evidence convincingly that it was not slain as a sacrifice to Yahweh.[105] Presumably, then, it was regarded as a sacrifice to the ghost of the murdered man, offered by the inhabitants of the town in question in order to appease this dreaded spirit in its relations to them, and thus free them from all danger from it.

Closely related to this rite in many ways is the ceremony of the red heifer. This relationship has been recognized by many scholars.[106] Numbers 19 prescribes that whatever, whether persons or inanimate objects, touches a corpse or is touched by someone who has previously come in contact with a corpse, or the open vessels which have been in the vicinity of a corpse—presumably, therefore, in the house in which the corpse lay—are unclean. They must be sprinkled with the ashes of the red heifer upon the third and seventh days and thereby become purified. For this purpose a heifer, red in color, which has never been used for any service, shall be burned outside the camp, and with it cedarwood, hyssop, and scarlet thread. The ashes shall be carefully collected and stored up in a clean place. When the time for purification arrives, a portion of these ashes is mixed with living waters, and this mixture is sprinkled by means of a bunch of hyssop upon the person or object to be purified. The ceremony is performed by a clean person who, however, is rendered unclean thereby and must in turn be purified. This is accomplished quite simply, by a ritual bath taken at eventide of the day of the ceremony.

This ceremony, these scholars have recognized, was performed originally in honor of, or as a sacrifice to, the ghost of the dead person.[107] In the present text of Numbers 19 the role of the priest and the provisions for performing this rite in honor of Yahweh are very obviously redactorial in character, the work of the Priestly editor who incorporated this ancient, non-Yahwistic ritual into the Priestly Code. In this ceremony too, just as in that of Deuteronomy 21, the animal sacrificed is, unlike the vast majority of Biblical sacrifices, a female, and one which has never been employed for profane service. Above all, the outstanding feature of this ceremony is the insistence upon the color of the animal—red. Moreover, the importance of the color red in this ceremony is emphasized by the role played by the cedarwood, which is likewise deep-red in color, by the scarlet thread, and also by the hyssop.[108] As we have already seen,[109] this color red plays an important role in ceremonies of expulsion of evil spirits. There is no reason whatsoever to doubt that just this was its function in this ceremony.[110]

With these facts in mind, there is no difficulty at all in determining the original character and purpose of this strange ceremony. It was very obviously performed immediately after a death occurred in the house or, perhaps more probably, immediately after the corpse had been removed therefrom. The reference to the uncovered vessels which required purification implies the belief, as Elhorst has seen, that the ghost of the dead might have taken refuge in one of these and might from this hiding place work mischief to the inhabitants of the house upon their return thither. Therefore, all such possible hiding places must be purified, and the ghost must be completely expelled from the dwelling. While this is not explicitly stated, it is an unavoidable inference. Presumably, therefore, until this ceremony has been performed, the relatives may not return to their former abode. This was, of course, upon the seventh day after death. In this respect, this ceremony has much in common with similar practices among Semitic peoples which we have already considered.

In the same way, the inmates of the house, who had presumably come into contact with the corpse and had therefore become subject to the power of the evil spirit, if not actually possessed by him, had to be purified. And finally, by an extension of these ceremonies, whoever or whatever came into contact with any corpse or part of a dead creature required similar purification. The entire ceremony partook partly of the character of a rite of expulsion of, and partly of that of a sacrifice to, the evil spirit or ghost.

7 The Cult of the Dead in Ancient Israel

This same conclusion holds true likewise with many other ancient Israelite rites of burial and mourning. Most of these, it seems, had their origin in early, pre-Yahwistic beliefs and practices and continued to be observed in Biblical and Rabbinic times, many even down to the present day. As we have remarked earlier, particularly in matters related to death and the dead the human mind is intensely conservative. In modern practice this conservatism rests very largely upon sentiments of reverence and affection for the dead and the desire to promote their well-being in the other world. But, unquestionably, the real origin of this conservatism must be found in the primitive fear of the spirits of the dead, which, as we have seen, was so firmly rooted in the beliefs and practices of the early Semites.

Thus, in ancient Israel the rites of wailing for the dead—frequently, if not usually, by professional wailing women—shaving off or tearing out the hair, making incisions in the flesh so that the blood might flow forth, were regular and seemingly indispensable elements of the funeral ceremony.[111] We have seen that a common method of warding off evil spirits was by making loud noises.[112] Elhorst has suggested the very plausible theory that the original purpose of these professional wailings at funerals was to frighten away the ghost of the dead.[113] We have likewise seen that the cutting off of the hair[114] and the making of incisions in their bodies by the relatives of the dead person as funeral rites partook of the character of a taboo-sacrifice, designed to redeem the sacrificer from the power of the dread ghost.[115]

Unquestionably, too, the institution of sacrifices to the dead, which, so the numerous Biblical and Apocryphal references indicate,[116] must at one time have been offered regularly in ancient Israel, implied recognition of the dread power of the ghost of the dead and the necessity of appeasing him by offering him all that he could ask for in the way of food for his cold and hungry sojourn in the nether world. Certainly these sacrifices were originally offered directly *to* the dead, and not, as is so frequently interpreted, merely *for* them.[117] In all likelihood these sacrifices to the dead were not all of one class, but, just as we have seen is the case among the modern Bedouin,[118] were offered at different moments and with slightly varying purposes with relation to the entire ritual of burial and mourning.[119]

This same conclusion with regard to the dread power of the ghost and the wisdom of providing him with those things which he might need in the nether world, thus disposing him favorably to his former relatives and friends, which we have drawn in regard to the institution of sacrifices to the dead, is even more obvious with regard to the parallel institution of putting various objects in their coffins or tombs[120] and of making burnings for them after burial. The Bible mentions such burnings for various kings of Judah.[121] In Rabbinic literature we read that such burnings of bed clothes and toilet articles were made for kings, but not for common people.[122] And as late as Rabbinic times, we are told, such things as a man's pen, ink, keys, and ledger were occasionally placed in the coffin with him.[123]

Of particular significance in this connection is the *maṣṣebah,* the sacred stone. Occasionally it is spoken of in the Bible as if it were an altogether regular and legitimate institution in the worship of Yahweh.[124] More frequently, however, and especially in the late Deuteronomic and post-Deuteronomic writings, it is looked at askance, and its use is forbidden as incongruous with Yahweh-worship and utterly abhorrent to Him.[125] It is usually referred to in such manner as to imply that it had no place in Yahweh-worship.[126] Recent excavations in Palestine establish beyond all question that the sacred standing-stone played an important role in Baʿal-worship, apparently in some symbolic connection with the cult of the sun.[127] However, despite all this, there is considerable evidence that these sacred stone pillars were no more primary in the cult of Baʿal than in that of Yahweh, that they were borrowed by Baʿal-worship, just as by early Yahweh-worship, from an even more primitive cult, and were given by these borrowing religions a new interpretation and a place in the ritual which they did not possess originally.

Unquestionably, the *maṣṣebah* was identical with the *bet 'el,* the sacred stone, in which, as the name implies, a deity or spirit or supernatural power of some kind was thought to dwell.[128] Such a belief must, of course, have had its origin in the remote period of animistic religion. In the earliest stages of Semitic religious evolution, sacrifices were offered to these sacred stones, blood was sprinkled upon them, and they were anointed with oil. It need scarcely be said that these sacrifices were offered to and these rites were performed in honor, not of the stones themselves, but rather of the *'el,* the spirit, which was thought to be dwelling in them. So Jacob sets up as a *maṣṣebah* the stone upon which his head had rested while he slept, and anoints it with oil, because, as the original story must have told, and as some vestiges thereof in the present text imply, he recognized that an *'el,* which the later form of the story identified with Yahweh, dwelt in it.[129] Jacob likewise erects a *maṣṣebah* over the grave of Rachel.[130]

It is impossible not to identify this *maṣṣebah* over Rachel's grave, and presumably over other graves as well, with the *naṣaba*-stone of the modern Bedouin. The two words are etymologically closely related and in a way practically identical. We have seen that the blood of the sacrifice offered to the ghosts of the dead is spread by the Bedouin upon these stones. In this way it is transmitted to the spirits for whom it is intended. Upon Aramaic and Nabataean monuments[131] and in Rabbinic[132] and Syriac[133] literature, the stone over a grave is frequently designated as *nefeš,* literally "soul." This designation could have developed only if at one time the soul or spirit of the person buried in the grave was thought to have in some manner taken up its abode in the stone. This would then have been, in the earliest stage of Semitic religious evolution, the *'el,* or spirit, residing in the sacred stone, or at least in such sacred stones, *maṣṣebôt,* as were connected with graves or tombs; and to this *'el,* or spirit, sacrifices and worship in their primitive form would have been directed.

In course of time this primitive Semitic spirit-worship evolved into higher forms among the Canaanites as well as in Israel. It underwent various modifications and took on new interpretations. Thus, it was incorporated into Baʿal-worship on the one hand and into Yahweh-worship on the other. In Baʿal-worship the sacred standing-stone, the *maṣṣebah,* became an important symbol and cult object. But, seemingly, in Yahweh-worship its foreign, incongruous character was never lost sight of entirely; and eventually—although apparently not without a bitter struggle—the use of the *maṣṣebah,* except as a simple, meaningless gravestone, was abrogated completely in Israel.[134]

All these considerations confirm the conclusion which we have drawn, that in early Israel, precisely as among practically all other primitive Semitic peoples, the ghost of the dead was conceived of as a dangerous and hostile spirit, who had to be dealt with carefully and wisely in order that the living might be protected from his wrath and malice. On the one hand, he had to be appeased by gifts and sacrifices, usually of a taboo character. On the other hand, he had to be frightened off by noises and other apotropaic methods. Against this primitive, pre-Yahwistic cult of the dead in ancient Israel the developing Yahweh-worship came in time to protest. Apparently the realization of the basic incompatibility of this cult of the dead with the purest Yahweh-worship evolved only slowly and gradually, even in the minds of the most ardent and far-seeing champions of Yahwism, the prophets. Hosea[135] apparently believed that eating of the bread of mourners put one into a state of taboo, whereby he could not participate in the established worship of Yahweh, but he does not seem to have demanded in any way the cessation of such rites. To Jeremiah, too, the traditional mourning rites seemed natural and normal, even those of shaving the head and making incisions in the flesh.[136] And Ezekiel also, so it seems, would have observed most of the established rites of mourning, even those of letting the hair fly loose and eating the bread of mourners, had he not been expressly forbidden by Yahweh to mourn for his wife in the customary manner.[137]

However, the Israelite people seem to have perceived quite clearly at a fairly early date that, even though the two cults might exist side by side, they could not be commingled, and that accordingly participation in the cult of the dead defiled a person and disqualified him for the entire period of his defilement from participation in the worship of Yahweh.[138]

Apparently the full consciousness of the incongruity of this cult of the dead with the pure and unadulterated worship of Yahweh did not dawn upon the people, nor even upon the prophets, until the Deuteronomic reformation, with its program of absolute and uncompromising Yahwism. This is the implication of the very precise language of Deuteronomy 14 : 1 f.: "Ye are children of Yahweh, your God; [therefore] ye shall not cut yourselves nor put a bald spot between your eyes [as a ceremony] for a dead person. For a people taboo unto Yahweh art thou" [and therefore must not have relations with or participate in the worship of any other deity or spirit]. This injunction is repeated in the Holiness Code,[139] although with somewhat less directness and obviousness of purpose.

But, just as was to be expected and as invariably happens in such a case, the reformation of the Deuteronomists and their successors could not be thoroughgoing. The cult of the dead was too deeply rooted in the religious and social life of Israel to be eradicated completely. Some of the grossest and to Yahweh-worship most repugnant rites, such as making incisions in the flesh and letting blood flow for the dead, were probably abrogated or else modified considerably. But other rites, the non-Yahwistic character of which was more or less obvious, persisted in folk-practice. In time, as the principle of pure Yahweh-worship became established more and more firmly and uncompromisingly, the true origin of the ancient cult rites for the dead became increasingly obscure, and their purpose was gradually reinterpreted. In the first period of reinterpretation a few ceremonies continued to be performed for the purpose of purifying the living from the defilement of contact with the dead, which now more than ever disqualified them for the time from participation in the worship of Yahweh.[140] Later, those ceremonies which survived came to be regarded as performed in a sentimental way in honor of the dead, rather than as rites of worship offered to them; they now expressed the reverence, grief, and persisting affection of the living for the dead, or they were thought to bring consolation to the living for the loss which they had suffered.

8 The Duration of Burial and Mourning Rites

In Chapter VII only birth rites were cited to posit our conclusion that according to primitive Semitic belief the power of evil spirits was thought to endure for three, seven, or forty days, usually reaching its greatest intensity upon the seventh day. Elsewhere we have shown that other sacrificial ceremonies, such as cutting off the hair and marriage rites, also conformed to this same principle. Now, a brief consideration of the time and duration of burial and mourning rites will round out our conclusion that this same belief was basic to almost all primitive Semitic rites.

We have seen[141] that among the Bedouin a sheep or goat is usually sacrificed on the day of death. This sacrifice has various names among the tribes: *'aša'-l-majet,* "the supper of the dead";[142] *sdâdet el ḳabr,* "the closing of the grave"; *hbûṭa,* "sinking (into the grave?)"; *rutbe 'an rûḥ,* "ceremony for the spirit"; *'awnâse* or *wanîse,* both words meaning "association" and probably signifying the last association of the dead with his living relatives. Among some tribes a goat is sacrificed on the second night, in addition to the first-night sacrifice, and among others another sacrifice, called *wanîeh,*[143] is offered just as the grave is about to be closed.

Among some of the tribes of the Sinaitic peninsula and the Hauran the period of extreme mourning seems to last for only three days,[144] during which time these Arabs do not return to their own homes but remain with strangers, where they receive visits of condolence.[145] In the Hauran during the first three days after death relatives and friends of the deceased assemble every morning about the tomb and there take their coffee.[146] "It is customary among the peasants of Upper Egypt for the female relations and friends of a person deceased to meet together by his house on each of the first three days after the funeral, and there to perform a lamentation and a strange kind of dance. They daub their faces and bosoms, and a part of their dress, with mud; and tie a rope-girdle, generally made of the coarse grass called 'halfa,' round the waist. Each flourishes in her hand a palmstick, or a *nebboot* (a long staff), or a spear, or a drawn sword; and dances with a slow movement, and in an irregular manner; generally pacing about, and raising and depressing the body. This dance is continued for an hour or more; and is performed twice or three times in the course of the day. After the third day the women visit the tomb and place upon it their rope-girdles; and usually a lamb, or a goat, is slain there, as an expiatory sacrifice, and a feast made, on this occasion."[147] At Merrâkech, in Morocco, the women likewise visit the tomb during the first three days after death and interment.[148] And among some of the Arab tribes of northern Syria a goat or sheep is sacrificed upon the third day.[149] The Mandaeans celebrate a seven-day period of prayer for the deceased, beginning on the third day after death and concluding therefore on the tenth day.[150]

In Damascus, immediately after death, the nostrils and ears of the corpse are stopped up. A gift of money is made to the poor to atone for all possible sins of the deceased.[151] Alms and food are likewise given to the poor after the funeral and again on the third, seventh, and fortieth days thereafter. The relatives also revisit the tomb on these days. The funeral meal given to the mourners on the evening of the interment consists of a sweet dish, composed of *semoule,* butter, and honey. Immediately after death the soul goes up to heaven and prostrates itself before the Creator; then it returns and hovers over the head of the corpse until a certain moment in the funeral rites, when the angels Munkhir and Nekir are supposed to pass judgment upon it. Then it goes back to heaven, and, if it finds the gate closed, it goes to purgatory.[152]

"The funeral-ceremonies of the Copts resemble, in many respects, those of the Muslims. . . . Hired wailing-women are employed to lament in the house of the deceased for three days after the death (though this custom is disapproved of by the clergy and many others, being only a relic of ancient heathen usages); and they renew their lamentations there on the seventh and fourteenth days after the death; and sometimes several weeks after."[153]

An interesting and illuminating account of the ceremonies of mourning at Tlemcen, in Morocco, is given by Bel:[154] "During the seven days which follow the interment the relatives and friends come to the house in which the death has occurred and bring, in the guise of an offering, some coffee, some sugar, and some food. Upon the third night after the interment, called *lilet-el-r'eriba,*[155] all the near relatives come to pass the night in the chamber in which the death has occurred, and there they weep. The belief is very widespread here that the soul of the deceased remains for these three days in this death chamber, beneath the door. In many families on the morning following the *lilet-el-r'eriba* they bring some *kouskous* as food to the *tolbas,* who are at the grave. These spread out upon the grave the remains of the meal which has been brought to them. It is also believed that during forty days the spirit of the dead person comes back to visit his house a moment before sunrise, and also visits his grave. But after the fortieth day it seldom revisits the grave except upon particular occasions. This is why on those days the women visit the graves. In addition to these occasions the women visit the graves frequently and plant flowers or bring food to the deceased, which they then give to the first beggar who may pass by. The tombstone is set up upon the fortieth day in the presence of relatives and friends. If the widow remarry, she must not pronounce the name of the deceased in the presence of the second husband or his relatives, nor may she again visit the grave of the deceased."

The Yezidis bury their dead facing the east. On the first three days after the funeral, and again on the seventh and fortieth days, sacrifices are offered and the flesh and other food and alms are given to the poor.[156] Among the Persians, also, special rites of mourning are performed upon the third, seventh, and fortieth days after death.[157] The Maronites, too, perform ceremonies in honor of the dead on the third, twelfth, twentieth, thirtieth, fortieth, and fiftieth days, and at the end of the first year after death.[158]

The Falashas make a lamentation for the deceased in his house every morning for seven days. On the third and seventh days they offer the sacrifice of *tazkir,* "remembrance," for the soul of the dead. They say that when a man's soul leaves his body it goes down to *ge' ṣalmawet,* "the valley of the shadow of death," and remains there until the first *tazkir*-sacrifice is brought on the third day. Then it goes up to heaven and comes to Abraham, our father, and remains there with him and the rest of the righteous. During these seven days of mourning they may not cook food in their houses, but their friends and relatives bring food to them. Particularly upon the first day it is strictly forbidden for a mourner to eat any of his own food.[159] They cut off their hair as a mourning rite. On the last day of the seven a sacrifice is offered, and the mourners are required to take a ritual bath.[160] This last is obviously in preparation for the return to the condition of daily, profane existence.

We have quoted Jaussen[161] that at Maʿān the spirits of the dead are thought to roam about the tombs for the first seven days after death. Also among the Nosairis on the evening of the sixth day after the funeral a feast is held, and the next morning a sacrifice is offered in the house of the dead man, after which the soul may pass out through an opening over the door into the body of a male child that is to be born. Obviously, the Nosairis believe that for the first seven days after death the soul remains in the house in which the deceased had lived.

Among the Bedouin tribes, sacrifices are offered and ceremonies of mourning are performed, as we have seen, for at least seven days, and sometimes even for fifteen days, after death. According to Jaussen, the sacrifice at the end of this period is called *d̲abīḥet el-ʿazā,* "the sacrifice of consolation," because it terminates the mourning;[162] according to Schumacher,[163] it is called *fakku-l-waḥdati,* "the redemption of isolation," implying that the mourners are now to be free of the ghost. The Otäbe tribe, as we have also learned,[164] sacrifice an old, toothless goat upon the seventh day after death in order to avert evil.

Among some Arabs in Upper Egypt of the *Rowadjeh* and *Djaafire* tribes, who live about Esne, "if any person of the family die, the women stain their hands and feet blue with indigo, which demonstration of their grief they suffer to remain for eight days, all that time abstaining from milk and not allowing any vessel containing it to be brought into the house; for they say that the whiteness of the milk ill accords with the sable gloom of their mind."[165] In Tangiers, too, the period of mourning is eight days.[166] The implication of both these last rites is plainly, just as in the case of birth rites, that the actual period of mourning, and therefore of taboo, extends over seven full days, and that the eighth day marks its culmination and termination.

A curious mourning custom was formerly practiced by the Druses. They would dress a stick or a bundle of straw in the garments of the deceased and would carry this about during the seven days immediately following death.[167] This figure undoubtedly represented, not so much the dead person himself, as rather his spirit or ghost, thought to be still present among his relatives and associates and within his former home during the first seven days after death.

In Abyssinia funeral banquets are held during the seven days immediately following the funeral, and food is given to the guests in descending rank each day. On the first day the priests alone are fed, but the poor at the gate receive a piece of bread and a portion of the entrails and the liver of the animal sacrificed at the banquet. On the seventh and last day the women are fed.[168]

Occasionally, rites of mourning are performed not only upon the seventh day after death but also upon multiples of seven days thereafter. Thus, as we have learned, among the Ṣẖûr the name of the deceased is mentioned at the evening meal on every eighth day during the first month after death, and some drops of water or crumbs of food are poured out as a sacrifice for, or perhaps to, him.[169] Among the Ẓullâm these ceremonies are performed on the evening of every Wednesday or Thursday of the first month after death.[170] Elsewhere, we are told, from the day of burial until the following Thursday the women go to the cemetery to wail at the grave. On this day oil-cakes are made and are eaten by everyone at the cemetery. Men never join in these wailings. This continues for seven consecutive Thursdays, or until the Great Thursday of the Dead, which comes in the spring at about the time of the Greek Easter.[171]

Occasionally the ceremonies of mourning terminate upon the tenth day after death, although this is far less common than their conclusion upon the seventh day. As we have seen, the Mandaeans begin a seven-day period of mourning upon the third day after death and terminate it upon the tenth day. Among the Saʿîdijjîn the wailing for the dead by the women ceases upon the tenth day.[172] The Tijâha offer the *ʿaza*'-sacrifice upon the tenth and (or?) thirtieth days.[173]

Among some tribes sacrifices are offered to the dead on the thirtieth day after death, or sacrifices which have been offered on an earlier day are repeated on this day. In addition to the *ʿaza*'-sacrifice of the Tijâha, just cited, upon the tenth and (or?) thirtieth days, the Saʿîdijjîn likewise offer this same sacrifice upon the memorial day of the deceased at the close of the first month after death.[174] The Ṣẖûr offer the sacrifice *ʿaša-l-majet,* "the supper of the dead," upon the thirtieth day.[175] The Copts, too, performed ceremonies in memory of the dead upon the close of the fourth week after burial.[176]

Some peoples apparently prefer the fortieth day for the sacrifice. We have already seen that on this day the ʿAzâzme Bedouin offer the *raḥma,* or "sacrifice of pity."[177] And at Tlemcen, in Morocco, and among the Persians, Yezidis, and Copts certain rites which are performed upon the third and seventh days are repeated upon the fortieth day. The Copts have an interesting superstition in regard to the first forty days after death: "They say that an angel takes the soul, so soon as it has left the body, conducts it across a great sea of fire, and plunges it into this sea a number of times, depending upon the degree of its sinfulness. A pure soul passes over this sea so high that it is not touched thereby. The angel then presents it before the Creator, who sends it back for a period of forty days, at the close of which it will receive its last judgment. The poor soul returns to its former home and wanders about there for three days, seeking its body. It goes to the grave, then returns to the house, and remains there for three more days. Then the priests go to the house, recite prayers there, and drive the poor soul from the house. The angel then takes it again and accompanies it into Paradise and into Hell and shows it the various dwelling places of the blessed and the damned. Thirty-seven days are consumed in these visits. It is then presented to God again, who pronounces its final judgment."[178]

Among the Christians of Palestine mourning is likewise celebrated for forty days. During this time the women may neither wash nor change their garments. On the fortieth day a religious ceremony is performed at the grave. The priest prays, blesses the food which has been brought along, and then distributes the grain among the poor.[179]

Among the Moslems of Egypt, too, ceremonies are performed at the tomb by the female relatives of the deceased on the first three Thursdays and Fridays following the interment, "and again, on the Thursday and Friday which complete, or next follow, the first period of forty days after the funeral: whence this Friday is called 'el-Arbaʿeen,' or Ġumʿat el-Arbaʿeen,' "[180] i.e., "the Forty," or "Friday of the Forty."

9 The Festival of the Dead

Finally, an important moment in the ceremonies of mourning is the close of the full year after death. In most cases it seems to mark the completion of all rites and obligations of mourning, and the full return of all relatives and associates to the state of daily, profane existence. At this time the Arab widow in particular performed peculiar ceremonies of purification.[181] Likewise among some Arab tribes the ceremony *taftaddu bihi* was, or is, held at the close of the year of mourning. As Goldziher says,[182] the meaning of this ceremony is obscure, although its ostensible purpose is the casting away of the animal and the dung. But, as the name implies,[183] it is certainly a ceremony of redemption, presumably in origin redemption from the power of the ghost of the deceased.

This ceremony, with the sacrifice which as a rule accompanies it, is, as we have seen,[184] generally known by the name *ḍaḥîyyeh*. But this term has a rather wide range of meanings, and the ceremony itself has assumed many forms. Usually it is performed, it would seem, only once, upon the close of the first year after death, and is designed only for the welfare of the soul of the particular relative who has just died. In such case, as we have seen, the dying person, particularly if he has no near-relative upon whom he can rely with assurance to perform this ceremony for him, ofttimes makes full provision himself therefor before his death. In fact, as we have also seen, instances are not unknown where he sacrifices the *ḍaḥîyyeh* for himself in anticipation of his death. The reason for this solicitude, as we have indicated, is that the animal, usually among the Bedouin a camel, and all the equipment which is customarily loaded upon it, are thought to be necessary for the happy, or, perhaps better, the least miserable, existence of the deceased in the world beyond the grave. Frequently the *ḍaḥîyyeh* ceremony is performed on the successive anniversaries of the death of a near relative; and, as we have seen, Doughty found it continued into even the third generation.

Most frequently, however, the *ḍaḥîyyeh* is performed, not upon the anniversary of a particular relative, but at a regular season in the year, usually in the early spring, which time-honored custom and tradition have sanctified for this purpose. Occasionally at this annual festival this sacrifice is offered in honor and on behalf of those members of the tribe or clan who have passed away within the year. Their names are recited solemnly during the ceremony, and generally the formula is repeated, that this sacrifice is intended specifically for them.[185]

Of this festival, Doughty writes as follows:[186] "At Christmas time there fell a pious Mohammedan festival, *eth-thaḥia,* when a sheep is slaughtered in every well-faring household, of which they send out portions to their poorer neighbors. The morning come, they all shot off their guns in the kella and sat down to breakfast together. The nomads devoutly keep this feast: there is many a poor man that for his father, lately deceased, will then slaughter a camel."

The following description of the *ḍaḥîyyeh*-festival and ceremonies was given by a native of Central Arabia: "When the day of the *ḍaḥijeh*-festival comes we sacrifice to the dead; whoever has a son, that son sacrifices for him; and whoever has no one, he appoints (before his death) an agent, in order to sacrifice for him. In this way, every year when the *ḍaḥijeh*-festival comes around sacrifices are offered for the dead. A third part of the flesh of the *ḍaḥijeh*-sacrifice is given to beggars and strangers; a third part is distributed to relatives and neighbors; and the final third is reserved for the inmates of the house. The flesh is taken and cut into large, flat slices and long, thin strips and laid upon the cross-beams of the rooms, where it dries; it remains there for five or six months; every day whatever is needed is taken, is beaten with a mallet, and is cooked for supper. From the skins of the animals sacrificed, water containers are made; during the summer these are filled with water and are carried out into the streets for public distribution; the people at large drink from these, and the reward [thanks?] therefor falls to the lot of the dead."[187]

But most commonly the *ḍaḥîyyeh* is celebrated annually in honor or for the welfare of all the dead of the family, clan, or tribe, both those recently deceased and those whose demise was more remote. In this case, it seems, no individual names are mentioned, but the dead are addressed collectively as "our dead," and are urged to accept and enjoy their sacrifice. In this case these *ḍaḥîyyeh*-rites naturally take on the character of a general festival for the dead, and must therefore be celebrated, not upon the anniversary of the death of any particular person or tribal hero, but upon some fixed moment or occasion of the year. As has been said, this is usually in the early spring. This has become accordingly a fixed, annual clan or tribal festival, with established, conventional rites, in which, however, the *ḍaḥîyyeh*-sacrifice is central.

As we have seen,[188] in his description of the *ḍaḥîyyeh*-festival Musil says, "Every year the people of Arabia Petraea visit the graves of their ancestors, about which other graves may lie." It is there and then that the *ḍaḥîyyeh*-festival is celebrated. Of the ʿAmârîn in particular he says that every spring they make a pilgrimage with their sheep to the graves of their ancestors, where they encamp for a considerable time and offer sacrifices and food to their ancestors and give them milk to drink.

The name *ḍaḥîyyeh* is applied to the sacrifice at Mina on the tenth of Dhû-l-Ḥiǧǧeh.[189] This is in certain respects the culmination of the *Ḥaǧǧ,* or sacred pilgrimage to Mecca, the most characteristic institution of Islamic ritual. As Wellhausen has shown, in the days of Arabic heathenism before the rise of Islam this ceremony was performed in the month or season of Raǧab, i.e., in the early spring, at exactly the time that the *ḍaḥîyyeh*-festival is celebrated by the Bedouin of Arabia still today. Islam has sought to reinterpret this sacrifice at Mina to make it commemorate the traditional sacrifice of Ishmael by Abraham, but the pre-Islamic, heathen origin of the rite is self-apparent.[190]

This sacrifice at Mina has come to be known in Islam as *al-ḳurbân,* "the sacrifice" par excellence, and the tenth of Dhû-l-Ḥiǧǧeh, the day upon which it is offered, as the *ʿId al-ḳurbân,* "the Festival of the Sacrifice." Of this, Burckhardt, describing the customs of the Aeneze Bedouin, says:[191] "On the day of the *korbán,* the great sacrifice on Mount Arafat, each Arab family kills as many camels as there have been deaths of adult persons during the last year in that family, whether the deceased were males or females. Though a dead person should have bequeathed but one camel to his heir, that camel is sacrificed; and if he did not leave one, his relations kill one of their own camels. Seven sheep may be substituted for a camel; and if the whole number can not be procured for the *korbán* of the death year, the deficiency may be supplied by killing some on the next or subsequent year. The *korbán* is therefore always a day of great feasting among the tribes." Elsewhere,[192] Burckhardt tells that during this festival horse races are run, among the Bedouin always a part of the celebration of their few festivals. "The daily fare during the festival is rather better than usual, even among those families that have no sacrifice to make for relations who have died during the course of the preceding year."

Similar ceremonies are observed at the same time by the urban Moslems. Of these, Curtiss says:[193] "There is a great difference . . . between the orthodox sacrifices of the Moslems and those offered by the people at the various shrines.

"The sacrifices offered by orthodox Moslems are in connection with the pilgrimage to Mecca, on the tenth of the pilgrim month, about three miles from the sacred city, at Muna. These sacrifices are called *ḍaḥîyyeh.* The meaning of the term is not clear. It comes from a root which signifies 'early in the morning,' so it is supposed to indicate those sacrifices which are offered about ten o'clock in the morning. These sacrifices are in commemoration of the sacrifice of Ishmael by Abraham, his father. They are not used at all for feasting by those who are most pious, but are buried, or are appropriated by the Bedouin.

"Besides the *ḍaḥîyyeh* at Muna, the faithful all over the Moslem world are required to offer sacrifices in commemoration of Abraham's sacrifice on the tenth of the pilgrim month. Hence the strange scene may be witnessed of sheep and goats slaughtered in the streets of Damascus, on this day; though otherwise it is contrary to law to slay animals outside the slaughter-houses. They are also put to death in cemeteries and in the courts of private houses.[194]

"Through the influence of ancient Semitic custom this great sacrifice has come to be diverted from its original use. It is employed for the dead, though the people make the distinction between the ordinary sacrifice for the dead and the *ḍaḥîyyeh* by saying that the blood of the latter is holy and that it is of use on the judgment day."

Wilson[195] describes the procedure in Palestine in these words: "In Palestine, however, the yearly sacrifice of the *Dthahiyeh,* which is offered at the same time as the *Hajj* (pilgrims to Mecca) are slaying the victims at Mount Arafat, is regarded by the Moslem peasants as a *Kifarah* . . . , that is, a satisfaction for their sins. In some villages, moreover, they put the blood of this sacrifice on the doorposts and upper lintels of their houses. In one village near Jerusalem I have seen many houses with the blood thus sprinkled on the doorposts, while some had in addition two of the victim's feet stuck in a hole in the door, these being left the whole year till the next feast comes round."

Another reliable observer describes the same institution as follows:[196] "There is a Moslem Feast of Atonement that resembles the Passover of the Jews and their Feast of Atonement. It commemorates Abraham's contemplated sacrifice of a son, not of Isaac, but of Ishmael, according to Moslem teaching. A lamb is slain by each householder, the blood of the sacrifice is sprinkled on the doorpost, and an olive-branch is fixed over the door as a sign of peace."

In his description of this same festival, Baldensperger[197] adds a few significant details. On this festival the fellahin of Palestine kill a goat or a lamb and eat it, together with rice and bread. They then assemble in the mosque and listen to a sermon preached by the Khateeb. He continues: "The Feast of Atonement is evidently copied and mixed up from Judaism. It has this peculiarity that the blood of the sacrifice is sprinkled on the doorposts and olive-branches are stuck over the door as a sign of peace. The sacrifice here is not all eaten upon the spot, but parts are distributed to relatives away, as any of the female relatives married in another village." This last custom Baldensperger compares very properly with the ancient Jewish custom, recorded in the Bible,[198] of sending gifts and portions to friends and relatives upon the various festivals.

But it is not only the Moslems of Palestine who offer this annual sacrifice, but the Christians of Palestine as well. Wilson continues his account of the *ḍaḥîyyeh*-sacrifice with these words:[199] "In two or three mixed hamlets (Moslem and Christian) with which I am acquainted, the Christians, either just before Lent or at Easter, kill a goat or sheep, and put the blood on the upper lintel in the form of a cross, and on the side-posts in spots. These villages are all situated in the district known as that of the Beni Zeid, whose Moslem inhabitants always observe this custom at the feast of the *Dthahîyeh,* as described above. The custom seems to be a very local one, but whether it has been derived by the Moslems from the Christians or *vice versa* I cannot say."

The Christians of Kerak also, as we have seen,[200] "on the eighth day before the beginning of the forty-days fast designate an animal which they slaughter on the following Saturday evening, with the words, 'This is your supper, O our dead!'"

It is a superstitious belief among the Christians of Palestine that "during the period between the Carnival and Palm Sunday the souls (ghosts) of the departed have permission to visit their living friends."[201] The period, Thursday to Friday, which comes eight days before Good Friday is commonly called by them, and also by their Moslem neighbors, *ḫamîs* or *djumʿet el-amwât* or *ḫamîs* or *djumʿet el-bêḍ,* i.e., "Thursday (or Friday) of the dead" or "Thursday (or Friday) of the eggs."[202] Among the Moslems it corresponds to the Christian All Souls' Day.[203]

The folk procedure on this occasion is described by an authoritative observer:[204] "In *djumʿet el-amwât,* better known as *ḫamîs el-amwât,* the women of Jerusalem go on Thursday afternoon to the cemeteries to visit their dead. They take with them dyed eggs, sweets, and even cooked food and meat. The greater part is distributed to the poor—who gather on such a day—as an *adjr* (recompense). The meaning is that, since some help is given to the needy in the name of the deceased, God will reckon such an act in his favor. In some villages the women go before sunrise to the cemetery, believing that a visit after this time is not so good. Soon after sunrise they go home. The children of the peasants go on Thursday afternoon to the houses of their neighbors and beg:

a'tûni bêḍa 'an amwâtkum, 'give me an egg in the name of your dead.'[205] Those in the house give an egg, dried figs, raisins, or a piece of bread. The children express their thanks with the words *allah yirḥamhum,* 'God be merciful to them.' This day, therefore, bears also the name *ḫamîs el-bêḍ* (Thursday of the eggs)."

Of this "Thursday of the Dead" or "Thursday of the Eggs," Baldensperger says:[206] "Thursday is the universal day for visiting tombs. Townspeople are the most assiduous to do it, Fellahin come next, and Bedouin last. As a rule, the tombs are visited the day after the burial of the dead, and for seven following days, and on the next Thursday. Food is distributed at the tomb to anybody passing, and by many this food-distributing, *rahmy* (mercy), is carried on till the Great Thursday of the Dead when everybody visits tombs and distributes food for the repose of the soul. Any food is good for those who can not afford many and good things, but most commonly oil pancakes, *Zalâbíe,* are distributed. This Thursday is always in spring, and is a movable feast-day, or *duty*-day; they do not call it feast. It is, as closely as I could observe, either on Maundy Thursday or next to it (Greek calendar). I could not make out why they in this follow the Greek calendar, but most probably the spring of the year is the occasion, which would not happen if they would follow the lunar months and have a fixed date."

The strong hold which these festivals of the dead have upon the Christians of Syria is best evidenced by the fact that, despite numerous prohibitions and interdicts, the Jacobite Church has been able to limit the practice only slightly, and has failed absolutely to abrogate it entirely. And the fact that one interdict in particular forbids the observance of these festival rites during Lent, and especially upon Saturdays and Sundays therein, may be regarded as further corroboration that this was formerly, if it is not still today, the usual time for the performance of these rites of memorial for the dead.[207]

Among the Nestorians, too, "the better classes sacrifice a lamb a week or a month after the death of a relative, with the object of bettering the condition of the soul of the departed, and bread and other provisions are distributed among the poor." Moreover, among these same Nestorians, "a kind of love-feast to commemorate the dead is celebrated once a year in all the mountain villages. The feast is prepared in the churchyard, where the most wealthy families bring their offerings, consisting of bread and a number of lambs. After the sacrament is administered, the deacons swing the burning censers, into which locks of wool, cut off from the fleece, are introduced, and the priests are chanting a long anthem over 'the lambs that are slain in the sacrifice for the dead.' The prayer is concluded with the recital of the legend of the seven sleepers of Ephesus. As soon as the religious service is concluded, the bread and the lambs' flesh are distributed among the villagers assembled on the occasion."[208]

Festivals of the dead are celebrated in other parts of the Moslem world. At Tlemcen, in Morocco, there are certain annual festivals called *nefqas.*[209] A meal of flesh is eaten in a ceremonial manner. Some of this flesh is given to the poor by the head of the family. A strict fast of a single day's duration is likewise observed, especially by old people who expect to die soon, and who therefore feel impelled to prepare in this manner for their demise.

"The *nefqas* at Tlemcen are also festivals in honor of the recent deceased of the family. On these days the women go to the cemetery to visit the graves of their relatives.[210] They weep together while reciting the merits of the departed; for they believe that on this day the soul of the deceased returns to his house. A common meal is also prepared, similar to the funeral meal (on the third and seventh days after the interment). Every female visitor ought to bring with her a gift of some article of food. Apparently this gift constitutes the contribution of each one to the funeral meal, of which the soul of the deceased is thought to partake. Whoever does not bring an offering may become the object of the anger of the soul of the deceased person. The character of this offering is indicated by the formula which each woman recites while presenting her gift, 'This is alms for the soul of So-and-So.'" Twelve such *nefqas* are held in the course of the year, in connection with the different main festivals.

In Merrâkech, in Morocco, both men and women visit the tombs in great numbers on the annual Ashura-festival, on the tenth of Moḥarram, and on the twenty-seventh of Ramadan, i.e., just before the close of the great fast and the celebration of the Bairam-festival. Only the women visit the tomb during the three days following death and interment.[211]

The Falashas and the Christians of Abyssinia likewise observe a festival for the dead. "Once in his lifetime every faithful one among them must observe a memorial festival for all his dead relatives and friends. The poorest Falasha will sacrifice his very last possession in order to discharge this duty. In accordance with his means the festival meal is luxurious or simple. Generally a young animal is sacrificed, which, because it is a sacrifice for the dead, may not be prepared by the women. At the close of the festival the skin of the animal is burned with all manner of ceremonies and prayers. The closing prayer of this *Teskar* (memorial festival) is called *Fetat,* and asks for forgiveness of the sins of the deceased."[212]

The Sabaeans of Ḥaran also observe a festival for their dead. En-Nadim describes it in the following words:[213] "The first Teschrin (October). In the middle of this month the burning of food for the dead takes place. It is performed in this manner; every one buys all kinds of eatables, which the market offers, as, for example, different kinds of flesh, and fresh and dried fruits. They cook various kinds of food and sweetmeats, and burn all these during the night for the dead. The thigh-bone of a camel is burned with these. It is intended for the dog of the mistress of the nether world, in order that he may not bark at the dead, and they thus become worried. They also pour out mixed wine upon the fire for their dead, so that these may drink it, just as, according to their opinion, they eat the burned food."

The Persians, too, have their festival of the dead, called *Tîrdjân*. They believe that on this festival the dead assemble to receive the food and drink which the living have prepared for them. This is called "the food of the dead." This festival, too, is observed in the spring, on the twenty-sixth of the month of Aban, which corresponds to May.[214]

10 The Departure of the Soul and the Return of the Dead

A careful analysis of all these rites and ceremonies establishes one fact beyond all question: at the bottom of all of them lies the belief, either partly outgrown or else still openly affirmed, that death does not mark the absolute separation of the dead from the living. For a certain period the soul or spirit of the dead person is thought to hover about the corpse or in the vicinity of the grave, or in his former earthly abode, or in some other contact with his former relatives, neighbors, or friends. It is clear that this continuing sojourn of the ghost of the dead man in the land of the living is thought to endure for varying periods inasmuch as, as we have seen, these ceremonies are performed at various times after death and burial.

Or rather, since certain ceremonies are usually performed by one and the same group of people on different days after death, it seems that the departure of the soul from the land of the living to its eternal abode in the nether world was generally conceived of as being gradual and in stages, instead of sudden and complete in a single step. These ceremonies, which consisted in most cases of offering a sacrifice to the dead, were and are generally performed upon the third, the seventh, the thirtieth, or the fortieth days after death, and then upon the completion of the first year and upon this annually recurring day, or else at an annually recurring festival which comes regularly in the early spring.[215]

The thought basic to all this is that for the first three days after death the soul or spirit is believed to hover about the corpse, in immediate contact with it, presumably seeking to re-enter its former earthly envelope, the body. Apparently during these first three days the soul is not regarded as being particularly dangerous to its surviving relatives and friends; and in some circles, as we have seen, an attempt, or at least a pretense thereat, is made to continue the association between the living and the spirit of the dead person. It is during this period that the sacrifice *wanîse,* or *'awnâse* ("association") is offered, and, in Tlemcen, in Morocco, the night of the third day is known as *lilet-el-r'eriba,* "the night of departure." At the end of this three-day period, by which time signs of decomposition of the corpse are as a rule unmistakably apparent, the soul realizes that return to the body is denied it forever; that, in other words, it is really dead.[216]

Now the next stage of the spirit's retirement from its former earthly associations and associates begins. But apparently the poor ghost does not yield and depart without a struggle. When he sees at last that he can not re-enter his former body and that he must wend his way to the realm of the departed, his anger is aroused. This continues for the next four days, until the close of the seventh day after death. During this four-day period the soul or ghost is generally conceived of as a raging demon, inimical to all with whom it may come into contact, whether relatives or friends or total strangers. During these seven days rites of deep mourning are performed, such as additional sacrifices, wailing, covering the head with ashes, wearing old garments, letting the hair grow and fly loose and uncombed, and the like. These ceremonies probably have a twofold character; they are undoubtedly intended in part to appease the dangerous ghost and make him realize that he is not forgotten but is being sincerely mourned for by the survivors, and in part they are also undoubtedly designed to ward off his attacks. During this period the living become increasingly eager day by day to be rid of the now hostile spirit. They speed his going in every way possible; and at the end they offer the sacrifice *fakku-l-waḥdati,* "the redemption of isolation," or by whatever other name it may be called. It is unquestionably a taboo-sacrifice, which redeems the living from the taboo, or power, of the ghost, to which they are exposed until the close of this seventh day. And at that time, very appropriately, the taboo-sacrifice of the hair is offered,[217] and the living return to the condition of everyday, profane life, from which they have been excluded since the death of their relative.

Apparently from the seventh to the thirtieth or fortieth day after death the living have little or nothing to fear from the ghost of their dead. The mourning during this period seems on the whole quiet and reserved and to express grief and reverence for the dead rather than actual fear of him. Perhaps the sacrifices and ceremonies upon the thirtieth day mark the complete and final departure of the ghost to the realm of the dead in the nether world; or perhaps, what is not at all unlikely, they mark the close of the period of danger from a ghost which was thought to be exceptionally powerful, perhaps because its possessor had been extraordinarily powerful or wicked during life.[218]

And finally, the ceremonies at the close of the complete year after death mark the complete cessation of mourning. Apparently the living have nothing more to fear from the ghost of the deceased, which is now firmly, even though perhaps not quite permanently, located in the nether world. The living may now go about their daily tasks undisturbed, or at least almost so.

But on the recurrent anniversaries of the death, continuing frequently through three generations, or more generally at an annual festival, which, with but very few exceptions, falls in the early spring, the dead are remembered with reverence, either individually and personally, or collectively and impersonally, and ceremonies are observed in their honor. The reason for this is clear. In many of the forms of celebration of this festival which we have analyzed, the thought is definitely expressed, or else clearly implied, that on these annual occasions the dead are thought to return for a brief period to the world above, to associate once more in a distant, shadowy way with their former relatives and friends. If the dead are treated with fitting honor and hospitality, the living have nothing to fear from these visits. But if the proper due of sacrifice and ceremonies is omitted, then once more the wrath of these otherwise harmless dead may be kindled against their living kinsmen, and woe betide them; therefore the *ḍaḥîyyeh*-sacrifice[219] and other kindred ceremonies, such as that practiced by the Eben Rašid Bedouin, of cutting the throat of the animal appointed as the *ḍaḥîyyeh*-sacrifice and then leading it around the tent so that the blood drips to the ground and forms a protecting circle about the tent, across which the evil spirit dare not pass.

Here, the expressed purpose of this ceremony is to protect the inmates of the house, human and animal both, from the attacks of the dangerous spirits. Usually, however, it seems that this sacrifice has the effect of protecting chiefly the herds and flocks. Curtiss tells[220] that there are many Bedouin tribes which mark their best camel mares on the *ḍaḥîyyeh* festival with the blood of the *ḍaḥîyyeh*-sacrifice with a characteristic mark, or *wasm*. Elsewhere,[221] he says that in the month of Reġeb[222] most of the members of the Ruala tribe, a branch of the large Aeneze group, sacrifice a sheep or a goat in order to protect their herds from pestilence or robbery, and mark the camels with stripes of blood from the sacrifice. Doughty found the custom practiced by the Bedouin (among whom he happened to be sojourning at the time), in the fall. His account is as follows:[223] "At evening he [Mishwat] offered a young sheep for the health of his camels. . . . Some of the spouting blood he caught in the bowl, and with this he passed devoutly through the troop; and putting in his fingers, he bedaubed with a bloodstreak the neck and flank of every one of his couching great cattle.[224] The mutton went into the pot."

A similar practice is commonly observed in Palestine. Dalman says:[225] "To the Arab religious practice belongs the custom, observed by me at various places in Palestine, of sacrificing a *fedu* at the beginning of the year on behalf of both the men and animals of a household. Frequently the blood of the sacrifice is smeared upon the lintel of the door, the foreheads of the children, and upon the animals. Furthermore, the custom, very commonly observed by Christians and Moslems in Palestine, of daubing with some red color the cattle and other animals on the Good Friday of the Greeks, i.e., on the Passover day, where in all certainty this red dye is the substitute for blood, must have the same purpose, to serve as a protection of both men and animals."

This last custom is described in considerable detail by Canaan:[226] "In *djumʿet el-ḥaiwânât,*[227] better known as *djumʿet el-maghrî*[228] (but never as *ḫamîs*), the useful animals (cows, horses, sheep, and goats)[229] are dyed with red. The frontal portion, between the horns, is the part chosen for dyeing, but the horns and the back, especially of sheep, may also be dyed. All animals enjoy a yearly rest day. They are not sent to work, and the milk is not sold, but is used or distributed to the poor. *Lêlatu djumʿah*[230] and Friday morning the animals are not milked. This is done about noon. In some places even the jars where milk and its products (butter, sour milk, etc.) are stored, are dyed with *mighrî.* Cattle are protected on this day against serpent bites."[231]

In this custom, or ceremony, one procedure is of particular interest and significance. The facts that on this day the animals are not sent out to work but enjoy a complete rest, that they are not milked until noon, and that the milk is not sold but is either used at home or given to the poor, indicate clearly that on this day the animals and their products and labors are thought to be in a state of taboo. This is borne out by the fact that they are not milked during the night, nor early in the morning, as is usually done, but that this is deferred until noon. As we have learned, evil spirits, and especially the spirits of the dead, are thought to be most powerful at night;[232] with the coming of the dawn their power wanes rapidly; certainly by noon it has departed completely; after that time it is safe to milk the animals without fear that these evil spirits may affect them in any way. But even then this milk is still taboo; therefore it may not be sold in the usual manner, but must either be used at home or else—and what, in the light of all that we have learned thus far, may be better—given to the poor.

A somewhat similar ceremony is performed by the inhabitants of Moab at the festival of the important wely Ǧaʿfar, at his shrine situated about three hours' journey south of Kerak. "Once each year, in the spring, a solemn festival brings together about the *mazar* all the inhabitants of the country and the pious pilgrims who come to offer their homage and to demand a favor of the great *wely*. The festivities proceed joyously about the tomb; the tournaments in the broad plain stimulate the curiosity of the assistants and the enthusiasm of all the warriors, while the many sacrifices of fat sheep evidence the devotion of all and gladden the heart of the multitude invited to partake of the festal meal. No one is denied admission to the table where rice and flesh in abundance are consumed lavishly in the name of Ǧaʿfar. The blood of the victims upon the threshold, the doorposts, and the lintel testify to the piety of the visitors."[233] While this festival, with its interesting ceremonies, is celebrated by the semi-agricultural inhabitants of Moab in honor of the wely Ǧaʿfar, and there is no mention of the spirits of the dead as the recipients of the sacrifice, nonetheless a striking similarity may be noticed between this and the *ḍaḥîyyeh* festival celebrated by the pre-agricultural, nomadic ancestors of the present inhabitants of Moab.

A kindred ceremony is practiced by the Yezidis. They celebrate their New Year's Day on the first Wednesday after the spring equinox. On this day, it is thought, the fate of human beings is sealed. On the day preceding, the young people go to the mountains and gather scarlet anemones, which they fashion into small bunches and fasten above the doors of the houses, in order to guard the house and its inmates against all evil during the year just beginning.[234]

11 Periods of Mourning in Ancient Israel

When we examine the rites of mourning in ancient Israel in the Biblical and Rabbinic periods, we find the same basic beliefs and the same customs observed as among other Semitic peoples. In the Israelite practice the third, seventh, and thirtieth days after death and the first anniversary of death are of particular significance. In fact, traditional Judaism divides the time of mourning into four periods, marked off by these four significant days.

The first three days after death and interment are given to violent weeping and lamentation.[235] During the next four days, i.e., during the second half of the first seven days after death, extreme rites of mourning are observed.[236] The mourners may not leave the house and may sit only upon the ground or the floor or, at the very most, upon a low stool, but not upon an ordinary chair; nor may their beds be prepared in the ordinary manner for them to sleep in. They may not go about their regular tasks and duties, even within the house. These are neglected or else are performed by friends. And even the food for the first meal after the burial is sent in from without. During this period the mourners wear torn and disheveled garments, and in the Orient even strew ashes upon their heads,[237] and keep the mouth and nostrils covered.[238] The ostensible reason for this last custom is in order not to work harm to visitors who come to condole with them. But, obviously, the original reason was to prevent the ghost of the deceased from attacking them and slipping into their bodies through the openings of the mouth and nostrils. And finally, during this entire period the mourners give way to, or indulge in, expressions of loud and excessive grief.

With the close of these seven days this extreme mourning, with its many restrictions and taboos, comes to an end and the next period, that of milder mourning, begins and continues until the end of the thirtieth day after death. During this period the immediate relatives of the deceased are still subject to certain restrictions. They may not, for example, wash their garments or cut their hair or marry.[239]

Finally, the fourth and last period follows after the thirtieth day and continues for eleven months, to round out the full year of mourning. During this period only the most immediate relatives, particularly children mourning for parents and parents mourning for children, are subject to certain mild restrictions. They may not indulge in excessive joy or visit places of amusement, or wear any but black outer garments. With the completion of a full year after death, or, among certain groups, of eleven months as the substitute for the full year, the formal mourning automatically ceases entirely and all restrictions and taboos are ended.

It is easy to recognize the ideas and principles which underlie these various mourning rites, which conform so closely to those of the present-day Arabs, which we have already analyzed. It was commonly believed in ancient Israel that on the third day after death decomposition of the body became definitely noticeable. So it was customary to observe the corpse carefully during the first three days after entombment in order to establish the certainty of the death.[240] A superstitious belief, frequently cited in Rabbinic literature, was that for the first three days after death the soul hovers about the body, seeking to re-enter it. But when, on the third day, it seems that the appearance of the body is changed, that, in other words, decomposition has set in, and therefore that entrance into the body is denied it forever, it goes away.[241] For this same reason, it was likewise held that the most extreme grief and mourning endured for the first three days.[242]

The antiquity of this belief may be inferred from a variety of Biblical evidence. The ceremonies of purification of one who has touched a corpse or any dead object are performed upon the third and seventh days after such contact.[243] After Elijah had been carried away in the chariot of fire, the people searched for him for three days; then they desisted from their search, undoubtedly concluding that now the prophet was surely dead.[244] Hosea 6 : 2 represents resurrection from death as taking place upon the third day, unquestionably because this day was thought to mark the complete separation of the soul from the body.[245]

This seems also to be the implication of the tradition recorded in Luke 24 : 37 (but missing in the other gospels), that when the apostles see Jesus in their midst upon the third day after his death their first impulse is to fear him, for they imagine him to be a spirit, and thus now dangerous to them, until he convinces them to the contrary.

The seventh day marked the conclusion of the period of intensive mourning[246] and the beginning of lighter or negative mourning. In the Revelation of Moses[247] the following significant passage occurs: "And when she [Eve] was dead, the archangel Michael stood beside her; and there came three angels and took her body, and buried it where the body of Abel was. And the archangel Michael said to Seth: Thus bury every man that dies, until the day of resurrection. And after having given this law, he said to him: Do not mourn beyond six days. And on the seventh day, rest and rejoice in it, because in it God and we angels rejoice in the righteous soul that has departed from earth." In Rabbinic literature references to the seven-day period of mourning are frequent.[248] There, too, we find the tradition that during the first seven days of mourning it is as if a drawn sword is held over the mourners; during the remainder of the first thirty days it is as if this sword is brandished toward the mourners; and not until the close of the full twelve-month period is this sword returned to its scabbard.[249]

It is impossible not to correlate these mourning periods in ancient Israel with parallel customs among other Semitic peoples and with the principle underlying them, which we have established, that the dread power of the spirit, or ghost, of the dead was thought to extend, with greatest and most immediate danger to his living relatives, over the first seven days immediately following death and burial; and particularly from the third day—when the soul realizes the futility of its attempts to regain entrance into its former body, and that it must now seek admission into the nether world—until the seventh day. We have seen that in ancient Israel the belief existed that the souls of the *r^e^fa'im*, i.e., the ghosts of the dead, became evil spirits which injured the living.[250]

The Talmud likewise records the belief that the soul mourns over the body for the first seven days after death.[251] It proves this by the story of a soul which at the end of the seven days appeared to the mourners and thanked them for their solicitude in its behalf. Moreover, it was generally believed that the corpse heard and understood everything that was said in its presence by the mourners and visitors. According to some, this power of the corpse continued until it was interred; according to others, until it had decomposed.[252] Therefore it behooved the mourners, particularly those closely related to the deceased, to "speak no ill of the dead" and to perform most punctiliously the various rites of mourning on his behalf. Otherwise it might be expected that, instead of thanking them for their solicitude, he would vent his wrath upon them for their disrespect for his corpse and their disregard of his welfare in the hereafter.

Occasionally these extreme mourning ceremonies, typical of this first period, were continued for the first thirty days after death.[253] The children of Israel mourned for Moses and Aaron for this period,[254] and the woman taken captive in war was charged to mourn for her parents for a like period.[255] In the Talmud we read that the first three days after death are given over to lamentation for the dead; the remainder of the first seven days are for deep mourning; on the thirtieth day the rents made in the garments at the moment of death are sewed up, the garments are cleaned, and the hair is cut.[256] In the case of a sage or a great man, the intense mourning may endure, as in the cases of Moses and Aaron, up to the thirtieth day after death, but not later.[257] This custom, or at least a modified survival of it, seems to obtain still today among the native Jews of Palestine.[258] According to the Talmud, the soul goes up and down for the first year after death, but after that time it ascends to heaven and does not return.[259] The first anniversary of the death marks the close of the entire period of mourning. On all subsequent anniversaries of the death the deceased is lovingly remembered by near-relatives by the kindling of a small light in the home,[260] which is kept burning through the entire day, and by the recital of a traditional prayer, known as the *Ḳaddiš*, "Sanctification," because the name of the Deity is sanctified therein.

12 The Festival of the Dead in Ancient Israel

The striking similarity, close relationship, and common origin of the beliefs and ceremonies of mourning in ancient Israel and of those of other Semitic peoples naturally suggest the question whether there was any institution in ancient Israel akin to the *ḍaḥîyyeh* festival and its ceremonies. In other words, was there an ancient Israelite festival of the dead, when the souls of the dead were supposed to return, to renew for a short time and in either a friendly or a hostile relationship their association with their former kinsmen?

This question is not new. Schwally discussed it at some length[261] and concluded that the Purim festival was in origin such a Jewish festival of the dead. His arguments, however, are gratuitous and far from convincing, and have been conclusively refuted by Grüneisen.[262]

We have seen that the *ḍaḥîyyeh* festival is normally celebrated in the early spring, that the outstanding feature thereof is the sacrifice of an animal, among the Bedouin usually a camel and among the urban inhabitants of Palestine a sheep. It is expressly stipulated that this animal must be physically perfect, with no part of its body maimed or missing. Frequently the blood is sprinkled upon the lintels and doorposts of the houses, or is applied in some other manner as a safeguard against evil. These procedures remind us strongly of certain Biblical prescriptions for the celebration of the Passover festival and suggest quite forcibly that it alone, of all the ancient Israelite festivals, might once have been celebrated, in some measure at least, as a *ḍaḥîyyeh* festival, as a festival of the dead.

It is a generally accepted fact that the Biblical Passover is the result of the amalgamation of two ancient festivals, quite distinct from each other, the original *Pesaḥ* and the *Ḥag Hamaṣṣôt*.[263] The latter was in origin an agricultural festival, celebrated during the last seven days of the year of the ancient pentecontad calendar, which marked therefore both the end of the old and the commencement of the new calendar year, and also the beginning of the harvest season.[264] The *Pesaḥ* was a shepherd festival in origin, observed by the Israelite clans or tribes before their entrance into Canaan, during the night of the new moon immediately preceding the advent of the vernal season,[265] at, or shortly after, the time when their sheep, and probably also their camels, cast their young. Wellhausen has correlated this original *Pesaḥ* festival with the Raġab ceremonies and sacrifices among the Arabs,[266] which, as we have seen, were identical in origin with the *ḍaḥîyyeh* festival and sacrifices of the modern nomad and urban Arabs. This fact suggests further the correlation of the original *Pesaḥ* with the *ḍaḥîyyeh* festival of the dead.

A careful analysis of the Passover legislation in Exodus 12, and particularly that portion which deals with the ceremony of the Paschal lamb, will confirm this hypothesis completely. It is readily apparent that, from a literary standpoint, the chapter is composite. This fact has been recognized by practically all Biblical scholars. The main body of the chapter comes from the Priestly Code.[267] But verses 21–24 and possibly also verse 42 are from J, and must have been part of the older J legislation, which in the early pre-Exilic period regulated the manner of celebration of this important festival. Moreover, verses 25–27a are easily recognizable as Deuteronomic in character and origin.

This fact points to a Deuteronomic revision of the older J Passover legislation. It was from this Deuteronomically revised J legislation that verses 21–24 and 42 in their present form were taken and incorporated into the Priestly legislation.

A comparison of the legislation in these verses from the J Code with that in the Priestly portions of the chapter establishes the fact that the ceremonial provided for in the J legislation was decidedly more primitive than that of the P Code.

In the older J ritual the sacrifice of the Paschal lamb and the sprinkling of the blood from it upon the entrance of the house is the central theme. The ritual is quite simple, and its purpose is obvious. A sheep is selected by each family[268] for its Paschal sacrifice and is slaughtered. The place where this sheep is sacrificed is not specified, but from the verse immediately following it is perfectly clear that the animal is slaughtered in such position and manner that the blood flows over the threshold of the house.[269] Then a bunch of hyssop is taken and dipped in the blood upon the threshold, and with this the blood is daubed upon the lintel and the two doorposts, thus forming a bloody circle about the doorway. Under no condition may any member of the family go forth from the house during that entire night. Instead, within the house every person is to observe a watchnight. These are the details of the ancient Passover ritual recorded in the J Code.

The later P Code ritual of the Paschal sacrifice and ceremony[270] has modified the older J ritual in a number of significant respects, suppressed some ritual details, and likewise prescribed others not mentioned in the J ritual. These last may be either P innovations or modifications, or else they may have been a part of the older, pre-J ritual for the festival and have been suppressed by J in favor of its own formulation of these ceremonies; or they may have been regarded by the J legislators as ceremonies so universally observed that specific provision for them in their festal legislation was unnecessary.

The P ritual prescribes that the animal for the Paschal sacrifice must be selected on the tenth day of the month, four days before the actual moment of sacrifice.[271] During these four days it must be carefully guarded, presumably to ensure that no accident befall it which would render it unfit for sacrifice. For it is especially prescribed that the animal must be a perfect male, entirely without blemish. This was undoubtedly an ancient ritual requirement, even though it is not recorded in the J ritual.

Furthermore, the P Code has changed the original character of the ceremony as a family sacrifice to that of a household sacrifice. Under the provisions of the J ritual, the sacrificial unit was the *mišpaḥah,* the family or clan, all the members of which were close blood kin. Under the provisions of the P Code the unit of sacrifice is the *bêt 'ab,* the household—in this particular instance, all the inmates of one single house. Presumably in most cases these, too, are all blood-relatives. But the fact that it is provided that in case the inmates of the house are too few to consume an entire lamb or kid by themselves, the nearest neighbor—and with him, of course, his entire household—shall be invited to join in the sacrifice, indicates that the emphasis is no longer laid upon the family or clan relationship and unity for sacrificial purposes, but rather upon the number of persons who are to participate in the Paschal meal. This number must be sufficient to consume the entire animal during the course of the night, so that no portion, or at least as little as possible, may remain over until morning. Obviously, just in order to satisfy this ritual prescription does the P legislation provide for the combining of two households in the Paschal meal. Apparently the disposal of the entire animal in this manner during the course of the night is here a more important element of the ritual than the older character of the ceremony as a family or clan sacrifice.

Apparently in thus stressing the fact that the animal must be completely consumed during the night, and that whatever remains uneaten in the morning must be burned, the P legislators were trying to bring the sacrifice under the head of a "peace-offering" given as a thank-sacrifice, according to the ritual prescriptions in Leviticus 7 : 11–15, offered out of gratitude to the Deity for His miraculous deliverance of the people of Israel from Egypt. But the very facts that this animal is slaughtered, not at the sanctuary but at the home, that it is sacrificed, not during the day but just at nightfall, that no priest need play any role in the ritual connected with it, and that no part of it whatever comes upon the altar, but that it is consumed entirely within the house and during the night, show that this is no real sacrifice according to the P Code principles governing sacrifices, and even, in all likelihood, that originally it was not offered to Yahweh.

The animal is to be sacrificed at twilight, i.e., just before nightfall. The place where it is to be sacrificed is not stated, but merely that the blood is to be smeared upon the doorposts and lintel of the house in which the animal is to be eaten. Obviously the sacrifice takes place at the house, and presumably, therefore, despite the lack of explicit mention thereof, upon the threshold. Quite probably the P legislators suppressed the reference to the threshold because of the implication of the association of the threshold with non-Yahwistic religion. Probably for the same reason they omitted all reference to the hyssop with which the blood is sprinkled upon the doorposts and lintel, according to the J ritual.

Furthermore, the sacrifice must be roasted in fire; and it must be entire, with no bone broken[272] and with nothing missing, not even the head or the lower part of the limbs or the entrails. This is exactly the manner in which the *ḍaḥîyyeh*-sacrifice is disposed of today. As we have seen, it is thought by those Bedouin who still offer the *ḍaḥîyyeh* consciously as a sacrifice to the dead, that passing the animal through fire or consuming it in fire enables the dead to gain possession of it. Similarly among the Sabaeans of Harran,[273] food offered to the dead, at the annual festival of the dead in the fall, was conveyed to them by being burned in the fire, and even the wine intended for them was poured upon the fire.

The P legislation stipulates explicitly that under no condition may the animal be eaten raw or boiled in water. This last provision is in all likelihood a repeal of the Deuteronomic law, which specifies that the Paschal lamb is to be boiled.[274] Obviously the aim of this P legislation is to reinstitute in large measure the original method of presenting this sacrifice to the dead, as it had obtained in the pre-Deuteronomic period.

Furthermore, the sacrifice must be eaten hastily by the worshipers during the night and while clad in a particular garb. Their loins must be girded, their sandals must be on their feet, and their staves in their hands. This is indeed strange equipment for men who are expressly charged not to go forth during the entire night from the house in which these ceremonies are being performed. They are, as it were, ready to set out upon a journey, but at the same time they are indirectly forbidden to do so. This particular rite is not mentioned in the J ritual of this festival, at least not in that portion which has been preserved. Seemingly it is an archaic Paschal rite, the true origin and meaning of which had long been forgotten, and which had been prescribed, or perhaps reinstated, by the P legislators in their attempt to revive, or at least to permit, the observance of this ceremony in something approximating its most ancient form.

The implication here is that the people are ready to set out upon a journey. This cannot, however, refer to the Exodus from Egypt, for, as Eduard Meyer has shown,[275] the Passover was an ancient shepherd festival, the origin of which far antedates the Exodus, and the connection of which with the Exodus is only incidental. The garb of the worshipers is simple indeed and suggests the old garb of the nomad in the desert. In all likelihood, therefore, this particular prescription is a survival from the ancient, nomadic practice of this ceremony, which, under the conditions of Palestinian agricultural life, had entirely lost its original significance, whatever that may have been, and had continued to be observed mechanically as a meaningless reminiscence.

This comparison of the Passover ritual of the J Code in Exodus 12 with that of the Priestly Code in the same chapter makes clear what the historical evolution of this festival during the Biblical period must have been. Between these two codes the Deuteronomic Code intervened with a number of significant modifications of the older ceremony to conform to the conditions of the centralized worship which it instituted, such as permitting the use of large cattle for the sacrifice in addition to sheep or goats, and boiling the flesh instead of roasting it. It is obvious that this Deuteronomic form of the ceremony changed its original character completely. It now ceased to be a family or household ceremony, performed on behalf of all the members of a family or clan or the inmates of a house. The blood of the sacrifice was no longer sprinkled upon the doorposts and lintel; the bunch of hyssop was no longer used, nor could the sacrifice be eaten any longer within the home and in haste by the worshipers, with their loins girded, their staves in their hands, and their sandals upon their feet; nor could the prohibition of leaving the house during the entire night be observed in any manner. The Deuteronomic reform, it is clear, divested the festival ritual of all its original, distinctive character and meaning and made of it an almost conventional celebration at the central sanctuary, which differed but little from the celebration there of the other festivals.

Now this journey to the central sanctuary and the subsequent return home from there, with the consequent loss of precious working days just at the commencement of the harvest season, must have interfered seriously with the preparations for the important harvest activities, particularly if the worshipers came from a considerable distance. Moreover, as we shall see, it tended to abrogate a custom of long-established practice, upon which in great part the safety and protection of every home and all its inmates were popularly thought to depend. In all likelihood, therefore, this Deuteronomic reformation of the Passover celebration was not popular and probably was never fully accepted, particularly in rural circles, despite the royal enforcement which it received. Probably the old ceremonies continued to be practiced quite extensively in homes throughout the land, although now in unsanctioned and probably therefore in somewhat modified and varied forms.[276]

This Deuteronomic reformation of the Passover ritual, it is clear, the P legislation in its turn sought to abrogate. Obviously, in accordance with its pronounced conservative and archaistic tendencies, it aimed to reinstitute the old, pre-Deuteronomic form of the ceremony, so far as this was possible under the religious conditions of its own day. Therefore it incorporated a portion of the old J Passover legislation into its own code and restored the character of the celebration as a ceremony centering about the home. It likewise reverted to some of the old, pre-Deuteronomic rites, such as using only small cattle and roasting the animal, and even prescribed certain ancient ritual details which are not mentioned in the portion of the J ritual which it incorporated. And in addition thereto, the Priestly Code added the new prescription—not met with in any of the earlier Passover legislation and certainly not a part of the original Passover practice—that the sacrifice must be a yearling lamb or kid.[277] The reason for this innovation will become clear very soon.

However, as was to be expected, it was impossible to restore completely the old, pre-Deuteronomic character of the Passover festival, even had the P legislators desired to do this. And it is not at all likely that this was their real aim. In fact, it seems most probable that this P legislation was largely a concession on the part of the P legislators to the folk-practice of the people, who had persisted in observing many of the old Passover rites in their homes despite the Deuteronomic centralization of the Passover observance in the Temple in Jerusalem. The very idea of a sacrifice to the Deity offered elsewhere than at the central sanctuary was so fundamentally contrary to the basic principle of the P sacrificial system that it is difficult to believe that the P legislators altogether voluntarily restored the old character of the Passover as a purely home ceremony.

One thing the Deuteronomic reformation had done for the Paschal sacrifice. It had divested it entirely of its original character as a sacrifice offered for the protection and welfare of the family or members of the household. It had made it partake largely of the character of a typical festival-sacrifice at the central sanctuary, offered as a thank-sacrifice by the worshiper and his family out of gratitude for the many blessings which the Deity had already conferred upon them and for the continuance of which they hoped.

Probably, too, the Deuteronomic practice tended to gradually associate, and perhaps even to ultimately identify, the old firstling sacrifice with this characteristic Passover sacrifice. As has been stated, it is generally recognized by scholars that in the nomadic period the Passover festival was celebrated at about the time when the sheep, goats, and camels gave birth, early in the spring, and that upon this festival, in addition to the regular Passover sacrifice, the firstlings of domestic animals, recently born, were sacrificed. That this custom continued to obtain in the Southern Kingdom as late as the ninth century B.C. is evidenced by the intimate association of the institution of firstling sacrifices with the observance of the Passover in Exodus 34 : 18 ff. It is clear from the wording of this law that originally every first-born domestic animal was sacrificed, regardless of its physical condition. The Deity had created it; therefore it belonged to Him and of course had to be given back to Him as a redemption-sacrifice for all subsequent offspring of these same mother-animals.

But the Deuteronomic legislation introduces something new into the sacrificial ritual of firstlings when it provides, in Deuteronomy 15 : 19 ff., that only perfect firstlings may be brought to the central sanctuary and offered as a sacrifice, while those firstlings which have any physical defect, regardless of their firstling, taboo character, may not be used sacrificially, but may instead be consumed at home as ordinary, nonsacrificial food. The Passover legislation in the Deuteronomic Code follows immediately upon this firstling legislation. This association justifies the conclusion, even though it is not expressly stated, that the Deuteronomic legislators regarded the Passover festival as the regular and proper occasion for the offering of these firstling sacrifices.

Now this *novum* in the Deuteronomic firstling legislation, viz., that only physically perfect animals may be offered, tends very naturally to correlate for us this firstling sacrifice with the original *Pesaḥ-ḍaḥîyyeh* sacrifice. We have seen that the present-day Bedouin practice insists that the animal for this sacrifice must be physically perfect, with no member maimed or missing. And the P legislation in Exodus 12 : 5 likewise insists upon this condition in the Passover sacrifice. Therefore, even though this Deuteronomic legislation makes no mention of this condition in its Passover legislation, it may be safely inferred that it, too, took for granted that only physically perfect animals were suitable for this Passover sacrifice, just as it prescribed this for the firstling sacrifice.

Thus it follows that theoretically, under the provisions of the Deuteronomic Passover legislation, at this one festival two sacrifices, the regular Passover sacrifice and the firstlings, were to be offered almost simultaneously; and probably one requirement was that both must be perfect animals. But with the passing years, as the people advanced further and further in their economic development, and sheep- and cattle-raising gave way more and more to agriculture, the tendency would be for the number of firstling animals offered at the annual Passover festival to decrease. Under the conditions of the Deuteronomic legislation, very many families must have discharged their religious obligations of the Passover festival at Jerusalem without offering a single firstling sacrifice. But all of them offered their regular Paschal sacrifice, likewise a perfect animal.

Furthermore, the practical condition of the anticipated presence of multitudes at Jerusalem for the annual Passover celebration and the necessity of feeding them all, coupled with the additional consideration that it would have been a physical impossibility either to burn all the firstling sacrifices upon one occasion in a single sanctuary, no matter how large and well equipped, or to have them all eaten by the priests, no matter how numerous these may have been, brought about another necessary and significant change in the method of disposing of firstling sacrifices under the conditions of the Deuteronomic legislation. Inasmuch as these firstlings were in origin pure taboo-sacrifices, it follows that originally they could not have been eaten by the sacrificers. They must either have been burned entirely, and thus given over completely to the Deity, or, in a later stage of development, like other taboo-sacrifices, a part thereof must have been burned upon the altar and the remainder given to the priests, or other earthly representatives of the Deity. Under the Deuteronomic legislation, at the central sanctuary both procedures were physically impossible. Therefore the Deuteronomic legislators were constrained to alter radically the original prescription of the firstling sacrifice in order to ensure its complete disposal during the first night of the festival. The only way possible, so it seemed, was to provide that this sacrifice might now be eaten by the sacrificer and his associates.

Consequently, under this Deuteronomic legislation the interesting condition obtained of two kinds of sacrifice being offered in theory at the central sanctuary on the Passover festival, viz., the original Passover sacrifice and the firstling sacrifice. Both sacrifices consisted of the same kind of animal, but with one difference, viz., the firstling sacrifices consisted, of course, of only yearling animals, while no specification as to age existed originally, so it seems, for the animals of the Passover sacrifice. Furthermore, in all likelihood both sacrifices could now consist of only perfect animals, and both were now eaten by the sacrificer and his associates. And in practice, as we have seen, there must have been very many families which offered only one sacrifice, viz., the original Passover sacrifice.

The natural and almost inescapable tendency, therefore, under the conditions of the centralized worship, was eventually to merge the identity of these two sacrifices, both of which had lost almost completely their original distinctive characteristics and purpose, and which were now externally so strikingly similar in almost every respect.

Just this is apparently what has happened in the P legislation for the Passover in Exodus 12. The P Code provides for the institution of firstling sacrifices,[278] but nowhere does it associate these with the Passover festival.[279] In fact, the seemingly incidental character of the P legislation for firstling sacrifices conveys the impression that they had come to play only a comparatively minor role in the P sacrificial system. On the other hand, the Passover legislation of the P Code requires not only that the Passover sacrifice be a perfect animal, but also that it be a yearling.

For many of the people, as we have suggested, it was quite a hardship to come up to Jerusalem each year for the celebration of the Passover, as required by the Deuteronomic legislation. Moreover, in all likelihood the people had never completely discontinued their ancient Passover practice of killing animals upon the thresholds of their homes and smearing the blood upon the doorposts and lintels, a ceremony which the Deuteronomic Code undoubtedly sought to abrogate as non-Yahwistic and idolatrous, and which the Holiness Code[280] unquestionably classed under the head of sacrifices offered to *s^eʿîrîm*, or evil spirits. Influenced by both these considerations, the P Code now, even though this was contrary to the fundamental principle of its sacrificial system, revived and legitimized the old Passover home-sacrifice and ceremony, even, on the one hand, with the archaic rite of smearing the blood upon the doorways, but also, on the other hand, with considerable modification of the character of the sacrifice itself, due to the influence upon it of the Deuteronomic legislation and the changed economic conditions which we have pictured. The new insistence of the P legislation that the Paschal sacrifice must be a yearling animal is, as we have seen, the most striking instance of this modification.

In this way the Passover legislation and ceremonial must have evolved from the J Code, through the Deuteronomic and the Holiness Codes, to the P Code.

But it is self-apparent that the Passover festival, with its many strange and obviously originally non-Yahwistic rites and practices, had a history long antecedent to the form which it had assumed under the J legislation. The question therefore arises: if the Passover sacrifice proper was not originally offered to Yahweh, and if many of the peculiar rites of the festival were not originally performed in honor of Yahweh, then to what deity or supernatural power was this sacrifice originally offered, and in whose honor were these rites originally performed?

Especially indicative of the original character and purpose of this sacrifice and of the entire Passover ceremonial is the reason ascribed in the two codes, J and P, for its observance. The reason given by P in Exodus 12 : 12 f. is as follows: "And I shall pass through the land of Egypt in this night, and I shall smite every first-born in the land of Egypt, both man and beast, and against all the gods of Egypt I shall exercise judgments, I, Yahweh. But the blood will serve you as a sign upon the houses in which you are; and I shall see the blood, and I shall pass over you; and there will not be against you a plague as a 'destroyer,' when I smite the land of Egypt."

The meaning of this entire passage is clear except for one point. The expression "a plague as a destroyer" is strange indeed, and requires explanation. But such explanation is not forthcoming from the present context.

However, the parallel passage in the J Code throws considerable light upon this difficulty. After commanding the sprinkling of the blood upon the doorposts and lintel and charging the people that under no condition may they come forth from their houses during the entire night, verse 23 continues: "For Yahweh will pass by to smite Egypt; and he will see the blood upon the lintel and the two doorposts, and Yahweh will pass over above the door, and He will not permit the Destroyer to enter your houses to smite."

From this passage it is more apparent just what the *mašḥît,* "the Destroyer," is. It is that supernatural power or being which is abroad during this night, bent upon destruction. Into every house which has no blood smeared upon the door-frame this Destroyer enters and works evil upon the inmates. Specifically, it takes the lives of all the first-born in that household.[281]

In the J text this Destroyer functions as the agent of Yahweh, or at least as subject to Yahweh's control. It is Yahweh who permits him to enter the unmarked houses and to work his will. In fact, the implication of the passage is even stronger than the language; for the narrative implies that Yahweh not only permits the Destroyer to do all this, but that this is Yahweh's purpose, and that He sends the Destroyer into the unmarked houses to carry out this purpose.

This inexactness of expression can be readily explained. The blood upon the door is represented as a sign in the P Code, verse 13. It is not stated of what it is a sign, but from the context, that Yahweh is bent upon destroying the first-born in every Egyptian household, presumably the blood upon the door is the sign that this is an Israelite household, which Yahweh means therefore to spare. This, too, is the implication of the J passage (verse 23), even though the term "sign" is not used there. But this is indeed a strange way in which to indicate an Israelite household; and had this been the original and sole reason for this strange sign, something far simpler and more natural would have served the purpose equally well.

It is clear then that both the P and J accounts of this entire ceremonial represent modifications of an ancient and primitive rite and concept, the character and purpose of which can be readily determined. Unquestionably, this ceremony of sprinkling upon the door or door-frame the blood of an animal, slaughtered upon the threshold in connection with the observance of an important festival in the early spring, is exactly the same as the ceremony which we have encountered so frequently, of offering the *ḍaḥîyyeh*-sacrifice as a part of the ritual of the *ḍaḥîyyeh* festival, likewise celebrated, as a rule, in the early spring. We have seen also that, particularly among the fellahin of Palestine, the custom exists of smearing the blood of this *ḍaḥîyyeh*-sacrifice upon the doorposts and lintels of the houses. Frequently, too, the blood is smeared upon the foreheads of the children and upon the backs or other parts of the bodies of cattle in order to protect them against pestilence or robbery.

Now it is clear that just this was the original purpose of this Passover ceremony. The blood upon the door-frames was originally something quite other than a sign to Yahweh that this was an Israelite household. The blood of the slain animal, poured forth upon the threshold and then sprinkled or daubed upon the two doorposts and lintel, formed a complete circle about the entrance into the house, through which the evil spirit could not pass. Thus, the circle of blood protected the inmates of the house, just as the circle of the camel's blood in the *ḍaḥîyyeh*-sacrifice protected the tent of the Eben Rašid Bedouin and its inmates. But outside this circle of the sacrificial blood about the doorway lurked the evil power, doubly wrathful, no doubt, because it was barred from entering and working its fell purpose. Therefore it behooved all persons to remain carefully within the house, and also to keep awake and on guard; in other words, to observe a watchnight. Not until dawn appeared and banished the evil power to the realm of eternal darkness did the danger pass.[282]

Clearly it is this evil power, or spirit, which is designated in the Biblical text as the *mašḥît*, the "Destroyer." In the original form of the ceremony it was not Yahweh at all who prevented the entrance of this *mašḥît* into the homes, but rather the blood upon the door-frame of each house, the blood of the sacrifice which had been offered to this very *mašḥît* itself.[283] Originally this *mašḥît* had no connection with and no dependence whatever upon Yahweh.

As the concept of Yahweh evolved in Israel, this ancient ceremony was gradually modified and reinterpreted, and was thus eventually incorporated into the Yahweh-religion and ritual. In the J version of the Passover ritual it is still the *mašḥît*, the "Destroyer," who enters the houses of the Egyptians and kills their first-born, and is prevented from entering the houses of the Israelites for the same purpose. It is Yahweh, however, who notices the sign of the blood upon the doors and, according to the J writers, apparently by passing over them forbids entrance to the *mašḥît*. Thus the *mašḥît* no longer acts independently; he is now merely the agent of Yahweh, fulfilling mechanically Yahweh's purpose by destroying the first-born of the Egyptians. But the *mašḥît* is at the same time the enemy of Yahweh, as it were, in that he would likewise destroy the first-born of the Israelites did not Yahweh protect them. Thus, in the J ritual the blood no longer serves the purpose of preventing the entrance and the evil work of the *mašḥît,* as in the original ceremony. In fact, it is no longer even associated with him.[284] It has become only the sign to Yahweh that in this house faithful Israelites dwell, who have hearkened to His word and have slain the Passover sacrifice.

And in the P version of the Passover ritual the role of the *mašḥît* has been weakened still further. There it is no longer the *mašḥît* who destroys the first-born of Egypt, but Yahweh Himself. And Yahweh passes over the houses of the Israelites, no longer to protect them against the attack of the *mašḥît,* but merely to approach the houses of the Egyptians. He passes over or by the Israelite homes and spares their inmates, but He enters the Egyptian homes and slays their first-born. In the P ritual the name *mašḥît* has survived as a pure archaism, a vague reminiscence of a term and a concept which had once been associated with the Passover tradition and ritual, but the true origin and nature of which had long been almost completely forgotten; hence in P the vague, difficult, and practically meaningless expression, "a plague as a destroyer."

What then was this *mašḥît* in the original Passover ritual and tradition? In the light of all the evidence presented there can be only one answer to this question. In the early, nomadic period of its existence Israel must have believed, just as have other Semitic nomads in more recent times, that early in the spring, presumably upon the first new moon of the spring season and at about the time of the spring equinox, after the great majority of the sheep, goats, and camels had cast their young, the souls of dead ancestors returned from the realm of the dead and revisited their former haunts. But they returned, not as friendly powers to be greeted happily by their living kinsmen, but as evil, hostile spirits, contact with whom was dangerous indeed and therefore to be avoided. In particular, their malevolence was directed against the first-born members of their former households.

Accordingly, the living shut themselves up within their homes, nor dared to venture forth during the entire night. And they guarded themselves against the possible entry of these unfriendly spirits into their homes by sacrificing a sheep or goat upon the threshold and sprinkling a circle of the sacrificial blood upon the doorposts and lintel as well. Through this blood-encircled doorway no evil spirit could possibly pass. Moreover, the blood upon the threshold and doorposts was the unmistakable sign to the dread spirit that he had received his full due from his living relatives and could have no further claim upon them.[285] This fear-inspiring spirit was itself, or at least was the forerunner of, the Biblical *mašḥît*.[286]

The animal thus sacrificed was physically perfect, with nothing broken and no member missing. It was sacrificed originally to the spirit, or ghost, of the dead which threatened. Presumably its sacrifice rendered the existence of the soul of the dead in the nether world a degree easier and happier. It was apparently in all respects identical with the annual *ḍaḥîyyeh*-sacrifice of the present-day Bedouin.

Possibly, too, this blood was sprinkled not only upon the threshold, doorposts, and lintel, but also upon the inmates of the house, or at least upon those whose lives were most immediately threatened, viz., the first-born, just as in the modern Samaritan form of the ceremony the blood of the sacrifice is smeared not only upon the entrances to the tents, but also upon the foreheads of the children, particularly the first-born.[287] This blood served not only as the unmistakable sign that the sacrifice had been offered, especially on behalf of those upon whose foreheads the blood had been smeared, but also brought upon them a *baraka,* a blessing.[288]

The fact, too, that the blood of the sacrifice was sprinkled upon the doorposts and lintel with hyssop is further confirmation of the conclusion that the sacrifice and the entire ceremony were directed originally against the ghosts of the dead, conceived of as evil spirits. For, as we have already learned, both of the other Biblical ceremonies in which hyssop played a role were directed against evil spirits, viz., the ceremony of the cleansing of the leper,[289] and that of the red heifer.[290] In fact, as we have also learned, the latter ceremony was designed particularly to safeguard the living against the contagion of dead bodies, and, unquestionably, in the earliest form of the ceremony, from the danger which threatened thereby from the spirit, or ghost, of the dead person whose body had been touched.

Still another fact points to this same conclusion, viz., that the people are commanded to observe a watchnight. Exodus 12:42 prescribes that this watchnight is to be observed in honor or on behalf of Yahweh. But both the thought and the language of the verse are so involved that it is clear that this, too, represents an attempt to adapt to the worship of Yahweh a ceremony which in origin had no connection whatsoever therewith, but which must have been a part of the ceremonial of protection against the dreaded spirits. The people are to remain awake and on watch the entire night in order to guard themselves, and especially the first-born, against the attacks of the evil spirits.[291] In the same way and for the same reason, as we have seen,[292] a watchnight is frequently observed on the night before a circumcision.

Still today, faithful Moslems, performing their pious duty of the *ḥaǧǧ,* or pilgrimage to Mecca, observe the night at Muzdalifa very punctiliously as a watchnight.[293] The relationship of the *ḥaǧǧ* to the old, nomadic Israelite Passover on the one hand, and, on the other hand, to the present-day *ḍaḥîyyeh* festival in honor of the dead, has already been commented on. Similarly, the Mandaeans observe the night of their New Year's Day as a watchnight. A considerable portion of the ceremonies performed upon this occasion are in honor of the dead.[294]

All this evidence taken together points strongly to the conclusion which we have suggested: that in remote ages, when the Israelite tribes, or clans, were still living as nomads in the desert, the Passover festival, which they celebrated, in part at least, in honor of their dead, corresponded in practically every essential with the present-day Bedouin *ḍaḥîyyeh* festival. It was celebrated upon the night of the first new moon in the spring, after their sheep, goats, and camels had given birth. This was the moment when in each succeeding year the souls of the dead, perhaps only those who had died within the year, or perhaps also the souls of ancestors for generations back, were supposed to return, as malevolent spirits, to their former abodes. The Paschal sacrifice offered to these spirits, and also all the peculiar Passover rites performed in their honor, were intended to protect the living from the sinister designs of these dead ancestors and relatives of the *mišpaḥah,* or clan.[295]

Several additional bits of evidence of extra-Biblical provenance lend support to this hypothesis. The tradition seems to be old in Israel that the dew will revive the dead. A reference to this belief seems to be contained in the very difficult and obscure passage Isaiah 26 : 19. The Talmud records the tradition that only through the efficacy of the dew can the dead be restored to life.[296] This dew is stored up in the highest heaven, *ʿArabôt,* with the souls of those destined to be born.[297] On the first night of the Passover festival the storehouses of the dew are unlocked.[298] And in the ritual of the Synagogue for the first day of Passover the prayer for dew is solemnly recited.[299]

Probably, too, the association of the Passover with the return of the souls of the dead has, in part at least, given rise to the concept of the Passover as the Festival of Resurrection. Perhaps, too, in half-conscious anticipation of and preparation for this return of the souls of the dead, the custom arose of whitening the sepulchres during the month of Adar,[300] the month preceding that in which the Passover festival falls.

All these facts taken together may well be regarded as establishing with a very large measure of certainty the conclusion that, in part at least, the Passover was originally a festival celebrated in honor of the dead, at the moment when in each succeeding year they were thought to return, with more or less malevolent intent, to their former abodes, and corresponded in practically every essential respect with the present-day Bedouin *ḍaḥîyyeh* festival.

XV

A Historical Survey

Our investigation is almost completed. We have considered rites practiced by various Semitic peoples, not only through the full span of human life from birth to death, but also through the entire course of their cultural evolution from prehistoric to modern times.

We have devoted extensive study to the institution of circumcision. The remoteness of origin of this peculiar custom has long been perceived by Biblical scholars. The persistent use of stone or flint knives[1] in performing the circumcision, long after the use of iron and steel had become normal in daily life, has pointed unmistakably to this conclusion. Our own study has shown the close connection which the rite of circumcision had in its origin and the early stages of its history with the institution of *beena* and *môṭaʿa* marriage and the important role which it played in the primitive social life and organization of the early Semitic peoples. As the abundant evidence which Robertson Smith[2] presents indicates and our own research confirms, this institution of *beena* and *môṭaʿa* marriage belongs, particularly in its origins and fundamental practices, to the remote, prehistoric period of Semitic cultural evolution. Whenever we meet it in historic times, it is invariably as a survival, almost completely outgrown and but half understood. This fact, more than all else, proves the extreme antiquity of the origin of the rite of circumcision.

We have seen, too, that other important birth rites, notably those of *ʿaḳîḳah, taḥnîk,* and *tasmîyya,* which have survived in certain Moslem circles even, with various modifications, down into historic times, likewise had their origin in the institution of *beena* and *môṭaʿa* marriage.

Furthermore, we have seen that in their earliest form these ceremonies were performed upon children in order to free them from the condition of taboo or possession by some deity or spirit, in whose power they were thought to be at birth. The underlying principle in all these rites was that the sacrifice of a part or of an appropriate substitute redeemed the tabooed object, whether child, animal, crop, or work of human hands, and permitted it to enter into the state of ordinary existence and to participate in or be used for daily, profane life. These rites were manifestly an integral and indispensable part of the religious and social practice of the cultural stage in which they had their origin. Therefore it follows that they carry us back not only to the stage of *beena* and *môṭaʿa* marriage but also to that of spirit-worship, or animism, i.e., to what must have been the very earliest, the most primitive stage of Semitic religion.

But, as has become clear in the course of this investigation, not only did these cognate birth rites have their origin in the worship of spirits, but likewise practically all other rites which bear upon the important and critical moments of life which we have considered. Rites of the removal of taboo and redemption in all their countless forms, the closely related rites of ritual purification,[3] the myriad primitive birth and marriage rites, and, above all, the equally numerous and varied rites of death, burial, and mourning, all had their origin and have their only possible logical and historical explanation in the cult of spirits among the earliest Semites.

This fact is particularly manifest in the peculiar and, to moderns, almost incomprehensible institution of child-sacrifice. Here, too, the underlying principle was that the sacrifice of a part, particularly the first part, redeemed the remainder—in this case, all future offspring of the same mother. It is noteworthy that this taboo was always reckoned from the standpoint of the mother, and that fatherhood played no part therein. It was the *peṭer reḥem,* "the opener of the womb," the first-born of the mother, that was sacrificed.[4] Of course, the origin in Israel of this institution of the sacrifice of the first-born offspring of every human mother might be accounted for as springing from analogy with the sacrifice of the first-born of animal offspring, particularly since in both Exodus 22 : 28 f. and 34 : 19 f. they are grouped together in one law. But such grouping is, of course, a matter of convenience of statement, much later than the origin of the institution itself, and consequently of no particular moment. Still, it is undoubtedly significant that under the normal conditions of *baʿal* marriage, where the father was the recognized head of the family, as a rule not only was the first-born male child not sacrificed, but also he enjoyed a position of high honor and importance in the household. He was regarded as the first-fruit of the manly strength and vigor of his father,[5] and therefore endowed with a double portion of his father's nature and entitled to a double share in the division of the paternal estate.[6] These considerations seem to justify the inference that the institution of child-sacrifice had its origin under the conditions of *beena* and *môṭaʿa* marriage, when fatherhood was either an unknown or an unstable and inconsequential matter. We have even ventured to suggest[7] that it was the transition from *beena* and *môṭaʿa* marriage to *baʿal* marriage which tended to break down the ancient institution of child-sacrifice and to cause its eventual disappearance.

The facts of history bear this out. Among all the Semitic peoples at the beginning of the historic period, where we find that *beena* and *môṭaʿa* marriage have either disappeared entirely, as among the Assyrians and Babylonians, or else still exist only in a transition stage and are well on the way to disappearance, as among the ancient Israelites, Canaanites, and Arabs, we find the institution of child-sacrifice in a corresponding stage. In Israel the oldest Biblical legislation[8] forbids it, but in such manner that it would seem that the period of child-sacrifice was not too far in the past. Moreover, this legislation did not suffice to terminate the practice.[9] Seemingly, not until after the Babylonian Exile did it die out completely in Israel.

Likewise in Moab, it would seem, the institution of child-sacrifice was in process of dying out in historical times; for, instead of sacrificing his first-born son shortly after birth, the king of Moab permitted him to live, intending to make him his successor upon the throne, but later sacrificed him as an extreme offering to avert the complete overthrow of his kingdom by Israel.[10] Even among the Carthaginians, among whom, so the historical evidence indicates, the institution of child-sacrifice was deeply rooted, we find it in the process of decay and on the way to eventual complete abandonment. This is best indicated by the oft-cited account of the procedure of the Carthaginians after their defeat by Agathocles. They attributed their defeat to the anger of Saturn because they had substituted slaves as sacrifices to him in lieu of their first-born children. Accordingly, they now sacrificed two hundred of these children in the vain hope that, having at last received his due, Saturn might be appeased.[11]

With this evidence before us we need not hesitate to correlate the waning of the institution of child-sacrifice among the Semites with the transition from *beena* and *môṭaʿa* marriage to *baʿal* marriage. And, conversely, this confirms our primary conclusion that the institution of child-sacrifice, like that of circumcision, had its origin under the conditions of *beena* and *môṭaʿa* marriage and the primitive social and religious concepts which underlay them, and, further, that the origins of the institution of child-sacrifice, again like circumcision, antedate by far the beginning of the worship of the great gods and lie in the primitive Semitic cult of spirits.

We find the same principle and the same course of development in the evolution of marriage rites among the Semites. Certainly basic to these also is the belief, which we have seen amply evidenced, that originally a spirit had dominion over every woman, and in particular had an indisputable right to the first act of sexual intercourse with her and to her hymeneal blood. Therefore this first act of sexual intercourse was always fraught with danger both to the maiden and to the man associating with her. Consequently, various rites were performed, all protective in character and all acknowledging in one way or another the prior right of the spirit over the maiden.

Thus the maiden was yielded to initial sexual intercourse with a stranger. Either he was regarded as the representative of the spirit, or else, since he was unknown to the members of the maiden's clan and presumably therefore unknown to the evil spirit also, he ran a minimum risk of reprisal from the spirit. This union, performed at some secret place and without cognizance thereof by the maiden's kin, was naturally of the briefest duration. It constituted plainly a marriage of the *môṭaʿa* type and, under the conditions of the most primitive Semitic civilization, was regarded as the normal and proper procedure.

Or, instead of this, the hair of the maiden might be cut off and given to the spirit on the principle that the sacrifice of a part of a tabooed object redeems the remainder. The question, by whom the hair was cut off and where, as well as all other details of this sacrifice of the maiden's hair and its obvious purpose, need not be raised.[12]

And in the third place, as we have seen,[13] an animal sacrifice, known today as the *ḥellîyeh*-sacrifice, "the sacrifice of profanation," was and still is offered in connection with the first act of sexual intercourse.[14] It might be objected that it would be impossible to offer such a sacrifice upon this occasion, if this first act were altogether of the private and secret character of a *môṭaʿa* marriage. This objection is valid and presents a serious difficulty, a difficulty which can be obviated only by way of conjecture, since we are dealing with primitive conditions which obtained in prehistoric times and concerning which we have therefore no contemporary, authenticated information. It may be that these three rites of the sacrifice of an animal or of the maiden's hair or of her virginity through a form of *môṭaʿa* marriage were in origin alternative forms of payment to the spirit of that which was recognized as his due. In such case, the sacrifice of an animal, and with it also perhaps the sacrifice of the maiden's hair, would probably have been offered originally only when the first act of intercourse was intended to inaugurate a relationship between the maiden and the man of her choice somewhat more stable than a mere *môṭaʿa* marriage; in other words, this sacrifice would have been in origin the preparation for *beena* marriage between a virgin and a man of another clan, who took up his sojourn for the time being with the clan of the maiden—such a marriage, for example, as that of Moses with Zipporah, of the Kenite clan. Accordingly, in connection with a *môṭaʿa* marriage a sacrifice would not have been offered.

It is perfectly obvious that the primitive Semitic marriage rites of removal of the taboo resting upon the virgin bride, due to possession of her by a spirit, parallel exactly the rites of redemption of the newborn male child. First, the yielding up of this maiden to sexual intercourse with a stranger is the exact counterpart of the sacrifice of the tabooed child itself. Both represent the giving to the spirit that which was regarded as his actual due. Secondly, the sacrifice of the hair of the bride as the substitute for the sacrifice of her virginity parallels the sacrifice of the hair, or of the foreskin, of the child. And finally, the fact that the "sacrifice of redemption" became doubly effective if the blood of the animal was sprinkled upon the bride, or upon both bride and groom, parallels in every way the *ʿaḳîḳah*-sacrifice for the newborn child.

Moreover, as was but natural, just as the various rites of redemption of the child, so also these various redemption rites for the bride came in time to be repeated and combined. As we have seen, according to Lucian, the Syrian women might choose between the sacrifice of their hair or of their virginity; but not infrequently custom came to demand both rites simultaneously. We have likewise had instances of the offering of an animal-sacrifice as a marriage rite in conjunction with the sacrifice in some form or other of the hair of the bride. Not improbably, all three rites of redemption were occasionally combined. We have pointed out that the language of Herodotus in his description of the Babylonian marriage practice[15] is somewhat obscure, but that there is some reason for believing that the custom which he records, of the Babylonian women binding up their hair with cords preliminary to their first sexual intercourse with a stranger, and then the breaking of this cord following the sacrifice of virginity, as recorded in the Epistle of Jeremiah,[16] points to an original form of the ceremony in which the hair was cut off. Herodotus likewise speaks, although in very ambiguous language, of an expiatory sacrifice offered to the goddess by the woman after the completion of the first act of intercourse with the stranger and before her return to her home. The purpose of this sacrifice is not clearly stated, but it is not at all unlikely that it was of redemptive character and thus parallel to the *ḥellîyeh*-sacrifice.

In some localities and under certain conditions the old *môṭaʿa* marriage continued in a degenerate form, viz., in the practice of yielding virgins to strangers or slaves for the first act of intercourse, until comparatively late in historic times. But, as Semitic culture progressed and *baʿal* marriage gradually superseded *beena* and *môṭaʿa* marriage, the husband became, in theory at least, the permanent lord and owner of his wife. More and more the desire naturally asserted itself to have her completely for himself and to share her with no other being, not even a spirit. The effect of this was to discourage increasingly the practice of the sacrifice of virginity, and to develop various substitutes for it.

More and more now, it would seem, the custom of virgins sacrificing their hair preliminary to marriage became general, until among the Syrians, according to Lucian, it had become the normal practice, and the sacrifice of virginity was the substitute for it, instead of the reverse, as it must have been originally.

And still another substitute for the original sacrifice by all maidens of their virginity to strangers was the institution of sacred harlotry. There is ample reason for believing that, in the gross forms in which it was practiced in historic times, this to us thoroughly abhorrent institution was not native in Israel but was borrowed, together with many other elements of Canaanite agricultural civilization, when the Israelite tribes entered and settled in Palestine. The practice seems to have no exact parallel in pure Semitic nomadic culture and to be altogether contrary to the principles and standards of sexual relations and practices which obtained therein. This was a major reason why this institution was so completely out of accord with the true Yahweh-worship, the roots of which were set in nomadic culture and ideals, and was therefore so bitterly denounced and combated by the prophets of Israel.

But even though this practice seems to have had its widest usage under the conditions of early Semitic agricultural environment, it does not follow that its origin may not have been in remotest antiquity, and also have had its beginnings in animism. Undoubtedly, despite repeated acts of sexual intercourse on their part as a ritual procedure, these sacred harlots were regarded as representatives of the virgin-mother goddess, and therefore, in theory, as still virgins themselves. In precisely the same manner, the Levites are represented in the Bible as being the substitutes for the first-born of Israel.[17]

In time, too, other practices and safeguards for women against the evil spirits which were thought to naturally possess them developed, such as defloration of maidens by artificial means, the flight of the bridal couple to the mountains or some other inaccessible place and its later outgrowth, the wedding journey, the hiding of the bride under a veil, and the like. It is in these modified forms, for the most part, that we encounter the institution of the sacrifice of the virginity of maidens in historic records and authenticated practice, obviously in a process of decadence from its original form. And there can be no question whatsoever, in the light of the evidence which we have adduced, that this custom and its parallel rites—the sacrifice of the hair of virgins at the attainment of puberty and the offering of the *ḥellîyeh*-sacrifice—go back among the Semitic peoples, just as do the ceremonies of removal of taboo from and redemption of new-born children, to an origin in spirit-worship in the early days of *beena* and *môṭaʿa* marriage.

Even more apparent is the close relationship between rites attendant upon death, burial, and mourning, and the original concept of evil spirits and the worship of them. This was but natural and to be expected. The mystery of death is universal and eternal. Primitive man, no less than his modern and supposedly wiser descendant, was awed and even terrified by the dread stillness and uncertainty which accompany death, and he gave free reign to his affrighted fancy. All about the corpse and the grave he saw the ghosts of the dead hovering with malicious intent, and able, particularly at certain critical moments, to return from the realm of the departed to make demands upon, to annoy, or even to harm or destroy their surviving kin. In matters of death, as we have noted, the human mind is extremely reactionary and unreasoning. Accordingly, superstitions and ceremonies relating to death persist long after religion has advanced to a far higher stage in all other phases of belief and worship. It is therefore not at all surprising that the primitive character of many rites of death, burial, and mourning have been preserved with but little modification, and their first, lowly origin is easily recognizable even in an advanced stage of cultural development.

Our investigation has established that the basis of practically all rites of death, burial, and mourning among the Semitic peoples is the concept of the ghosts of the dead as evil spirits, particularly inimical to surviving kinfolk. The principle underlying the primitive worship of evil spirits in general, and of ghosts of the dead in particular, was simple and naïve. Their attacks must be warded off by the use of amulets, charms, and the like, and by the recital of incantations, prayers, and other, similar formulas. Their anger must be appeased and their hostility placated by according them due honor, by bewailing their passing, with either real or feigned grief, by giving them proper sepulture, by providing for their needs in the dark abode of the nether world, by offering them at the proper moment sacrifices of redemption in order to remove the taboo imposed by them upon the living, and by repeating these rites in proper manner whenever the occasion warranted, such as at those seasons of the year when the dead were thought to return to their former homes.

One fact, however, of apparent significance demands careful study at this point. It would seem that the primitive Semitic mind conceived of some intimate connection between ghosts of dead kin and both birth and marriage. We have concluded from considerable evidence that the primitive Israelites and their prehistoric ancestors regarded the annual Passover festival in the early spring as marking the particular moment when the ghosts of the dead were thought to return to associate with and terrify their living relatives. As we have seen, they called this evilly disposed ghost by the meaningful name *mašḥît,* "Destroyer." Now it is significant that, as the story of the Exodus implies, it was in particular the first-born of each family who was in most immediate danger from this dread spirit. Moreover, as we have learned, the Passover festival was also a circumcision festival in origin. This circumcision redeemed the child from the danger threatening from this *mašḥît.* In all likelihood, in ancient Israel, as we have suggested above, children were as a rule circumcised upon the first Passover-circumcision festival after birth. But whether circumcised at this first circumcision festival or at some other festival a year or two later, until circumcision was performed a child, and especially a first-born child, as the story of the Exodus reveals, was thought to be in immediate danger, not only during the first seven days after birth but again during the period of the Passover-circumcision festival.

But why should children in general, and first-born children in particular, be especially threatened by the *mašḥît,* the ghost of a dead relative, unless some immediate connection was thought to exist between the two? This conclusion is confirmed by the Orthodox Jewish superstition recorded in the *Šulḥan ʿArûk,*[18] that the birth of a male child within the twelve months following a death frees the family from all danger which threatens during that period, a danger which was, of course, thought to come from the ghost of the dead person. Quite similarly, as we have seen,[19] the Copt bride is not permitted to leave the house of her husband after marriage until after the birth of her first child. In both these cases, clearly, the birth of the child terminates the power of the evil spirit, or ghost of the dead, and frees the living from his malign influence.

What is more, as we have seen, the Passover festival originally not only marked the return of the ghosts of the dead and the circumcision of children, but it was also the occasion when, in primitive Israelite and, seemingly in general, primitive Semitic, pastoral practice, the firstlings of animals and the first-born of human beings were sacrificed. Can it be that originally these firstling and first-born sacrifices were offered to the ghost or ghosts of dead ancestors and relatives?

And why not? All the evidence points to just this conclusion. In the remote, prehistoric period of Semitic religious evolution, before the idea of great, personalized deities had evolved, the highest concept of the supernatural was that of the existence of powerful spirits. In their honor alone, as we have seen, were all these various rites from birth to death performed, and to them alone were these many primitive sacrifices offered. And since the particular spirit, or group of spirits, associated with the original Passover festival and the accompanying circumcision of male children was the *mašḥît,* the ghost or ghosts of dead kin, and since, moreover, it was first-born children who were most immediately threatened by this *mašḥît,* the conclusion is unavoidable that in the very oldest and most primitive form of the ceremony both firstling animals and first-born children were actually sacrificed to the *mašḥît.*

This conclusion is reinforced by the significant fact that in Israel as late as the Deuteronomic period the custom, rooted in pre-Yahwistic religion, persisted—or at least the memory of it as a living institution was still preserved—that the first-fruits of the soil were eaten by persons in mourning or were given as sacrifices to the dead.[20] This evidence establishes with certainty that the spirits of the dead had an immediate connection with and a pressing claim upon the firstlings of animals, the first-born of human beings, and, under the conditions of agricultural life, the first-fruits of the soil.

Other considerations strengthen this conclusion. We have seen that a momentous rite in the life of the Bedouin infant, closely related to the ceremonies of *taḥnîk* and of circumcision, and marking one stage in the removal of the taboo thought to rest upon newborn infants, is the *tasmîyya,* the naming of the child. We have seen also that among some Bedouin tribes still today this rite, too, is performed at the annual *ḍaḥîyyeh* festival, the intimate relationship of which to the ancient Passover festival we have established.

Likewise, as we have seen, this Passover-*ḍaḥîyyeh* festival was, and still is, the occasion for the dances of the maidens of the clan or tribe who are candidates for marriage. The antiquity of this rite is amply attested by Biblical and Rabbinic evidence. Not only was it performed upon two of the annual harvest festivals which came near the end of the agricultural and calendar year,[21] but also upon the annual Passover-*Maṣṣôt* festival, as the story of the dances of Miriam and the maidens of Israel proves.[22] Still today, as we have seen,[23] the

Bedouin virgins dance in similar manner at the annual circumcision festivals. The fact that these dances, the regular preliminaries, as Doughty puts it, "to happy marriage and the blessed motherhood of sons," were and are celebrated in connection with the festival of the dead, probably points again to and supports our conclusion: that among the early Semites the spirits of the dead were thought to have some close relationship with the marriage of the living members of their clan or tribe, with the first act of copulation attendant thereon, with the subsequent birth of children, and also with the parturition of their flocks and herds.[24]

And finally, one further consideration points to this same conclusion. Excavations in Palestine have shown how general was the custom among the ancient, pre-Israelite inhabitants of the land of burying the corpses of little children beneath the thresholds of their homes.[25] These can hardly have been in every instance foundation sacrifices, for they seem to have been too numerous for such use. Rather, in all probability, these infants had died before they could be redeemed, either by circumcision or by the sacrifice of the first hair or by some other parallel ceremony, and therefore were not yet "blood-kinsmen," *ḥatᵉne damîm;* thus their bodies could not be consigned to the regular clan or tribal burying-place. Now we have seen that the threshold was regarded as the place where household spirits resided, also as the place where the approach of evil spirits should be checked. It was upon the threshold, as we have noted, that the Paschal lamb was sacrificed in order to protect the first-born within the house from the threatening *mašḥît* without. What place, accordingly, more appropriate than beneath the threshold for the burial of the bodies of the little ones who had died unredeemed, whose lives had been claimed by these evil spirits, especially the dread *mašḥît,* as their own? This was tantamount to actually turning the little corpse over to the powerful spirit which had claimed it. But if this chain of argument is correct, it points again to the conclusion that some intimate connection existed between these spirits—especially the *mašḥît,* the ghost of the dead—and the birth of children.

There can be only one conclusion. If at the annual Passover-*ḍaḥîyyeh* festival first-born and firstling sacrifices were offered for the redemption of all future offspring of the same mothers, if likewise at this festival children were circumcised and thereby redeemed in a different manner, and if at this same festival maidens, clad in borrowed garments, danced their peculiar, sacred dances in anticipation of approaching marriage and eventual motherhood, the conclusion is unavoidable that originally all these sacrifices were offered to, and these ceremonies were performed in honor of, the ghosts of dead relatives and ancestors.

From this it would follow logically that the earliest Semites, in the remote, prehistoric period of animistic belief, must have conceived of the ghosts of their dead kinsmen as powerful spirits, who presided in particular over the critical moments of life within the family, clan, or tribe—over birth, the attainment of puberty, marriage, and death. It was these spirits who apparently were thought, in the early period of Semitic cultural evolution, to cause the sheep, goats, and camels of the clan or tribe to give birth. And to them, therefore, at the proper moment the firstlings were offered as a taboo-sacrifice to redeem the flocks and herds from the possession of their supernatural creators and to permit their use and increase for the satisfaction of the needs of clan or tribal life.

It was likewise these spirits of the dead who caused the birth of children within the family or clan; or, if not quite that, who were thought at least to have power over the lives of infants, particularly the first-born, especially during the first seven days after birth and again at the time of the annual Passover-*ḍaḥîyyeh* festival. From their power these children had to be redeemed at the proper moment by means of the established ceremonial, in order that they might live and participate in, and thereby strengthen, the ordinary, profane clan or tribal existence.

It was these same spirits of the dead who apparently also had power over the maidens of the clan or family, who had first claim upon their virginity from the moment of the attainment of puberty until the actual consummation of the marriage, or perhaps even until the birth of the first child. And from their power these maidens had to be redeemed at the attainment of puberty, again at marriage, and finally at the birth of children, particularly of the first child, through the performance, either by them or on their behalf, of the proper, traditional ceremonies and the offering of the conventional sacrifices.

And finally, when death expelled the spirit from its earthly home, and the body lay cold and still, the disembodied spirit hovered about the corpse or the tomb, trying to re-enter its former home, until at the end of a full year, realizing at last the futility of its efforts, it wended its way to its final dwelling place, the nether world. One new member was added to the countless ranks of the ghosts of the dead, one new spirit but recently departed and vividly remembered by the living, and therefore all the more to be feared and placated and guarded against. Hence the speedy burial with all its peculiar rites; hence, too, the countless and varied rites of mourning; and hence, also, the peculiar ceremonies at the annual festival, when the spirits of the dead were thought to return for that one night.

Just because of the actuality of their former existence and association with the living, these ghosts of dead kinsmen were regarded by the primitive Semites as the most real, powerful, and omnipresent of all spirits, with something akin to individuality and personality, likewise with closer and more compelling relations with the living, whose former kinsmen they were, than with people with whom they had had no personal association during life. Therefore they would be more dangerous under certain conditions, more beneficent under other conditions, than spirits of other kinds and classes. Ordinarily, it seems, these ghosts were regarded as hostile, maleficent spirits, whose rights had to be scrupulously recognized, whose attacks had to be guarded against, who had to be placated in every way possible, and to whom due honor had to be paid. But if accorded all this in proper and generous manner, they could be changed into kindly disposed, beneficent spirits, who, instead of a curse, would bring benefit and blessing, *baraka,* upon the living. They could even be compelled, by the proper performance of certain rites, to function in behalf of the living. They could be summoned from their abode in the nether world and be made to reveal things unknown and incomprehensible to the little minds of mortal man.[26]

These concepts, strange though they may seem, not only to the ordinary reader but also to the conventional student of Semitic religion, are not without precedent and parallel in other primitive religions. Paton has pointed out[27] that among the ancient Greeks the spirits of the dead were thought to give offspring to the living. The Babylonians too, among the Semitic peoples, conceived of the spirits, or gods of fertility, as dwelling in the nether world, the realm of the dead.[28] In all probability, the Semites must in the very earliest times have identified the two mysteries of birth and death and have believed that it was these ghosts of the dead who caused the earth to bear her produce and, in still more primitive belief, both animals and human beings to give birth to young.

Is this, then, to be identified with ancestor-worship? And shall we say that the early Semites, in common with so many other primitive peoples, worshiped the spirits of the dead? It can mean nothing else. Not that the primitive Semites believed that the ghosts of the dead were the only powerful, supernatural agencies who controlled all the circumstances and destinies of human life. There is ample evidence that they conceived also of spirits of other categories, dwelling in various places and objects—in trees, in springs, in stones of unusual size and appearance—spirits with varying powers and discharging various functions, and therefore to be feared, placated, and worshiped in manifold ways. But among these supernatural beings, and certainly not the least real among them in power and in potential animosity or friendship, and therefore not the least to be feared, placated, and worshiped, were the ghosts of the dead. We may not say that the religious belief and practice of the primitive Semites consisted solely of ancestor-worship. But we must certainly conclude that in primitive Semitic religious belief and practice ancestor-worship, the cult of the spirits of the clan dead, played a large and conspicuous role.[29]

XVI

Conclusion

This has been a lengthy and detailed investigation and it has led far afield. But it has established various facts of significance for the history of Semitic religion in general and especially for the history of the religion of Israel and of the Judaeo-Christian heritage therefrom, and of Islam, and of many of the conventional ritual practices of these religions in the present day.

It has established in particular that the religion of the Semitic peoples began with animism, the belief in spirits. Long before the Semitic mind conceived of gods, and especially of gods of supreme, world-wide power, spirits were thought to be swarming everywhere, incorporeal, unsubstantial beings, for the most part hostile to men and intent upon their hurt. Some of these spirits were impersonal beings; but in large measure these spirits were the souls, the intangible personalities, of dead relatives, persisting after death and maintaining a close and active contact with their living kinsmen, a contact which was perhaps benevolent to some small extent, but which in the main was compelling and threatening in its demands upon the living, and which on the whole was far more of a burden, or even a constant danger, than it was a happy promise of potential blessing.

For the most part, the relations of these ghosts were with individuals or small groups of people, with clans, or, eventually, with families. In fact, the belief in spirits, in a positive sense, was, so it seems, current and active primarily in that earliest stage of Semitic cultural evolution when *beena* marriage prevailed, and the clan was the normal unit of social organization. During this period the very first Semites roamed as nomads through the vast stretches of the Arabian Desert and derived a meager and precarious living from their scanty flocks and the sparse products of occasional oases, with the food supply in consequence adequate for only a limited population, and the normal folk unit, the clan, therefore relatively small in size.

In time, however, with the gradual settlement of Semitic clans in the comparatively fertile lands which border the Arabian Desert, the evolution of Semitic agricultural civilization began. As the food supply became more and more abundant, stable, and varied, a much larger population and larger folk units could be sustained, with people dwelling closely together in fixed abodes in villages and towns, and, consequently, with a much more rapidly evolving culture. Now with the resultant transition from *beena* to *ba'al* marriage and the evolution of the tribe, and eventually of the nation, as the larger folk unit, and of the family, under the headship of the father, as the smaller, constituent unit, the concept of gods, as contrasted with spirits, gods personal and name-bearing, with relations not only with individuals but also with the larger folk unit, began to evolve. Along with this, so it would seem, came the birth and the expansion of the concept of the universe as a whole, as the maximum unit of existence, and with this of the activities of the gods, as contrasted with those of the spirits, as the controllers and administrators of the various constituent parts of the universe and of their functions, of the sun, the moon, the planets, the rain, the wind, the vegetation, and the like, and all this in behalf of mankind as a whole. This development of the concept of gods, as contrasted with spirits, marked the birth of positive religion as contrasted with what may well be called negative religion, with the protection and prospering of mankind as the particular function of these gods, as contrasted with the endangering and harming of men as the work of spirits. This seems, speaking broadly, to have gone hand in hand among the early Semites with the transition from *beena* to *ba'al* marriage and the attendant cultural reorganization of society.

And as nations grew and expanded and international relations began to evolve, as society developed and human culture progressed, the belief in spirits, and especially evil spirits, receded more and more into the background. As we have seen, many beliefs, rites, and institutions whose origin was in the cult of the spirits gradually took on new form and meaning and became incorporated into the content and formal expression of positive religion in doctrine, ceremony, and ritual. Other beliefs and rites of like origin died out completely. Still others lived on in conventional manner, partly as superstitions and partly as customs and institutions invested in varying degree with new meaning and purpose. Even a religious institution so fundamental as the Sabbath day had its origin, as we have learned, in the connection of the number seven with the belief in and the cult of spirits.

But its origin is only one moment in the history of a religious doctrine or rite, an important moment, it is true, one which frequently gives content and imparts direction to the subsequent evolution. But it is only one moment, nevertheless; and history consists of an endless succession of important moments. Doctrines and ceremonies must be evaluated, not only by what they were and meant at the moment of origin, but also, and even more, by what they grew into and came to mean at every stage of their history, and, above all else, by what they are and mean today and may become and mean tomorrow. As the flower springs from the soil, so the most exalted ceremony or doctrine, richest in inspiration and uplift, may have its roots in the most primitive and abhorrent belief and practice. What more loathsome to our modern sense than the prostitution of women in the name of religion? Yet it marked one stage in the evolution of civilization and in the gradual elevation of the position of woman from the sex relations of savagery to the equality, dignity, and respect which she enjoys today. Or what more horrifying than child-sacrifice? Yet this institution, too, marked a stage in the evolution of the human family. To have left these stages far behind and to have reached the concepts which we cherish today of the position of women, of the sanctity of human life, and of the abundant meaning and rich blessing of the family relationship are the best indications of the progress of civilization through time and history. They tell in new terms that there are divine wisdom and purpose, which lead man on and on to ultimate truth and good. They tell, too, that we do not stand still even for a moment; and they bid us expect and plan for a tomorrow for our children and our children's children as much brighter and richer than today in knowledge, in vision, in hope, and in faith as our today surpasses the yesterday of our primitive ancestors.

Chapter Notes

Notes to Chapter II

1. Samter, *Geburt, Hochzeit und Tod;* Scheftelowitz, *Das stellvertretende Huhnopfer,* p. 7.
2. Abēla, "Beiträge zur Kenntniss abergläubischer Gerbräuche in Syrien," *ZDPV,* VII (1884), 79–118.
3. Featherman, *The Aramaeans,* p. 64.
4. *Niniveh and Its Remains,* I, 228.
5. *Ibid.,* I, 248.
6. Newman, *Babylon and Niniveh,* p. 399.
7. Menzel, "Ein Beitrag zur Kenntniss der Jeziden," in Grote, *Meine Vorderasienexpedition,* I, 144, 156.
8. Pierotti, *Customs and Traditions of Palestine,* p. 191.
9. G. Wad-el-Ward, *Palestine through the Eyes of a Native,* p. 68.
10. Hardy, *The Unvarying East,* p. 69.
11. Canaan, "The Child in Palestinian Arab Superstition," *JPOS,* VII (1927), 163.
12. "The Curse in Palestinian Folk-Lore," *JPOS,* XV (1935), 257.
13. Bauer, *Volksleben im Lande der Bibel,* p. 59; so also Whiting, "Village Life in the Holy Land," *NGM,* (1914), p. 261.
14. Grant, *The Peasantry of Palestine,* p. 66.
15. Wilson, *Peasant Life in the Holy Land,* p. 89.
16. It is referred to also in the Talmud (Šab. 129b), and seems therefore to have been practiced in Palestine uninterruptedly through the centuries.
17. For the widespread use of the sieve in ceremonies such as this, cf. Fehrle, "Das Sieb im Volksglauben," *ARW,* XIX (1916), 547–551; cf. also Scheftelowitz, *Alt-Palästinensischer Bauernglaube,* pp. 65 f.; Blackman, *The Fellaḥin of Upper Egypt,* pp. 63, 79; Westermarck, *Ritual and Belief in Morocco,* II, 390, 402.
18. Klunzinger, *Upper Egypt, Its People and Products,* pp. 185–187.
19. *Arabian Society in the Middle Ages,* pp. 186–192; cf. also *The Manners and Customs of the Modern Egyptians,* pp. 467 f.
20. A. Bel, "La Population Mussulman de Tlemcen," *RES,* I (1908), 214 f.

21. Jaussen, *Naplouse,* pp. 33–35.

22. Garnett, *The Women of Turkey and Their Folklore,* II, 473–476.

23. *Ibid.,* II, 243–246.

24. From Socin, *Diwan aus Centralarabien,* p. 40; 1, 10, the inference may be drawn that among the Bedouin the custom of binding a cloth around the arm of the child immediately after birth was practiced fairly generally. This partook probably of the character of a talisman to guard against evil spirits.

25. Adams, *Darkness and Daybreak,* pp. 120 ff., 231.

26. "To defend themselves from a Jinnee . . . the Arabs often exclaim, 'Iron! Iron!' . . . or 'Iron, thou unlucky!' as Jinn are supposed to have a great dread of that metal" (Lane, *Arabian Society in the Middle Ages,* pp. 36 f.). Among the nomad Bedouin a piece of steel is placed at the side of the newborn babe; Dickson, *The Arab of the Desert,* pp. 160, 175; cf. also Basset, *Le Culte des Grottes au Maroc,* p. 65; Stevens, *Folk-Tales of Iraq,* pp. 22, 293 f. Already among the ancient Assyrians iron and bronze played a distinct role in magical rites; Ebeling, "Aus dem Tagewerk eines assyrischen Zauberpriesters," *MAOG,* V (1931), 3.

27. Cf. Samter, *Geburt, Hochzeit und Tod,* pp. 151–161; Jirku, *Materialien zur Volksreligion Israels,* pp. 13–20; Bertholet, *Kulturgeschichte Israels,* p. 116 and note 15. Many instances of the use of salt for this purpose in the Semitic world can be cited. Pococke says (*Travels,* in *A Compendium of the Most Approved Modern Travels,* II, 38): "The Egyptians are very credulous with respect to talismans, charms and every species of magic. Should you praise one of their children without blessing it, they are sure to suspect that you mean it no good, and immediately use some superstitious ceremonies to prevent the effects of the evil eye; one of these is throwing salt in the fire."

Elsewhere (*Arabian Society in the Middle Ages,* p. 269, note 1), Lane says that at funerals "Two customs, viz., tying the toes of a corpse and placing a knife, or rather a sword, upon the body, are still common in some Moslem countries, but I did not hear of their being observed in Egypt, nor the custom of putting salt with knife or sword." Iron and salt are both believed to repel genii and to prevent their approach, and hence, perhaps, are thus used. (So also Baldensperger, "Peasant Folklore of Palestine," *PEF* [1893], p. 205.) It is a Sunna ordinance among the Moslems that corpses must be washed in salt water in order to preserve them longer from turning to dust (Clerk, *Ilam-En-Nas,* p. 135). Probably the real reason for this custom is to reduce the power of the danger from the evil spirit or spirits associated with the dead body. That salt played a role, at least occasionally, in the funeral rites of ancient Israel may be inferred from the provision that a dying man might not be moved or placed upon sand or salt until the life had departed completely from his body (*Semaḥôt* I, 3). It is a common superstition among some Jews in many parts of the world still today that salt can repel evil spirits or the evil eye or avert evil influences (*JE,* X, 661; Lauterbach, "The Ceremony of Breaking a Glass at Weddings," *HUCA,* II [1925], 357 f.).

Similarly in Palestine during the marriage procession of the bride to the house of the bridegroom salt is frequently cast upon the heads of those in the procession to guard against the evil eye (Rothstein, "Moslemische Hochzeitsgebräuche," *PJB* (1910), p. 21; Bauer, *Volksleben im Lande der Bibel,* p. 199).

Likewise in Mecca (Snouck Hurgronje, *Mekka,* II, 141 ff.) at a circumcision, big drums are beaten in the street in front of the house in which the circumcision is to take place. The obvious purpose of this ceremony is to frighten off the evil spirits by means of the deafening noise. Then the boys who are to be circumcised are led through the streets on horseback. At their head rides the boy whose father is to pay the costs of the entire operation and the attendant ceremonies and festivities. Immediately in front of him marches an old black female slave of his father, usually she who has had most to do with the lad's upbringing. Upon her head she carries a large, metal firepan in which, upon the wood of the fire, *Fasūch* (an ill-smelling resin) mixed with salt is laid and is constantly replenished. The burning of this causes a loud crackling and a very bad odor. It is thought that this will render harmless the evil eye, so greatly feared, especially upon occasions such as this.

In Mecca a standard remedy against the evil eye is fumigation with an ill-smelling resin mixed with salt and burned in a firepan. The bewitched person fumigates his hands, face, and feet three times, and then steps over the pan seven times so that the smoke may saturate him thoroughly; for further results, he puts his trust in God (*ibid.,* II, 122). In Northern Africa both salt and alum are used to ward off the evil eye (Doutté, *Magie et Religion dans l'Afrique du Nord,* p. 324). Likewise, at the setting out of an Ababde caravan in Upper Egypt, "just before the lading commenced, the Ababde women appeared with earthen vessels in their hands, filled with burning coals. They set them before the several loads, and threw salt upon them. At the rising of the bluish flame, produced by the burning of the salt, they exclaimed, 'May you be blessed in going and coming.' The devil and every evil genius are thus, they say, removed" (Burckhardt, *Travels in Nubia,* p. 169). In Southern Palestine the Terâbîn and the Ẓullam bring salt from Sabha and from the Dead Sea. When they buy salt, they take a handful, spread it out in the tent, and say, "O God, grant us freedom from trouble" (Musil, *Arabia Petraea,* III, 146). Moreover, the unique character of salt may be inferred from the fact that among the Bedouin it is never stolen, nor is the salt merchant ever touched. Of him the Bedouin say, "Whoever robs him Allah will rob" (*ibid.,* pp. 146 f.).

In Northern Abyssinia one of the ceremonies performed upon the day of the reappearance of the new moon is this: the women take a few grains of salt with their finger tips and pour them into the fires upon their hearths. As the grains of salt split with a cracking sound and fly up in the air, they say, "May he who is envious of our herds and our children also split into pieces" (Littmann, "Sternensagen und Astrologisches aus Nordabessinien," *ARW,* XI [1908], 314.

Interestingly enough, Kahle records just the opposite practice. He tells (*PJB,* VII [1911], 109) that in driving out evil spirits, among other details of the ceremony, the sick person is given food from which salt has purposely been omitted. Possibly the principle underlying this practice is that in such ceremonies the salt belongs entirely to the evil spirits, and therefore must not be eaten or enjoyed by mortals. In none of the salt ceremonies cited above is the salt eaten by human beings. Likewise in the *Peḥta,* the bread of the Mandaean eucharist, no salt may be used (Brandt, *Mandäische Religion,* p. 109). According to Basset (*Le Culte des Grottes au Maroc*, pp. 90, 93, *et passim*), salt may under no condition be used in sacrifices to the *jann*.

For further instances of the use among the Semites of salt to ward off evil spirits, cf. Blackman, *op. cit.*, p. 220; Scheftelowitz, *Alt-Palästinensischer Bauernglaube*, pp. 78 f.; Trachtenberg, *Jewish Magic and Superstition*, p. 160; and, above all, Westermarck, *Ritual and Belief in Morocco*, Index under "salt." Behrens (*Assyrisch-Babylonische Briefe Kultischen Inhalts*, p. 18) records the use of salt in an Assyrian rite of exorcism of the eighth century B.C.

Supplementary accounts of birth rites among modern Semitic peoples, which, however, while corroborating fully, actually add little to the material cited above, may be found in Goodrich-Freer, *Arabs in Tent and Town*, pp. 62, 67, 78, 305; Blackman, *op. cit.*, pp. 68–86; Jaussen, *Naplouse*, pp. 31–41; Canaan, "Mohammedan Saints and Sanctuaries in Palestine," *JPOS*, V (1925), 196.

Notes to Chapter III

1. *Arabia Petraea*, III, 215 ff.
2. Offered at the annual festival of the dead; cf. Musil, *op. cit.*, III, 451 ff.; Jaussen, *Coutumes des Arabes au pays de Moab*, pp. 371 ff.; and below, pp. 126 ff., 133.
3. *The Manners and Customs of the Rwala Bedouins*, p. 243; cf. also, by the same author, *In the Arabian Desert*, p. 98; also Raswan, *The Black Tents of Arabia*, p. 56.
4. *Primitive Semitic Religion Today*, pp. 178, 200 ff.; in the German translation of this work, pp. 201, 231 ff.
5. Jaussen, *op. cit.*, pp. 55 f. In a footnote Jaussen shows that camel-urine is apparently thought to possess magical properties and is therefore effective in warding off evil spirits.
6. For the meaning of *'aḳîḳah*, cf. below, pp. 36 ff.
7. Not impossibly also, the blood upon the child's forehead partakes somewhat of the nature of a deceit practiced upon a gullible deity, making it seem that the child itself has actually been sacrificed, and that this is its own blood. For a concrete and illuminating discussion of this important subject of redemption by substitution, or *fedû*, cf. Curtiss, *op. cit.*, pp. 194 ff. (English ed.); pp. 226 ff. (German ed.); also Jaussen, *op. cit.*, pp. 362 f.

Notes to Chapter IV

1. So also Bertholet, *Kulturgeschichte Israels*, p. 48.
2. "Eisen als Schutz gegen Dämonen," *ARW*, X (1907), 43; cf. also Scheftelowitz, "Die Sündentilgung durch Wasser," *ARW*, XVII (1914), 405, 412, and the reference cited there; Canaan, *Aberglaube und Volksmedezin im Lande der Bibel*, pp. 84, 90. That the same practice was observed in ancient Israel is clear from the reference to it in *Tôsefta Šabbat*, VI (ed. Zuckermandel), 117, 26), where the custom is denounced as of heathen origin (cf. also *Pesaḥîm* 112a). In Israel dur-

ing the same period the kindred custom of fastening a piece of iron to the bed of a woman in childbirth was known, but was frowned upon as being of heathen origin and nature (*Tôsefta, ibid.*, p. 11; cf. Krauss, *Talmudische Archäologie*, II, 7, and *JE*, article, "Childbirth," IV, 28 ff.; Blau, *Das altjüdische Zauberwesen*, pp. 159 f.; Trachtenberg, *Jewish Magic and Superstition*, Index under "iron." Likewise, for the use of iron among Semitic peoples, ancient and modern, to ward off evil spirits, cf. Ebeling, *Aus dem Tagewerk eines assyrischen Zauberpriesters*, pp. 29, 44; Westermarck, *Ritual and Belief in Morocco*, II, Index under "iron"; Stevens, *Folk-Tales of Iraq*, XVI, 22, 293 f.; Basset, *Le Culte des Grottes au Maroc*, p. 65; Thomas, *Arabia Felix*, p. 209; Stephan, in *JPOS*, XII [1932], 64, note 3).

3. Samter, *Geburt, Hochzeit und Tod*, p. 132.

4. Luncz, "The Customs of Our Brethren in the Holy Land" (Hebrew), *Jerusalem*, I (1886), 2, 27.

5. Garnett, *The Women of Turkey and Their Folklore*, II, 22.

6. "Palestinian Animal Folk-Lore," *PEF* (1904), p. 266.

7. Cf. Isa. 34 : 14, a passage coming from the second quarter of the fifth century B.C.; also Syr. Apoc. Bar. 10, 8.

8. Cf. *JE*, IV, 30; VIII, 87 f.; Grunwald, in *MGWJ*, LXXVII (1933), 244; Trachtenberg, *op. cit.*, index under "Lilith."

9. Goodrich-Freer, *Arabs in Tent and Town*, p. 67.

10. Cf. Zimmern and Winckler, in *Die Keilinschriften und das Alte Testament*, p. 460.

11. *Midrash Rabba* to Num. 16, ed. Wilna, p. 119, col. 4.

12. *'Erubin* 100b.

13. Baldensperger, "Peasant Folklore of Palestine," *PEF* (1893), pp. 206 f.; "The Immovable East," *PEF* (1910), p. 89; Bliss, *The Religions of Modern Syria and Palestine*, p. 290; Jaussen, *Coutumes des Arabes au pays de Moab*, p. 30; *Naplouse*, p. 35; Canaan, *op. cit.*, pp. 23 f., 48; also in *JPOS*, III (1923), 125; VI (1926),57; VII (1927), 171, 181, 185; XI (1931), 130–138; Klunzinger, *Upper Egypt, Its People and Products*, pp. 185, 383; Blackman, *The Fellaḥin of Upper Egypt*, pp. 54, 65, 68–75, 102; Westermarck, *op. cit.*, I, 402.

14. Cf. Canaan, *Dämonenglaube im Lande der Bibel*, pp. 47 ff.; Grunwald, in *MGWJ*, pp. 241–245. In the superstitions of Egypt and Northern Africa, Karīneh seems to manifest some relationship to the ancient Egyptian concept of the *ka*, or the soul-being of a person; cf. Blackman, *op. cit.*, pp. 68–75; Westermarck, *op. cit.*, I, 402, note 1.

15. Cf. Zwemer, *Arabia the Cradle of Islam*, p. 203; Jaussen, *Naplouse*, p. 35; Canaan, *Aberglaube und Volksmedezin im Lande der Bibel*, p. 27; *Dämonenglaube im Lande der Bibel*, p. 49; Westermarck, *op. cit.*, I, 400 f.

16. *Mekka*, II, 124.

17. *Magie et Religion dans l'Afrique du Nord*, pp. 112 f., 115 ff.

18. *Ibid.*, p. 221, note 1.

19. Westermarck, *op. cit.*, I, 400.

20. *Op. cit.*, I, 401; II, 382.

21. Canaan, "Mohammedan Saints and Sanctuaries in Palestine," *JPOS*, VI (1926), 133; *Aberglaube und Volksmedezin im Lande der Bibel*, p. 32; "The Palestinian Arab House," *JPOS*, XIII (1933), 27.

22. Canaan, "The Child in Palestinian Arab Superstition," *JPOS,* VII (1927), 181.

23. Musil, *The Manners and Customs of the Rwala Bedouins,* p. 416.

24. *Ibid.,* p. 417.

25. Cf. Myhrman, "Die Labartu Texte," *ZA,* XVI (1902), 141–200, and particularly pp. 180–181, lines 33–36; Thompson, *Semitic Magic,* p. 41 f.

26. Thonnelier, *Le Livre des Dames de la Perse,* I, 76 ff.; cf. also Grünbaum, "Beiträge zur vergleichenden Mythologie aus der Hagada," *ZDMG,* XXXI (1877), 335. According to Stevens (*Folk-Tales of Iraq,* XVII), in Armenian folk tales *Ḳarīnah* is usually called the *Al,* and is directly related to the ancient Akkadian *c rdat Lilî.*

Notes to Chapter V

1. Above, pp. 15 f. Among various tribes or folk groups of Morocco the third day after birth plays a role of considerable importance. Upon this day the mother is painted with henna, and the child also is frequently so treated. Upon this day, too, the mother rises from her bed, presents are given to the child, it receives its name, and, in connection with this ceremony, a sheep is sacrificed. Also the mother's first milk is given to the child upon either the third or the eighth day (Westermarck, *Ritual and Belief in Morocco,* II, 384, 391, 392, 396, 397, 400).

2. Baldensperger, "Woman in the East," *PEF* (1901), pp. 262 f.; cf. also Westermarck, *op. cit.,* II, 386–398; Rutter, *The Holy Cities of Arabia,* II, 60 f.; Blackman, *The Fellaḥin of Upper Egypt,* p. 80.

3. Cf. above, p. 15.

4. *Sanhedrin* 32b; *Jer. Ketûbôt* I, 25c; cf. Levy, *Neuhebräisches und chaldäisches Wörterbuch,* I, 238b, and IV, 499b. *Babba Qama* 80a, and *Babba Batra* 60b, give *yešûʿa haben* as the equivalent of, or variant for, *šᵉbûʿa haben.* Etymologically at least, this term, if it is correct, designated the act of circumcision as a "deliverance of the son"; but, deliverance from what? we may well ask. Cf. also Mann, in *HUCA,* I (1924), 324 ff.; Bergman, in *MGWJ,* LXXVI (1932), 465–467; Press, *ibid.,* p. 575. In Morocco, too, the day is known, with minor dialectic variations among the different tribes, as "the day of the seven" (Westermarck, *op. cit.,* II, 387, 389, 391, 392, 394, 408).

5. Daumas, *La Femme Arabe,* pp. 6 ff.

6. *Ibid.,* pp. 88 ff.; cf. the Biblical provisions for a domestic animal upon the eighth day after birth, recorded in Exod. 22 : 29; Lev. 22 : 27.

7. Featherman, *The Aramaeans,* p. 650.

8. Palmer, *The Desert of the Exodus,* p. 84.

9. The material immediately following is cited from Westermarck, *op. cit.,* II, 370–433; cf. also Blackman, *op. cit.,* pp. 68–79, 121, 287; Klunzinger, *Upper Egypt, Its People and Products,* p. 186; Scheftelowitz, *Die altpersische Religion und das Judentum,* p. 70; Palmer, *op. cit.,* p. 84.

10. *Op. cit.,* p. 394.

11. Cf. Johnson, "Here and There in Northern Africa," *NGM,* XXV, No. 1 (January, 1914), 32b; also Nilsson in *ARW,* XIV (1911), 425, note 2, and the references there cited.

12. Baldensperger, "The Immovable East," *PEF* (1910), p. 259.

13. Of the number five, Canaan says (*Aberglaube und Volksmedezin im Lande der Bibel,* p. 94): "The number five is greatly feared and we have seen how it is frequently avoided. Often, and especially in North Syria, but also in Palestine, this fear extends also to manifestations of five. For this reason, the number five and the hand have a certain mysterious relationship. In representations of the 'hand' (cf. *ibid.,* p. 64) the number five finds its application in the superstition of amulets." Elsewhere (*ibid.,* p. 48), Canaan tells how the utterance of the number five is avoided when inquiry is made concerning the age of a child who happens to be five years old. "The mysterious relationship between the dread number five and the age of a child, or the supernatural powers [connected therewith], I am unable to explain. Often short formulas are employed [in answer to the question; How old is the child?], such as *ʿadad aṣâbîʿak* or *ʿadad idêk,* 'the number of your fingers' or 'the number of (what is upon) your hand.' From this it is apparent how greatly feared is the number five, and how one seeks to avoid pronouncing it." Cf. also Doutté, *Magie et Religion dans l'Afrique du Nord,* p. 327; Westermarck, *op. cit.,* II, 239 ff.

14. Wilson, *Peasant Life in the Holy Land,* pp. 212 f.; cf. Frazer, *Folk-lore in the Old Testament,* II, 559. For the observance of the same custom in the province of Oran in Algeria, cf. Doutté, *op. cit.,* p. 180. For the general fear of attracting evil spirits at the measuring of the grain, and with this the possible need of employing unlucky numbers, and the precaution taken by the fellahin against this, cf. Musil, *Arabia Petraea,* III, 305 f.

15. Cf. Morgenstern, "The Doctrine of Sin in the Babylonian Religion," *MVAG,* III (1905), 11; Grimme, *Das altisraelitische Pfingstfest und der Pleiadenkult,* p. 40. The natives of modern Palestine likewise know of seven evil spirits. They control the seven planets and the seven days of the week. But corresponding to them and contending against them and combating their evil designs are the seven good spirits or angels, who also rule the planets and the days of the week (Canaan, *op. cit.,* pp. 7, 22 f., 94).

16. Brünnow, *List of Ideographs;* no. 12,195.

17. Cf. Morgenstern, *op. cit.,* p. 90; Hehn, *Siebenzahl und Sabbat bei den Babyloniern und im Alten Testament,* p. 25.

18. Cory, *Ancient Fragments,* p. 19.

19. In this connection, Movers (*Die Phönizier,* I, 530) very properly quotes the Roman superstition with regard to the seven stars of the Great Dipper cited by Ovid (*Fasti* iv.70), "Quae septem dici, sex tamen esse solent."

20. Deut. 7 : 1; Josh. 3 : 10; 24 : 11.

21. It is significant, however, that with the exception of but five passages in which the Massoretic text mentions the names of only six of the seven traditional, pre-Israelite nations of Palestine, *G* contains all seven names, although in two passages, Exod. 34 : 11 and Josh. 9 : 1, the order of the names in *G* differs from that of the Massoretic text. Of the five passages in which *G* also contains only six names, in four (Deut. 20 : 17; Josh. 12 : 8; Judg. 3 : 5 [all these

passages are Deuteronomic]; Neh. 9 : 8) the order of the names in both *MT* and *G* is the same, and in only one (Exod. 33 : 2, where *G* omits "the Canaanite" of *MT* and instead inserts "the Girgashite") is there any divergence in the content of the list and the order of the names. Moreover, Gen. 15 : 20 f., in a longer list of the pre-Israelite peoples of Palestine and the vicinity, mentions only six of the traditional seven nations, while *G* mentions all seven. It is clear from this that the regular enumeration of the seven names in *G* is due to emendation of the original Hebrew text, in accordance with the probable fact that the Jews of Alexandria, for whose use the *G* translation of the Bible was made, did not entertain the same superstition about the number seven as the Jews of Palestine obviously did, and so did not hesitate to supply in the majority of cases the name of the missing nation.

According to Eduard Meyer (*Die Israeliten und Ihre Nachbarstämme,* p. 331, note 1), the mention of the six names is original, and the addition of the seventh name, wherever it occurs, is in every case the work of the Deuteronomist. However, in the light of the evidence we have adduced bearing upon the widespread superstition among the Semites with regard to the use of the number seven, particularly in the enumeration of groups consisting of seven members, we may safely regard our conclusion as established, that already the older sources knew of seven nations, but, fearing the unlucky number seven, ventured to enumerate only six, and therefore purposely omitted one, usúally "the Girgashite."

22. *Voyages;* text and translation by Defrémery and Sanguinetti, I, 146.

23. *Arabic Proverbs,* V. In this connection, mention may also be made of the ninety-nine (i.e., the hundred less one) "beautiful names" of Allah, which play such an important role in Moslem theology; cf. Doutté, *Magie et Religion dans l'Afrique du Nord,* p. 199. According to Chwolsohn, *Die Ssabier und der Ssabismus,* II, 243 f. and 782, even numbers were frequently considered unlucky; cf. also Blau, *Das altjüdische Zauberwesen,* p. 77, and the Talmudic references there given.

24. A most illuminating and convincing instance of the purposed avoidance of the number seven, in one case by using six, and in the other, parallel case by using eight, is recorded in Brandt, *Die jüdischen Baptismen* (Beiheft zur *ZAW,* XVIII), pp. 105 f.

25. Cf. also Cruickshank, in Hastings, *ERE,* IX, 416, quoting Hilprecht. This may also account for the institution of the Sabbath every seventh day, originally a day of ill omen, probably thought to belong to the evil spirits, a day when therefore it was expedient to do no work. Hence the Babylonian designation of the seventh, fourteenth, nineteenth, twenty-first, and twenty-eighth days of the months Elul II and Marḫešwan as *ūmu limnu,* "evil day," and the prohibition of work upon these days (*IV R,* 32 and 33), and the further designation of each of these days as *ūm nūḫ libbi,* "day of appeasing the heart (of enraged and therefore hostile deities)"; cf. Zimmern and Winckler, *Die Keilinschriften und das Alte Testament*[3], pp. 592 ff.; Hehn, *Siebenzahl und Sabbat bei den Babyloniern und im Alten Testament,* pp. 106 ff.; Meinhold, *Sabbat und Woche im Alten Testament,* p. 18; Webster, *Rest Days,* pp. 223 ff.). By a natural expansion of the idea, the seventh year would similarly be regarded as unlucky and sub-

ject to the evil spirits, and therefore no agricultural labor would be performed in it (Exod. 23 : 10 f.; Lev. 25 : 1–7).

This suggests also that this evil import of the number seven was basic to the ancient, West Asiatic, agricultural calendar, the so-called "pentecontad calendar" (cf. J. and H. Lewy, "The Origin of the Week and the Oldest West Asiatic Calendar," *HUCA,* XVII [1942–43], 1–152*c*; also Morgenstern, "The Chanukkah Festival and the Calendar of Ancient Israel," *HUCA,* XXI [1948], 365–374; "The Calendar of the Book of Jubilees, Its Origin and Its Character," *VT,* V [1955], 34–76). This calendar divided the year into seven periods of fifty days each, seven pentecontads. Each pentecontad consisted of seven periods of seven days each, i.e., seven weeks, plus one extra day, the final, the fiftieth, day of this time-unit, a day which stood outside the week and was celebrated as the closing festival, the *ʿaṣeret,* of this pentecontad, and which accordingly bore its own distinctive festal name. At the end of the fourth and again at the end of the seventh pentecontad, i.e., then at the very end of the year, a festival of seven-days' duration was celebrated. These two festal weeks were not reckoned to any of the seven pentecontads, but were additional time-units within the year. And finally, the day immediately following the close of the second seven-days' festal period—in other words, the day following the formal close of the year—was a day of supreme sanctity. It, too, stood outside the week, and likewise was not reckoned to any one pentecontad but bore its own distinctive festal name. Upon it, the first day of the new year—the New Year's Day, in other words—the first sheaf of the grain crop of the new year was cut with fitting ritual celebration. Thus, this ancient agricultural calendar reckoned the year as of 365 days. In this calendar the seventh day of each week, and likewise, so it seems, every seventh year, were periods when no work whatsoever, except perhaps that which was absolutely essential to daily existence, was performed. Likewise, it is clear, within the year of this agricultural calendar the seventh pentecontad would coincide with the latter portion of the winter season, when agricultural activity was practically at a standstill. From all this evidence it is reasonable to assume that the primary import of the number seven basic to this calendar was that it was an evil number, probably related directly to evil spirits, who were themselves probably thought to be seven in number and to be particularly active and powerful during every seventh time-unit, whether day, week, pentecontad, or year.

In time, however, with cultural advancement and under the expanding influence of evolving Yahweh-religion, the significance of the number seven in Israel gradually underwent a complete transformation. The principle became established eventually that everything that came in groups of seven was pleasing to Yahweh, and therefore propitious, and of the seven members of such a group the seventh and last was the most propitious (cf. *Leviticus rabba* XXIX, 9 [ed. Wilna]). The most significant manifestation of this process of transformation was the new interpretation of the Sabbath, the seventh and final day of the week, as no longer an evil day, upon which the power of evil spirits was transcendent, but a day of good, pleasing unto Yahweh, and therefore hallowed by Him for His honor and worship. The abstention from work and consequent rest which characterized this day, originally out of a very lively fear of the evil spirits, was reinterpreted correspondingly as something commanded by Yahweh for His honor and glorification. A careful consideration of the Biblical evidence seems to indicate that this transformation did not take place, or at least was not completed, in Israel until the time of the Deuteronomic Reformation in 621 B.C.

26. In Palestine today the seventh, fourteenth, and twenty-first days, but especially the seventh, of every illness are regarded as of the deepest and most far-reaching import. On these days, and especially on the seventh, the patient may under no condition receive visits from friends (Canaan, *Aberglaube und Volksmedezin im Lande der Bibel,* p. 95).

27. Cf. Westermarck, *op. cit.,* pp. 384, 391, 392, 396, 397, 400; Jaussen, *Naplouse,* p. 37; Canaan, in *JPOS,* VII (1927), 165.

28. Granquist, *Birth and Childhood among the Arabs,* p. 100; cf. also pp. 104 f., 245.

29. Dickson, *The Arab of the Desert,* I, 173.

30. Jaussen et Savignac, *Coutumes des Fuqarâ.*

31. Jaussen, *Coutumes des Arabes au pays de Moab,* p. 56.

32. Schmidt and Kahle, "Volkserzählungen aus Palästina," *Forschungen zur Religion und Literatur des Alten und Neuen Testaments,* p. 196, note 10; Canaan, *Aberglaube und Volksmedezin im Lande der Bibel,* p. 37; "Unwritten Laws Affecting the Women of Palestine," *JPOS,* XI (1931), 195 f.; Stephan, "Studies in Palestinian Customs and Folklore," *JPOS,* VIII (1928), 214-222; Musil, *Arabia Petraea,* III, 208; Granquist, *op. cit.,* pp. 100, 104 f.

33. Bauer, *Volksleben im Lande der Bibel,* p. 198; Canaan, *op. cit.,* pp. 69, 128.

34. Cf. also Blackman, *op. cit.,* p. 76.

35. Dandini, in Paulus, *Sammlung der merkwürdigsten Reisen in den Orient,* II, 235.

36. DuBernat, in Paulus, *op. cit.,* IV, 254 f. According to Blackman (*op. cit.,* pp. 83 f.), among the Copts a boy is baptized and receives his name upon the fortieth day after birth, but a girl only upon the eightieth day.

37. Rathjens, *Die Juden in Abessinien,* p. 85.

38. Grant, *The Peasantry of Palestine,* p. 66. An especially interesting form of the baptism ceremony, in which salt plays a peculiar and significant role, is found in the ritual of the Syrian-Catholic (Jacobite) Church. "The priest takes the child from the hands of the godfather and godmother in the door of the church and carries him into the church, lays the child on a white veil on the floor, then prays over a handful of salt, and puts salt into the child's mouth. Then he pinches the child's nostrils, saying, 'Open, ye nostrils and inhale the heavenly odors!' "

39. Adams, *Darkness and Daybreak,* p. 231.

40. Doutté, *Merrâkech,* pp. 343, 348; Westermarck, *Ritual and Belief in Morocco,* II, 402.

41. Westermarck, *op. cit.,* II, 382, 395, 402; cf. also pp. 394, 398; cf. also Musil, *Arabia Petraea,* III, 208.

42. Featherman, *The Aramaeans,* p. 400; cf. Von Maltzan, *Mekka,* II, 131 f.

43. Crichton, *History of Arabia Ancient and Modern,* II, 224; Ali Bey, *Travels,* II, 129.

44. Snouck Hurgronje, *Mekka,* II, 120 f.

45. *Ibid.*, 140 f.; Rutter, *The Holy Cities of Arabia*, II, 62, 65. On this same ceremony, Canaan ("The Child in Palestinian Arab Superstition," *JPOS*, VII [1927], 167) offers the following interesting comment: "Palestinian women believe that the best way to decide whether a child is legitimate or not is that practiced in Mecca, namely, to lay the child, at its fortieth day, after washing it and dressing it in white after the evening prayer has been said, in the so-called Prophet's Niche, where it is left for three to five minutes. If it remains all the time quiet it is a legal child of its father; otherwise it is illegal and the poor mother is despised despite her innocence."

46. Cf. below, pp. 44 f.

47. In this light, the dictum of R. Simon b. Gamaliel becomes fully comprehensible: "A newborn child which lives for thirty days (based upon Num. 18 : 16) or an animal which lives for eight days (based upon Exod. 22 : 29; Lev. 22 : 27) should not be regarded as prematurely born"; in other words, it is thought that it will surely live a natural existence (*Jer. Yᵉbamot* XI, 12b; *Sabbat* 135b; cf. Aptowitzer, "The Rewarding and Punishing of Animals and Inanimate Objects," *HUCA*, III [1926], 126, note 21). Occasionally, too, in Northern Africa the period of possession of the child by, or its subjection to the power of, evil spirits, at least in some slight degree, seems to be thought to endure for seven years. Here and there in Morocco the child's hair is cut in ceremonial fashion, and sometimes for the very first time, at the end of the seventh year (Westermarck, *op. cit.*, II, 409). And in Upper Egypt, we are told (Blackman, *op. cit.*, p. 72; cf. also p. 73), "A woman's *karīneh* may do good or evil to her children till they have passed the age of seven years." In all likelihood such extension of this period of abnormal and uncertain existence of the child over a full seven years is due primarily to the supposed evil symbolism of the number seven rather than to any other, more fundamental consideration.

48. That with the eighth day a new period of life was thought to commence for the child may be inferred also from the following instance: Burckhardt (*Travels in Arabia*, I, 424 f.) tells that "the Sherifs, or descendants of Mohammed, resident at Mecca and in the neighborhood, who delight in arms and are often engaged in civil broils, have a practice of sending every male child, eight days after its birth, to some tent of the neighboring Bedouins, where it is brought up with the children of the tent, and educated like a true Bedouin for eight or ten years, or till the boy is able to mount a mare, when his father takes him back to his home. During the whole of the above period the boy never visits his parents, nor enters the town, except when in his sixth month; his foster-mother then carries him on a short visit to his family, and immediately returns with him to her tribe. The child is in no instance left longer than thirty days after his birth in the hands of his mother; and his stay among the Bedouins is sometimes prolonged till his thirteenth or fifteenth year."

Notes to Chapter VI

1. Cf. Morgenstern, "The Doctrine of Sin in the Babylonian Religion," *MVAG*, III (1905), 69 ff.

2. Cf. Additional Notes, A.

3. Samter, *Geburt, Hochzeit und Tod,* pp. 184 ff.

4. It is quite significant that Mālik in the *Muwaṭṭa* (ed. Zurqānī, 1280, IV, 116) regards circumcision and paring the nails as religious rites of the same nature, belonging to the domain of natural religion (*fiṭra*) (quoted from Margoliouth, article, "Circumcision, Muhammadan," in Hastings, *ERE*, III, 677*a*). Similarly, the pilgrim to Mecca, when donning the *iḥram,* or sacred garment, upon entering the consecrated territory, was required, among other rites, to cut the nails of his fingers and toes (Von Maltzan, *Meine Wallfahrt nach Mekka,* I, 175).

5. Num. 6 : 9 f.

6. Num. 19 : 11–19; cf. also 31 : 19, 24; Ezek. 44 : 26. For the same practice among the Falashas, cf. Epstein, *Eldad ha-Dani,* p. 172.

7. Lev. 15 : 19 ff.; cf. also Epstein, *op. cit.*

8. Lev. 15 : 13 ff.; cf. Num. 12 : 14 f.

9. Acts, 21 : 23–27.

10. Exod. 29 : 30, 35, 37; Lev. 8 : 33, 35; Ezek. 43 : 25 ff.; cf. also II Chron. 7 : 9.

11. It is significant that ceremonies almost identical in character and purpose were common in Babylonian religious practice. One text reads as follows (83-1-18, 37, Harper, *Letters*, p. 355; cf. Morgenstern, "The Doctrine of Sin . . .," pp. 138 f.; Hehn, *Siebenzahl und Sabbat bei den Babytoniern und im Alten Testament,* p. 43):

obverse

. . . Seven days
in the tent
shall he remain; expiatory rites
shall be performed; the prayer for him,
the ceremony for him, like that of a sick person
shall be performed.

reverse

During the seven days supplication
(offered) unto the gods of the night
and the NAM-BUR-BI rites for all kinds of evil
shall be performed together.
During the seven days which [he passes] within the tent prostrate
and submissive
to his god and his goddess
shall he show himself.
Just as
the king will now command
it shall be done.
The eighth day is favorable for performing [the rites].

It should be noted that this text states explicitly that these ceremonies, including probably the confinement in the tent for seven days, were the same as those performed on behalf of a sick person. It is likewise noteworthy that the number seven plays a conspicuous role in Babylonian ceremonies of expulsion of evil spirits and ritual purification (cf. Morgenstern, *op. cit.,* p. 128).

It may be added here that these NAM-BUR-BI rites, to which reference is made in this letter, played a very important role in Babylonian religio-magical practice (cf. Morgenstern, *op. cit.,* pp. 137 ff.). They were, beyond all question, ceremonies of purification, designed to remove all evil, particularly of a ritual nature. Analytically the ideogram NAM-BUR-BI designates these as rites for the removal of sin or death (cf. Brünnow, *A Classified List of All Simple and Compound Cuneiform Ideographs,* nos. 344, 2094, 2095, 2100, 2103). In view of the widespread belief in evil spirits current in ancient Assyria and Babylonia, we need not hesitate to infer that in origin these were taboo-rites primarily designed to expel evil spirits, and as such were closely related in form and content to parallel rites, such as we have already considered, practiced by other Semitic peoples for the same purpose.

12. Marett (*ARW,* XII [1909], 87 ff.) called this, respectively, "tabu" and "mana," and designated it as negative and positive modes of the supernatural. Webster says of it (*Rest Days,* p. 86): "As we pass from savagery to barbarism and from animism to polytheism, the notion of taboo, at first vague and indeterminate, tends to differentiate into the twin concepts of impurity and holiness. This differentiation, indeed, is never perfectly accomplished, even by peoples which have reached some measure of civilization; and the lower races find still greater difficulty in distinguishing between what is dangerous because polluted, and what is dangerous because sacred. The 'holy' thing and the 'unclean' thing possess alike the mystic potency, the magico-spiritual power." Cf. also Brandt, *Die jüdischen Baptismen* (*ZAW,* Beiheft XVIII), pp. 5 f., 12, 26, 123; Grüneisen, *Der Ahnenkultus und die Urreligion Israels,* pp. 91–94, 105 ff.

13. Num. 6 : 1–21.

14. Lev. 13–14.

15. Lev. 14 : 10–20; Num. 6 : 13–21.

16. Num. 19.

17. For this reason, the customary translation of *ṭame',* "unclean," hardly fits every Biblical passage in which the word occurs. It would be more correct to translate it simply "taboo," with the understanding that, while it usually designates subprofane taboo (i.e., ritual defilement), it does occasionally designate superprofane taboo (i.e., ritual sanctity) as well.

Notes to Chapter VII

1. *Reste des altarabischen Heidentums*[2], pp. 173 f.

2. The first food or object to pass the child's lips seems to have played a role of considerable importance in that it was thought to impart to the child certain qualities or powers which endured throughout life. Thus, we are told of the children of the Sinaitic Bedouin: "He, the manchild, has much before him, even before he tastes his mother's milk. If his parents wish him to be lucky through life, he must swallow a finely chopped feather of the long-

eared or eagle owl. This is mixed with milk, and the child has to swallow it. To become scorpion-proof the baby must also swallow, in the same way, the ashes of a burnt scorpion, which are mixed with milk and given to the child. Both these charms must be taken before anything has crossed his lips. This method of rendering a child invulnerable to the poison of scorpions is believed in by all, but, luckily for the babies, not always put into practice" (W. E. Jennings-Bramley, "The Bedouin of the Sinaitic Peninsula," *PEF* [1907], p. 22).

3. Westermarck, *Ritual and Belief in Morocco,* I, 41. For the magical power of saliva, either as a prophylactic or to drive out evil spirits, cf. *ibid.,* index under "spitting"; Doughty, *Travels in Arabia Deserta,* I, 527, II, 164; Ebeling, *Aus dem Tagewerk eines assyrischen Zauberpriesters, MAOG,* V (1931), 3, 14 f.; Blau, *Das altjüdische Zauberwesen,* pp. 162 f.; Trachtenberg, *Jewish Magic and Superstition,* pp. 120, 159, 162, 203; cf. also Mark 7 : 33; 8 : 23; John 9 : 6.

4. Westermarck, *op. cit.*, I, 41.

5. Above, p. 16.

6. Canaan, "The Child in Palestinian Arab Superstition," *JPOS*, VII (1927), 166.

7. Blackman, *The Fellaḥin of Upper Egypt,* p. 65.

8. Bacon (*Hibbert Journal* [Jan., 1919], p. 266, note 1) holds that the fundamental meaning of *ḥanak* is "to be narrow." Rankin (*The Origins of the Festival of Hanukkah: the Jewish New-Age Festival,* p. 28) contends that it is "to initiate; to begin." But from what has been established above, it is certain that neither interpretation reaches back to the commencement of the etymological evolution of the word and uncovers the interesting and significant ritual procedure implicit therein.

My good friend Dr. Joshua Finkel, an eminent Bible student and Arabist, has suggested to me in a letter that *ḥanîkâw* of Gen. 14 : 14, obviously a technical term, presumably of ancient origin, since it had to be interpreted by the gloss *yelîdê bêtô* ("those who were born in his household"), were those persons upon whom, as the head of the clan, Abraham had performed the rite of *taḥnîk*. If this explanation is correct—and it has much to commend it—then it would follow that this rite of *taḥnîk* must have been actively current in Israel, at least in the earliest period of its history.

Notes to Chapter VIII

1. Cf. Lane, *An Arabic-English Lexicon,* I, 2097a; Robertson Smith, *Kinship and Marriage in Early Arabia*², pp. 181 f.; *The Religion of the Semites*³, pp. 328 ff., 610; Nöldeke, in *ZDMG,* XL (1886), 184; Wellhausen, *Reste des altarabischen Heidentums*², p. 174; Doutté, *Magie et Religion dans l'Afrique du Nord*, p. 458; Kahle, in *PJB* (1912), 150–152; Westermarck, *Ritual and Belief in Morocco,* II, 397 f.

2. Apparently the ancient name *'aḳîḳah* is gradually falling into disuse in the language of ordinary Arabic life. Although the sacrifice upon the seventh day after birth is, as we have seen, referred to quite frequently, the name *'aḳîḳah* is used but rarely. By Doughty and Curtiss it is not used at all, and by Musil and Jaussen but once each, while Kahle seems to imply that *'aḳîḳah* is the official, theological name given to the sacrifice by Islam, and was borrowed from ancient, pre-Islamic usage, but is scarcely the term in common use today. In Morocco the sacrifice is usually called, with slight, dialectic variations, *s-saba'*, i.e., "the sacrifice of the seventh day" (cf. Westermarck, *op. cit.*, pp. 387–398, and especially p. 389). Seemingly this trend had commenced already in pre-Moslem times, for "Mohammed . . . preferred that the *'acîca* should be called *nasîka,* that is, simply 'a sacrifice' " (Robertson Smith, *Kinship and Marriage in Early Arabia*[2], p. 152).

3. Above, pp. 11, 17.

4. *Op. cit.*, p. 174; cf. also p. 121, note 2.

5. Doughty's own words are: "When a man child is born, the father will slay an ewe, but the female birth is welcomed in by no sacrifice" (*Arabia Deserta,* I, 452).

6. *Kinship and Marriage in Early Arabia*[2], pp. 152–154.

7. Above, p. 11; cf. also Curtiss, *op. cit.*, English edition, p. 158; German edition, pp. 177f.

8. Above, p. 15.

9. Above, p. 16.

10. *Op. cit.*, English edition, pp. 202 f.; German edition, p. 233.

11. Above, p. 12; also Westermarck, *Ritual and Belief in Morocco*, II, 379, 380, 412. For another form of the substitute sacrifice, likewise offered at Tlemcen, to protect the newborn child against evil spirits, cf. Doutté, *Magie et Religion dans l'Afrique du Nord,* p. 455.

12. *Op. cit.,* English edition, pp. 158, 202; German edition, pp. 177 f., 233.

13. *Naplouse,* pp. 37–39.

14. In this connection, it may be remarked that, according to Musil (*Arabia Petraea,* III, 219), even for an unweaned child which has died the *'aḳîḳah* sacrifice must still be offered. Not improbably, this is a survival of the original custom of offering the *'aḳîḳah* upon the seventh day to redeem the child, continued mechanically after the original purpose thereof had been largely forgotten, and it had come to be thought that upon the seventh day after birth of every child, whether living or dead, the sacrifice must be offered. Perhaps coupled with this is the additional thought that the *'aḳîḳah* was secondarily a redemption-sacrifice for the mother and even for the entire family or clan; consequently, even though the babe itself had died, the sacrifice must still be offered on behalf of the remaining kinfolk. Moreover, as we have seen, in Mecca the offering of the *'aḳîḳah* sacrifice is occasionally deferred until after the death of the person for whom it is given.

15. Snouck Hurgronje, *Mekka,* II, 138–140.

16. The practice, common among primitive peoples, of frightening off evil spirits by means of loud noises is so well attested that it will suffice here to illustrate the procedure among Semitic peoples by only a few instances: cf.

Midr. Lev. Rab. 24, par. 3; Doughty, *Arabia Deserta,* I, 289; Scheftelowitz, *Alt-Palästinensischer Bauernglaube,* pp. 76 f.; Westermarck, *Ritual and Belief in Morocco,* Index under "Noise."

17. Doutté, *Merrâkech,* pp. 341 f., 348 f.
18. *Ibid.,* p. 97.
19. *Ritual and Belief in Morocco,* II, 387–398.
20. *Op. cit.,* pp. 393, 402.
21. *The Nile Tributaries of Abyssinia,* p. 186.
22. Above, p. 29.
23. Cf. Lev. 17 : 11, 14; Deut. 12 : 23.
24. Cf. Nöldeke, in *ZDMG,* XL (1886), 184.
25. "Beiträge zur Kenntniss abergläubischer Gebräuche in Syrien," *ZDPV,* VII (1884), no. 27.
26. *Op. cit.,* German edition, pp. 189 f.; not in the English edition.
27. *PJB* (1912), pp. 150 ff., and below, p. 87.
28. *Op. cit.,* German edition, p. 218; not in the English edition.
29. Kahle, *PJB* (1912), p. 152.
30. Cf. below, pp. 100 ff., for a full discussion of this subject.
31. *Op. cit.,* p. 146.
32. Manifestly, the cutting off, upon the seventh day after birth, of the first hair of Moslem and Christian Albanian babes, recorded above (p. 13), serves a similar purpose and is therefore actually a persistent form of the old *ʿaḳîḳah* ceremony, and that too in one of the peripheral Moslem lands.
33. *Coutumes des Arabes au pays de Moab,* p. 94.
34. There is nothing surprising or illogical in the linking of two rites of redemption, viz., the substitute sacrifice of an animal and the cutting off of the first hair. Duplication of religious ceremonies, particularly such as are designed to ward off evil spirits or to safeguard human life, is, as we have said, natural and common. We shall have many additional, striking instances.

Notes to Chapter IX

1. For an excellent résumé of the various hypotheses, cf. Gray, in Hastings, *ERE,* III, 659–670; Toy, *Introduction to the History of Religions,* pp. 68–74.
2. *Principles of Sociology,* II, 67.
3. *History of Human Marriage*[5], pp. 201–206.
4. *Op. cit.*
5. "The Origin of Circumcision," in *IR,* IV (1904), 204–218; *The Golden Bough*[3]*; The Magic Art and the Evolution of Kings,* I, 95 ff.; *The Belief in Immortality and the Worship of the Dead,* I, 426 f.
6. *IR,* IV (1904), 218.
7. *Das Leben nach dem Tode,* p. 85.
8. *The Religion of Israel,* pp. 67–70.
9. See also Mahler, "Der Sabbat, seine etymologische und chronologisch-historische Bedeutung," *ZDMG,* LXII (1908), 61; Gunkel, "Ägyptische Paral-

lelen zum Alten Testament," *ZDMG,* LXIII (1909), 533 (note the references there cited); Haupt, "Midian and Sinai," *ZDMG,* LXIII (1909), 523.

10. Josh. 5 : 2–9.

11. *A Sketch of Semitic Origins,* pp. 98 ff.; Hastings, *ERE,* III, 679 f.

12. "Die Bedeutung des Beschneidungsritus und Verwandtes," in *Philologus,* LXII, 91 ff.; *Geburt, Hochzeit und Tod,* p. 176, note 1.

13. It may be remarked in passing that the modern Arabs have no definite conception of the origin and purpose of circumcision. Thus, Samter states (*Folk-Lore of the Holy Land,* p. 33) that "according to Mohammedan tradition, circumcision began with Ibrahim, and was introduced in order that corpses of Moslems slain in battle might be distinguished from those of unbelievers, and receive decent burial"; cf. also the act of al Mugheira, after the battle of Hunain, cited by Wellhausen (*Reste des altarabischen Heidentums*[2], p. 174). Doughty, too, says (*Arabia Deserta,* I, 341 f.): "The nomads imagine even the necessity of circumcision; graziers, they will allege the example of all cattle, that only in the son of Adam may be found this manner of impediment. When they questioned me I have said, 'You can amend then the work of Allah!' . . . 'Of that we speak not,' they answered, 'but only of expediency.' "

14. "De Besnijdenis," in *TT,* 6 Jaargang (1907), Aflevering 2, 163–191 (quoted from Schwally's review in *ARW,* XII [1909], 562).

15. Gen. 17 : 12; 21 : 4.

16. According to some scholars, circumcision thus became a distinctive and indispensable sign of tribal membership. It needs only a moment's consideration to show how preposterous this theory is. For, unless we presume that the men among the early Semites who first practiced circumcision habitually went naked, or at least with the penis exposed (so Bertholet, *Kulturgeschichte Israels,* p. 81), it would have been impossible to tell whether a man was circumcised or not, and therefore did or did not belong to this or that clan or tribe. Moreover, if circumcision, as a sign of tribal membership, had been intended to distinguish the members of one tribe from those of another tribe, we would be compelled to assume the possibility of various distinctive styles and modes of circumcision, just as there may be different styles or modes of cutting or wearing the hair. The ridiculousness of this assumption shows the utter untenability of this hypothesis (so also Gray, in Hastings, *ERE,* III, 659 ff.).

17. *Religion of the Semites*[3], pp. 328 ff.

18. *Reste des altarabischen Heidentums*[2], p. 175; *Prologomena zur Geschichte Israels*[6], pp. 338 f.

19. *ZAW,* VI (1886), 132–143.

20. *Lehrbuch der alttestamentlichen Religionsgeschichte*[2], pp. 150 f.

21. *Geschichte der israelitischen Religion*[5], pp. 51 f.

22. *Exodus,* pp. 35 f.

23. *La Famille dans l'Antiquité Israélite,* pp. 45, 77, 174.

24. *Merrâkech,* pp. 353 f.

25. *The Religion of Israel,* p. 38.

26. *The Religion of the Hebrews,* p. 391.

27. This hypothesis is, of course, in its ultimate analysis based primarily

upon Robertson Smith's theory of a covenant-relationship between deity and worshipers, established by means of a covenant-sacrifice and the attendant shedding of blood, as the basic institution of primitive Semitic religion. But while not denying for a moment that this covenant-relationship and the accompanying covenant-sacrifice were fundamental institutions of Semitic religion, they were not, as we have shown (above, p. 31), the only fundamental institutions thereof. The principle of taboo and the attendant taboo-sacrifice and other related taboo-rites were equally fundamental. And, as evidence still to be presented will establish conclusively, circumcision was in origin just such a taboo-rite, paralleling in every way the sacrifice, originally, as we have seen, upon the seventh day after birth, of the first hair with which a child was born.

28. *Reste des altarabischen Heidentums*[2], p. 175.

29. *Prolegomena zur Geschichte Israels*[6], p. 339, note.

30. *Travels in Arabia Deserta,* I, 128 f.

31. Snouck Hurgronje, *Mekka,* II, 151.

32. *Reisen im Orient*[2], I, 101.

33. *Personal Narrative of a Pilgrimage to Al-Madinah and Mekka,* II, 110 f.

34. *Palestine through the Eyes of a Native,* p. 79.

35. Granquist, *Birth and Childhood among the Arabs,* pp. 201–209, 285 f.

36. *The Manners and Customs of the Modern Egyptians*[3], p. 47 and note.

37. *Arabian Society in the Middle Ages*, p. 192; cf. above, p. 12.

38. *Travels in Ethiopia,* p. 192.

39. *Études sur le Folklore Bedouin de l'Egypte,* p. 38.

40. Pococke, in *A Compendium of the Most Approved Modern Travels* (Dublin, 1757), II, 30.

41. Schulz, in Paulus, *Sammlung der merkwürdigsten Reisen in den Orient,* VI, 193.

42. *The Manners and Customs of the Modern Egyptians* (1890 reprint of the 3rd ed.), p. 495.

43. Rathjens, *Die Juden in Abessinien,* p. 56.

44. Cf. Gray, in Hastings, *ERE,* III, 662 ff.

45. *Arabia Petraea,* III, 219.

46. *Arabia Deserta,* I, 340 f.

47. *Coutumes des Arabes au pays de Moab*, p. 363.

48. *Notes on the Bedouins and Wahabys,* p. 50.

49. *A Journal of Travel in Egypt, Arabia Petraea and the Holy Land,* p. 173.

50. *The Arab of the Desert,* pp. 175, 507.

51. *Traditions and Beliefs of Palestine,* p. 190.

52. Margoliouth, in Hastings, *ERE,* III, 678, quoting Ghazāli, *Ihya' ulûm al-dîn,* 1306, I, 115.

53. *The Religions of Modern Syria and Palestine,* p. 288.

54. *Palästinischer Diwan,* p. 172.

55. *Primitive Semitic Religion Today,* English edition, p. 178; German edition, p. 202.

56. Baldensperger, "Religion of the Fellahin in Palestine," *PEF* (1893), p. 312.

57. Von Maltzan, *Reisen in Arabien,* I: among the Fodli, p. 266; the Audeli,

p. 282; the Yafiʿ tribes, p. 299; the Rezaz, p. 309; the ʿAqareb and ʿAuwaliq, p. 319; the Sobehi, p. 383; at Laheg, p. 346; the Qaʿtaba, p. 370; in Hogreya-land, p. 396. Cf. also Featherman, *The Aramaeans,* p. 423. According to Snouck Hurgronje (*Mekka,* II, 141 ff.), on the other hand, the people of Hadhramaut, who have migrated to Mecca, circumcise their children on the fortieth day after birth. The native Meccans practice circumcision between the ages of five and seven years.

58. Featherman, *op. cit.,* p. 608; Parkyns, *Life in Abyssinia,* II, 35; Rathjens, *op. cit.,* pp. 56, 83. Hoskins (*op. cit.,* p. 192), however, says that in Abyssinia circumcision is usually performed when the child is from four to six years of age.

59. Parkyns, *op. cit.,* I, 33.

60. Epstein, *Eldad-Ha-Dani,* p. 167.

61. Adams, *Darkness and Daybreak,* pp. 122, 226.

62. *Ibid.,* p. 258.

63. Mustafa Nûrî Pascha, "Die Teufelsanbeter" (translated by Menzel), in Grote, *Meine Vorderasienexpedition 1906 und 1907,* I, 157.

64. *Ibid.,* p. 156.

65. *Ibid.,* p. 144.

66. *Travels of Ali Bey,* I, 378.

67. Döbel, *Wanderungen im Morgenland,* p. 326.

68. *Upper Egypt, Its People and Products,* p. 195.

69. Featherman, *op. cit.,* p. 510; Bel, "La Population Mussulmane de Tlemcen," in *RES,* I (1908), 200–225, 417–447; Certeux and Carony, *L'Algérie Traditionelle; Contributions au Folk-Lore des Arabes,* I, 207 f.

70. Certeux and Carony, *op. cit.*

71. *Merrâkech,* pp. 262 f.

72. *Ibid.,* p. 351.

73. Gen. 17 : 25. The statement of Josephus (*Antiquities,* I, XII, 2) that the Ishmaelites circumcised in the thirteenth year is probably based upon this passage in Genesis rather than upon personal knowledge of Ishmaelite practice, and is consequently of little or no significance; cf. Barton, in Hastings, *ERE,* III, 679.

74. Gen. 21 : 4.

75. Gen. 17 : 24.

76. Gen. 25 : 1–4.

77. Gen. 17.

78. Gen. 12 : 4.

79. Gen. 16 : 16.

80. V. 14; for the probable reason for the disgrace, cf. below, p. 298.

81. Cf. Gunkel, *Genesis*[2], for a critical analysis of the chapter; but cf. also Meyer, *Die Israeliten und Ihre Nachbarstämme,* pp. 415 ff., for an altogether different analysis.

82. Against this, Richter ("Zwei alttestamentliche Studien, I, Der Blutbräutigam," *ZAW,* XXXIX [1922], 124 f.) contends, and correctly, that there is no proof at all that the circumcision of adults was ever practiced in Israel.

83. *Beena* marriage, as abundant evidence indicates, was a type of marriage practiced by primitive Semitic peoples in the earliest stages of their cultural

evolution, and which persisted among the Arabs until shortly before the time of Mohammed (cf. Robertson Smith, *Kinship and Marriage in Early Arabia,* pp. 63 ff.). In *beena* marriage the concept of fatherhood was unknown, or at least totally disregarded. Kinship was traced solely through the mother, and the basic social unit was the clan—in Hebrew, *mišpaḥah.* (There is ample evidence that the Hebrew verb-root *šapaḥ*—in Arabic, *safaḥa,* "to pour out; to practice fornication [Lane, *Arabic-English Lexicon,* I, 1369]—was, in the earliest stages of the evolution of the Hebrew language, the word which connoted "to participate in the sexual relationship of *beena* marriage." This verb-root had died out completely in the usage of the Hebrew language even before the commencement of Biblical writing, except for this one noun, *mišpaḥah,* derived from it, and the closely related noun *šifḥah,* "a female servant or slave, particularly one used as a concubine" [cf. Morgenstern, "Beena Marriage {Matriarchat} in Ancient Israel," *ZAW* {new series}, VI {1929}, 91–110]. Clearly, the primary connotation of *mišpaḥah* can only have been "clan," i.e., a closely related and integrated group of persons resulting from the *beena* marriage practice.) All children, male or female, born to a woman under the conditions of *beena* marriage belonged to her clan, as did likewise the children of her sisters and of her and their daughters, continuing through the generations. The head of the clan was always the senior uncle or brother of these women. Marriage within the clan, i.e., endogamy, was abhorrent and strictly forbidden. A man would leave his own clan for a time to live with a woman of another clan and thus satisfy his sexual instinct. Such a marriage might endure for only a single sexual act and be known to only its two participants. This specific type of *beena* marriage was called by the Arabs *moṭaʿa* marriage. Or the union might endure over a protracted period, even for years. This was the normal form of *beena* marriage. In such a *beena* marriage the husband lived openly with his wife's clan and shared the regular activities of their daily existence. But this made him in no way a member of that clan, nor did it affect in any way his membership in the clan of his mother, to which, as a rule, he returned sooner or later.

Gradually, however, as culture advanced and society evolved among the various Semitic peoples, *beena* marriage was superseded by another type of marriage in which the male member of the sexual union, i.e., the father, was the dominant figure, and kinship was traced through him. This type of marriage called into being two new and distinct social units: the family, consisting of the father and all his children (in Hebrew, *bêt ʾab,* literally, "a father's house; a household"); and the tribe (Hebrew, *šebeṭ*), consisting of all families related on the male side, i.e., of fathers, brothers, sons, and male cousins, and also their sisters and daughters so long as these did not contract marriage with men of other tribes and thus become each a member of her husband's tribe. The head or master (*baʿal*) of the family was, of course, the husband and father; hence the designation of this type of marriage, to distinguish it from *beena* marriage, as *baʿal* marriage. Under the conditions of *baʿal* marriage, marriage within the tribe, i.e., the marriage of cousins, was not only not forbidden but was even approved and encouraged, probably because it kept the woman within the tribe into which she had been born.

The transition from *beena* to *baʿal* marriage among the various Semitic peoples was slow and gradual. Among the Babylonians and their national antecedents, this process seems to have been completed and *ba'al* marriage to have become dominant already by the second half of the third millennium B.C. In Israel, *beena* marriage seems to have persisted, at least among the clans of Judah, until the time of David, i.e., until near the beginning of the tenth century B.C. In fact, David's marriage with Michal, the daughter of Saul, was, in its early stages, until David himself became king, a typical *beena* marriage (cf. Morgenstern, *op. cit.*; "David and Jonathan," *JBL*, LXXVIII [1959], 322–325).

Even after *ba'al* marriage had completely supplanted *beena* marriage among the great majority of the Semitic peoples, and the nation had replaced the tribe as the largest and the dominant social unit, nonetheless, various customs and institutions rooted in *beena* marriage persisted in the evolving folk practice—such institutions as the role of the relatives (and particularly of the senior uncle) on the mother's side in circumcision, name-giving, and other rites attendant upon the birth of a male child, and also rites attendant upon marriage and upon death and burial. Of these, we shall have numerous instances in the course of this investigation.

84. V. 26b is almost certainly an editorial appendage to the original text.

85. Cf. Morgenstern, "The Oldest Document of the Hexateuch," *HUCA*, IV (1927), 51–54.

86. Cf. Morgenstern, "The 'Bloody Husband' (?) (Exod. 4 : 24–26) Once Again," *HUCA*, XXXIV (1963), 35–70.

87. Cf. Gen. 17 : 12; Exod. 22 : 28 f.; Lev. 12 : 3; Luke 1 : 59, 2 : 21.

88. *B. Babba ḳama'* 80a; *Babba baṯra* 60b.

89. P. 18.

90. Schwarz, *Das heilige Land*, p. 340; Luncz, "The Customs of Our Brethren in the Holy Land," *Jerusalem*, I (1882), 3.

91. Luncz, *op. cit.*, p. 66.

92. Benjamin, *Eight Years in Asia and Africa*, p. 285; cf. also Feldman, *The Jewish Child*, p. 212.

93. Samter, *Geburt, Hochzeit und Tod*, p. 153, quoting Tuchmann. For the use of salt to ward off evil spirits, cf. above, pp. 7–17, 34, 196–198, 204.

94. Canaan, *Aberglaube und Volksmedezin im Lande der Bibel*, p. 78.

95. *The Desert of the Exodus*, pp. 84 f.

96. Oesterley (*The Sacred Dance*, pp. 144 f.) maintains that these dances were designed to ward off the evil which threatened upon such occasions. Certainly the name, *daḥa*, is closely related to the word *daḥîeh;* the primary connotation of the verb-root is "to be in or to enter into the sunshine" (Lane, *op. cit.*, I, 1772 f.).

97. *Arabia Petraea*, III, 219–223.

98. The Talmud (*B. Sanhedrin* 32b), too, speaks of the sound of the hand-mill in the village of Burni in Palestine as being the sign of a circumcision. The meaning of the passage is obscure. Both Rashi and the Tosafists explain it as meaning that during the Hadrianic persecution circumcision was forbidden on pain of death. Nonetheless, the people continued to circumcise secretly. But since the edict made it impossible to publicly announce the circumcision and invite guests thereto, there was a secret understanding among the villagers of

Burni that the sound of the hand-mill would serve as the signal of such an occasion. This explanation is obviously fanciful and improbable, for, on the one hand, why should this practice have existed in only this one village, and, on the other hand, the sound of the hand-mill must have been heard almost daily, when the instrument was used for ordinary, household purposes, and when no circumcision was implied. It is interesting to note that the Tosafists correlate the reference in Jer. 25 : 10 to the sound of the hand-mill (which, together with the voices of the bridegroom and the bride, was no longer to be heard in the streets of Jerusalem) with the ceremony of circumcision. Whether there is any foundation for this correlation it is impossible to tell, nor is it vital to this discussion. But may it not be that in this village of Burni some old custom, similar to this of the Arab women carrying the hand-mill upon their heads during the circumcision ceremony, survived until, or almost until, Talmudic times, the original meaning and purpose of which were completely forgotten, and that this is what is referred to in this passage? If so, it would be, because of its antiquity, an interesting instance of this custom, even though it sheds no light upon its original meaning and purpose. (I owe this reference to the kindness of my dear friend and former colleague, now long deceased, Professor Jacob Z. Lauterbach.)

99. Lane, *op. cit.,* I, 2097*a*.

100. Above, p. 41.

101. *Op. cit.,* I, 396.

102. *Notes on the Bedouins and Wahabys,* p. 114. Among the Bedouin of Beersheba, *ġaḏa* designates a camel in its fourth year (Haefeli, *Die Beduinen von Beerseba,* p. 113); this same usage is current among the Rwala Bedouin (Musil, *The Manners and Customs of the Rwala Bedouins,* pp. 333 f.). However, according to Musil (*Arabia Petraea,* III, 367), among the Ṭerâbîn and the Tijâha Bedouin of the Sinai Peninsula *ġaḏa* designates a camel in its fifth year. According to Kennett (*Bedouin Justice,* pp. 50 f.), *ġaḏa* designates a camel in its sixth year. In all these cases, except among the Ṭerâbîn and the Tijâha Bedouin, *ġaḏa* designates the camel during the year before it becomes a *ṯanîy,* i.e., before it enters upon the second stage of life.

According to Socin (*Diwan aus Centralarabien,* I, 300), in Negd the one-year-old sheep, when it still has its milk teeth, is called *ġaḏaʿ*; in the following year, when it has lost these teeth, it is called *ṯanîy*.

103. Apparently the sacrifice of firstlings, called *faraʿ* by the ancient Arabs, when the animal was still so young that the flesh was like glue and stuck to the skin (cf. Robertson Smith, *The Religion of the Semites*^{3}, pp. 462 f.)—i.e., while still in the initial period of its existence, before it became a *ġaḏaʿ*—constituted the only, and a most natural, exception. Mohammed sought to abolish this sacrifice, but apparently with only partial success.

104. Exod. 22 : 29; Lev. 22 : 27. A partial parallel to this custom may be seen in the Bedouin practice (Musil, *Arabia Petraea,* III, 195) not to sacrifice a sheep which has just given birth to young until at least seven days after the birth. Probably during these seven days the mother sheep, just like its young, is thought to be in a state of ritual uncleanness or taboo.

105. Lev. 19 : 23 ff.

106. Cf. the Biblical Hebrew verb *ṭihher.*

107. Lane, *op. cit.,* I (1887); Lagarde, *Übersicht über die im Aramäischen übliche Bildung der Nomina,* p. 117, note; Doughty, *Arabia Deserta,* I, 342, 391; Klunzinger, *Upper Egypt, Its People and Products,* p. 195; Musil, *Arabia Petraea,* III, 219, 222; Jaussen, *Coutumes des Arabes au Pays de Moab,* p. 361; Haupt, "The Etymology of Mohel, 'Circumciser,'" *Hebraica,* III (1905), 252.

108. Whether this will account for the origin and practice of circumcision and kindred rites in all parts of the world, we do not venture to say, even though it is difficult to conceive of any satisfactory argument against such wide and general application. However, for the reasons stated in the Introduction, it seems best to limit this investigation solely to the Semitic peoples, even to the exclusion of the ancient Egyptians. Therefore these conclusions have validity only with regard to the Semites. Whether this investigation and these conclusions will shed any light upon the question of the origin and history of Egyptian circumcision and its possible relationship to Semitic circumcision, we must of necessity leave to Egyptologists to determine.

This much, however, may be affirmed with certainty as a result of this investigation: that Semitic circumcision could not have been borrowed from an older, Egyptian practice. For we have seen that among the Semites circumcision had its roots in the remote period and primitive social conditions and relations of *beena* marriage, native in Semitic culture, and which seem to antedate, from a cultural standpoint, all that we know of Egyptian social life and institutions. From this it follows that, if there is any relationship at all between Semitic and Egyptian circumcision, it must be that Egyptian circumcision was borrowed from the primitive Semitic practice, or else, what may be far more probable, that both go back to a very remote, common origin. (Eduard Meyer, *Die Israeliten und Ihre Nachbarstämme,* p. 449, maintains quite strongly that Israelite circumcision must have been borrowed from the Egyptians; so also Mahler, "Der Sabbat, seine etymologische und chronologisch-historische Bedeutung," *ZDMG,* LXII [1908], 61; Gunkel, "Ägyptische Parallelen zum Alten Testament," *ZDMG,* LXIII [1909], 533; Haupt, "Midian und Sinai," *ZDMG,* LXIII [1909], 523.)

It may be added that not all Semites seem to have practiced circumcision (cf. Barton, in Hastings, *ERE,* III, 679). The ceremony was not observed in many parts of Syria (Chwolsohn, *Die Ssabier und der Ssabismus,* II, 10, 114, and note 86), nor among the Druses (with the exception of the Shehab family, who observed the rite out of deference to Islam; Burckhardt, *Travels in Syria,* p. 203), nor by the Assyrians and Babylonians (cf. Barton, *op. cit.;* Peters, *The Religion of the Hebrews,* p. 109). However, as we have seen, the Syrians, and not improbably also the Assyrians and Babylonians, practiced the cognate rite of cutting off the first hair as a taboo-sacrifice, while the practice of offering substitute sacrifices is attested for the Druses (Curtiss, *Primitive Semitic Religion Today,* pp. 233, 242, 264, German ed.), and for the Assyrians and Babylonians (cf. Morgenstern, "The Doctrine of Sin in the Babylonian Religion," *MVAG,* III [1905], 3). Among the Assyrians and Babylonians, too, the lives of little children seem to have been regarded as being peculiarly endangered by the demon Labartu. In other words, the belief seems to have existed among practically all the ancient Semitic peoples that the lives of little children, generally for the first seven days after birth, but occasionally for longer periods, were exposed to attacks by hostile deities and evil spirits. Accordingly, various taboo-rites, all designed to redeem the children from these maleficent powers, were performed by practically all Semitic peoples. Of these rites, the sacrifice of the foreskin, of the first locks of hair, and of a substitute animal seem to have been most common.

109. Cf. Baentsch, *Exodus,* pp. 89 f.; Holzinger, *Exodus,* p. 93.

110. Cf. Meinhold, "Indogermanen in Kanaan" in the *Baudissin Festschrift,* pp. 342–346.

111. Cf. Bertholet, *Kulturgeschichte Israels,* p. 100.

112. Cf. Morgenstern, "The Foundations of Israel's History," *Yearbook of the Central Conference of American Rabbis,* XXV (1915), 256–287; *As a Mighty Stream,* pp. 3–67.

113. II Kings 16: 3; 21 : 6; Jer. 7 : 31; 19 : 5; 32 : 35; Ezek. 16 : 20 f.; 20 : 26, 31.

114. Cf. Morgenstern, "The Oldest Document of the Hexateuch," *HUCA,* IV (1927), 1–138.

115. Cf. Holzinger, *Genesis,* p. 165; Gunkel, *Genesis*², p. 213; Skinner, *Genesis,* p. 332.

116. Exod. 34 : 20.

117. Num. 18 : 15 f.

Notes to Chapter X

1. The practice among Jews and Abyssinians of circumcising upon the eighth day, and the practice in southern Arabia of circumcising upon the seventh day, after birth, constitute the most noteworthy exceptions.

2. Barton, *A Sketch of Semitic Origins,* pp. 99 f.

3. *Arabia the Cradle of Islam,* p. 266.

4. Ordinarily, as Burckhardt says (*op. cit.,* p. 29), "the Bedouin ladies half cover their faces with a dark-colored veil, called *nekye,* which is so tied as to conceal the chin and mouth."

5. *Notes on the Bedouins and Wahabys,* p. 147.

6. Featherman, *The Aramaeans,* pp. 380 f., quoting almost literally Burckhardt, *op. cit.,* pp. 50 f.

7. W. E. Jennings-Bramley, "The Bedouin of the Sinaitic Peninsula," *PEF* (1906), p. 28.

8. Above, pp. 59 f.

9. *Arabia Deserta,* I, 340 f.

10. *Op. cit.,* I, 391 f.; II, 118.

11. *The Bedouins of the Euphrates,* p. 350.

12. *Primitive Semitic Religion Today,* p. 48 (German ed.; not in the English ed.). For further details, cf. note 4 to this passage in Curtiss.

13. *Coutumes des Arabes au pays de Moab,* p. 364.

14. *RB* (July, 1910), p. 395.

15. For instances of dancing the *daḥa,* or *daḥîeh,* dances on these and parallel occasions, cf. also Olin, *Travels in the East,* II, 383 f.; Euting, *Tagebuch einer Reise in Inner-Arabien,* pp. 139 f.; Doughty, *Arabia Deserta,* II, 118; Jennings-Bramley, *op. cit.,* p. 32; Musil, *Arabia Petraea,* III, 221; Dalman, *Palästinischer Diwan,* p. 254.

16. *Palestine under the Moslems,* p. 88.

17. In 1910, from April 22nd through the 29th.

18. *PJB* (1912), pp. 176 f.

19. *Primitive Semitic Religion Today,* English edition, p. 178; German edition, p. 202.

20. *Aberglaube und Volksmedezin im Lande der Bibel,* p. 74.

21. *Travels,* I, 7.

22. Bel, "La population Musulmane de Tlemcen," *RES,* I (1908), 207, 215.

23. According to Doutté (*Magie et Religion dans l'Afrique du Nord,* p. 500), in northern Africa the Ashoura ushers in a protracted period of festal celebration which endures throughout the month. This is characterized chiefly by the *takoûka,* a dance of a rather strenuous and wild character, participated in mostly by the young women of marriageable age. Moreover, in Ouargla marriages are solemnized only at this season of the year and at no other time.

24. Quite similarly, among the Tsūl of Morocco the sheep sacrificed for the bride, as a part of the marriage ceremonies, must have been previously ridden by her (Westermarck, *Marriage Ceremonies in Morocco,* p. 146).

25. Musil, *Arabia Petraea,* III, 222.

26. "Three Hebrew Synonyms for 'to Dance,'" *JAOS,* XXXVI (1916), 321–333; "Two Ancient Israelite Agricultural Festivals," *JQR* (new series), VIII (1917), 31–55.

27. Cf. the statement of Jennings-Bramley (*op. cit.,* p. 32): "The Dahia and Harbi are their only dances, and these are danced not only at the Rubieh, but whenever there is a fantasia for a marriage or other festivity, or in the evenings of the days spent at a Neby's tomb. On these occasions during the day they have camel races and games." And again (*ibid.* [1909], pp. 254 ff.): "The nearest approach to general social intercourse between men and women takes place during the Rûbiaʿ. . . . At this season of the year—the only one when many collect together in one place—the Dahieh is danced, or rather sung, in the evenings. . . . The Hashi (the maiden who leads in the dance) can never be a married woman. I have heard that in the Ababda she is not veiled, and that, instead of a sword, she holds out her own long hair to its full length. . . . These dances and amusements are only indulged in at the time of the Rûbiaʿ, or on such special occasions as a circumcision or marriage." The Rûbiaʿ is the season of the early spring, just after the close of the rainy season, when the vegetation, even in the desert, is green and fresh and fairly plentiful, and the sheep and goats cast their young; cf. Wellhausen, *Reste des altarabischen Heidentums*², p. 97; Irby and Mangles, *Travels in Egypt and Nubia, Syria and the Holy Land,* p. 85; Blunt, *The Bedouin Tribes of the Euphrates,* p. 364; Doughty, *Arabia Deserta,* I, 429; Bauer, *Volksleben im Lande der Bibel,* p. 153.

28. Quite similarly, the Ruâla, "whose pasture ground extends to Nedjd in the Arabian Peninsula, but who in summer pitch their tents in the Hauran, and

whose patron saint is Abu' d-Duhûr in Djôf, celebrate a great religious festival at the birth of the first camel. At this festival men and women dance in spirited manner" (Curtiss, *op. cit.,* p. 204, German ed.; not in the English ed.).

29. *Ta'anit* IV, 8.

30. This custom is not without its significant parallels in Semitic religious practice. II Kings 10 : 22 tells explicitly that the devotees of Ba'al might not participate in the festival there referred to in their own garments. For this reason, garments, which were probably ordinarily kept stored for this purpose in the closets of the sanctuary, were lent to them. Zeph. 1 : 8 likewise seems to refer to the wearing of strange, and perhaps borrowed, garments as a ritual act abhorrent to the true worship of Yahweh. Whether something of the same import lies at the bottom of the reference in Gen. 35 : 2 to the change of garments in preparation for the performance of ritual acts at the sanctuary at Bethel, it is difficult to determine; but it is by no means impossible. Certainly Exod. 11 : 2 f. and 12 : 35 f. imply that for the contemplated celebration of the festival in honor of Yahweh—the festival which was coincidental with the Passover—for which, ostensibly, they were about to go forth from Egypt out into the desert, the Israelites borrowed garments from their Egyptian neighbors. This implies further that wearing borrowed garments and jewelry was a regular ritual procedure of this festival, and also that the Egyptians, duped by the Israelites, believed that the latter would return from the desert after the conclusion of the festival and restore the borrowed articles to their owners. Wellhausen has shown that in the pre-Islamic worship of Al-Jalsad in Hadramaut, as well as occasionally in the celebration of the *Ḥaġġ* at Mecca, the worshipers performed the various rites either naked or in garments which they had borrowed for this purpose from the priests or keepers of the sanctuary (*op. cit.,* pp. 55, 110, 143). This is precisely the same custom as that recorded in II Kings 10 : 22. Robertson Smith's explanation of the meaning of this custom, that it may have been in order to prevent the ordinary, daily garments of the worshipers becoming taboo through contact with the sanctuary (*Religion of the Semites*[3], pp. 451 f.), may be correct. If so, then the long-established ceremony of Islam of wearing the *iḥram* during the sojourn in the sacred territory while performing the *Ḥaġġ* at Mecca must be linked with this custom. But be that as it may, the evidence is ample that the wearing of borrowed garments during the celebration of certain festal rites was an established institution of early Semitic religion.

A partial parallel to this custom may be found, perhaps, in the following statement: "It is the custom for one going on the pilgrimage (i.e., the *Ḥaġġ* at Mecca) to borrow money from all; this is paid back (the sum being entered in a book) either at the time of marriage or when the lender goes on a pilgrimage." (Jennings-Bramley, *op. cit.,* pp. 1912, 63).

31. Gen. 17 : 12; 21 : 4.

32. The tradition of the circumcision of the son of Moses and Zipporah, in Exod. 4 : 24–26, which we have already considered, is, as we have intimated, not the work of J, as most Biblical scholars hold, but a fragment of a much older document, the greater portion of which was suppressed by later J editors, but a small portion of which was incorporated by them into a secondary stratum of

the J Code (cf. Morgenstern, "The Oldest Document of the Hexateuch," *HUCA,* IV [1927], 1–138).

33. Here the sources are immaterial, since all are based upon the same primary tradition.

34. A survival of this original concept of the peculiar relation of the first-born to the Passover celebration may be seen in the practice, still observed by Orthodox Jews, of all first-born males fasting on the day preceding the night of the Passover celebration (*Šulḥan ʿArûk, ʾÔraḥ Ḥayyîm* 470; cf. Morgenstern, "The Origin of *Maṣṣoth* and the *Maṣṣoth* Festival," *AJT,* XXI [1917], 285).

35. Still today, we are told (Burckhardt, *Travels in Nubia,* p. 328; Doughty, *op. cit.,* I, 555), black slaves, purchased by Arab masters and adopted into their households, are circumcised, and thus admitted into Islam; this is exactly the same rite as that prescribed for ancient Israel. Here, too, just as in the case of a proselyte to Judaism or Islam, circumcision marks the passage from a state of uncleanness or ritual taboo into one of ordinary Jewish or Moslem profane life.

36. *Die Israeliten und Ihre Nachbarstämme,* pp. 32–40.

37. A moment's consideration may offer the explanation of this otherwise unaccountable fact. It is generally admitted by even the most conservative Biblical scholars that the oldest sources of the Hexateuch reveal nothing at all of the forty years of wandering in the wilderness. Instead, they tell that the tribes of Israel, emerging from Egypt, came directly to the mountain of Yahweh, there received the revelation of the fundamental principles of Yahweh-life and -worship, and thence, at Yahweh's bidding, proceeded onward and, after a few days' journey, entered the Promised Land (cf. Num. 10 : 29–33). According to the oldest sources, therefore, the entrance into Canaan would have followed shortly after the celebration of the first Passover in the desert, with its circumcision of all the males. The second Passover, a year later, would have been the first celebrated after the entrance into Canaan; and at this second Passover the children who had been born during the year intervening since the last Passover, and who were at least eight days old, would naturally be circumcised. Just this is what is told in Josh. 5. In other words, this narrative in its original form was based upon the oldest tradition of the Exodus, which told nothing of the forty years in the desert. It implied very obviously that the Passover festival was the regular occasion for circumcision in ancient Israel. Later, however, after the tradition of the forty years of wandering in the wilderness had developed, and perhaps also after the custom of circumcising newborn children—no longer upon the Passover festival but instead upon the eighth day after birth—had been instituted, the original narrative of Josh. 5 had of necessity to be so recast as to explain, with at least seeming satisfaction, why this was only the second occasion of circumcision in Israel; hence the insertion of vv. 4–7.

38. Meyer (*op. cit.,* p. 92) has shown quite conclusively that, just as Exod. 15 : 21 states, v. 1b constituted the original nucleus of the so-called Song of Miriam and that the entire remainder is the result of later amplification. This picture, therefore, of Miriam leading the dances of the women of Israel on the seventh day of the Passover festival, while they chant in alternate refrain a song of a single verse, is identical in every respect with that which we have already witnessed, of the *haši*-maiden leading the *daḥa*-dances of the women at the

daḥîyyeh festival, and likewise at circumcision festivals, while they, too, repeat in alternate chant their song of a single verse.

39. *Šemôt rabba,* par. XIX, near end; cf. also the entire discussion of this matter in Morgenstern, "The Origin of *Maṣṣoth* and the *Maṣṣoth*-Festival," *AJT,* XXI (1917), 281–284.

40. Below, p. 297. Moreover, as Doughty tells us with regard to the dances of the Arab maidens at their circumcision festivals, and as the Mishnah records with regard to the dances of the maidens of Jerusalem in the vineyards on the 15th of Ab and the 10th of Tishri, these dances were preparatory to marriage, which ordinarily followed very soon, if not immediately, thereafter. These maidens participating in these dances on these festivals, clad in borrowed garments, may therefore be regarded, in a sense, as brides, potentially speaking at least. With this ceremony, therefore, may very profitably be compared the modern, widespread superstition—undoubtedly a survival from an ancient custom, and perhaps even from the very custom which we have here explored—that during the solemnization of the marriage the bride must wear some object of apparel which has been borrowed for the occasion. Frequently it is the bridal veil which is thus borrowed, and that too from a bride of only a few years earlier. And with this the additional superstition is commonly associated, that, if the preceding wearer of this veil or other borrowed object has already borne children, so the new bride, the latest wearer of the garment, will likewise be fruitful.

An interesting parallel to this custom is the Ottoman practice of decorating the boy who is about to be circumcised with precious ornaments which have been borrowed for the occasion (Garnett, *The Women of Turkey and Their Folk-Lore,* II, 479 f.). Perhaps the idea underlying this practice of wearing borrowed garments or ornaments is that thereby the person wearing them is disguised and his identity obscured; thus he may not be recognized by, and so will be enabled to escape the dangers threatening from, malicious evil spirits.

41. Later writers or editors, no longer understanding the real nature of this peculiar rite, yet remembering that the original tradition had told of the borrowing of the garments and ornaments, explained it as a mere spoliation of the Egyptians and attempted to justify it by saying that it was commanded by Yahweh, and also by implying perhaps that it was no more than deserved compensation, insufficient at the best, for Israel's enforced and bitter labors in Egypt.

42. Cf. Gesenius-Buhl, *Handwörterbuch über das Alte Testament* under *psḥ* II; Köhler-Baumgartner, *Lexicon in Veteris Testamenti Libros,* p. 769a.

43. The later editors, who recast the original tradition, interpreted it very simply and naturally as implying that these means of redemption were revealed to Israel by Yahweh on this occasion in Egypt, but not having been revealed to the Egyptians likewise, and so not being practiced by them, the *mašḥît* was able to enter every Egyptian house and kill every first-born male child therein.

44. In other words, this *mašḥît* had no part at all in the original form of the one tradition of the slaying of the Egyptian first-born, and the subsequent Exodus and the institution of the *Maṣṣôth* festival, but played a role only in the

other tradition of the Exodus previous and preliminary to the celebration of the old, nomad *Pesaḥ* festival in the desert. Not until after the original Passover tradition was reinterpreted and antedated, and the scene was shifted from the desert and after the Exodus to Egypt and before the Exodus, could the legend have arisen that while the first-born of Israel were saved through the efficacy of the blood upon the door, the first-born of Egypt, not protected in this manner, became the victims of the *mašḥît,* or, eventually, the objects of Yahweh's wrath and punishment.

45. *Pirqe de Rabbi Eliezer,* XXIX (translation of Friedlander, p. 210).

46. I.e., the use of the strange and seemingly otherwise inexplicable plural, *dâmayik;* cf. Rashi to this passage and also to Exod. 12 : 6.

47. Cf. Beer, *Das Leben Abrahams,* p. 36 and notes.

48. The basis of this tradition is, in all likelihood, the interpretation of the word *mô'ed* in Gen. 17 : 21 and 21 : 2 in the specific sense "festival," rather than in the more general meaning, "appointed time." Either meaning would be appropriate and perfectly justified in both passages. If, therefore, the Priestly author had in mind the connotation "festival" when he used the word *mô'ed* in these two verses, it may well be that he meant to imply that the Passover festival was the occasion for this circumcision, just as the Midrashic tradition states. According to Jub. 15 : 24 and 16 : 13, this happened at Shabuot. This variation in the tradition, however, is unquestionably due to the marked, sectarian predilection of Jub. for the Shabuot festival.

49. Cf. Morgenstern, "The Bones of the Paschal Lamb," *JAOS,* XXXVI (1916), 146–153, and "The Origin of *Maṣṣôth* and the *Maṣṣôth*-Festival," *AJT,* XXI, (1917), 275–293.

50. Cf. the retention of the term *Pesaḥ* for the festival in v. 25.

51. Cf. Morgenstern, "The Oldest Document of the Hexateuch," *HUCA,* IV (1927), 1–138.

52. Cf. Morgenstern, "The Origin of *Maṣṣoth* and the *Maṣṣoth*-Festival," *loc. cit.* Note also that in Exod. 23 : 18, the Northern parallel of Exod. 34 : 25, the *zebaḥ ḥag happesaḥ,* "the Passover sacrifice," has become *ḥeleb ḥaggi,* "the fat of My festal sacrifice," i.e., any festival-sacrifice.

53. It might well be asked: Why should just the foreskin, in preference to some other part of the body, be offered by so many Semitic peoples as a taboo-sacrifice to redeem the life of the male child? The answer is not far to seek. As we have said, the principle underlying the ceremony of circumcision, just as that underlying that of cutting the hair or some other comparable part of the body, is the idea that the sacrifice of a part of the tabooed object redeems the remainder. Of course, the part of the body thus offered had to be one which could be dispensed with without too greatly inconveniencing or crippling the child. And the sacrifice of the foreskin had two distinct advantages over that of any other part of the body, even the hair. For it was an actual part of the physical organ which played an essential role in the process of human procreation, and for this reason alone it might seem the most natural and appropriate part of the body to be so sacrificed to redeem the life of the child. Moreover, whereas in the hair-sacrifice no blood was shed, the sacrifice of the foreskin

entailed the shedding of some of the blood of the child, for whom the foreskin was the taboo-offering. (Note that in the Jewish circumcision ritual, in addition to cutting off the foreskin itself, the inner membrane must also be broken in order to ensure the shedding of at least a minimum amount of blood; *Šulḥan ʿArûk; Yôreh Dēʿah* 264.) And since the blood was regarded primarily as the seat of life (cf. Morgenstern, "The Bones of the Paschal Lamb," *op. cit.*, pp. 151 ff.), the sacrifice of the foreskin, particularly when accompanied, as in the Jewish ritual, by the shedding of some blood, must have implied in fact what it symbolized in theory, the giving of the life of the child to the deity.

Not impossibly, there may have been associated with the origin of the rite of circumcision the fact that not only the blood but also the penis and the semen which comes from it were likewise regarded to a certain extent as the seat of life, just as is the case occasionally among other primitive peoples (cf. O. Waser, "Über die äussere Erscheinung der Seele," *ARW,* XVI [1913], 381 f.). This would account for the fact that, while evidence of actual phallic worship among the Semites is rare and questionable, nonetheless a certain measure of sanctity was attached to that organ. This is attested by the oath by the genitals, and kindred practices.

Thus, Doughty notes (*Arabia Deserta,* I, 237): "There is a strange custom (not only of nomad women, but in the Arabic countries even among Christians, which may seem to remain of the old idolatry among them), of mothers, their gossips, and even young maidens, visiting married women to kiss with a kind of devotion the *hammam* of the male children."

Of the oath by the genitals, we are told, "In Palestine today there is also an oath, 'My hand below thy girdle'" (Baldensperger, "The Immovable East," *PEF* [1910], p. 261). Musil likewise relates (*Arabia Petraea,* III, 339): "The following form of oath is considered inviolable: The one who demands the oath lays his left hand upon the head of him who swears, and puts his right hand under the latter's girdle, seizes his genitals, and says: 'I cause you to swear by your girdle and by your genitals, by (your children) which you already have or can yet have, by your relatives and by your posterity.' Then there is added what the other obligates himself to do.

"Their love for their children and above all the desire to have numerous and fortunate posterity forbid the one who swears to ever perjure himself."

Again Musil tells (*ibid.*, p. 341) that, "With the most solemn oath, one who demands the oath causes him who swears to lay his left hand upon his head and his right hand upon his genitals, and says, 'I submit you to God, and I separate your back from God, and I lay my hand between your girdle and your genitals.'" This is, of course, the very same oath by the genitals of which mention is made in Gen. 24 : 2 and 47 : 29 (cf. Pedersen, *Der Eid bei den Semiten*).

These illustrations show that, as is to be expected, the idea underlying these ceremonies with the male organ is that of its relation to reproduction and the obtaining of numerous posterity. Therefore, the foreskin, the portion of the male organ which can be easily removed without affecting the functioning of that organ, may well have suggested itself to the primitive Semites as the part of the body most appropriate in every way to be offered as the taboo-sacrifice in order to redeem the life of the child.

Notes to Chapter XI

1. Therefore, as already pointed out, the Christian Arabs of Palestine designate the baptizer by the same term, *muṭahher* (literally, "purifier"), as the Moslems use to designate the circumciser. Unquestionably too, the role of the godfather at baptism is quite the same as that of the *sandiḳ* at the Jewish circumcision and of the *ṣaḥeb el-baḫt* at the Bedouin ceremonies of naming the child, and, like them, probably had its origin in the ancient practice of tracing kinship through the mother alone.

2. Cf. Ezek. 35 : 25 f. and Morgenstern, "The Doctrine of Sin in the Babylonian Religion," *MVAG* III (1905), 30–63; Brandt, *Die jüdischen Baptismen*, pp. 70, 97; Goldziher, "Wasser als Dämonen abwehrendes Mittel," *ARW*, XIII (1910), 20–46; Scheftelowitz, "Die Sündentilgung durch Wasser," *ARW*, XVII (1914), 353–412.

3. Cf. Scheftelowitz, *op. cit.*; Petermann, *Reisen im Orient*², I, 116; Ploss, *Das Kind*, I, 295 ff.

4. Constantine, however, was not baptized until just before his death (Socrates, *Historia Ecclesia*, I, 39). Many of his successors followed his example in this. Commenting upon this passage of Socrates, Zenos says: "It was the belief of many in the earlier ages of the church that baptism had a certain magical power, purging away the sins previous to it, but having no force as regards those that might follow. This led many to postpone their baptism until disease or old age warned them of the nearness of death; such delayed baptism was called 'clinic,' and was discouraged by the more judicious and spiritual-minded Fathers, some of whom doubted its validity, and rebuked those who delayed as actuated by selfishness and the desire to indulge in sin. The church, however, encouraged it in the case of gross offenders." Cf. Bingham, *Ecclesiastical Antiquities*, IV, 3; XI, 11; Bennett, *Christian Archaeology*, pp. 407, 409; Zenos, in *A Select Library of Nicene and Post-Nicene Fathers of the Christian Church* (ed. Schaff and Wace), II, 35. Comparable to this is the custom, not uncommon at Mecca, of deferring the performance of the *ʿaḳîḳa* rites until late in life, or even until after death (above, p. 39).

5. Parkyns, *Life in Abyssinia*, II, 35.

6. Among the Falashas, however, water is poured upon the child immediately after birth, while the rite of circumcision is performed upon him by the women upon the eighth day, unless this is a Sabbath, in which case it is performed upon the next day (Epstein, *Eldad Ha-Dani*, p. 167).

7. Sicard, in Paulus, *Sammlung der merkwürdigsten Reisen in den Orient*, V, 63. According to Wansleb, however (in Paulus, *op. cit.*, III, 83), among the Copts children are baptized normally at the age of seven months, but this may be deferred even until the seventh year; so also Du Bernat, in Paulus, *op. cit.*, IV, 254 f. Lane says (*The Manners and Customs of the Modern Egyptians*³, p. 494): "The Coptic Church recommends baptizing boys at the age of forty days, and girls at the age of eighty days, if they continue so long well and healthy; but earlier if they be ill and in apparent danger of death: for it is a prevailing belief among the Copts, that, if a child die unbaptized, it will be blind in the next life, and

the parents are held guilty of a sin, for which they must do penance, either by repeating many prayers, or by fasting: yet people of the lower orders, if living at an inconvenient distance from a church, and even in other cases, often neglect baptizing their children for a whole year." It may be inferred that this blindness in the next world of a child unbaptized in this world would be caused by the evil spirit, from whose power he had not been redeemed by the rite of baptism.

8. Du Bernat, in Paulus, *op. cit.,* IV, 255, 257.

9. Wansleb, in Paulus, *op. cit.,* III, 83; Du Bernat, *op. cit.,* pp. 272 ff.; Lane, *op. cit.,* p. 495.

10. Du Bernat, *op. cit.,* p. 275.

11. Or the third, assuming that the first period ended on the third day, and the second period on the seventh day; cf. above, p. 22.

12. *Life of Adam and Eve,* I, 5–8; according to *Pirqe de Rabbi Eliezer* XX, the river in question was the Giḫon.

13. Matt. 4:1–11; Mark 1:13; Luke 4:1–13.

14. Brandt, *Mandäische Religion,* pp. 98–102; cf. Petermann, *Reisen im Orient*[2], II, 117. So also among the Maronites baptism is frequently deferred until the fiftieth or sixtieth day after birth; but if the child dies unbaptized, its soul is irretrievably lost (Dandini, in Paulus, *op. cit.,* II, 233). For the same principle among the Copts, cf. above, p. 81.

15. Brandt, *op. cit.,* p. 113.

16. Cf. above, pp. 7 f.

17. Menzel, "Ein Beitrag zur Kenntniss der Jeziden," in Grote, *Meine Vorderasienexpedition, 1906 und 1907,* p. 156.

18. Socrates, *Historia Ecclesia,* V, 22.

19. Zacharias of Mitylene, *Syrian Chronicle,* IV, 1.

20. Notes of the translators of St. Gregory Nazianzen, "Oration on the Holy Baptism," *The Nicene and Ante-Nicene Fathers of the Christian Church* (ed. Schaff and Wace), VII, 368.

21. Lev. 15:2–13, 19 ff.

22. *Ibid.,* vv. 16 f.

23. *Ibid.,* v. 18. For the same practice among the Bedouin, cf. Doughty, *Arabia Deserta,* I, 572.

24. II Sam. 11:2–4.

25. Lev. 16:26, 28.

26. Num. 19:7, 8, 19.

27. Num. 31:19.

28. Lev. 17:15 f.

29. Cf. also Lev. 22:6.

30. *Sibylline Oracles,* IV, 164.

31. Cf. Krauss, in *JE,* II, 499 f.; X, 222; Scheftelowitz, *op. cit., ARW,* XVII (1914), 366; Brandt, in Hastings, *ERE,* II, 408 f.

32. Above, p. 221, note 35.

33. Brandt, *Mandäische Religion,* pp. 95 f.

34. Cf. Morgenstern, "The Doctrine of Sin in the Babylonian Religion," *MVAG* III (1905), pp. 28–63. Likewise, before participating in the complex ceremonies of the New Year festival in Babylon the high-priest was required

to undergo repeatedly a ritual bath (Langdon, *The Epic of Creation,* pp. 21 ff.).

35. II Kings 5 : 10–14.

Notes to Chapter XII

1. Cf. Tylor, *Primitive Culture*[3], II, 401; Robertson Smith, *The Religion of the Semites*[3], p. 324, note 2, and the references there given; Curtiss, *Primitive Semitic Religion Today,* German edition, pp. 189 f. (not in the English ed.); Frazer, *The Golden Bough*[3], *The Scapegoat,* pp. 252–287; *Balder the Beautiful,* II, 103 ff.; *Folk-lore in the Old Testament,* II, 184 ff.; III, 303; Clemen, "Miszellen zu Lukians Schrift über die syrische Göttin," in *Baudissin, Festschrift,* pp. 87 f.

2. Goldziher, *Muhammedanische Studien,* I, 250. Still today among the Ṭerâbîn, Beli, and Tijâha, the man who swears the particularly solemn oath *'al-ḫuṭṭa* must shave, cut off his hair, and wash himself (Musil, *Arabia Petraea,* III, 342). In other words, at the moment of swearing he is regarded as having entered into a state of consecration.

3. *Op. cit.* (German ed.), pp. 246–251.

4. Jennings-Bramley, "The Bedouin of the Sinaitic Peninsula," *PEF* (1907), pp. 34 f.

5. *Reisebeschreibung nach Arabien und anderen umliegenden Ländern,* II, 431.

6. *Coutumes des Arabes au pays de Moab,* pp. 94 f.

7. Perhaps this was the implication of the sign put by God upon Cain, the murderer of his brother, when he was let go free as an outcast among the peoples (Gen. 4 : 15). Whoever would see this sign of the cut-off hair would know that technical and formal vengeance had been visited upon Cain for his brother's murder, and so no one would seek to kill or harm him further; but cf. Stade, "Das Kainzeichen," in *Akademische Reden,* pp. 229–273; also Bauer, *Volksleben im Lande der Bibel,* pp. 6 f.

8. Cf. also Goldziher, "Sacrifice de la chevelure chez les Arabes," in *RHR,* XIV (1886), 49; *Muhammedanische Studien,* I, 250; Robertson Smith, *op. cit.*, p. 337. Likewise among the ancient Arabs the custom of shaving the hair, or the hair and the beard, of prisoners of war was common, as is proved by the numerous references thereto in the Antar romance (cf. *Antar, A Bedoueen Romance,* translated by Hamilton, I, 149; II, 30; III, 92, 117, 155, 203; Goldziher, *op. cit.*, p. 250). This practice is there represented as an indignity visited upon the prisoners and a sign of profound disgrace. But in all likelihood in origin the cutting off of the hair was the substitute for taking the life of the prisoner, as might quite properly have been done. In this way the cutting off of the hair became among the Arabs the substitute for the loss of freedom (cf. Pedersen, *Der Eid bei den Semiten,* p. 67).

9. *Loc. cit.*

10. The most compelling form of oath among the modern Moslems; cf. Rassam, *Assur and the Land of Nimrod,* p. 115.

11. A slightly different account of the sacrifice of the hair in the termination of a blood-feud is given by Haddad ("Die Blutrache in Palästina," *ZDPV,* XI [1917], 228 f.; reprinted in English translation in *JPOS,* I [1921], 107): "Only in

case a truce has been arranged between the two hostile parties, and then this truce is violated by one of the parties disregarding the truce oath and killing a member of the opposite party, does the following procedure take place when the occasion for making the final and lasting peace comes about. The man or men who have broken their oath are brought, according to a previous arrangement made by representatives of both parties, into a circle of their enemies, with their heads bare, as a sign that they submit themselves completely to their enemies. Their turbans are unrolled and hung about their necks, and their *fes* and the white caps which are under these are laid upon their breasts. . . . They may not greet nor converse with any of those present. They kneel down in the midst of the circle. Then, if the party who has been true to the oath is inclined to forgive his enemies, he stands up and says to one of his followers, 'Stand up and shave their heads, for I have forgiven them.' After this sheep are killed and a meal is prepared for them; only then may they cover their heads again." To this, Haddad adds the note that shaving the head is considered a great disgrace, if it is performed as a punishment, and so likewise the shaving of the beard, which is performed upon the man who has violated a woman's honor.

12. *Op. cit.,* pp. 189 f.; cf. Bauer, *Volksleben im Lande der Bibel,* p. 59.

13. In *PJB* (1912), pp. 150–152.

14. According to Canaan (*Aberglaube und Volksmedezin im Lande der Bibel,* p. 74), when the child is four years old or more. This is also the practice of the native Jews of Jerusalem (cf. below, p. 88). Apparently the age limit varies somewhat in different localities.

15. The 18th of Iyyar, the thirty-third day after the second day of the Passover festival, celebrated by Orthodox Jews, particularly in Palestine, as a minor festival.

16. I.e., the second through the sixth days of the Passover week, regarded by Orthodox Jews as of semi-sacred character.

17. Luncz, "Customs of Our Brethren in Palestine in Religion and Daily Life" (Hebrew), *Jerusalem,* I, (1886), 4 f.

18. The native Jews of India; cf. *JE,* III, 17.

19. Cf. also Baldensperger, "Peasant Folklore of Palestine," *PEF* (1893), p. 203.

20. *De Dea Syria* (Tooke's translation), p. 60.

21. Petermann, *Reisen im Orient*², I, 277.

22. An interesting parallel to this ceremony, and one not altogether without significance, may be found in the rite of baptism as practiced in the Greek Orthodox church at Myconi. There the priest cuts off some of the hair from the child's forehead and then some from above each temple, presses these together with wax, and deposits them in the most holy part of the church (Schulz, in Paulus, *Sammlung der merkwürdigsten Reisen in den Orient,* VI, 21).

23. *Coutumes des Arabes au pays de Moab,* p. 94.

24. Benjamin, *Eight Years in Asia and Africa,* pp. 285 f.

25. The ceremony for boys at the attainment of the thirteenth year, which marks their passing from the state of childhood into that of manhood.

26. III, 8.
27. Cf. also Wellhausen, *Reste des altarabischen Heidentums*², pp. 198 f.
28. (Ed. Zuckermandel) *Šabbat,* VI, 1 (p. 117); cf. also *D^ebarîm Rabba* (ed. Wilna), II, 10.
29. *ʿAbôda Zara,* I, 3.
30. Manifestly the very same custom as that described by Lucian.
31. *Babba Qama* 83a.
32. *Ḳómê* (Greek, κόμῃ), according to Rashi, "the hair which grows in front, just over the forehead"; cf. Krauss, *Talmudische Archäologie,* I, 646, note 841.
33. *Tent Work in Palestine*², II, 233 f.
34. Chwolsohn, *Die Ssabier und der Ssabismus,* II, 307, quoting Shehab-ed-din in the *Kitâb-el-Ġômân.*
35. *Arabia Deserta,* II, 239; cf. also I, 469, and the two representations of bas-reliefs of figures with streaming horns, *ibid.,* I, 169, and also Doughty, *Documents épigraphiques recueilles dans le nord de l'Arabie,* plate XII. These figures make it immediately apparent why these temple locks should have received the characteristic name "horn," for their resemblance to the horn of a goat is unmistakable. Not improbably *ḳeren* in Biblical Hebrew may occasionally designate these locks above the temple, particularly in Job 16 : 15, and possibly also in Jer. 48 : 25 (cf. 48 : 45), Lam. 2 : 3.
36. *Arabia Petraea,* III, 160.
37. *Ibid.,* p. 396.
38. *Notes on the Bedouins and Wahabys,* p. 133.
39. For a magical procedure quite similar, cf. II Kings 13 : 15–19.
40. Among the Aeneze tribes, however, it seems to be the custom to wear the tresses of hair throughout life. Burckhardt (*op. cit.,* pp. 27 f.; cf. also p. 58) says: "The Aenezes are distinguished at first sight from all the Syrian Bedouins by the long tresses of their hair. They never shave their black hair, but cherish it from infancy, till they can twist it in tresses that hang over the cheeks down to the breast; these tresses are called *keroun* (horns)." Euting (*Tagebuch einer Reise in Inner-Arabien,* I, 45) likewise tells that the Bedouin usually wear four braids, called *ḳurûn* (horns), two in front, one over each temple, and two at the back of the head. Wellsted (*Travels in Arabia* [German translation by Roediger], II, 200) also remarks upon the two braids which the Bedouin of the Hedjaz, in contrast to those of Oman, wear hanging from their temples; also Burckhardt, *op. cit.,* p. 133; Keane, *Six Months in Mecca,* p. 11.
41. Lev. 19 : 27; 21 : 5; cf. also Gressmann, "Die Haartracht der Israeliten," *Budde Festschrift* (1920), p. 65.
42. Jud. 16 : 13, 19.
43. Exod. 19 : 6.
44. Lucian, *De Dea Syria,* p. 6.
45. Cf. Additional Notes, B.
46. *Historia Ecclesia,* V, 10; cf. also II, 5, and Socrates, *Historia Ecclesia,* I, 18, 7–9, and Robertson Smith, *Religion of the Semites*³, p. 329, note 3.
47. Quoted from Barton, *"The Semitic Ishtar Cult," Hebraica* X (1893), 58 f.
48. So Barton; perhaps "lustful" would be better; cf. the meaning of *faḳara*

in the *'etpa'*. and *'af.* (Brockelmann, *Lexicon Syriacum,* 283b). It should be noted also that in this passage Ephraem uses the feminine, *pitkarta'*, instead of the masculine, *pitkara',* and indicates thereby that these ceremonies were performed in the worship of a goddess instead of a god. This is borne out by the reference to the star, meaning undoubtedly the planet Venus, associated in the Babylonian religion and its offshoots with the mother-goddess.

49. "Aegyptica," in *Nöldeke Festschrift,* I, 418 ff.; cf. also Burckhardt, *Arabic Proverbs,* p. 117.

50. Burckhardt, *op. cit.,* p. 145.

51. Snouck Hurgronje, *Mekka,* II, 134.

52. Cf. Ploss, *Das Weib,* I, 302; Schwally, *Semitische Kriegsaltertümer,* pp. 76 ff.; Toy, *Introduction to the History of Religions,* p. 79.

53. I, 199.

54. XVI, 1, 20.

55. Cf. Hartland, "Concerning the Rite in the Temple of Mylitta" in *Anthropological Essays Presented to Edward Burnett Tylor,* pp. 189 ff.; Nilsson, *Études sur le culte d'Ishtar;* Delitzsch, "Zu Herodots Babylonischen Nachrichten," in *Festschrift für Eduard Sachau,* pp. 87–102. Delitzsch holds, chiefly upon the basis of the evidence of Babylonian literature, that Herodotus' statement is entirely without historical basis (cf. also Zimmern, *Die Keilinschriften und das Alte Testament*^{3}, p. 423), and he cites the fact that both Herodotus (I, 196) and Strabo (*op. cit.*) describe the Babylonian marriage market, at which virgins were disposed of for marriage. However, the custom described by Herodotus is, as our discussion shows, attested too widely to be disposed of in Delitzsch's summary manner, and Herodotus' account must be accepted as having a considerable measure of historical truth. (So also Sumner, *Folkways,* p. 538, and Langdon, *Tammuz and Ishtar,* p. 73, the latter of whom has, however, entirely misunderstood the origin and significance of the rite.)

56. Herodotus reads: στέφανον περὶ τῆσι κεφαλῆσι ἔχουσαι θώμιγγος πολλαὶ γυγαίκες. Strabo reads: θώμιγγι δ'ἔστεπται ἑκάστη. Whether the *agū* which Ishtar wore about her head, and which was the first object of apparel removed from her when she was admitted into the nether world, may be identified with this cord is uncertain (*Ishtar's Descent to Hell,* obv. pp. 42 f.; cf. Jensen in *KB,* VI, 82 f. and 349, 1.14). But if so, it would, on the one hand, shed additional light upon the question now under consideration, and, on the other hand, it would probably indicate that Ishtar is here represented as the virgin-goddess. It is noteworthy, too, that the goddess Nin-Tu, another form of the Babylonian virgin mother-goddess, is described as wearing a fillet (?) and a horn about her head (*CT,* XVII, plate XLII, obv. II, 2; cf. Thompson's translation in *The Devils and Evil Spirits of Babylonia,* II, 146 f.). *Qarnu,* "horn," is probably a colloquial term for a lock of hair of peculiar shape (cf. above, p. 91). Assuming the correctness of Thompson's emendation, [*ku-u*]*b-šu,* this fillet, too, would probably be identical with the cord around the head of the Babylonian maidens in the ceremony described by Herodotus, and therefore probably also with the *agū* of Ishtar.

57. It may be noted that the messengers of Ben Hadad to Ahab, sent to intercede for favorable terms of submission, are clad in sackcloth and have cords

bound about their heads (I Kings 20 : 31 f.). Just what the import of this latter rite, or manner of garb, may have been in this particular instance, it is difficult to determine.

58. XVIII, 5, 4, upon the authority of Trogus Pompeius, a lost writer of the Augustan age (quoted from Hartland, *op. cit.*, pp. 189 f.).

59. I, 93.

60. Cf. Arnobius, *Oratio contra Gentes*, VI, 19.

61. *Op. cit.*, p. 26.

62. The present composite text of Num. 25 : 1–9 preserves, of course, only a confused and vague reminiscence of the original tradition. On the one hand, it first represents these sacrifices and rites as being performed in honor of the Moabite deities, and, on the other hand, it represents them, in the Priestly addendum, as being performed in immediate vicinity to the Tabernacle of Yahweh, and therefore in the midst of the camp of Israel, and presumably therefore in connection with false Yahweh-worship, rather than in the vicinity of some Moabite shrine and in connection with the worship of Moabite deities, as the two opening verses state. The original tradition, it is clear, must have told simply and directly that the Israelite men cohabited with the Moabite maidens in the celebration of a festival, observed with all the regular and characteristic rites, in honor of Moabite deities.

63. Though why Wellhausen *(Composition des Hexateuchs*[3]*)*, Baentsch *(Exodus)*, and Holzinger *(Exodus)*, following Popper, should call the insertion aggadic is by no means clear.

64. This is the opinion of Rashi also, who likewise associates these mirrors with the discharge of the sexual function. He records, in his commentary on this passage, the interesting tradition that "the daughters of Israel used to have mirrors in their hands, with which they would look at themselves while they were adorning themselves. Nevertheless they did not refrain from offering them as a free-will sacrifice to the sanctuary; but Moses rejected them, because they were made for the satisfaction of the evil inclination. Thereupon God said to him: 'Accept them, for they are more precious to Me than aught else, for by means of them the women brought many myriads of people into existence in Egypt. For when their husbands were toiling under forced labor, they would bring them food and drink and cause them to eat; and they would take their mirrors with them, and every one would look at herself in company with her husband in the mirror, and would seduce him with such words as these, "I am more beautiful than thou"; and because they thus brought their husbands into a state of desire, and were united with them, they became pregnant and gave birth there; as it is said (Cant. 8 : 5), "Under the apple-tree have I stirred thee up"' (or perhaps 'stripped thee naked'); this is what is meant by the expression, *b^e^mar'ôt haṣob^e'^ôt.*"

65. Note also the presence of mirrors in the toilet equipment of the women of Jerusalem (Isa. 3 : 23). For the important role played by the hand mirror in the toilet of the Moslem women of Algeria today, cf. Daumas, *La Femme Arabe*, p. 50.

66. So Hos. 4 : 13 f.; here the adultery of the daughters and daughters-in-law

may well refer to just this sacrifice of virginity as a necessary preliminary to marriage.

67. Whether II Macc. 6 : 4 refers to a similar practice of the Graeco-Syrian religion introduced into the Temple at Jerusalem cannot, of course, be determined with certainty, although it is very probable, since the ceremonies here cited are represented as part of the celebration of an annual festival.

Gen. 34 probably offers still another instance of the practice of the sacrifice of virginity by maidens on the occasion of some great, annual festival. The chapter begins very suggestively with the statement that Dinah, the daughter of Leah (who bore her to Jacob), went out to watch the native Shechemite maidens, and then proceeds to recount how upon this occasion she was seized by Shechem, the son of Ḥamor, and forcibly violated, after which act he was inflamed with love for her and desired her for his wife. V. 1 does not state what the Shechemite maidens were doing that merited such attention. But from the continuation of the story and in the light of what we know was the regular procedure at such festivals in ancient Israel and in still more ancient Canaan (cf. Morgenstern, "The Etymological History of the Three Hebrew Synonyms for 'to Dance,'" *JAOS,* XXXVI [1916], 321–333, and "Two Ancient Israelite Agricultural Festivals," *JQR* [new series], VIII [1917], 31–54), we may assume with reasonable certainty that the maidens of Shechem, just as the maidens of the nearby city of Shiloh (Judg. 21 : 19–23), were celebrating one of their important, annual festivals (so actually Josephus, *Antiquities,* I, 21, 1) with the characteristic dances in the vineyards, which, in turn, were followed, as was customary, by the seizure of the maidens by the young men, concealed and waiting nearby, and the pairing off for purposes of sexual intercourse and sacrifice of virginity, and, in many cases at least, ensuing marriage. So here Shechem, beholding Dinah and manifestly attracted by her, and mistaking her for one of the maidens of his city, seizes her and violates her, only to learn too late that she is not a Canaanite maiden. Nevertheless, there is not the slightest conception on his part that he has done anything improper or contrary to custom. And finding Dinah all that he desires for a wife, he proceeds, still in accordance with established custom, to demand her hand in marriage. Only then does he learn that the customs and standards of Israel differ from those of his own people.

It is true that there is nothing here of the idea of first intercourse with a chance stranger, who was himself ineligible for subsequent marriage with the maiden. But this, it seems, was by no means the universal practice among the ancient Semites, but was rather the local custom in certain districts; in others, the custom prevailed of the maidens being seized in the dances and carried off by the young men of their own city, each of whom, at least in the majority of cases, after the sacrifice of the virginity of the maiden in this manner, took her as his wife.

At any rate, what has been said makes the probability strong that v. 1 implies the celebration of some annual festival by the people of Shechem, one of the important ceremonies of which was the dancing of the maidens in the vineyards, their seizure by the young men, and the attendant sacrifice of their virginity. Such an assumption makes the entire story far more intelligible and realistic. This becomes especially clear in the light of Gunkel's comment on this passage.

He says: "The statement that Dinah goes out to watch the daughters of the land is intended to explain how it came about that she left the protection of her father and so came into Shechem's power; the motive is not very happily devised." But the statement motivates far more than this, for it explains, not only how Dinah came into the power of Shechem, but also how the idea of seizing and violating her was suggested to him by all that was going on around about him between the other youths and maidens, and also how, in accordance with the established practice, he came subsequently to demand her hand in marriage. Therefore, contrary to Gunkel, we must conclude that the motive given, that Dinah went out to watch the daughters of the land, is indeed effectively devised, in that it gives us the complete setting for the entire narrative.

68. Cf. also Frazer, *Adonis, Attis and Osiris*[2], pp. 32 ff.

69. *Silius Italicus,* III, 28; *Pausanias,* VII, V, 3.

70. *Primitive Semitic Religion Today,* p. 191 (German ed.; not in English ed.).

71. Gesenius-Buhl, *Hebräisches und aramäisches Wörterbuch über das Alte Testament*[17], p. 234 (following Socin); Koehler-Baumgartner, *Lexicon in Veteris Testamenti Libros,* p. 303.

72. "The Etymological History of the Three Hebrew Synonyms for 'to Dance,'" *JAOS,* XXXVI (1916), 321–333.

73. Cf. Additional Notes, C.

74. Frazer, *The Golden Bough*[3]; *The Magic Art and the Evolution of Kings,* I, 28 ff.

75. Chwolsohn, *Die Ssabier und der Ssabismus,* II, 42; quoting En-Nadim, *Fihrist,* VII.

76. Snouck Hurgronje, *Mekka,* II, 165.

77. Jaussen, *Coutumes des Arabes au pays de Moab,* p. 54.

78. *Reisen im Orient*[2], I, 275.

79. *JE,* XII, 518 f.

80. Cf. Krauss, *Talmudische Archäologie,* I, 195.

81. *Yôma* 47a.

82. Conversely, among the Palestinian Jews today on the night before the marriage ceremony the hair of the bridegroom is cut off (Luncz, *Jerusalem* [Hebrew] I [1886], 6). Among some Arab tribes, too, the same custom seems to obtain, and, in addition, the bridegroom is required to take a ritual bath (Socin, *Diwan aus Centralarabien* quoting Wetzstein, II, 144, note a.)

83. Isa. 47 : 2; cf. I Cor. 11 : 5–15; cf. Krauss, *op. cit.*

84. Cf. Additional Notes, D.

85. Num 5 : 18.

86. *JE,* XII, 518; Krauss, *op. cit.,* I, 195, 650. Among the Aeneze today the hair of a maiden is allowed to hang loose only at her marriage or in battle (Wetzstein, "Sprachliches aus den Zeltlagern der syrischen Wüste," *ZDMG,* XXII [1868], 98).

87. Goldziher, "Wasser als Dämonen abwehrendes Mittel," *ARW,* XIII (1910), 32.

88. Similarly among the Moslems today, when a slave is given his freedom, he cuts off his hair (Burckhardt, *Notes on the Bedouins and Wahabys,* p. 103). If the slave is of non-Moslem origin, the act of manumission implies also admission to Islam.

89. Lev. 14 : 8.

90. Cf. Kohler, "Seltsame Vorstellungen und Bräuche in der biblischen und rabbinischen Literatur," *ARW,* XIII (1910), 79 ff.; Frazer, *The Golden Bough*[3]*; Taboo and the Perils of the Soul,* p. 34 f.

91. *Reste des altarabischen Heidentums*[2]*,* p. 31; Robertson Smith, *Religion of the Semites*[3], p. 331; Goldziher, *Muhammedanische Studien,* I, 249.

92. *Mô'ed Ḳaṭôn* III, 1.

93. Similarly among the ancient Arabs, and apparently also in Israel, it was customary for warriors, returning home after the close of a campaign, to cut off their hair (cf. Wellhausen, *Reste des altarabischen Heidentums*[2], p. 123, note 2; Pedersen, *Der Eid bei den Semiten,* p. 121, note 2.

94 *Mô'ed Ḳaṭôn* 15a. The prohibition against changing the garments was probably only the necessary preliminary to the complete change of garments at the close of this period as a ritual act.

95. The *Mishnah* (*ibid.* III, 2) likewise provides that all these, as well as others who were in a state of ritual uncleanness or taboo, viz., persons with an issue, menstruating women or women in childbirth, or, in general, all who passed from a state of ritual uncleanness to one of purity were permitted to wash their garments on these middle days of the festivals. This is obviously a ceremony performed primarily for ritual purposes rather than for the sake of mere physical cleanness; cf. Num. 19 : 7, 8, 10, and Goldziher, "Wasser als Dämonen abwehrendes Mittel," *ARW,* XIII (1910).

96. *Nazîr* 18a.

97. Rathjens, *Die Juden in Abessinien,* p. 85. It may be inferred that the Bible implies (Num. 12 : 9–14) that Miriam had to undergo some procedure such as this when she was shut up outside the camp for seven days to be cured of her leprosy, even though it is not stated that her hair was cut off.

98. This is, as a moment's consideration will show, exactly the same condition as that of boys, vowed by their parents to a saint or *wely,* and freed from the obligation of the vow by the sacrifice of the first hair and of a proper substitute animal, discussed above, p. 87.

99. *Primitive Semitic Religion Today* (English ed.), p. 177.

100. *Ibid.,* p. 200; cf. also the additional instances of this sacrifice, cited in the German edition, pp. 200 f., 221, 234, and the sacrifice of victorious warriors upon their return home, discussed in detail by Robertson Smith, *The Religion of the Semites*[3], p. 491 f.

101. As is implied by the obvious relationship, and, in fact, the original identity, of the two stems *nadar* and *nazar* (cf. Robertson Smith, *op. cit.,* pp. 482 f.; Wellhausen, *Reste des altarabischen Heidentums*[2], pp. 142 f.). Similarly with the extreme oath taken by the Bedouin within the magic circle outside the camp, he must be freshly washed, shaved, and with hair newly cut (von Landberg, *Arabica,* V, 124 f.; quoted from Pedersen, *op. cit.,* p. 153). He takes the oath to free himself from the suspicion of extreme guilt. Obviously it marks his passing from a state of theoretical taboo into one of ordinary profanity.

102. *Primitive Semitic Religion Today* (English ed., p. 153; German ed., p. 173).

103. Comparable to the institution of the Nazirate is the following practice,

none too well authenticated, however, of the Ismailis: "Every female child born on the 27th of Rajab is set apart and held to be an incarnation of the divinity. She is called the Rozah. She does not work, her hair and nails are never cut, her family share in the respect that is accorded her, and every man in the village will wear a piece of her clothing or a hair from her body folded in his turban. She is not permitted to marry" (Bell, *The Desert and the Sown,* p. 233). This Rozah is obviously in a state of permanent consecration, from which she can never emerge; hence, her hair and nails are never cut. Quite similarly, the Mandaean priests are forbidden to cut their hair. They must let it grow long throughout their lives and, probably for convenience' sake, wear it braided. In other words, they too, as this prohibition shows, are in a permanent state of consecration (Brandt, *Mandäische Religion,* p. 92).

104. *De Dea Syria,* p. 53.

105. *Mô'ed Ḳaṭôn* III, 1; cf. above, pp. 101, 234, note 92, and Krauss, *Talmudische Archäologie,* I, 643, note 82.

106. Cf. Ali Bey, *Travels,* II, 45; Burton, *Pilgrimage to Al-Madinah and Mekka,* II, 205, 243, 286, 289; Wellhausen, *Reste des altarabischen Heidentums*², pp. 25, 62, 64, 80, 123; cf. also p. 31.

107. *Op. cit.,* p. 124.

108. Hartmann, "Volksglaube und Volksbrauch in Palästina," *ARW,* XV (1912), 150. In a number of localities of northern Africa today, certain classes of religious devotees refrain from cutting their hair or their nails from the first day of Muḥarram until the close of the Ashura festival upon the tenth of the month (Doutté, *Magie et Religion dans l'Afrique du Nord,* pp. 508 f.).

109. Above, pp. 100 ff.

110. So also Doutté, *op. cit.,* p. 471.

111. *The Land and the Book,* II, 492.

112. Tobler, *Topographie von Jerusalem und seinen Umgebungen,* II, 324, quoting Ewald, *Journal of Missionary Labor in the City of Jerusalem,* II, 250.

113. This should read, of course, "the thirty-third."

114. Cf. above, p. 88; also Additional Notes, E.

115. Cf. Robertson Smith, *op. cit.,* pp. 323 ff.; Wellhausen, *Reste des altarabischen Heidentums*², p. 81; Goldziher, "Le culte des ancêtres et le culte des morts chez les Arabes," *RHR,* XI (1884), 351; *Muhammedanische Studien,* I, 247–251.

116. So the Syrians of Hierapolis in honor of the dead Adonis, Lucian, *De Dea Syria,* p. 6.

117. Burckhardt, *Notes on the Bedouins and Wahabys,* p. 58; Jaussen, *Coutumes des Arabes au pays de Moab,* p. 94; Musil, *Arabia Petraea,* III, 427 ff.; Bauer, *Volksleben im Lande der Bibel,* p. 211. On the other hand, Musil (*op. cit.,* III, 428) tells that among the Ẓullâm and the Ḥêwât the men do not fix their hair or beard or have them cut during the period of mourning. The implication is that when the period of mourning is past the hair is cut once more. While there is here no trace of the sacrifice of the hair, nonetheless the act of cutting it off marks here the close of the period of mourning and taboo.

118. Lev. 21 : 5; Deut. 21 : 12 (unless the cutting off of the hair here be

regarded as designed to remove the condition of taboo resting upon the woman by reason of her previous non-Israelite associations, or as a rite regularly performed upon captives taken in war; cf. above. However, since the verse especially enjoins mourning for her deceased, and presumably slain, parents, it is best to regard this and the accompanying and kindred rite of cutting off the nails as a ceremony of mourning); Isa. 22 : 12; Jer. 16 : 6; Ezek. 7 : 18; Amos 8 : 10; while Deut. 14 : 1 expressly forbids the shaving of the eyebrows in honor of the dead, on the ground, of course, that it is not a Yahwistic rite (cf. Schwally, *Das Leben nach dem Tode,* pp. 10, 16; Grüneisen, *Der Ahnenkultus und die Urreligion Israels,* pp. 144 ff.; Lods, *La Croyance à la Vie Future et le Culte des Morts dans l'Antiquité Israelite,* pp. 124 ff.; Doutté, *op. cit.,* p. 446; Frazer, *Folk-Lore in the Old Testament,* III, 270–274; Gressmann, "Die Haartracht der Israeliten," in the *Budde Festschrift* [1920], pp. 61–88). It is perhaps worthy of note that the Mandaeans are forbidden to cut their hair in honor of, or as a sacrifice to, the dead (Petermann, *Reisen im Orient*[2], II, 119; Brandt, *Mandäische Religion,* pp. 80 f.). Neither may their priests shave their heads (Petermann, *op. cit.,* II, 115), nor do they practice circumcision (Zwemer, *Arabia the Cradle of Islam,* p. 298). In ancient Israel the priests were permitted to wear their hair trimmed, but were forbidden to shave their heads (Ezek. 44 : 20).

119. *Religion of the Semites*[3], pp. 323 ff.

120. Frazer, *The Golden Bough*[3], *The Scapegoat,* Index under "ghost," and for the practice among Jews, Scheftelowitz in *ARW,* XVII (1914), 405.

121. Below, pp. 117 ff.

122. "De doodenvereering bij de Israeliten," *TT,* XV (1881), 356.

123. *Geburt, Hochzeit und Tod,* pp. 179–184.

124. "Die israelitischen Trauerriten," in *Festschrift für Julius Wellhausen,* p. 121.

125. *Das Leben nach dem Tode,* pp. 16 ff.; cf. also Paton, *Spiritism and the Cult of the Dead in Antiquity.*

126. Schwally suggests further (*op. cit.,* p. 17) that, since the wearing of the hair long was the privilege of the free man, the cutting off of it as a mourning rite signified that the mourner thus became, as it were, the slave of the deceased. Grüneisen (*op. cit.,* pp. 101 f.) suggests that the purpose of cutting off the hair may have been to disguise the mourner and thus permit him to evade the dread claim and power of the ghost (so also Scheftelowitz, "Der Seelen- und Unsterblichkeitsglaube in Alten Testament," *ARW,* XIX [1916], 222).

127. A possible exception to this general principle seems to be the well-established practice of pre-Islamic Arab warriors of cutting off their hair as a sign that they consecrated themselves to death for the honor of the tribe (cf. Goldziher, "Le Sacrifice de la chevelure," *RHR,* XIV [1886], 49 ff.; *Muhammedanische Studien,* I, 249). Here, contrary to the general rule which we have posited, the cutting off of the hair apparently marks the beginning, rather than the close, of a period of consecration or taboo.

It is a well-known fact that among the early Semites warriors upon a campaign or in battle were regarded as being in a state of consecration and subject to taboos, similar in every way to the conditions affecting a pilgrim during the celebration of a festival (cf. Robertson Smith, *op. cit.*, p. 455). Nevertheless, we know that in ancient Israel (cf. Deut. 32 : 42; Judg. 5 : 2; Wellhausen, *Reste des altarabischen Heidentums*[2], p. 123, note 2) and among the Assyrians (cf. the representations of kings and warriors upon numerous reliefs) just the opposite practice prevailed, and that warriors went into battle with their long locks of hair flying loose. Nonetheless, they were in a very real state of consecration, or taboo (cf. I Sam. 21 : 5 f.), at the termination of which they had to purify themselves in the regular, prescribed manner (cf. Num. 31 : 24). Probably, therefore, in ancient Israel the hair of warriors was cut off at the close of a battle or campaign, i.e., at the close of the period of taboo, as an integral and important part of the rites of purification, and the hair was allowed to grow long during this period in preparation for this ceremonial cutting of it at the period's close. But this makes it all the more difficult to account for the seemingly altogether irregular practice of the ancient Arab warriors.

Another exception to the general principle and practice of cutting off the hair seems to be furnished by the custom of Christian monks and nuns of sacrificing their hair at ordination and keeping it cut, or at least keeping a portion of the head shaved, during the remainder of their lives. This practice seems to be just the opposite to that of the Hebrew Nazirite, particularly the Nazirite vowed for life, with which the Christian institution has apparently the most pronounced affinities. For this reason it is all the more surprising and inexplicable.

Inasmuch as no satisfactory explanation of these two apparently isolated instances of the rite of cutting off the hair suggests itself, we must perforce regard them as exceptions, and the only striking exceptions which we have been able to discover, despite diligent search, to this general rule governing the rite of cutting off the hair among the Semites, which we have established. Certainly these two seemingly unique exceptions do not weaken the validity of our conclusion that the cutting off of the hair marks the passing out from a state of consecration, or taboo, into a state of ordinary, profane existence.

An interesting instance of the rite of cutting off the hair is the following ancient Babylonian practice (quoted from Jastrow, "Older Elements in the Code of Hammurabi," *JAOS,* XXXVI [1916], 6, note 16): "Again in Poebel, *Legal Documents of the First Dynasty,* No. 48, 14–16, the wife stipulates that she is to receive one half mina of silver in case of divorce by her husband, whereas if she says to her husband, 'thou art not my husband,' she is to be shorn of her hair and sold. Such appears to have been the practice in Nippur." It is interesting to note that almost the same custom survives still today in another part of the Semitic world. Burckhardt (*Travels in Nubia,* p. 146) relates that "among the Arabs of Upper Egypt it is the law that if a wife oblige her husband to give a divorce, her dowry and all her clothes are taken away, and the husband shaves her head completely before he dismisses her." Until her hair has grown again she may not remarry. In both these cases, however, the shaving of the head seems to be rather a sign of disgrace than a rite of removal of taboo. For a like practice among the pre-Islamic Arabs, cf. Goldziher,

Muhammedanische Studien, I, 185. This, too, seems to be the principle underlying the additional Babylonian practice of cutting off the hair as a punishment for raising a finger against a priestess, for bringing an action at law improperly, and for bearing false witness (Pinches, *ERE,* IV, 259).

128. The offering of the hair and the nails as taboo-sacrifices differs in one very essential respect from the offering of other parts of the body, in that the hair and the nails grow again after cutting and so this form of sacrifice may be repeated at regular intervals throughout life, whenever conditions necessitate such a sacrifice, while other parts of the body—such as the foreskin or a tooth or a joint of a finger or toe, which do not grow again—can, of course, be offered only once during a lifetime. This fact makes the frequency and appropriateness of the offering of the hair or the nails as a taboo-sacrifice all the more apparent. Thus, in northern Africa the hair and nails of a sick person should not be cut (Doutté, *Merrâkech,* p. 97; *Magie et Religion dans l'Afrique du Nord,* p. 445). This is undoubtedly in anticipation of the moment when the sick person will be pronounced cured, which would be the natural and proper time for the offering of the hair and nails as a taboo-sacrifice to the evil spirit who had caused the sickness.

Notes to Chapter XIII

1. Wellhausen, "Die Ehe bei den Arabern," *GGN,* XI (1893), 442; cf. also Gen. 29 : 27 f. The relationship of this term with *sabûʿ,* the designation for the rites upon the seventh day after birth, is self-apparent.

2. Quite obviously the bride is thought to be more subject to danger from evil spirits than the groom, and therefore in greater need of protection in every way possible against their attacks; cf. Gaudefroy-Demombynes, *Cérémonies du Marriage chez les Indigènes de l'Algérie,* pp. 36, 37, 38, 49, 59, 60; Canaan, *Aberglaube und Volksmedezin im Lande der Bibel,* pp. 23, 57, 77.

3. Jennings-Bramley, "The Bedouin of the Sinaitic Peninsula," *PEF* (1907), pp. 24 f.; cf. also Robinson Lees, *The Witness of the Wilderness,* p. 123.

4. *Coutumes des Arabes au pays de Moab,* p. 54.

5. I.e., "bridal chamber"; cf. Morgenstern, "The Etymological History of the Three Hebrew Synonyms for 'to Dance,'" *JAOS,* XXXVI (1916), 321–332.

6. *Arabia Petraea,* III, 195 f., 206.

7. Elsewhere (*op. cit.,* III, 321 f.), Musil relates a story, which he had heard from the Arabs, of a man whose young wife was stolen away from him by a *ǧinn* on the seventh night after marriage, but was recovered by him through the favor of the *ǧinn* chief.

8. Musil, *op. cit.,* III, 373.

9. Cf. Deut. 20 : 7.

10. *Notes on the Bedouins and Wahabys,* p. 152; but cf. Wetzstein, "Sprachliches aus den Zeltlagern der syrischen Wüste," *ZDMG,* XXII (1868), 109, where the bride is not thus secluded.

11. It is interesting to note in this connection that the marriage festivities

of Tobias and Sarah are represented as also continuing for fourteen days (Tobit 8 : 18 f., 10 : 7). May the inference be drawn that this is intended to emphasize the fact that despite her previous marriages Sarah was still a virgin at the time of this marriage?

12. *Coutumes des Arabes au pays de Moab,* pp. 53, note 1, 55.

13. Featherman, *The Aramaeans,* p. 368; Hartland, *Primitive Paternity,* II, 16.

14. Von Maltzan, *Reisen in Arabien,* II, 262 f.

15. Cf. also above, Chapter XII, note 84, and below, note 39, and also Wellhausen, *Reste des altarabischen Heidentums*², p. 196. According to Grüneisen, *Der Ahnenkultus und die Urreligion Israels,* p. 97, and Klippel, *Études sur le Folklore Bedouin de l'Egypte,* p. 37, just the opposite was the case, and the veil was worn by brides to protect them against evil which threatened them from without, particularly the evil eye. It is quite as logical that the veil should protect the person under it from danger from without as that it should protect all persons without from maleficent influences emanating from the person veiled. But since, as we have seen, the bride, as a virgin, was certainly regarded as being subject to the power of an evil spirit, so that contact with, or even the sight of, her was dangerous to others, it is quite likely that something of both ideas lies at the bottom of the institution of wearing the veil by brides; on the one hand, it protected the bride, and where worn in some form by the groom also (cf. Lauterbach, "The Ceremony of Breaking a Glass at Weddings," *HUCA,* II [1925], 355 f.), then him as well, from danger threatening from without; and, on the other hand, it protected the family and friends, and perhaps in a way even the groom also, from the evil influence emanating from the bride, or from the evil spirit which possessed her. In some localities the one motive would tend to be accentuated and the other motive would eventually be almost completely forgotten, while in other localities the opposite tendency would prevail. Such is the opinion also of Doutté (*Magie et Religion dans l'Afrique du Nord,* pp. 321 ff.). Of course, where the veil is worn by mourners in rites of death and burial, and particularly by the nearest relatives of the deceased, it can originally have had only the one purpose: to protect them from the evilly disposed ghost of the dead (cf. Lods, *La Croyance à la Vie Future et le Culte des Morts dans l'Antiquité Israélite,* pp. 81 f., 103 f.; also below, p. 248, note 54). For the veiling of the bride, and also of other women as well, among the ancient Assyrians, cf. Jastrow, "An Assyrian Law Code," *JAOS,* XLI (1921), par. 39, pp. 34 ff.

16. *Peasant Life in the Holy Land,* p. 114.

17. Baldensperger, "Woman in the East," *PEF* (1901), p. 174.

18. Schwarz, *Das Heilige Land,* p. 341; cf. also Luncz, in *Jerusalem,* I (1886), 6, 9; Lauterbach, *op. cit.,* p. 355.

19. Benjamin, *Eight Years in Asia and Africa,* p. 287. This seems to have been the practice at the marriage of Jacob with the daughters of Laban (Gen. 29 : 21–28) and also at the marriage of Samson with the Philistine woman (Judg. 14 : 10 ff.). So also, in *Joseph and Asenath* XXI, Pharaoh makes a great banquet which continues for seven days, during which time all work is forbidden; the marriage is consummated on the first night.

20. Snouck Hurgronje, *Mekka,* II, 186.

21. Daumas, *La Femme Arabe,* p. 44. Among the Arabs a widow was and is regarded as a dangerous person, contact or association with whom is liable to work mischief. Apparently she was thought to be possessed by evil spirits, for Wellhausen ("Die Ehe bei den Arabern," *GGN,* XI, 454 f.; *Reste des altarabischen Heidentums*[2], p. 171) records the practice that before remarriage a widow was required to bring a bird into contact with her body and then let it fly away, presumably carrying the evil spirit or influence with it, just as in the rituals of the leper in ancient Israel (Lev. 14 : 4–7) and of the sick or possessed man in ancient Babylonian practice (cf. Morgenstern, *The Doctrine of Sin in the Babylonian Religion, MVAG,* III [1905], 60, note 3, and the references there cited). Quite similarly at Jewish marriage ceremonies during the Middle Ages it was a common practice to let a cock and a hen fly away over the heads of the bride and groom (cf. Scheftelowitz, "Das stellvertretende Huhnopfer," *ARW,* XIV [1911], 11; Lauterbach, *op. cit.,* p. 359, note 11). Even more explicit is the purpose of this rite in the following ceremony: at Tlemcen, in Morocco, "when a woman is pregnant, in order to protect her offspring and to ward off the *ǧinn,* a black hen is carefully guarded in the house from the end of the seventh month to the accouchement. At this moment the oldest woman in the house takes the hen and goes to the Jewish quarter and there lets it fly away; the hen carries the *ǧinn* away with itself" (Doutté, *Magie et Religion dans l'Afrique du Nord,* p. 455).

But to return to the widow, Burckhardt (*Notes on the Bedouins and Wahabys,* p. 152) tells that "the Arabs regard everything connected with the nuptials of a widow as ill-omened and unworthy of the participation of generous and honorable men. For the space of thirty days, or a whole month, the husband will not eat of any provisions belonging to his wife, nor even use any of her vessels at meals. During that time she herself and everything appertaining to her are stigmatized as being *geràn* . . . ; and the Arabs believe that any infraction of this custom could be the sure road to perdition. If the husband makes coffee for the Arabs, every one of his guests brings with him his own cup, that he may not drink of one belonging to the new-married widow." In Palestine today the superstition is common that three things shorten life, walking behind funerals, going through deserts, and marrying widows or divorced women (Canaan, "Folklore of the Seasons," *JPOS,* III [1923], 25).

22. Daumas, *op. cit.,* p. 44.

23. Featherman, *The Aramaeans,* p. 509.

24. Westermarck, *Marriage Ceremonies in Morocco,* p. 291.

25. *Merrâkech,* p. 264.

26. *Ibid.,* p. 336.

27. *Ibid.,* p. 338.

28. Lane, *The Manners and Customs of the Modern Egyptians*[3], p. 505.

29. Featherman, *op. cit.*

30. *Arabic Proverbs,* pp. 117 f.

31. "Aegyptica," in the *Nöldeke Festschrift,* I, 418 ff.

32. Similarly, and undoubtedly for the same purpose, in Algeria the wedding guests assemble and make a loud noise outside the chamber in which the marriage is being consummated (Daumas, *La Femme Arabe,* p. 42;

Gaudefroy-Demombynes, *Les Cérémonies du Marriage chez les Indigènes de l'Algérie,* p. 64; according to the latter authority, the marriage candle is also kept burning outside the marriage chamber for the same purpose; *ibid.,* p. 58). Precisely the same custom is observed by the Druses (Kelly, *Syria and the Holy Land,* p. 148). And at marriages in Morocco, "the constant firing of guns, the loud music, and the quivering noise of women . . . obviously serve the same purpose of purifying the atmosphere and frightening away evil spirits by the noise and, in the case of the powder play, also by the smell of the powder, of which the *jinn* are believed to be much afraid. For the same reason the bridegroom carries a sword, dagger, or pistol; and the crossing of swords over his head or in front of him is likewise intended to ward off *jnûn,* who are afraid of steel and, especially, of weapons of this metal. The same is the case with his wearing of various charms and the use of salt, which is also a common safeguard against evil spirits" (Westermarck, *op. cit.,* pp. 122 f.). For noise as part of the ceremonies attendant upon the birth of a child and also at circumcision, cf. above, pp. 39, 60, 209, note 16.

33. Featherman, *op. cit.,* p. 422.

34. Dye, *Egypt and Abyssinia,* pp. 94 f.

35. Scheftelowitz, "Das Fischsymbol in Judentum und Christentum," *ARW,* XIV (1911), 377 (upon the authority of Leo Africanus, *Africae Descriptio,* Leyden, 1632).

36. Samter, *Geburt, Hochzeit und Tod,* pp. 93 f.

37. Cf. Westermarck, *op. cit.,* pp. 271 ff. for the practice in Morocco; also the supposedly Emorite custom recorded above (p. 93), that she who has just been married must offer herself for prostitution for seven days at the gate of the city.

38. Westermarck records that in Morocco the bride, and to a certain extent the groom also, are thought to be in a condition of taboo, and therefore in a state dangerous to others. Accordingly, ceremonies of varying character are performed to safeguard the people from their contact or glance. Thus, in the Hiaina "the bride's eyes must be covered, because it is believed that misfortune would befall any person or animal the bride looked at, before she has seen her husband on her arrival at his house" (*op. cit.,* p. 148). In Andjra it is believed that whoever would look at the bride would become blind. Therefore she is kept covered and shut up in order not to be seen (p. 169). Among the Tsul she keeps handkerchiefs over her face. "She must not look at anybody; if she did, there would be fighting and manslaughter at the wedding that very day. Nor must she turn her head, lest her husband should die" (p. 172). The Ait Ndêr have the same belief and custom (p. 181; cf. also pp. 189 f., 198, 219).

In Algeria the husband may not address a word to his bride until after the marriage has been consummated (Gaudefroy-Demombynes, *op. cit.,* p. 61). The wife may not visit her relatives until some five or six months after the marriage, nor may the husband see his relatives until nine months have elapsed. Should he by chance meet any of them, he must hide himself from them (*ibid.,* p. 75).

39. Cf. above, pp. 99 f.

40. Among the Moslems of Algeria the bride remains secluded in the house

for seven days after marriage. During this time she is not permitted to bathe, because, so the sages say, "she is then in Paradise, and so free from sin." At the close of this period she is compelled to take a bath (Certeux and Carony, *L'Algérie Traditionelle; Contributions au Folk-Lore des Arabes,* I, 211 f.). Unquestionably, bathing is here a rite to remove ritual uncleanness and taboo. Among the Mandaeans, also, both bride and groom are regarded as unclean for the first seven days after marriage, and at the close of this period both must take a ritual bath (Brandt, *Mandäische Religion,* p. 96; Petermann, *Reisen im Orient*², II, 118).

41. *Primitive Semitic Religion Today,* pp. 204 f. (English ed.); pp. 234 f. (German ed.).

42. *Notes on the Bedouins and Wahabys,* p. 151.

43. *Op. cit.,* pp. 61, 151.

44. *The Desert of the Exodus,* p. 83.

45. *Arabia Petraea,* III, 205 f.

46. *Op. cit.,* p. 195.

47. *Coutumes des Arabes au pays de Moab,* p. 54.

48. *Ibid.,* pp. 346 f.

49. Cf. Morgenstern, "The Etymological History of the Three Hebrew Synonyms for 'to Dance,'" *JAOS,* XXXVI (1916), 321–332.

50. Jaussen's translation is "Sois deliée; Allah t'a deliée."

51. However, this does not follow necessarily; for we shall soon see (below, p. 144) that certain other sacrifices, originally offered to evil spirits, and notably the sacrifice of the red heifer (Num. 19) and the heifer whose neck was broken (Deut. 21 : 1–9), had to be female animals, even though there was no question of the redemption of women, for whom they might be the substitutes, in connection with these sacrifices. Moreover, Jaussen gives one other instance when this sacrifice is offered (*op. cit.,* p. 358); "When in a tribe the sheikh has made a vow, in consequence of some great calamity, to sacrifice a victim every year, his descendants feel obligated completely and perpetually. If it is the common ancestor who made such a seeming promise, the entire tribe is obligated to carry out this agreement, or else the greatest misfortune must be expected. Sheikh Musallem at Irak never neglects to sacrifice each year many sheep at the tomb of Sheikh Ia'koub because of a vow made by one of his ancestors; this is called the 'sacrifice of satisfaction.'" The Arabic name of this sacrifice recorded by Jaussen is *dabîḥet ḥullîye.* Obviously this is only another form, or rather the occasion for the offering, of the redemption sacrifice which we have already discussed. In this case it averts the calamities which would certainly befall the tribe, so it is believed, were it not offered.

52. Samter, *op. cit.,* pp. 45–48; Bertholet, *Kulturgeschichte Israels,* p. 137.

53. Cf. also Frazer, *Folk-Lore in the Old Testament,* I, 498 ff. The following peculiar incident bears in some respects a certain resemblance to this one motif of the Tobit story: "The strangest marriage I have heard of was one, which, I have good authority for saying, occurred here some years ago. A man had married several wives, all of whom had died in childbirth. Thinking he was under some magical spell, he went through the form of marriage with a cow, the wedding ring being actually placed on the cow's horn. The

cow was then killed, and he immediately married a bride in the ordinary way . . . the curse having, as he thought, been removed" (Masterman, "Jewish Customs of Birth, Marriage, and Death," *BW,* XXII, 252). Quite similarly, it is customary at Artas, to the south of Bethlehem, that at the marriage of a woman who has been married several times before, but all of whose husbands have died shortly after marriage, a donkey is brought in in the procession of the bridegroom, along with the bridegroom himself, and the donkey is presented to the bride as if he were the real bridegroom. The purpose of this rite is, of course, to deceive the evil spirit which has wrought all the previous mischief and cause him to play his destructive pranks upon the donkey, and thus deliver the real bridegroom from impending death (Canaan, *Aberglaube und Volksmedezin im Lande der Bibel,* p. 69; cf. also Samter, *Geburt, Hochzeit und Tod,* pp. 98 ff.; Burckhardt, *Notes on the Bedouins and Wahabys,* p. 152; Frazer, *Folk-Lore in the Old Testament,* I, 525, for other, similar practices). An interesting gypsy parallel to the Tobit story is recorded by Garnett, *The Women of Turkey and Their Folk-Lore,* II, 379.

54. Quoted from *JE,* II, 217.

55. *B^e^rakôt* 54b.

56. Bauer, *Volksleben im Lande der Bibel,* p. 196.

57. Featherman, *op. cit.,* pp. 421 f. Among the Persians too, we are told, the bride wears a veil at her wedding in order to protect her against the evil eye (Chardin, *Voyages en Perse,* II, 234). The Midrash relates similarly the parable of a king who gives to his daughter at her marriage an amulet to protect her against the evil eye (*Bammidbar rabba* III, 4, near end). Among the Arabs of Moab, when the bride is being brought in festal procession to the house of her future husband, she holds a dagger in her hand, which she keeps pressed against her forehead in order to ward off the evil eye (Jaussen, *Coutumes des Arabes au pays de Moab,* p. 53).

58. Rothstein, "Moslemische Hochzeitsgebräuche in Lifta bei Jerusalem," *PJB* (1910), p. 116; cf. also Wilson, *Peasant Life in the Holy Land,* pp. 113 f.

59. Cf. also Samter, *op. cit.,* pp. 45–48. It is noteworthy in this connection that dancing is seemingly an important part of the marriage celebration in all the lands and among practically all the peoples and creeds of the Near East today. This matter has been adequately, although by no means exhaustively, discussed by Oesterley (*The Sacred Dance,* pp. 177–193). He concludes that the purpose of such dances at wedding feasts, and particularly of the sword dance, is to ward off the evil spirits which on such occasions threaten the bride and the groom.

Probably with this we may correlate an ancient and rather obscure Jewish ceremony. The Talmud (*Yer. K^e^tûbôt* I, 25a) states that while ordinarily it was customary to appoint only one bridal attendant or companion, and that this was the rule in Galilee, in Judea two were appointed, who discharged certain particular functions at the actual marriage ceremonies. One of these represented the groom and the other the bride. Among other duties, these two slept in the place of the bride and the groom. The meaning and purpose of this strange procedure are not clear. But it seems that these two representatives of the bridal pair slept in the bridal chamber, where supposedly the marriage would be consummated, while the bridal pair themselves actually slept elsewhere, probably in some place not generally known. If such was the real meaning of the practice, then the fact that the bride and groom slept in some unknown place and there consummated their union would parallel the Bedouin practice, which we have already noted, of the flight of the bride to some secret place in the desert, her pursuit and discovery by the groom, and their consummation of their marriage in that remote and previously unappointed spot. And if this interpretation is correct, then the fact that the two representatives of the bride and the groom slept in the place of the bridal pair—presumably in the bridal chamber, where the marriage should have been consummated—can have had only one purpose: to deceive the unsuspecting evil spirit and make him think that these were actually the bride and groom, so that he could direct, vainly of course, his evil machinations against them, while the bride and groom would be delivered from all danger from him. This is possibly the origin of the role of the best man and matron (or maid) of honor in modern marriage ceremonies.

In modern Palestine the best man frequently plays still another role in protecting the bridegroom against evil spirits. Among the Christians "meal is ofttimes strewn in the church before the bridegroom by some enemy. Should he tread upon it, the evil spirits immediately have him in their power. Therefore he is carried by a strong friend, usually one of the bridal attendants, in order that he may not touch the ground." "Frequently, too, immediately after the close of the marriage ceremony one of the bridal attendants suddenly lifts the bridegroom high in the air and shakes him quite vigorously three times, in order that all magical charm or fear thereof may be removed." (Canaan, *Aberglaube und Volksmedezin im Lande der Bibel,* pp. 25 f.)

60. Cf. Additional Notes, F.

61. Benjamin, *op. cit.,* p. 115.

62. Jaussen, *Coutumes des Arabes au pays de Moab,* p. 346.

63. Lane, *The Manners and Customs of the Modern Egyptians*[3], p. 152.

64. In *The Acts of Andrew and Matthias* (*Ante-Nicene Fathers,* VII, 520) we are told that after every act of sexual intercourse the priests were required to purify themselves for seven days. The passage does not state what priests these were. But undoubtedly the same principle as that stated above lies at the bottom of this ceremony.

65. Lev. 12 : 2; 15 : 19–24; 18 : 19; Ezek. 18 : 6.

66. II Sam. 11 : 4.

67. Schmidt and Kahle, "Volkserzählungen aus Palästina," *Forschungen zur Religion und Literatur des Alten und Neuen Testaments,* p. 196, note 10; cf. also Musil, *Arabia Petraea,* III, 208.

Notes to Chapter XIV

1. Schwally, *Das Leben nach dem Tod,* pp. 41 f.

2. Robertson Smith, *Religion of the Semites*[3], pp. 322 f.; Marti, *Geschichte der israelitischen Religion*[5], p. 41; Duhm, *Die bösen Geister des Alten Testament,* p. 24; cf.

in particular Goldziher, *Muhammedanische Studien,* I, 255, and the custom of the ancient Arabs, there described, of erecting over the grave a tent, in which the mourners remained in order to defer for as long as possible the final leave-taking from the deceased. However, this must have been the exceptional, and not the regular, practice and more a matter of deep sentiment than of belief and ritual.

3. Samter, *op. cit.,* pp. 28 ff.; Grüneisen, *Der Ahnenkultus und die Urreligion Israels,* pp. 98 f.; Marti, *op. cit.,* p. 49; Scheftelowitz, "Die Sündentilgung durch Wasser," *ARW,* XVII (1914), 405; "Seelen- und Unsterblichkeitsglaube im Alten Testament," *ARW,* XIX (1916), pp. 222 f.; Bertholet, *Kulturgeschichte Israels,* p. 139.

4. *Primitive Semitic Religion Today,* pp. 206 f. (English ed.; German ed., p. 236).

5. *The Koran,* Preliminary Discourse, IV, 55 f.

6. For *Borbût,* Lane would read *Barahoot* (*The Manners and Customs of the Modern Egyptians*[3], p. 486, note). Perhaps this belief in the sojourn of the spirits of the dead in a well immediately after death may be paralleled by the common Bedouin tradition, cited below, that immediately after death the souls enter the Well of the Souls, also known as the Well of the Spirits, in Jerusalem.

7. *Coutumes des Arabes au pays de Moab,* p. 103.

8. However, Jaussen tells also (*op. cit.,* p. 101) that "among some Arab tribes, before carrying the corpse of a little child from the house, a piece of silver is put into its mouth, in order that it may not attempt to return from the cemetery to carry away the property of the family."

9. *Arabia Petraea,* III, 448 ff.

10. Another observer says, "The souls of those who during their lifetime have not visited Jerusalem, have to go there directly after death, remain there a short time, and then return to the grave" (Jennings-Bramley, "The Bedouin of the Sinaitic Peninsula," *PEF* [1906], p. 25).

11. For the possibility of a similar belief by the ancient Babylonians in a two-compartment nether world, cf. Zimmern and Winckler, *Die Keilinschriften und das Alte Testament*[3], p. 638.

12. For the probable meaning of this imprecation, cf. Morgenstern, "The Bones of the Paschal Lamb," *JAOS,* XXXVI (1916), 146–153.

13. *Op. cit.,* p. 429.

14. *Aberglaube und Volksmedezin im Lande der Bibel,* pp. 11 f.

15. To this, Canaan adds the note that this superstition is gradually dying out.

16. Whereas, as we have seen, the modern Bedouin frequently conceive of the souls of the dead as having the form of flies.

17. *Ancient Arabian Poetry,* p. 67.

18. Cf. also Damîrî, *Ḥayât al-Ḥayawân* (Constantinople ed., 1330 Heg.) I, 285 (translation of Jayakar, I, 347); Crichton, *Arabia,* I, 207; Certeux et Carony, *L'Algérie Traditionelle; Contributions au Folk-Lore des Arabes,* I, 231; Doughty, *Arabia Deserta,* I, 168; Goldziher, *op. cit.,* II, 297 f.; Nicholson, *Islamic Poetry,* p. 90, note 2. For the same belief in Judaism, cf. Lods, *La Croyance à la Vie Future et le Culte des Morts dans l'Antiquité Israélite,* p. 71; Kohler, *Jewish Theology,* pp. 214 f.; also Waser, "Ueber die äussere Erscheinung der

Seele," *ARW,* XVI (1913), 348 f. For the same belief among the ancient Assyrians and Babylonians, cf. Jastrow, *Die Religion Babyloniens und Assyriens,* II, 957. It is interesting to note that the female of the species of the owl called *ṣada* in Arabic was sometimes known as *umm-aṣ-ṣibyân.* We have seen that this was the name also of one of the evil spirits which was thought to threaten the lives of little children (above, p. 19).

19. *Reste des altarabischen Heidentums*², pp. 185 f.

20. *Nubia,* p. 197.

21. *Arabia Deserta,* I, 349.

22. Jennings-Bramley, *op. cit.,* pp. 26 f.; cf. also Goldziher, "Wasser als Dämonen abwehrendes Mittel," *ARW,* XIII (1910), 20 ff.; Nicholson, *op. cit.,* p. 136; Jaussen, *op. cit.,* p. 99; Jacob, *Altarabisches Beduinenleben,* pp. 142 f.; Burckhardt, *Nubia,* p. 197. Similarly, the fellahin of Palestine leave hollow places in the tops of tombs, in which rain water may collect and the dead, buried beneath, drink therefrom (Baldensperger, "Peasant Folklore of Palestine," *PEF* [1893], p. 217).

23. *Op. cit.,* p. 99.

24. *Op. cit.,* pp. 424 f.

25. *Ibid.,* p. 425.

26. *Ibid.,* p. 424.

27. *Ibid.,* p. 425.

28. Cf. Wellhausen, *Reste des altarabischen Heidentums*², pp. 183 f.

29. *Primitive Semitic Religion Today,* pp. 178 ff. (English ed.; German ed., pp. 202 ff.).

30. *Op. cit.*, p. 208; German edition, p. 237.

31. Pp. 224 f.

32. *Op. cit.,* p. 352.

33. Jaussen adds that the practice exists at Kerak also, even among the Christians.

34. I.e., the Belqâwîeh and the Ṣeḫur, two Bedouin tribes.

35. Jaussen adds in a note that some Arabs likewise sacrifice, just when the grave is about to close, a victim called *wanîeh;* this constitutes for them the real "sacrifice of death."

36. *Op. cit.,* pp. 451 ff.

37. *MDPV* (1904), pp. 75 f.

38. Hess, "Beduinisches zum alten und neuen Testament," *ZAW* (1915), p. 130.

39. *Arabia Deserta,* I, 240 f.; cf. pp. 293, 354, 442, 451, 452.

40. Above, p. 124.

41. *Op. cit.* (English ed., pp. 211 f.; German ed., p. 240).

42. *Op. cit.,* p. 353.

43. *Ibid.,* pp. 371 ff.

44. So also Burckhardt, *Notes on the Bedouins and Wahabys,* p. 57.

45. *Op. cit.,* pp. 450 ff.

46. For the *daḥîyyeh* festival and sacrifice, cf. also Goldziher, *Muhammedanische Studien,* I, 240 f.; Socin, *Islamischer Diwan,* p. 295.

47. Similarly, "in some parts of Barbary the custom is prevalent of distrib-

uting cooked food among the poor on the evening of the burial. This is called 'the supper of the grave'" (Featherman, *The Aramaeans,* p. 511).

48. Above, p. 127.

49. Cf. Musil, *op. cit.,* III, 425. Among the ancient Arabs also it was customary to leave the favorite camel to starve at the grave of its master, with its head bound to its tail and covered with the cloak of the deceased, so that the dead man might not be obliged to travel on foot in the other world. If the animal made its escape, it was held sacred and allowed pasture and water free; in other words, it was still regarded as taboo, forbidden for profane use by mortals, presumably because it was still thought to be the property of the ghost of the dead man (Crichton, *Arabia,* I, 207). Wellhausen is even more explicit in his account of the same institution: "Traces of the world-wide custom of putting in the grave with the corpse all manner of things which he had need of in life are found among the Arabs. . . . There are instances of breaking the kettle and plate of a man, as well as his weapons, over his grave. In particular, he is given his riding animal with him, for without it he would be inadequately equipped. 'The heathen Arabs believed that without it at the resurrection he would be compelled to go on foot,' the Muslim archaeologists said; quite correct, if only the reference to the resurrection be omitted. Occasionally his camel, together with its saddle and other equipment, was burned. Or it was fastened in a hole beside the grave of its master and left there unattended until it died. Usually, however, its hind tendons were cut so that it could not run away; this custom is evidenced by many examples. . . . In lieu of the camel, in exceptional and more recent cases, the favorite horse was put to death in this manner at the grave; this proves that we do not have to do with a sacrifice here, for the horse was not a sacrificial animal" (*Reste des altarabischen Heidentums*[2], pp. 180 f.).

50. According to Paton (*Spiritism and the Cult of the Dead in Antiquity,* p. 207), the ancient Arabs had no conception whatsoever of the nether world, and therefore the belief therein cannot have been primitive Semitic. Unquestionably, Paton is mistaken in both his premise and his conclusion, as the evidence which we have presented above shows clearly.

51. For the systematic opposition of early Islam to the cult of the dead implicit in these primitive rites of burial and mourning, and its attempt either to abrogate these ceremonies or to give them a new interpretation as rites in honor of Allah, cf. Goldziher, *op. cit.,* I, 232 ff., 251 ff.

52. This is also the import of the fact cited by Jaussen (*op. cit.,* p. 101), that one of the very worst curses which can be invoked upon a Bedouin is, "May God so bring it about that at thy death there will be no one to offer thee the supper of the dead!"

53. This fear of the vengeance of the ghost of the dead for a duty unperformed by the living probably accounts for a certain custom in modern Palestine described by Haddad ("Methods of Education and Correction among the *Fellaḥin,*" *JPOS,* III [1923], 41): "The *fellaḥin* believe that after a dying person tells relatives about the debts he owes others he is no longer responsible for them before God, but his relatives will be responsible if they do not pay the debts he owes. Hence they see that it is necessary to pay his debts to his

creditors after his death, even if they are obliged to sell the furniture of their house."

54. In the light of these facts it is not at all surprising to find that among the modern Arabs of Nejd the *nefs,* literally, "the soul," is regarded as an evil spirit which can work irreparable mischief to man (Doughty, *Arabia Deserta,* II, 384; cf. Wellhausen, *Reste des altarabischen Heidentums*², p. 157, for a kindred belief among the ancient Arabs). Undoubtedly, fear of the ghost of the dead prompted the ancient Arabs to cover their heads and faces in the presence of a corpse (Wellhausen, *ibid.,* p. 196).

55. *Arabia Petraea,* III, 425. For a kindred practice among the ancient Arabs, cf. Wellhausen, *ibid.,* pp. 182 f.

56. *Folk-lore in the Old Testament,* III, 270–303.

57. Deut. 12 : 23; cf. Morgenstern, "The Bones of the Paschal Lamb," *JAOS,* XXXVI (1916), 151 ff.

58. Musil describes the practice of the Bedouin women of scratching their faces until the blood flows as a mourning rite (*op. cit.,* p. 428). Likewise in Abyssinia, we are told (Rathjens, *Die Juden in Abessinien,* p. 55), in honor of the dead both men and women cut off their hair, and the women beat their breasts and scratch their faces until they bleed. An interesting instance of the practice of bodily mutilation as a mourning rite in modern Palestine is given by Wad-El-Ward (*Palestine through the Eyes of a Native,* pp. 112 f.): "When the days of mourning are over, the son or sons of the deceased rise early in the morning, and, accompanied by their relations, friends, and acquaintances, proceed to the cemetery, making a large circle by standing around the tomb, where they compose a low chant of prayer for the repose of the soul and its sure life in Paradise; towards the end they become very excited, acting as if they were in a delirium. Knives are drawn, each one cutting his neighbor's garment, and many use knives on their own bodies, cutting and slashing themselves. . . . This cruel part of worship is meant to show to God that they are willing to give up their bodies if He will hear their prayers. Many among the crowd take large skewers of iron and pierce through both cheeks from one side of the face to the other. They then spread themselves, making a large circle around the grave, and with bowed heads they keep silence. This ceremony is called *'Mautheem kever ha muath,'* meaning 'the dead burying the dead.'"

59. So also Elhorst, "Die israelitischen Trauerriten," in *Wellhausen Festschrift,* pp. 119 f.

60. Cf. the passage from Doughty, *Arabia Deserta,* I, 240 f., cited above, p. 126.

61. It is possible, and even probable, that the consideration that the cutting off of the hair and the various bodily mutilations practiced by the ancient Semites would so alter their appearance as to make them unrecognizable by the ghost was associated with the idea that the parts of the body thus cut off were taboo-sacrifices which redeemed the living relatives from the power of the ghost. Such is the opinion of Grüneisen (*Der Ahnenkultus und die Urreligion Israels,* pp. 98 f.). But, as Frazer has shown conclusively (*op. cit.,* III, 297 f.),

this is at best a secondary consideration and cannot have been a factor in the original practice.

62. *The Sacred Dance,* pp. 194–206; cf. also Döbel, *Wanderungen im Morgenland,* p. 331; Bauer, *Volksleben im Lande der Bibel*², pp. 244 f.

63. Jaussen, *op. cit.,* p. 71; Samter, *Geburt, Hochzeit und Tod,* p. 88.

64. Petermann, *Reisen im Orient*², II, 119.

65. Garnett, *The Women of Turkey and Their Folk-lore,* II, 32; cf. *Šulḥan ʿArûk, Yôreh Deʿah,* 376, 4, note of Moses Isserles.

66. Par. 12, 3. The Rabbis called Psalm 91, or rather the first nine verses thereof, recited in conjunction with Psalm 3, the *šîr šel pᵉgaʿîm,* "the song" or "psalm against misfortunes," or, possibly, "against evil spirits" (*Yer. Šabbat* VI, 8b; *Bab. Šᵉbûʿot* 15b).

67. This is probably the origin of the custom of reciting this psalm as a part of the Jewish funeral ritual just as the corpse is being carried to the grave. This psalm is recited also in the funeral ritual of the Greek Orthodox Church at Constantinople (Sicard, in Paulus, *Sammlung der merkwürdigsten Reisen in den Orient,* V, 72).

68. Canaan, "Folklore of the Seasons," *JPOS,* III (1923), 25.

69. *Op. cit.,* p. 101.

70. *Op. cit.,* III, 428; cf. also pp. 426 f.

71. H. M. Huxley ("Syrian Songs, Proverbs and Stories," *JAOS,* XXIII [1902], pp. 215 f.), quotes a song which runs thus:

> The house, oh Saʿid, we have forsaken,
> from the day of (your) departure, and we have not entered it;
> From the day of departure, oh handsome bridegroom,
> we have painted its doors with indigo.

To this, the author adds the note: "This song recalls the custom . . . of deserting a house after there has been a death in it, on account of the belief that the house is haunted by the spirit of the deceased."

It should be noted in this connection that in Egypt, as well as in Syria, indigo is the color of mourning; cf. Burckhardt, *Notes on the Bedouins and Wahabys,* p. 159; Lane, *The Manners and Customs of the Modern Egyptians*³, p. 487; Kahle, *Die Totenklage im heutigen Aegypten* (reprint from the *Gunkel Festschrift*), p. 11, note 3. For red regarded as the color of death, and therefore also of mourning, among the ancient Assyrians, cf. Olmstead, *History of Assyria,* p. 341, and also Additional Note F and below, pp. 144, 151, 162 f.

72. Curelly, in Flinders Petrie, *Researches in Sinai,* p. 230; Bauer, *Volksleben im Lande der Bibel,* p. 212.

73. Wellhausen, *Reste des altarabischen Heidentums*², p. 151; Lods, *La Croyance à la Vie Future dan l'Antiquité Israélite,* p. 188; Musil, *op. cit.,* III, 319 ff., 429; Canaan, *Aberglaube und Volksmedezin im Lande der Bibel,* pp. 8, 12.

74. Cf. Gen. 32 : 25.

75. *Ḥagîga* 3b; *Niddah* 17a.

76. Canaan, "Folklore of the Seasons," *JPOS,* III (1923), 25.

77. Guys, *Voyage en Syrie,* pp. 193 f.

78. *The Manners and Customs of the Modern Egyptians*[3], p. 507.

79. Probably fear of the ghost at night prompts the custom, recorded by Musil (*op. cit.,* p. 429), that at el-Kerak during the first night after a burial a lantern is kept burning upon the spot where the death occurred, "for it is not nice that the house (tent) should remain dark."

80. *Kulturgeschichte Israels,* p. 98; Lods, *Le Culte des Ancêtres dans l'Antiquité Hébraique,* pp. 83 f.; Paton, *Spiritism and the Cult of the Dead in Antiquity,* p. 235.

81. Cf. Additional Notes, G.

82. Cf. Morgenstern, *The Doctrine of Sin in the Babylonian Religion, MVAG,* III (1905), 12.

83. *Utukki Limnuti,* IV, col. IV, 42–col. V, 66; translation of Thompson, *The Devils and Evil Spirits of Babylonia,* I, 38–45 (with a few minor corrections in the translation).

84. King, *Babylonian Magic and Sorcery,* no. 53, contains the prayer for divine help of a man who has been possessed by the ghost of a dead person. This evil spirit gives him no rest either day or night, but subjects him to all manner of torment. He causes his hair to stand on end, lames (?) his side, makes his eyes fixed, causes pain in his head, and poisons his limbs. The afflicted man prays to Šamaš, the sun-god, to free him from the power of this demon, whether it be the spirit of a deceased relative, or of someone who has been murdered, or of anyone else. It is significant that here apparently the ghosts most to be feared are those of relatives or of some one who has been murdered. This accords fully with what we have previously established.

85. Cf. Jensen, in *KB,* VI, 264 f.; Ungnad, *Das Gilgameš-Epos,* p. 68; Jastrow, *Die Religion Babyloniens und Assyriens* I, 359, 371 ff.

86. *Annals,* VI, 75 f.; *KB,* II, 206 f.; cf. also Pedersen, *Der Eid bei den Semiten,* p. 71.

87. *Annals,* IV, 70–72; *KB,* II, 192 f.

88. The technical Babylonian term for a sacrifice to the dead seems to have been *kispu,* and the verb *kasāpu* (cf. Delitzsch, *Assyrisches Handwörterbuch,* p. 344; Meissner, *Supplement,* p. 49). These words seem, however, to have been used technically with various shades of meaning, so that their precise connotation and ritual significance are difficult to determine. In Zimmern, *Ritualtafeln,* p. 26, col. IV, 43, a *kispu* is offered to the Anunnaki, the great gods, as a part of a very long and complex ceremony of purification of the king from ritual uncleanness. Whether or not the term Anunnaki here designates a group of inferior, chthonic deities, as is occasionally the case, it is impossible to determine. For this reason it is impossible also to fix the significance of the role of the *kispu* in this ceremony, although it appears to have been rather incidental. Again in Zimmern, *op. cit.,* pp. 49, 11, a *kispu* is sacrificed as a part of a rather complex ceremony performed before the triad of deities, Ea, Šamaš, and Marduk; the sacrifice is, however, not necessarily offered to these three deities. Again, in *op. cit.,* p. 66, rev. 7, a *kispu* seems to be offered to the Anunnaki, also as a part of a larger, complex ceremony of purification. The remnants of food, cast out into the street, which the souls of the dead eat, are called *kusiptu* (Delitzsch, *op. cit.,* 345). This is obviously a related word;

cf. also Alfred Jeremias, *Die babylonisch-assyrischen Vorstellungen von Leben nach dem Tode,* pp. 53 ff.; Zimmern and Winckler, *Die Keilinschriften und das Alte Testament*³, p. 638.

89. *Pirqe d'R. Eliezer,* XXXIV (translation of Friedlander), 253; cf. Blau, *Das altjüdische Zauberwesen,* pp. 13 f.; Jirku, *Die Dämonen und ihre Abwehr im Alten Testament,* pp. 15 f.; Canaan, *Aberglaube und Volksmedezin im Lande der Bibel,* pp. 11 f.

90. *Beᵉrakôt* 51a.

91. *Babba Batra* 100b; *Šulḥan ʿArûk, Yôreh Deʿah* 376, 4, and Moses Isserles to the passage; also Scheftelowitz, "Die Sündentilgung durch Wasser," *ARW,* XVII (1914); Samter, *Geburt, Hochzeit und Tod,* p. 150, note 7.

92. *Šulḥan ʿArûk, Yôreh Deʿah* 357. Beyond all question, this was the original reason for not permitting the corpse of one who had been hung to remain suspended overnight; cf. Deut. 21 : 22 f.; Josh. 8 : 29; 10 : 26 f.; Matt. 27 : 57 ff.; and parallel passages.

93 Exod. 13 : 19; Josh. 24 : 32.

94. I Sam. 31 : 13; II Sam. 21 : 12 ff.; I Chron. 10 : 12.

95. Amos 2 : 1. This procedure of the king of Moab parallels closely in both principle and practice that of Ashurbanipal with the bones of the Elamite kings.

96. II Kings 23 : 14–20.

97. Jer. 8 : 1 f.; Ezek. 6 : 5; cf. Ps. 141 : 7. Probably here we have the reason for the opposition of the Jews and other Semitic peoples and religions to cremation of the dead. Jaussen says (*Coutumes des Arabes au pays de Moab,* pp. 103 f.): "Many Arabs despoil the corpses of their enemies, but they do not mutilate them nor insult them. They condemn openly the conduct of the Druses, who two years ago burned the corpses of some Arabs of Seïlam, whom they encountered and massacred at Mawqar near Zerqā. Neither the Ṣeḫour nor the Šarārāt nor any other Arabs would permit such atrocities." It is surprising to note in this connection, that, according to Certeux and Carony ("L'Algérie Traditionelle," *Contributions au Folk-Lore des Arabes,* I, 221), the Jews of Algeria, in contrast to the Moslems, practice cremation.

98. Above, p. 121. For the thought that the institution of blood-revenge, common and basic in primitive Semitic culture, was prompted by the fear felt by the living of the ghosts of their slain and unavenged relatives, cf. Lods, *Le Culte des Ancêtres dans l'Antiquité Hébraique,* p. 84.

99. Cf. Additional Notes, H.

100. Bauer, *Volksleben im Lande der Bibel,* p. 197.

101. Canaan, *Aberglaube und Volksmedezin im Lande der Bibel,* p. 17.

102. *Travels in Assyria, Media and Persia,* p. 173.

103. Above, p. 120.

104. Cf. Pedersen, *Der Eid bei den Semiten,* p. 186.

105. From this discussion it becomes clear that Deut. 21 : 1–9 records a ceremony of extremely primitive origin and character, which had primarily no relation whatsoever with Yahweh-worship. Apparently the main body of this passage was copied almost verbatim from some ancient, pre-Deuteronomic ritual prescription. Vv. 5–6a are quite obviously a somewhat disturbing

Deuteronomic insertion into an older text; and equally obviously vv. 8 f. reinterpret or supplant what must have been the concluding words of the formula recited by the elders of the town. And in all certainty these words must have been directed to the ghost of the dead man, just as the heifer which was slain must have been originally a sacrifice or a gift to the ghost. The slaughtering of this animal in this peculiar place was in complete disagreement with the fundamental Deuteronomic principle of the sacrifice of animals only at the central sanctuary (Deut. 12), and is the best indication that originally this animal was killed in honor of, not Yahweh, but the ghost of the dead man. (So also Bertholet, *Deuteronomy,* p. 64; Lods, *La Croyance à la Vie Future dans l'Antiquité Israélite,* pp. 169 f.). This is indicated likewise by the character of the place selected for the performance of this ceremony, viz., a valley or ravine through which a stream flowed but which had never been tilled, and also by the manner in which the heifer was killed, viz., by breaking its neck, for this seems to have been the conventional manner in which animals not suitable for sacrifice, or at least sacrifice to Yahweh, were slain; cf. Exod. 13 : 13; 34 : 20; Isa. 66 : 3. In Abyssinia today a ravine through which a stream of water flows is the usual place in which the Defterers or Scribes perform their incantations to call up spirits (Parkyns, *Life in Abyssinia,* II, 144).

106. Cf. Bewer, "The Rite of the Red Cow," *JBL,* XXIV (1905), 41–44; H. P. Smith, "Notes on the Red Heifer," *JBL,* XXVII (1908), 153–156, and *Religion of Israel,* pp. 32 f.; Elhorst, "Die israelitischen Trauerriten," *Wellhausen Festschrift,* pp. 125 f.; Scheftelowitz, "Das Opfer der roten Kuh," *ZAW,* XXXIX (1921), 113–123.

107. The ancient Rabbis also understood that this ceremony was either designed itself, or else was strikingly similar in character to heathen ceremonies designed, to expel evil spirits; cf. the interesting conversation between Rabban Yochanan b. Zakkai and the heathen, recorded in *Bamidbar Rabba* XIX, 4, end; *Pesikta* 40a.

108. In my article "Two Ancient Israelite Agricultural Festivals," *JQR* (new series), VIII (1917), 49, I have ventured to suggest that the hyssop may have been red in color. The reference to hyssop in Ps. 51 : 9 and Heb. 9 : 19 would seem to indicate an extensive use of this plant in purification ceremonies. In modern Palestine the hyssop is still used occasionally in rites of a magical character. The belief obtains that whoever eats of this plant in moderation, or rubs his forehead or the skull behind the ears with it, will improve his memory thereby. Whoever eats for forty successive days of the leaves of the hyssop in dried and pulverized form is freed from all danger of snake bite (Bauer, *Volksleben im Lande der Bibel,* pp. 194 f.; Canaan, *Aberglaube und Volksmedezin im Lande der Bibel,* pp. 131 f.). Moreover, hyssop plants are distributed to the worshipers in the procession in the Church of the Sepulcher in Jerusalem in the Festival of the Cross (Perry, *The Pilgrim in Jerusalem,* p. 102). Quite naturally, the hyssop was of old and is still today, to some extent at least, thought to possess a certain quality or power, largely magical in character, not possessed by other plants. This quality or power, precisely like the same quality or power inherent in the cedar tree, with its wood red in color, may well be ascribed to the hyssop because of its reddish color.

109. Cf. Additional Note F, p. 284.

110. In the same way, the cedarwood, scarlet thread, and hyssop play an important role in the ceremonies of the purification of the leper (Lev. 14 : 4 ff.). They have to do there, of course, with the expulsion of the evil spirit of leprosy.

111. Cf. Jer. 16 : 5–8. For the custom in the Talmudic period, cf. Krauss, *Talmudische Archäologie,* II, 63, and note 455, p. 480; also Lods, *La Croyance à la Vie Future dans l'Antiquité Israélite,* pp. 116–183.

112. Above, p. 39.

113. *Op. cit.,* pp. 117, 120.

114. Cf. above, pp. 105 f. The rite of cutting off the hair of a corpse immediately after death and in preparation for burial (cf. Krauss, *op. cit.,* II, 56) had, of course, an altogether different origin and purpose. It was probably cut off for much the same reason that all the openings of the body were closed up so soon as it was definitely determined that death had set in (*ibid.,* p. 53; for the same practice among the modern Bedouin, cf. Musil, *Arabia Petraea,* III, 423), in order to prevent the return of the soul into the decomposing body. The hair upon the body would have offered, theoretically, an excellent hiding place in which the soul might lurk while it awaited an opportunity to slip once more into its former earthly abode. Among the Bedouin, too, the hair on the head of a corpse is occasionally shaved off (Doughty, *Arabia Deserta,* I, 450). Not improbably, here too is the origin of the ancient custom of washing the corpse in preparation for burial (Krauss, *op. cit.,* p. 53). It was thought that the soul might have adhered in some way to the outside of the body; in such case the washing of the body would remove it. Probably for this reason this water with which the corpse had been washed was cleared away immediately, so that no one might step over it. Likewise, the board upon which the corpse had been laid during the washing was removed; for should it be overturned, someone might die during the next three days (Bender, "Beliefs, Rites and Customs of the Jews, Connected with Death, Burial and Mourning," *JQR* [old series], VII [1894], 260). The washing of the corpse in preparation for burial was practiced not only in Israel, but likewise by the Syrians, Samaritans, Mandaeans, and Abyssinians (Bender, *op. cit.,* pp. 264 ff.). We have already noted the same custom among the modern Bedouin (above, p. 122). In modern Palestine the water in which a corpse is washed should be poured into a hole in the ground in order to avoid pollution (Bliss, *The Religions of Modern Syria and Palestine,* p. 292).

115. Perhaps, too, the custom referred to in Rabbinic literature (*Šabbat* 151b; *S*^e^*maḥôt* I, 3) of placing the corpse upon sand or salt immediately after death was for the purpose of laying the ghost. We have already noted the belief that salt was thought to possess apotropaic powers (above, p. 14). Krauss (*op. cit.,* II, 63 and note 455) has suggested that the custom of mourners baring their shoulders, which obtained in Israel in the Rabbinic period, originated as a substitute for the older practice of making incisions.

116. Cf. Schwally, *Das Leben nach dem Tode,* p. 23.

117. It is obvious that not until the beliefs had become firmly established in Israel that Yahweh's power extended over Sheol and its inmates, and that He determined their ultimate fate, whether for reward or for punishment,

i.e., not until the late post-Exilic period could the idea have developed that these sacrifices were offered *for* or *on behalf of* the dead instead of *to* them.

118. Above, 124 ff.

119. Of these, the so-called "meal of consolation," offered to the mourners upon their return from the cemetery, alone has survived in present-day Jewish practice. This meal is prepared by friends of the mourners. Eggs, which are regarded as the symbol of life and resurrection, and lentils, thought to symbolize death, constitute the chief articles of food at this meal (cf. *JE,* IX, 102).

120. Josephus, *Antiquities,* XV, 3, 4; *Semaḥôt* 8; *Šulḥan ʿArûk, Yôreh Deʿah* 350; Perles, "Die Leichenfeierlichkeiten im nachbiblischen Judentum," *MGWJ,* X (1861), 377 f.

121. Jer. 34 : 5; II Chron. 16 : 14; 21 : 19.

122. *ʿAbôda Zara* I, 3; *Semaḥôt* 8; *Tôsefta Šabbat* VIII, 18; *Šulḥan ʿArûk, Yôreh Deʿah* 348; cf. Krauss, *op. cit.,* III, 478, note 442. The same custom has survived until the present day in the practice of burning garments and other articles of like character at the festivals celebrated by the native Palestinian Jews at the tombs of the Rabbis at Tiberias and a week later at similar tombs in the neighboring village of Meron. Both these festivals are observed in the spring, the latter on *Lag beʿOmer,* the thirty-third day after the first day of the Passover. This last festival is celebrated primarily in honor of Rabbi Simon b. Yochai, the great Tanna (cf. Oliphant, *Haifa,* pp. 74, 159 ff.; Luncz, in *Jerusalem,* I [1886], 49 ff.).

123. *Šulḥan ʿArûk, Yôreh Deʿah* 350; cf. Scheftelowitz, "Der Seelen und Unsterblichkeitsglaube im Alten Testament," *ARW,* XIX [1916], 224 f.; Krauss, *op. cit.,* II, 475, note 421.

124. Isa. 19 : 19; Hos. 3 : 4.

125. Lev. 26 : 1; Deut. 16 : 22.

126. Deut. 7 : 5; 12 : 3; I Kings 14 : 23; II Kings 17 : 10.

127. Driver, *Modern Research as Illustrating the Bible; The Schweich Lectures* (1908), pp. 62 ff.; Vincent, *Canaan d'après l'Exploration récente,* pp. 102 ff.

128. Paton, *Spiritism and the Cult of the Dead in Antiquity,* p. 235.

129. Gen. 28 : 18, 22.

130. Gen. 35 : 20.

131. Cf. Lidzbarski, *Nordsemitische Epigraphik,* I, 324a; Cook, *Glossary of Aramaic Inscriptions,* p. 82.

132. Cf. Levy, *Wörterbuch,* III, 426.

133. Cf. Brockelmann, *Lexicon Syriacum*[1], p. 210b; also Paton, *op. cit.,* p. 203.

134. Probably somewhat akin to this is the custom, fairly widespread among the Semites, of planting a myrtle or some other kind of tree or bush upon the grave (cf. Buckingham, *Travels among the Arab Tribes,* p. 316; *Travels in Assyria, Media and Persia,* p. 93). The same custom was observed by the Romans; they held that the spirit of the person buried in the grave took up its abode in the myrtle (Paton, *op. cit.,* p. 76). In Mecca a cypress is planted over every grave. After being planted it receives no individual attention, but, on the other hand, it is never harmed (Von Maltzan, *Mekka,* II, 314). The inhabitants of Medina stick palm branches upon the graves of their dead.

These are changed once each year, at the festival of Ramadan, when the family visits the graves of its relatives and frequently remains there for several days (Burckhardt, *Travels in Arabia,* II, 225 f.; cf. also Lane, *The Manners and Customs of the Modern Egyptians*^{3}, p. 443). At Merrâkech, in Morocco, myrtles are likewise planted upon the tombs, and in certain parts of Algeria squills are similarly planted. Doutté says that this custom of planting flowers upon tombs is universal; it is generally believed that the soul passes into these plants and there suffers less (*Merrâkech,* 364).

135. 9 : 4. Here, just as, as we have noted (above, p. 248, note 54), was the occasional usage in other Semitic circles, *l*^{e}*nafšam,* literally "for their soul," has unquestionably the connotation "for their dead one."

136. 16 : 5–8.

137. 24 : 15 ff.

138. Cf. Deut. 26 : 14; Ps. 106 : 28; Jub. 22 : 17.

139. Lev. 19 : 27 f.

140. As, for example, the rite of the red heifer. Very obviously the authors of the Priestly Code would have greatly preferred to abrogate this ceremony altogether, since its non-Yahwistic origin and character are so readily apparent. But, unable to do this, they endeavored to incorporate the ceremony into the Yahweh-ritual by giving the priest a role in the ceremony and providing likewise for the sprinkling of some of the blood of the sacrificed animal in the direction of the Temple. To what extent they succeeded in their purpose it is impossible to tell. Most, if not all, of the later, Rabbinic legislation and tradition bearing upon this rite of the red heifer seems to have been theoretical and speculative rather than to have dealt with a ceremony which was actually observed. Quite probably, by thus legitimizing this rite and giving the priest an important place in it and bringing it into direct relationship with the Temple, its original character and purpose were so modified that it gradually lost all significance and eventually ceased entirely to be observed. This may account for the tradition recorded in the Mishnah (*Parah* III, 5) that the sum total of red heifers offered in all Jewish history was only seven, one by Moses, one by Ezra, and five in the post-Ezranic period.

A similar procedure undoubtedly took place with the ceremony described in Deut. 21 : 1–9. There, too, as we have already noted, the role assigned to the priests in v. 5 is manifestly secondary and disturbing and controverts the original character and purpose of this peculiar ceremony altogether. In all likelihood this ceremony ceased to be observed in Israel at a period much earlier than that of the rite of the red heifer, due chiefly to changed social and economic circumstances, particularly the advance beyond the conditions of simple village life and organization there depicted and the rise and development of the idea, first presented in the Priestly Code, that all Israel, and not merely each single village, constituted one, closely integrated congregation and religious unit. The fact, too, that the very character of this ceremony prevented its ultimate correlation with the Temple cult must naturally have furthered its eventual disappearance.

141. Above, pp. 124 f.

142. This same sacrifice is offered upon this same occasion and is called by

the same name by the urban Moslems of Palestine. The sacrificial meal which follows consists of the sheep which has been sacrificed and lentils. It is often prepared by friends of the family of the deceased. The poor and the stranger are invited to partake of it (Schmidt and Kahle, *Volkserzählungen aus Palästina,* pp. 94–97, 250, note 3).

143. Literally, "weakness."

144. Jaussen, *Coutumes des Arabes au pays de Moab,* p. 101.

145. Above, p. 137.

146. Jaussen, *op. cit.,* p. 102.

147. Lane, *The Manners and Customs of the Modern Egyptians*[3], p. 488.

148. Doutté, *Merrâkech,* p. 365.

149. Above, p. 123.

150. Brandt, *Mandäische Religion,* p. 82.

151. This is undoubtedly equivalent to the above-mentioned sacrifices among the Bedouin tribes.

152. Guys, *Voyage en Syrie,* pp. 212–214.

153. Lane, *op. cit.,* pp. 506 f.

154. "La Population Mussulmane de Tlemcen," *RES,* I (1908), 221.

155. I.e., "the night of departure," or "the night of going far away."

156. Menzel, in Grote, *Meine Vorderasienexpedition, 1906 und 1907,* I, 158.

157. Adams, *Darkness and Daybreak,* p. 142.

158. Dapper, *Asia,* I, 46 f.

159. Epstein, *Eldad ha-Dani,* p. 171.

160. Rathjens, *Die Juden in Abessinien,* p. 84.

161. Above, p. 119.

162. Above, p. 124.

163. Above, p. 125.

164. Above, pp. 125 f.

165. Burckhardt, *Notes on the Bedouins and Wahabys,* p. 159.

166. Ali Bey, *Travels,* I, 25.

167. Niebuhr, *Reisebeschreibung nach Arabien und andern umliegenden Ländern,* II, 435.

168. Featherman, *The Aramaeans,* pp. 620 f.

169. Above, pp. 124 f.

170. Above, p. 125.

171. Cf. below, pp. 157 f., and notes 202–205.

172. Musil, *op. cit.,* p. 429.

173. *Ibid.,* p. 453. Probably this is the sacrifice referred to by Curelly (in Petrie, *Researches in Sinai,* p. 230), when he says: "The Bedawyn told me that the dead are buried without delay, if possible, but never at night. A sheep is then sacrificed and eaten, and another is sacrificed ten or thirty days later. It is a frequent custom for friends to leave a little hand-mill and a wooden mixing bowl by the side of the grave, so that the dead man may not lack suitable implements to prepare his food."

174. Above, p. 125.

175. Above, p. 124.

176. Wansleb, in Paulus, *Sammlung der merkwürdigsten Reisen in den Orient,* III, 86 f.

177. Above, p. 125; cf. also Ibn Batoutah, *Voyages;* text and translation (French) by Defrémery and Sanguinetti, II, 37.

178. Du Bernat, in Paulus, *op. cit.,* IV, 284. It is not clear whether this ceremony of the expulsion of the ghost from the house is performed at the close of the first period of three days or at the end of a second period of three days, i.e., presumably upon the seventh day after death. If the reference to the thirty-seven days, which are mentioned later in this passage, is correct, it must mean that this expulsion took place, not upon the seventh day, but upon the third day, after death. In either case, however, a continued sojourn of the soul in the vicinity of the body for a period of either three or seven days after death is implied.

179. Bauer, *Volksleben im Lande der Bibel,* pp. 215 f.

180. Lane, *Manners and Customs of the Modern Egyptians*[3], p. 488; cf. also Kahle, *Die Totenklage im heutigen Aegypten* (reprint from the *Gunkel Festschrift*), p. 2.

181. Wellhausen, "Die Ehe bei den Arabern," *GGN,* XI (1893), 454 f.

182. *Muhammedanische Studien,* I, 254.

183. Literally, "thou hast redeemed thyself therewith."

184. Above, pp. 126 ff.

185. Above, pp. 124, 126 ff.

186. *Arabia Deserta,* I, 136 f. Doughty likewise makes mention of the celebration of this same festival at Kheybar, apparently early in the following spring (*ibid.,* II, 91, 118). The celebration there was marked by much dancing throughout the day by all people and by the exchange of visits and hospitality. But no sacrifices were offered, due, according to Doughty, to the proverbial niggardliness of the people of Kheybar.

187. Socin, *Diwan aus Centralarabien,* I, 295 f.

188. Above, p. 128.

189. Wellhausen, *Reste des altarabischen Heidentums*[2], p. 80, note; cf. also Doutté, *Magie et Religion dans l'Afrique du Nord,* p. 457.

190. Lane, *The Manners and Customs of the Modern Egyptians*[3], p. 80; Socin, *op. cit.,* I, 295, note a. Goldziher (*Muhammedanische Studien,* I, 239 f.) discusses the origin of the great Moslem sacrifice at Mina during the *Ḥağğ* on the tenth of Dhu-l-Ḥiğğeh and suggests, with considerable corroborative evidence, that it developed out of the pre-Islamic sacrifice to the dead; so also Lods, *La Croyance à la Vie Future dans l'Antiquité Israélite,* pp. 163 ff.

191. *Notes on the Bedouins and Wahabys,* p. 57.

192. *Ibid.,* p. 51.

193. *Primitive Semitic Religion Today,* pp. 175 f. (English ed.; German ed., pp. 198 f.).

194. To this, Curtiss adds the note: "Ahmed Rindi of Damascus, who had been on a pilgrimage three times, said, 'They do not eat the sheep, but put it in a hole in the ground.' (Cf. Burton, *Personal Narrative of a Pilgrimage to Al-Madinah and Mekka,* II, 218). 'It is considered a meritorious act to give away the victim

without eating any portion of the flesh. Parties of Takruri might be seen sitting vulture-like, contemplating the sheep and goats, and no sooner was the signal given than they fell upon the bodies and cut them up without removing them.'" Cf. Burckhardt, *Travels in Arabia,* p. 276.

195. *Peasant Life in the Holy Land,* p. 22.

196. Hardy, *The Unvarying East,* p. 149.

197. "Religion of the Fellahin of Palestine," *PEF* (1893), p. 316.

198. Neh. 8 : 10.

199. *Op. cit.,* p. 22.

200. Above, p. 129.

201. Hanauer, *The Folk-Lore of the Holy Land,* p. 309.

202. Stephan, "The Division of the Year in Palestine," *JPOS,* II (1922), 165, note 7; Canaan, "Folklore of the Seasons in Palestine," *JPOS,* III (1923), 23; Baumstark, *Festbrevier und Kirchenjahr der syrischen Jakobiten,* p. 189.

203. Stephan, *op. cit.* So also Baldensperger, "Woman in the East," *PEF* (1901), p. 83. For "All-Souls' Day," cf. Frazer, *The Golden Bough*[3]*; Adonis, Attis and Osiris,* pp. 301–318.

204. Canaan, *op. cit.,* p. 25.

205. The egg is used also in Jewish mourning ceremonies, constituting the main portion of the first meal eaten by the mourners after a funeral (cf. above, p. 254, note 119). It also plays an important role in the Seder supper and ritual which ushers in the Jewish Passover festival, and an equally interesting role in the folk celebration of Easter, particularly in Palestine; cf. *JE,* V, 54.

206. "Religion of the Fellahin in Palestine," *PEF* (1893), p. 317.

207. Jaussen, *Coutumes des Arabes au pays de Moab,* p. 102, note 3.

208. Featherman, *The Aramaeans,* pp. 76 f.

209. Bel, "La Population Mussulmane de Tlemcen," *RES,* I (1908), 210 ff.

210. "The Arabs are convinced that whenever they visit the tombs of their dead, the spirits of these come forth in order to associate with them; the spirits of men and women seat themselves upon round pillars placed at the heads of the graves, and the spirits of infants take their places beneath the cloaks of their mothers, their sisters, or their grandmothers. Moreover, when the women rise in order to return home, they take pains to do this very gently out of fear of injuring the poor, little souls of the infants" (Certeux and Carony, *L'Algérie Traditionelle; Contributions au Folk-Lore des Arabes,* I, 220).

211. Doutté, *Merrâkech,* pp. 364 f.

212. Rathjens, *Die Juden in Abessinien,* p. 79. According to Littmann, "Sternensagen und Astrologisches aus Nordabessinien," *ARW,* XI (1908), 311, it was the duty of the surviving brother to celebrate this festival in honor of his dead.

213. *Fihrist,* V, 7; quoting Chwolsohn, *Die Ssabier und der Ssabismus,* II, 31 f.

214. Mehren, *Manuel de la Cosmographie du Moyen Age,* p. 406.

215. The only real exception to this noted was the practice of the Sabaeans of Haran, who observed their festival of the dead in the first Teshrin, i.e., in October.

216. This is obviously the meaning of the custom, frequently met with, of

closing all the openings of the body in some way or other, presumably because only through one of the bodily openings through which it had emerged could the soul re-enter the body (cf. also above, note 114). We have seen (above, p. 150) that this custom is practiced at Damascus. It is likewise observed in Egypt (cf. Klunzinger, *Upper Egypt, Its People and Products,* p. 201), in Palestine (cf. Bauer, *Volksleben im Lande der Bibel*[2], p. 244), and among the Bedouin (cf. Musil, *Arabia Petraea,* III, 423). The same custom obtained in ancient Israel (cf. Krauss, *Talmudische Archäologie,* II, 55 and notes 411 and 412). The reason given by the Talmud, viz., that this was to prevent the air entering the body, is, of course, a rationalistic interpretation of an ancient custom, the actual origin of which had been forgotten. Despite the objection of Krauss, the true origin of this custom must have been that just stated: to prevent the return of the soul or spirit into the body. Probably this was also the origin of the custom, likewise mentioned by Krauss, of putting a metal vessel upon the navel of the corpse immediately after death, instead of, as Krauss suggests, to prevent too rapid decomposition in the hot climate of Palestine. We have already noted the use of iron to ward off the attacks of evil spirits (above, p. 14). To the instances recorded by Goldziher ("Eisen als Schutz gegen Dämonen," *ARW,* X [1907], 41–46), the following may be added here as having significance for our present object of investigation. We are told (Abdullah Mansur [W. Bury], *The Land of Uz,* p. 320) that among the natives of southern Arabia "there are a lot of superstitions about iron. Few slaves or low-class raya will pass a graveyard in the dark unless they are wearing an iron ring above the left elbow to prevent the ghosts of the dead from jumping on their backs and strangling them." The cognate custom of casting pieces of iron among the graves, undoubtedly for the same purpose, to protect against evil, was known in ancient Israel, and was denounced as a heathen practice (*Tôsefta,* ed. Zuckermandel, p. 117; *Šabbat* VI, 25). Likewise, when the women of the Touareg go to consult the spirits of the dead they may wear upon their bodies nothing made of iron (Doutté, *Magie et Religion dans l'Afrique du Nord,* p. 412), presumably because the presence of iron would prevent contact with these spirits sufficiently close for purposes of communication and divination.

217. Above, p. 105 f.

218. Cf. above, p. 139.

219. The etymological history of the technical name, *ḍaḥîyyeh,* is obscure. The fundamental meaning of the stem, *ḍaḥay,* seems to be "to become visible through the growing light of the early morning sun" (Lane, *Dictionary,* pp. 1772 ff.). *Ḍaḥa'* or *ḍaḥiy* have the connotation "he was smitten by the sun," or "the sun came upon it," and also "he went forth into the sun." *Ḍuḥan* means "the early part of the forenoon, after sunrise, when the sun is yet low." In the second conjugation, *ḍaḥḥay* means "he pastured the sheep, goats, or camels during the time called *ḍuḥan.*"

The connection of all this with the name of the sacrifice, *ḍaḥîyyeh,* or, as Lane gives it, *'aḍḥîyyeh,* is by no means clear. It appears from Lane that the Arab lexicographers were inclined to the view that it was so called because it was offered at the time of day called *ḍuḥan,* early morning. This is not impossible. But while it may be most meritorious to offer this sacrifice in the early morning, this is by no means essential. Burton offered the sacrifice in the afternoon, and this was apparently regarded as perfectly proper (*Personal Narrative of a Pilgrimage to Al-Madinah and Mekka,* II, 217 f.). We shall shortly find good reason to surmise that this sacrifice was originally offered during the night, and that therefore the very early morning, just after sunrise, probably represented the very latest moment when this sacrifice might be offered. Accordingly, it may be doubted whether the Arab lexicographers have hit upon the true origin of the term.

Another hypothetical explanation of the origin of the term *ḍaḥîyyeh* for this particular festival and sacrifice in honor of the ghosts of the dead is suggested in this connection. As has just been stated, *ḍaḥay* has the fundamental connotations "to come forth into the sun; to appear; to become visible." The noun *ḍaḥîyyeh* would have the etymological connotation "the coming forth into the sun; the becoming visible." This etymological connotation might very well refer to the return of the spirits of the dead upon this occasion from the nether world—in the darkness of which they are confined during the entire remainder of the year—their coming forth literally into the sun, and their appearance to and association again for the moment with their former relatives and friends. The *ḍaḥîyyeh* festival and sacrifice would then be, as they actually are in fact, the festival of, and the sacrifice at, the annual coming forth or reappearance of the spirits of the dead—the primitive Semitic "All Souls' Day." This seems, all in all, the best grounded and most plausible explanation of this technical term; it must not, however, be forgotten that it is purely hypothetical.

Whether there is any direct relationship between this primitive Semitic *ḍaḥîyyėh* festival of the dead and the ancient Babylonian *ûm kispi, ûm nubatti, ûm bubbuli,* and *ûm idirti,* it is difficult to determine because of the scantiness of the evidence. Certainly this day or these days were festivals in honor of the dead, but whether only of supposedly dead deities, about to be revived, or of dead human beings as well, it is not at all clear at present.

220. *Ursemitische Religion im Volksleben des heutigen Orients,* p. 223 (not in the English ed.).

221. *Ibid.,* XVI (likewise not in the English ed.).

222. As Wellhausen has shown (*Reste des altarabischen Heidentums*², p. 97), Reğeb was the month which originally marked the commencement of the summer half-year, or the spring season.

223. *Arabia Deserta,* I, 499.

224. Here the blood is smeared upon the animals with the fingers. Occasionally, however, if not regularly, a bunch of herbs is used for this purpose. Thus: "At the time when the goat or sheep is being killed for the proposed feast, some of its blood is collected in a bowl, and with it, by means of a sort of brush made with twigs of *retm,* the camel of the guest, in whose honor the feast is given, is marked. Each tribe has its special mark for this ceremony, and it is not the same as the *wasm*" (Jennings-Bramley, "The Bedouin of the Sinaitic Peninsula," *PEF* [1907], p. 132). The use of this bunch of *retm* twigs here is strikingly similar to the use of the bunch of hyssop for the same purpose in the Passover and related rituals (cf. below, pp. 168, 178).

225. "Das Samaritanische Passah im Verhältniss zum Jüdischen," *PJB,* VIII (1913), 136.

226. "Folklore of the Seasons in Palestine," *JPOS,* III (1923), 26.

227. I.e., the week of "Friday of the Animals," or Good Friday.

228. "Friday of the Dying" or "Painting."

229. Canaan says that mules and asses are not marked in this manner, and that sheep and goats are the animals most frequently marked. This may perhaps indicate a pre-agricultural, nomadic origin for this custom.

230. I.e., the night from Thursday to Friday.

231. The following is a ceremony of kindred or derivative origin and meaning: "The best trees . . . are seen to be girt about with bands of red dye from the ground upward; this is said to be a power which renders ineffectual the 'eye' which may strike such trees. The dye is now procured from vegetable or mineral matter, but I have long suspected that in an early age blood was used in protecting the trees against the 'eye,' and from feelings of consideration or economy the custom has been changed" (Ghosn El-Howie, "The Evil Eye," *PEF* [1904], p. 149). The antiquity of this custom of painting trees red in order to avert evil and make them fruitful is attested by numerous Talmudic references (collected by Blau, *Das altjüdische Zauberwesen,* pp. 165 f.).

232. Cf. Lods, *La Croyance à la Vie Future dans l'Antiquité Israélite,* p. 191.

233. Jaussen, *Coutumes des Arabes au pays de Moab,* pp. 295 f.

234. Newman, *Babylon and Niniveh,* p. 403; Adams, *Darkness and Daybreak,* p. 268.

235. In Biblical Hebrew, *b^ekî* or *misped;* cf. Ezek. 24 : 16 f.

236. In Biblical Hebrew, *'ebel,* although this term is also extended to the ensuing period of mourning; cf. also Judith 16 : 25; Sir. 22 : 12.

237. *Šulḥan 'Arûk, Yôred De'ah* 380–400; *JE,* IX, 101 ff.; Krauss, *Talmudische Archäologie,* II, 54–82.

238. *Yôreh De'ah* 386.

239. *Yôreh De'ah* 390. Quite possibly the prohibition to cut the hair during the first thirty days of mourning may be based upon the fact that throughout this entire period the mourner is regarded as being in a state of extreme taboo, which, however, terminates automatically with the conclusion of the thirtieth day. Accordingly, the cutting of the hair would mark the passing out of this state of extreme taboo into a state which, with the exception of a few minor restrictions, is the same as ordinary, profane existence.

240. *S^emaḥôt* VIII, beginning. It is expressly stated there that this was also a custom of neighboring, non-Jewish peoples. According to the four Gospels this practice was observed at the death of Jesus; cf. Krauss, *op. cit.,* II, 62 and note 451; cf. also *Kôhelet Rabba* I, 36; likewise John 11 : 39, where Martha says of her brother Lazarus, "Lord, by this time the body decayeth (or "stinketh"), for he hath been dead four days." For this same reason it was forbidden to eat the flesh of the "peace-offering" on the third day, for by that time it had become *piggul,* i.e., decomposition had set in (Lev. 7 : 17 f.; 19 : 6 f.).

241. *Yer. Mô'ed Ḳaṭôn* III, 82*b*; *Yer. Y^ebamôt* XVI, 15*c*; *Wayikra' Rabba* XVIII, 1; *Kôhelet Rabba* XII, 6; likewise *B^ere'šit Rabba* C, 7, which, however,

says that the soul hovers about the grave, instead of about the corpse, as do the other passages cited. This divergence in reading is, of course, immaterial. Cf. also the references in the various apocalypses cited by von Baudissin, *Adonis und Esmun,* p. 412, note 5.

242. *Yer. Môʿed Ḳaṭôn* III, 82b, and other references to Rabbinic literature cited in the preceding note.

243. Num. 19 : 12, 19; 31 : 19. Among the Falashas, too, the purification ceremonies for a person who has touched a corpse last for seven days. On the third and seventh days they sprinkle upon him the waters of purification. This is, of course, in accord with the Biblical prescriptions. But in addition thereto he is required to shave his head upon the third day. This last rite is not enjoined in the Bible (Epstein, *Eldad ha-Dani,* p. 172).

244. II Kings 2 : 17; cf. *Gospel of Nicodemus,* 11 : 2 f.

245. So also von Baudissin (*op. cit.,* pp. 412 ff.); cf. Rev. 11 : 9–11. An interesting and illuminating expression of the idea of resurrection upon the third day is found in *The Acts of Philip* (*Ante-Nicene Fathers,* ed. Roberts and Donaldson, VII, 502 f.). There the crucified apostle Philip is represented as saying to his comrade, "See, O Bartholomew, where my blood shall drop upon the earth, a plant shall spring up from my blood, and shall become a vine, and shall produce fruit of a bunch of grapes; and having taken the cluster, press it into the cup; and having partaken of it on the third day, send up on high the Amen, in order that the offering may be complete. . . . And after three days the plant of the vine sprouted up where the blood of Philip had dropped. And they did all that had been commanded them by him."

Obviously, the doctrine of resurrection upon the third day is a relatively advanced theological concept, which had no primary connection whatsoever with the primitive notion that on the third day the separation of the soul from the body was effected completely and permanently. Once, however, the doctrine of resurrection and immortality of the soul found a place in Jewish sectarian theology, the precise moment of resurrection would very naturally be determined by the old, primitive superstition with regard to the exact time when the separation of the soul from the body became complete.

246. Gen. 50 : 10; I Sam. 31 : 13; I Chron. 10 : 12; Sir. 22 : 12; Josephus, *Antiquities,* XVII, 8, 4; *Wars,* II, 1, 1; also Ezek. 3 : 15 f.; Job 2 : 13.

247. In the *Ante-Nicene Fathers,* ed. Roberts and Donaldson, VII, 570.

248. *Môʿed Ḳaṭôn* 14b f.; 20a f.; *Yer. Môʿed Ḳaṭôn* III, 82c.

249. *Yer. Môʿed Ḳaṭôn* III, 83c; *Beʳreʾšit Rabba* C, 7, end; in *B. Môʿed Ḳaṭôn* 27b the same tradition is recorded in a slightly different form: during the first three days it is as a sword raised over the shoulders of the mourners; it is directed against them from the corner of the room until the end of the seventh day; until the end of the thirtieth day it passes them upon the street; and until the end of the full year it may strike any member of the family. However, the birth of a male child during the year redeems the entire family from all danger. (Cf. *Šulḥan ʿArûk, Yôreh Deʿah* 394, 4.)

250. Above, p. 141.

251. *Šabbat* 152a and b.

252. *Ibid.* 152b.

253. Cf. *JE,* article, "Mourning," IX, 101.

254. Num. 20 : 29; Deut. 34 : 8.

255. Deut. 21 : 13.

256. *Yer. Môʿed Ḳaṭôn* III, 82a; *Keṭûbôt* 130b; *Semaḥôt* IX.

257. *Šulḥan ʿArûk, Yôreh Deʿah* 394, 2. Probably the original and underlying principle here was that since the man had been abnormally great and powerful during his lifetime, his ghost, too, must be correspondingly powerful, and its influence must be potent, not merely during the customary first seven days, but also during the entire second period, until the end of the thirtieth day. Therefore it was proper and even expedient to prolong the period of mourning for a great man for the full thirty days (cf. above, p. 161). According to Jubilees 23 : 7, Isaac and Ishmael mourned for Abraham for forty days.

258. Cf. Luncz, in *Jerusalem,* I (1886), 15.

259. *Šabbat* 152b, 153a; cf. *Pirqe de R. Eliezer* XXXIV (translation of Friedlander, p. 257).

260. Additional Notes, I.

261. *Das Leben nach dem Tode,* p. 42–45.

262. *Der Ahnenkultus und die Urreligion Israels,* pp. 187–191; cf. also Lods, *La Croyance à la Vie Future dans l'Antiquité Israélite,* p. 228, who likewise refutes the Purim idea and suggests that we might as well think of any other festival, such as Tabernacles or Passover, but that it is best to admit total ignorance of any such institution in Israel.

263. Cf. Morgenstern, "The Origin of *Maṣṣoth* and the *Maṣṣoth*-Festival," *AJT,* XXI (1917), 275–293.

264. Cf. Morgenstern, "The Chanukkah Festival and the Calendar of Ancient Israel," *HUCA,* XXI (1948), 371 f.

265. Cf. Morgenstern, "Supplementary Studies in the Calendars of Ancient Israel," *HUCA,* X (1935), 45; also Exod. 23 : 15; 34 : 18, 25*b*; Deut. 16 : 1.

266. *Reste des altarabischen Heidentums*[2], p. 98.

267. Probably in the main, if not entirely, P2; cf. Morgenstern, "The Three Calendars of Ancient Israel," *HUCA,* I (1924), 62 f. and 64, note 84.

268. For the particular significance of *mišpaḥah,* cf. above, pp. 213 ff. The use of this term, *mišpaḥah,* in these J verses lends confirmation to our conclusion that this festival and ceremony are of ancient, desert origin. Moreover, this confirmation is strengthened further by the fact that the corresponding passages of the Priestly legislation in this chapter use instead the term *bêt ʿab,* literally, "father's house" (vv. 3 f.), a term, as we have learned, not only characteristic of Priestly authorship, but also indicating a form of social organization later than that implied in the term *mišpaḥah,* at least in its original connotation. The use of the older term, *mišpaḥah,* in these J verses seems to imply that this was originally a clan sacrifice and festival, and that only later, as the result of the social reorganization resulting from the transition from *beena* to *baʿal* marriage, and also in part as the result of eventual Priestly recasting of ancient rituals and ceremonies, did it become a household sacrifice. This is in complete accord with the hypothesis of Luther (in Meyer, *Die Israeliten und Ihre Nachbarstämme,* pp. 170 ff.), that the annual festival of David's clan (*mišpaḥah*) at Bethlehem—the necessity of his presence at which he suggests as

a plausible excuse for his absenting himself from Saul's new-moon festival (I Sam. 20 : 6)—was the Passover. If the celebration of this festival was at all connected with the cult of the dead of the clan, it is comprehensible that David's absence would be almost inexcusable. Furthermore, if this festival at Bethlehem was coincident with Saul's new-moon festival, it would follow, even as we have suggested, that originally the Passover was celebrated at the new moon of the first spring month.

269. Additional Notes, J.

270. Vv. 3–14.

271. With this may be compared the fact, noted above (pp. 129 and 157), that the Christians of Kerak select a lamb for the sacrifice, which among them corresponds to the *daḥîyyeh*-sacrifice, on the eighth day before the commencement of the forty-day fast, and sacrifice it on the following Saturday evening. This sacrifice bears a striking similarity to the Paschal sacrifice, not only in the facts that it is offered in the early spring season and in the evening, just at nightfall, but also in that in each case a period of four full days elapses between the moment of its selection and that when it is actually sacrificed.

272. This prescription that no bone of the Paschal lamb may be broken is of particular significance. The same prescription has been met in Lane's account of the *'aḳîḳah*-sacrifice (above, p. 38) and the sacrifice of the Otäbe Bedouin upon the seventh day after death (above, pp. 125 f.). It is closely akin to the other prescription of the Paschal sacrifice, that the animal must be perfect, with no part of the body defective or missing. We have met this prescription frequently in the various accounts of the *ḍaḥîyyeh*-sacrifice, and most significantly in the account of the sacrifice of the Ṣaẖâry Bedouin which was rejected by the dead ancestor to whom it had been offered because one of its feet was missing. Our discussion of the *ḍaḥîyyeh*-sacrifice shows conclusively that the sacrificial animal was supposed to pass into the possession of the spirits of the dead. And because these were very jealous of their rights and prerogatives, they would accept only animals complete and perfect in every way.

I have treated of this ritual prescription elsewhere ("The Bones of the Paschal Lamb," *JAOS*, XXXVI [1916], 146–153) and have shown that it implied the primitive belief in the eventual resurrection and reincarnation of the animal sacrificed. The evidence there adduced suffices to show that the belief was common and well established among the early Semites that so long as the bones were preserved intact, flesh might be brought back upon them and life restored to them. And the very fact that, even though the Priestly legislation for the Paschal lamb has already provided that the animal must be perfect and must be sacrificed whole, it still feels the necessity for an additional, specific provision that no bone may be broken, may well be regarded as indicating that to this last prescription it attached an added implication, viz., the ancient and probably half-outgrown belief in the eventual reincarnation of the animal sacrificed.

273. Above, p. 159.

274. Deut. 16 : 7. Possibly, too, in its insistence that the Paschal sacrifice may consist only of a sheep or a goat the P legislation is repealing the Deuteronomic provision that large cattle may likewise be used for this pur-

pose. Inasmuch as oxen and cows are practically unknown in the true nomadic life, and particularly as sacrificial animals, this, too, is obviously a reversion to the older, nomadic form of the ceremony.

275. *Die Israeliten und Ihre Nachbarstämme,* pp. 37 f.

276. The question arises here, Why should the Deuteronomic legislators have been more concerned with the reorganization of the celebration of the Passover than of the other festivals? For that such was the case may be inferred from the greater space and detail given in Deut. 16 to the legislation for the Passover than to that for the two other harvest festivals. The same inference may be drawn also from the fact that II Kings 23 : 21–23 states that the Passover festival in the eighteenth year of Josiah was selected as the occasion for the official promulgation of the Deuteronomic legislation, and particularly from the emphatic form of the statement that the Passover had never been celebrated in this manner, in such complete conformity with the written law—in other words, in a manner so completely and truly Yahwistic—since the days of the Judges. Certainly the Passover legislation in Deut. 16 inaugurated an altogether new and thoroughly Yahwistic manner of celebration of this festival. The suspicion obtrudes itself that to these Deuteronomic legislators the Passover celebration in the homes, with its many strange, and even archaic, rites, current until their day, may have seemed not altogether Yahwistic but to suggest origins and to contain elements reminiscent of other cults. These they sought to abrogate by new legislation, and particularly by focusing the sacrifice and initial celebration of the festival under the new regulations about the central Yahweh-sanctuary.

Unquestionably, in theory at least, these Deuteronomic legislators would have preferred greatly, had they been able, to make the entire seven-days' celebration of the *Maṣṣôt* festival center around the sanctuary, just as they did with the *Sukkôt* festival (v. 15). But circumstances made this impossible. The people could not remain longer at the central sanctuary than the first day, or rather the first night, of the festival; the exigencies of the impending harvest season compelled them to return to their homes without delay. Therefore the Deuteronomic legislation, probably making the best of the situation, sanctioned their departure from the central sanctuary upon the morning after the first night's celebration. But it was during just this night that the distinctive Passover rites, as contrasted with those of the original, independent *Maṣṣôt* festival were performed (cf. Lev. 23 : 5 f.). Obviously, therefore, the main object of these Deuteronomic reformers seems to have been to modify the peculiar Passover rites of the first night of the combined festival by concentrating them about the central sanctuary, and thus to give them an unmistakably Yahwistic coloring. But, as has been said, this very purpose points to the conclusion that previously these particular rites and ceremonies had possessed a distinctly non-Yahwistic flavor.

277. In this connection it is interesting and perhaps not without significance to recall the fact, already noted (above, p. 128), that at Ma'ān the yearling lamb is not regarded as an animal suitable for the *ḍaḥîyyeh*-sacrifice (Jaussen, *Coutumes des Arabes au pays de Moab,* p. 373).

278. Lev. 27 : 26; Num. 8 : 17; 18 : 15.

279. Unless perhaps in Num. 8 : 17, and also in Exod. 13 : 2, provided that the latter verse is P. This, however, despite the practically unanimous opinion of all modern Biblical scholars, I find very difficult to believe. The evidence pointing to the Priestly authorship of this verse seems to me quite insufficient and inconclusive. Certainly vv. 12 f. are not P, despite Baentsch's contention. The setting in which they are embedded, vv. 11 and 14 ff., is very obviously Deuteronomic. This proves that these verses themselves cannot be Deuteronomic or Priestly. On the other hand, the verses must be pre-Deuteronomic, for they still prescribe the sacrifice of all firstling animals, whereas, as we have seen, the Deuteronomic legislation permits the sacrifice of only those firstlings which are physically perfect animals. Nor is there here any reference whatever to the sacrifice of these firstlings at the central sanctuary. The provisions here show a direct dependence upon Exod. 34 : 19 f. Therefore, there need be no hesitation in assigning vv. 2, 12 f. to J2.

280. Lev. 17 : 5–7.

281. It is possibly not entirely without significance that the Targums render *mašḥît* in both verses of Exod. 12 by "destruction," or "the destroying angel," or "the angel of death to whom is given the power to destroy." This rendering is practically identical with the paraphrase in all three Targumic versions of Exod. 4 : 24–26 of Yahweh seeking to kill the son of Zipporah. Apparently, therefore, the Targums regarded the destroying agent in Exod. 12 : 13 and 23 as identical with the threatening deity or spirit in Exod. 4 : 24–26.

282. Manifestly, it was for precisely this reason that the Passover sacrifice was offered just at dusk and that all the peculiar Passover rites were performed during the night. For this was the exact period, as we have seen, in which the evil spirits were most powerful. The facts that this is the only sacrifice in the entire Biblical ritual which was offered after sunset, and that all the ceremonies centering about it were performed during the night, indicate more clearly than anything else its original, non-Yahwistic, demonic character.

283. For the very same ceremony still today, though with varying application, cf. Doughty, *Arabia Deserta,* I, 136, 452; II, 100; Curtiss, *Primitive Semitic Religion Today,* pp. 216–226 (German ed. only); Jaussen, *Coutumes des Arabes au pays de Moab,* pp. 54, note 3, 342, 371–373; Musil, *Arabia Petraea,* I, 372; III, 417, 450–454; Kohler, "Seltsame Vorstellungen und Bräuche in der biblischen und rabbinischen Literatur," *ARW,* XIII (1910), 81–84.

284. A further development of this idea is found in II Sam. 24 : 16 and I Chron. 21 : 15. Here the *mašḥît* has become a *mal'ak,* an angel or divine messenger—a "destroying angel," literally—who mechanically obeys Yahweh's command to destroy the people and desists therefrom again at Yahweh's command. Here absolutely nothing remains of the original idea, of which a reminiscence still lurks in Exod. 12 : 23, that the *mašḥît* was once an independent, evil spirit, and therefore the enemy of Yahweh. Still further developments of the idea, approximating more and more closely that of the Priestly Code, may possibly be seen in Jer. 51 : 1 and Ezek. 5 : 16; 9 : 6, 8; cf. also Isa. 54 : 16, and likewise I Cor. 10 : 10 and Wisd. of Sol. 18 : 25. In

Rabbinic literature the *mašḥît* is represented as one of the five destructive evil spirits, and has become identified with Satan and the angel of death; cf. Bender, "Beliefs, Rites, and Customs of the Jews, Connected with Death, Burial, and Mourning," *JQR* (old series), VII (1894).

285. So Musil, *Arabia Petraea,* III, 313; Scheftelowitz, "Das stellvertretende Huhnopfer," in *Religionsgeschichtliche Versuche und Vorarbeiten,* ARW, XIV (1911), 3, 49; Kahle, "Gebräuche bei den moslemischen Heiligtümern in Palästina," *PJB,* VIII (1912), 160.

286. As has been said, *mašḥît,* or, with the article, *hamašḥît,* literally means "the Destroyer." It is, of course, a *hif'il* participle of the verb *šaḥat,* "to destroy." But while etymologically unjustifiable, by a quite natural play on words one other interpretation of this fearsome evil spirit, quite significant for our thesis, may well have suggested itself to many early-Israelite minds. In Hebrew a common designation for the nether world is *šaḥat,* or, with the article, *hašaḥat.* Etymologically, this name has no connection whatever with the root *šaḥat,* "to destroy," but is derived instead from *šûaḥ,* "to descend." Etymologically, then, *šaḥat* has primarily the connotation "(the place of) descent," and the secondary connotation "pit, grave." But, used with the article (*hašaḥat*), the word has acquired the tertiary connotation "the nether world," and in Ps. 16 : 10; Sir. 51 : 2 it is used in parallelism with *šᵉ'ol,* the most common term in Hebrew for the nether world. Accordingly, by a quite natural and meaningful (although etymologically altogether incorrect) play upon words, the name *hamašḥit* may well have suggested to not a few ancient Israelite minds the connotation "he who brings down to the grave," or "to the nether world." And this connotation would, in turn, link the spirit bearing this name with the dead and the nether world and suggest his nature and function, so hostile to the living.

287. Petermann, *Reisen im Orient*[2], I, 237; Newman, *From Dan to Beersheba,* p. 324; Lindner, "Die Passahfeier der Samaritaner auf dem Berge Garizim," *PJB,* VII (1912), 111 f.; Dalman, "Das samaritanische Passah im Verhältniss zum jüdischen," *op. cit.,* p. 124.

288. Cf. Kahle, *op. cit.,* pp. 159 f. An indication that this idea, too, was not missing from the old Israelite tradition and ceremony may well be found in Pharaoh's words to Moses in Exod. 12 : 32, *uberaktem gam 'ôti.* These words are extremely difficult of interpretation other than in the sense, "And [by means of this sacrifice and ceremony] work ye a *baraka* [a blessing, a divinely conferred benefit] also for me."

289. Lev. 14 : 49 ff.

290. Num. 19 : 6, 18; cf. Additional Notes, F.

291. In fact, the Talmud (*Pᵉsaḥîm* 109b) preserves the tradition that just because this night was observed as a watchnight, evil spirits had no power to harm the living thereon. It may be noted in passing, as a matter of interest, that, in addition to celebrating the first night of the Passover as a watchnight, the native Jews of Jerusalem celebrate also the seventh night, the last night of the festival, in a somewhat similar manner. During this entire night the men remain in the synagogues. From midnight to dawn they recite various psalms and songs, and

just at dawn read from the Bible the passage extending from Exod. 13 : 17 to 15 : 26, describing Yahweh's salvation of Israel (Schwarz, *Das heilige Land,* p. 334).

292. Above, p. 18.

293. Wellhausen, *Reste des altarabischen Heidentums*², p. 80.

294. Zwemer, *Arabia, the Cradle of Islam,* pp. 289 ff.

295. This, too, is the conclusion to which Marti comes in part (*Geschichte der israelitischen Religion*⁵, pp. 47 f.). He holds, on the one hand, that the Passover rites were originally connected with the cult of the dead in prehistoric Israel, and, on the other hand, that the ceremony of sacrificing the Paschal animal and sprinkling its blood upon the door was designed to keep off the pest.

In this connection, the account of one particular sacrifice recorded by Curtiss (*Primitive Semitic Religion Today,* German ed., XV [not in the English ed.]), is of especial significance. Speaking of the Diab Arabs, he says: "Frightened by the outbreak of cholera in Tiberias in the spring of this year, they erected a primitive sanctuary in the open air to Diab, their ancestor. After it was finished each family sacrificed a white sheep, and sprinkled some of its blood upon the front of the sanctuary. They begged pardon of their ancestors that they had neglected to sacrifice to them and besought of them that the plague be kept far from them. Every owner of a house or tent slaughtered a sheep and with its blood smeared the foreheads of his sons. Even before the erection of this sanctuary they were accustomed to sacrifice a sheep about the middle of spring in order to protect their herds. Every shepherd offered a sacrifice and with its blood sprinkled his entire herd, so that God might protect it. They sacrifice to their ancestor, so that he might show favor to the whole tribe." The similarity of these sacrifices, here offered to the tribal ancestor, to the Passover sacrifice in its original form, as we have established this, is strikingly significant.

296. *Yer. Bᵉrakôt* V, 9b; *Yer. Taʿanît* I, 63d; also *Pirqe de R. Eliezer* XXXIV (Friedlander's translation), 259 f.

297. *Ḥagîga* 12b.

298. Ginzberg, *Legends of the Jews,* I, 331.

299. Cf. *JE,* IV, 552.

300. *Šᵉḳalîm* I, 1; cf. Schwally, *Das Leben nach dem Tode,* pp. 44 f. Not improbably a reminiscence of an original connection between the celebration of the Passover festival and the cult of the dead may be discerned in the words of Athanasius (*Festal Letters* [in Schaff and Wace, *The Nicene and Post-Nicene Fathers of the Christian Church,* V, 545], XIX, 1): "Even the heathen fancy that they keep the festival (i.e., the Passover) . . . . But the feast of the heathen He reproved as the bread of mourners."

Notes to Chapter XV

1. Exod. 4 : 25; Josh. 5 : 3; cf. Jacobs in *JE,* IV, 97.
2. *Kinship and Marriage in Early Arabia.*
3. Additional Notes, K.
4. Exod. 34 : 19 f.; Ezek. 20 : 26.

5. Gen. 49 : 3.
6. Deut. 21 : 15–17.
7. Above, p. 64.
8. Exod. 34 : 19 f.
9. Again and again, particularly in times of extreme national crisis, when it seemed that only the greatest and most elaborate sacrifices might avail to avert the threatening danger, the practice was revived; cf. Gen. 22; Exod. 22 : 28; II Kings 17 : 17; 23 : 10; Isa. 57 : 5; Jer. 32 : 35; Ezek. 20 : 26, 31.
10. II Kings 3 : 27.
11. Diodorus Siculus XX, 14; cf. Movers, *Die Phönizier,* I, 302.
12. Presumably the maiden's hair was cut off either by her mother or her mother's oldest brother, or, if he were no longer living, by her own oldest brother, the same person who later circumcised her children. Any one of these would have been, under the conditions of *beena* marriage, the logical person to perform this ceremony. But in case it was the maiden's oldest brother, we may not infer that the performance of this rite had any relation with his subsequent title of *ḥôten,* since the verb-stem *ḥatana* seems never to connote "to cut the hair," but only "to cut off the foreskin," i.e., "to circumcise."
13. Above, pp. 112 ff.
14. This sacrifice is redemptive in character and purpose. It is offered just immediately preceding and in preparation for the consummation of the marriage. Originally it was offered to the evil spirit who was thought to threaten the bride, or both bride and groom, at that moment.
15. I, 199.
16. Vv. 42 f.
17. Num. 3 : 44 ff.
18. *Yôreh De'ah* 394, 4.
19. Above, p. 111.
20. Deut. 26 : 14; cf. Frazer, *The Golden Bough*[3]; *The Spirits of the Corn and the Wild,* II, 109 ff.

From this it follows that in the very oldest form of the ceremony all first-born children were sacrificed to the *mašḥît.* They were given to him because he had an immediate and irrefutable claim upon them. The tradition of the Exodus, therefore, that the first-born of Israel were saved from the danger threatening from the *mašḥît* by the performance of the various Passover ceremonies, and that their lives were thus delivered, represents a manifest and very early departure from the original and seemingly invariable practice of actually sacrificing these first-born children. Even though the Exodus story is unquestionably a very ancient tradition, and though the rites and ceremonies of the Israelite Passover festival are of ancient origin, they do not carry us back to the primary form of the ceremony. They represent apparently the initial attempt to escape from the first and most mechanical and horrifying form of the ceremony by providing a method of redeeming the lives of first-born children. These Passover ceremonies, in other words, represent, it would seem, the first stage of cultural advance in ancient, prehistoric Israel—or, more precisely, among the clans which came later to constitute the nation, Israel—from the crude, revolting savagery of primitive Semitic ancestor-worship and child-sacrifice.

21. Cf. Morgenstern, "Two Ancient Israelite Agricultural Festivals," *JQR* (new series), VIII (1917), 31–54; "The Three Calendars of Ancient Israel," *HUCA*, I (1924), 13–78.

22. Exod. 15 : 1.

23. Above, p. 69.

24. Additional Notes, L.

25. Vincent, *Canaan d'après l'Exploration récente*.

26. Cf. Gilgamesh-Epic, XII (*KB*, VI, 256–265); I Sam. 28 : 3 ff.; Isa. 8 : 19; Musil, *Arabia Deserta*, III, 449 ff.

27. *Spiritism and the Cult of the Dead*, p. 91; cf. Dieterich, *Mutter Erde*, p. 48.

28. Jensen, in *KB*, VI, 479; Zimmern, *Die Keilinschriften und das Alte Testament*³, pp. 459 f.; Jastrow, *Die Religion Babyloniens und Assyriens*, I, 473, 482.

29. It is interesting to note that this is precisely the testimony of Sanchuniathon (cf. Cory, *Ancient Fragments*, p. 7), although he has perhaps assigned to ancestor-worship an unduly preponderant role in primitive Phoenician religion at the expense of the cult of other spirits. His exact words are: "And when all these men were dead, those that remained consecrated to them staves of wood, and worshiped stelae, or pillars, and celebrated feasts in honor of them every year." It is interesting to note also that Schwally (*Das Leben nach dem Tode*, p. 85), although on grounds altogether insufficient, derives both the rite of circumcision and the idea of the sanctity of the male organ among the Semites from primitive ancestor-worship.

Additional Notes

A[1]

Cf. also Lagrange, *Études sur les Religions semitiques,* pp. 268–283. Lagrange has stated the principle of divine possession and taboo very clearly and forcibly, although he has undoubtedly exaggerated somewhat its application. In fact, he has apparently taken a position the extreme opposite to that of Robertson Smith (*The Religion of the Semites*[3], pp. 213–440). The latter would derive all forms of sacrifice in Semitic religion from one source, viz., the covenant-sacrifice, by virtue of which a covenant was established or renewed between deity and worshipers. Lagrange also would derive all sacrifices in Semitic religion from one source. But this source, or this primary Semitic sacrifice, he holds, is that which we have chosen to call the "taboo-sacrifice."

He has formulated the principle of divine possession, taboo, and redemption clearly and forcefully. It is the same as that which we have posited above, that the offering of a part of the tabooed object, and particularly the first, and presumably therefore the best, part, or of an appropriate substitute for it, redeems it and renders it free for profane use.

Lagrange is correct when he asserts that many things are naturally taboo by virtue of the deity's prior claim upon them. But he errs in making the application of this principle practically universal. He makes this assertion gratuitously and altogether unsupported by evidence. And even he must admit that not all sacrifices partake of this taboo character. For example, the ancient Israelite "free-will offering" (Lev. 7 : 11 ff.) was in no sense a taboo-sacrifice and possessed nothing of the imperative, compulsory character thereof.

The solution of the problem is that both Robertson Smith and Lagrange err in trying to derive all Semitic sacrifices from one common source or original sacrifice. Rather it would seem that both forms, taboo-sacrifice and covenant-sacrifice, existed in Semitic religious practice from the very beginning and, so far as all available evidence indicates, were always clearly differentiated. The most marked external characteristic which distinguished the taboo-sacrifice from the covenant-sacrifice was that the latter was eaten almost entirely by the sacrificer and his guests, whereas the former, since it represented a solemn presentation to the deity, or spirit, of what was already his by right of original possession, had to be given in its entirety to him; under no condition, therefore, might the sacrificer partake of any part thereof.

[1] Chapter VI, note 2.

In the earliest form of the taboo-sacrifice it would seem that the blood of the victim was applied to the sacred stone or cult-object, while the carcass was left lying where it fell, to be consumed by birds or beasts of prey (Robertson Smith, *op. cit.,* pp. 225–229). In more cultured environments the sacrifice was burned entirely upon the altar. Later, as Semitic religion developed, as the concept of deity, as distinguished from that of mere spirits, evolved, and fixed sanctuaries with more complex and varied rituals and large bodies of priests arose, and economic need and instinct asserted themselves, the original practice was modified. Now frequently—though by no means invariably—only a part of the taboo-sacrifice was burned upon the altar. (In Hebrew, taboo-sacrifice is the *'azkarah,* the "reminder" or "symbol" of the original, whole sacrifice; Lev. 2 : 2, 9, 16; 5 : 12; 6 : 8; Num. 5 : 26; cf. with this connotation of *'azkarah* the Babylonian technical term of the *âšipu*-ritual, *zuqqurûtu,* the original connotation of which was probably "height, loftiness," but which, together with its synonyms, *pûḫu* and *dinânu,* came to be used in the ritual texts in the meaning of "substitute" [cf. Morgenstern, "The Doctrine of Sin, etc.," pp. 70 f.]). The remainder was given to the priest, to be consumed by him as "holy" food, i.e., food of which the ordinary, profane person might not partake, and which might not be eaten under profane conditions (Lev. 10 : 12–20). The priest was qualified to eat of this "holy" food because he himself was also "holy" and stood in immediate relation with the deity—was the deity's representative on earth, as it were, and the mediator between him and profane mankind. But equally with the priest, he who was in any way filled with the divine spirit or stood under the immediate protection of the deity—the prophet, the "man of God," the poor, the stranger, the orphan, and the widow—was qualified to eat of the taboo-sacrifice, or at least of certain forms thereof.

Thus, for example, the man from Ba'al Shalisha gives his first-fruit sacrifice to Elisha because he recognizes the prophet as a "man of God" (II Kings 4 : 42–44). The implication of the incident recorded in I Sam. 10 : 3 f. is to the same effect. Saul, on departing from Samuel, after the divine spirit had come upon him as the result of his being anointed with the holy oil, meets three men going up to the sanctuary at Bethel, each carrying what was apparently a taboo-sacrifice, to be offered to the deity. They give to Saul a portion of their sacrifices, attesting thereby that they recognize him as possessed of the divine spirit, therefore as a "man of God." This act not only strengthens Saul's confidence in Samuel's power, but also deepens his faith in himself and his conviction that the spirit of God has indeed come upon him and that the people at large can perceive this, and therefore must acknowledge his authority and leadership. Similarly, the corners of the field and forgotten sheaves and gleanings might not be gathered by ordinary persons and used for their profane needs, but had to be left for the poor (Lev. 19 : 9 f.; Deut. 24 : 19–21), which was tantamount to giving to the deity, since, in the steadily progressive evolution of the religion of Israel, the poor had come to be regarded as the immediate wards of the deity.

It seems that in ancient Israel the common designation for the taboo-sacrifice was *minḥah* (cf. Lagrange, *op. cit.,* p. 269, note 1), while the covenant-sacrifice was called either *zebaḥ* or *šelem,* or, with the two terms combined, *zebaḥ šelamîm.* The latter terms continued to be used in the Priestly Code (Lev. 3). Even before the Babylonian Exile, however, the taboo-sacrifices which were burned entirely upon the altar came to be distinguished, though seemingly rather loosely, from the taboo-sacrifices of which only a portion was burned and the remainder was eaten by the priests. The term *minḥah* continued to be applied generally to the latter form of the taboo-sacrifice, while the former was called either *kalîl* or *'ôlah.* Of these, *kalîl* seems to have been the older term and is seldom found in the later Biblical literature.

In the Priestly Code a marked change in the terminology of the taboo-sacrifice is noticeable. *'Ôlah* still designates the sacrifice which was burned entirely upon the altar (Lev. 1). But *minḥah* has ceased altogether to be a generic name for taboo-sacrifice, and has come to designate only a class, and that too a subordinate class, of taboo-sacrifices, viz., the so-called "cereal-offering." Apparently this was no longer offered as an independent sacrifice, except in the case of the oblation of first-fruits, but was always offered in connection with and dependent upon some other, larger, and more important animal taboo-sacrifice (Lev. 2). And two additional designations for other important classes of taboo-sacrifice were now regularly used, viz., *ḥaṭṭa't,* "sin-offering" (Lev. 4; used already by Hosea [4 : 8], though whether in its later, technical connotation it is impossible to determine with certainty; cf. also II Kings 12 : 17), and *'ašam,* "guilt-offering" (Lev. 5). In all these sacrifices the old principle was still scrupulously maintained, that the sacrificer might under no condition eat of his own sacrifice.

In this connection it is illuminating that, inasmuch as there was no one who stood higher in ritual rank than the high-priest or the entire community as a congregational unit, there was accordingly no one qualified to eat the customary portions of the sin-offerings of either of these. Hence, after the regular portions of these two sin-offerings had been burned upon the altar, the remainder, which in the ordinary sin-offering was eaten by the priests, was burned outside the camp at the ritual spot where the ashes from the altar were poured out (Lev. 4 : 12, 21). This bears out our contention that the prohibition of the sacrificer, or of the person or persons for whom the sin-offering or taboo-sacrifice was offered, from eating any portion of his sacrifice, was a fundamental and indispensable element, and therefore a distinguishing characteristic, of the ritual of the taboo-sacrifice.

Two very interesting traditions, recorded by Damîrî (*Ḥayât al-Ḥayawân,* trans. Jayakar, pp. 244, 280), may be cited here, since they furnish evidence, upon the authority of Mohammed himself, corroborative of this principle: "Muslim relates on the authority of Musa b. Salamah al-Hudhaili, who said, 'I and Sinân b. Salamah started on a religious visit to the sacred places at Makkah during the pilgrimage, and Sinân had a bulky she-camel with him which he was driving; she became fatigued on the road, and as I was thinking sorrowfully over it, she broke down entirely. We therefore went to Ibn-Abbâs to ask him regarding it, and he replied, "On the possessor of knowledge thou hast lighted." The Apostle of God once sent sixteen camels for sacrifice with a man and ordered him to sacrifice them; but the man asked, "O Apostle of God, what shall I do with any of them which may break down on the way?" and he replied, "Slaughter it and dye its feet with its blood, then apply the blood to its sides, but neither you are to eat it nor is any of your companions to do so." ' " It is clear that this animal was being driven to Mecca to be offered there as a sacrifice, either on the regular day of sacrifice, the 10th of Dhû'l Ḥijjeh, when each pilgrim offered his sacrifice, and of which he was not permitted to eat, or in payment of a vow. In either case, the prohibition of the sacrificer and his guests or companions from eating of the sacrifice is absolute.

The second tradition deals with a sacrifice offered in payment of a vow, where, again, the sacrificer does not, and therefore clearly may not, eat of his sacrifice, but instead distributes the flesh to the poor. "Ibn-al-Athir states that Khallâd b. Râfi' and his brother went forth, with the object of going to the battle of Badr, on a very lean camel, but when they went as far as near ar-Rawḥa the camel lay down on its breast; he [Khallâd] stated,

We then said, 'O God, we bind ourselves to Thee to slaughter it if we reach Badr.' The Prophet saw that, and said, 'What is the matter with you two?' and when we informed him of what had happened, he dismounted, performed the necessary ablution [for prayer], spat in the water of ablution, and ordered us [them] to open its mouth, which we [they] did; he then poured the water into its stomach [interior], then on its neck, then on the part between the neck and the hump, then on its hump, then on its rump, and then on its tail, and said, 'O God, take Rifâʿah and Khallâd on.' We then recommenced our journey and overtook the first rank of the camels. When we reached Badr, it lay down on its breast, and we slaughtered it and gave away the meat in charity." This last tradition is interesting also because of its account of the use made by the Prophet of his saliva, clearly to impart strength to the weak animal; just this was the purpose of the use of the Prophet's saliva in the rite of *taḥnik* (cf. above, pp. 34 f.).

Still another significant instance of the ancient Semitic practice of the sacrificer not being permitted to eat of his sacrifice is the following, cited by Lane (*Arabic Dictionary,* I, page 2379 f.), "When the camels (of a man's herd) amounted to the number for which their owner wished, they sacrificed (a firstling); or when one's camels amounted to a complete hundred, he sacrificed a he-camel thereof every year, and gave it to the people to eat, neither he nor his family tasting of it; or rather, it is said, he sacrificed a young, or youthful, he-camel to his idol; and the Muslims used to do it in the first part of El-Islam; then it was abrogated." This sacrifice, too, partook of the character of the payment of a vow. The hundredth camel, or the one over the wished-for number, was, as it were, vowed to the deity, and was therefore taboo for use and enjoyment by the man to whom the herd belonged; therefore he might not partake of its flesh when it was sacrificed.

B[1]

According to Valerius Maximus, II, 6, 15 (quoted from Selden, *De Dis Syris Syntagmata,* p. 314), at the shrine of Sicca Veneria, about a three-day journey from Carthage, matrons used to assemble, and "proceeding to make money, they collected gifts at the expense of their bodies." Eusebius (*Vita Constantii,* III, 58; *de Laude Constantii,* I, 15) likewise states that matrons as well as maidens were accustomed to prostitute themselves in the worship of the Syrian mother-goddess. The women of Cyprus also have always been reputed to hold the marriage bond very loosely (Ali Bey, *Travels,* I, 316). This accords completely with the statement of Lactantius (*Instit.,* I, 17, 10) that in the worship of Venus the Cyprian women used to make money by prostitution (cf. below, p. 95). Isaac of Antioch tells how the women of the city, Beth-Chur, submitted to prostitution in the service of the goddess Balthi (ed. Bickell, I, 212). Barhebraeus (on Ps. 12 : 9), too, speaks of the obscene feasts of the Edomites (Nabataeans ?), where the women made a sevenfold circuit, as at Arabian shrines, round an image of Beltis or Aphrodite, on the top of a Palestinian mountain, and then practiced promiscuous uncleanness (Robertson Smith, *Kinship and Marriage in Early Arabia*², p. 295). At Tabala, in Yemen, also there was, according to a tradition of the Prophet, recorded in Yâcût, II, 462, 24, a feast to which women of the Daus thronged, and at which, undoubtedly, similar rites were observed (*ibid.*). In this connection, the numerous Biblical references to sacred prostitution committed by the women of Israel

[1] Chapter XII, note 45.

upon the tops of mountains and under green trees in the practice of the borrowed agricultural Canaanite religion, so bitterly denounced by the prophets, may be cited.

Of the inhabitants of Martawan, a village on the road from Alexandretta to Aleppo inhabited by Nosairis, we are told (Volney, *Travels through Egypt and Syria,* II, 100) that "they let out their wives and daughters for a trifling sum. This prostitution, held in abhorrence by the Arabs, seems to me to have originated in some religious custom, which ought, perhaps, to be sought for in the ancient worship of the goddess Venus." Another traveler (Buckingham, *Travels in Assyria, Media and Persia,* pp. 63 f.; *Travels among the Arab Tribes,* p. 451) tells that the men of a Nosairi village on the road from Scanderoon to Aleppo, i.e., in close proximity to Martawan, if not that very village, prostitute their wives and daughters to strangers, "also a relic of the ancient devotion to Venus." Furthermore, an interesting tradition bearing upon a somewhat similar medieval practice in this same vicinity is recorded by Yâcût (III, 760; cf. also the *Marâsîd al-Ittilâ* of Safi ad-Din, quoted from Le Strange, *Palestine under the Moslems,* pp. 294 f.) as follows: "There was in the neighborhood of Halab a domain called Ain Jarah, and between this place and Al Haunah, which some also call Al Jaunah, was an upright stone, as might be for a boundary between the two domains. Now, whenever a quarrel fell out between any of the inhabitants of these two domains, the people of Al Haunah were wont to proceed and throw down the standing-stone. As soon, however, as the stone had fallen, the women-folk of the two domains would come out publicly and in all their ornaments, but as though deprived of their reason; and they would seek to commit fornication; neither were they to be restrained in the madness that possessed them by the sense of shame. To prevent this, the men would hasten to the stone and set it up again as it was before, standing erect and firm; after which the women would return to their houses, regaining the discrimination of matters such as are abhorrent to commit."

In most, if not all, of these practices there seems to be something of a religious implication, or, rather, of a survival thereof. The assumption of Volney and Buckingham may therefore be correct, that these practices represent survivals of ancient prostitution of women, both married and single, in the worship of the Semitic mother-goddess. And the standing-stone, mentioned by Yâcût, may well be an ancient sacred pillar or cult-object of a like nature, in the worship of which, under certain conditions, the prostitution of women played a certain role.

In even more recent times, and in fact down to the present day, similar rites seem to be practiced still. Curtiss (*Primitive Semitic Religion Today,* German ed., Introduction, xviii, note 3) tells, on excellent authority, that at the great festival celebrated annually at Nejjar in honor of Hasan and Hosein by the Shiites the servant of the shrine offers women as temporary wives to pilgrims for a week or more. The Persian girls come there for this purpose, and in order to distinguish themselves from other women they wear a peculiar earring. They are veiled also, precisely as was the sacred prostitute of ancient Canaanite religion. Similar rites were likewise practiced until quite recently during festival celebrations at Mount Carmel (cf. also Curtiss, "The Ancient Religion of Syria in Centers of Moslem and Christian Influence," *BW,* XXIII, 332 ff.).

Curtiss says also (*Primitive Semitic Religion Today,* English ed., pp. 154 f.; German ed., pp. 174 f.): "Nor are there those in Syria who vow themselves once, as Herodotus says was the custom among Babylonian women in their service of Venus, known as Istar. It is said that a Syrian woman vowed, in case the saint granted her request, she would serve as a prostitute three days. And a Syrian is authority for the statement that Egyptian women, in connection with the *molid* service, at a shrine in Tanta, follow the ancient custom of Babylonia." To this, Curtiss adds the note: "Such customs . . . are attested as existing in Baalbek by a missionary who has resided long in the vicinity. I have heard of such a practice among a tribe of the Bedouin, from what seems to be a trustworthy source." He also appends the following note: "Hanna Khizani of Hamath visited Tanta, Egypt, and saw the great annual festival of Seiyid Ahmed el-Bedawi, 'probably the most popular saint in Egypt,' when there were 'upwards of half a million persons' present, including singers, dancers, jugglers, and showmen of every kind. It is at this festival 'that some of the honorable women vow the use of their bodies to the first one who happens to approach them,' following precisely the custom described by Herodotus."

Furthermore, Curtiss tells (*op. cit.*, German ed., pp. 294; not in the English ed.) that frequently a saint or *wely* is thought to have a real property right over the body of a man or a woman. He then adds (*op. cit.*, p. 296): "Often a maiden can be redeemed therefrom by paying the whole, or at least a part, of her marriage price to the sanctuary. However, until quite recently, the same custom as the old Syrian or Babylonian one, existed in northern Syria, viz., that the festival pilgrim, when he had cast a coin in her lap, could deliver up a maiden to the temple of Astarte. In the same manner, the previously mentioned 'holy' man among the Nosairis could demand a new sacrifice every day. The practice of vowing maidens to ez-Zaʿbi and then to marry them to his priests is a survival of the ancient sacrifice of virginity" (cf. also *ibid.*, pp. 191 ff.). In this last instance Curtiss is speaking very obviously of the prostitution of virgins and the sacrifice of their virginity. But all the other cases which he mentions seem to deal with the prostitution of women, regardless of whether they are virgins or not, and who, in fact, seem in the majority of cases not to be such.

It is doubtful if this same inference of religious association and origin may be drawn from the well-known and oft-cited lewdness with strangers of the women of Jericho. Of the inhabitants of this city, Osborn (*Palestine, Past and Present,* pp. 441 f.) remarks: "The people here are almost a separate race from all around, and . . . are despised by all. The women have not modesty enough to wear the 'mendel' or hardly any dress at all; and the men seem careless in view of the infidelity of their wives, provided they are not forced to put their lazy bodies to the exertion of punishing them. And thus they often exhibit themselves in immodest dances and dresses for little reward." Robinson (*Biblical Researches in Palestine,* I, 552 f.) also testifies to the same effect: "Our Sheikh spoke of them (the people of Jericho) as hospitable and well-meaning people, but feeble and licentious, the infidelity of the women being winked at by the men. . . . At our encampment . . . the night before we reached this place, we overheard our Arabs asking the Khatib for a paper, or written charm, to protect them from the women of Jericho, and from their conversation it seemed that illicit intercourse between the latter and strangers who come here is regarded as a matter of course." (Cf. also Prime, *Tent Life in the Holy Land,* p. 218; Olin, *Travels in the East,* II, 223; Leary, *The Real Palestine of Today,* p. 133.) This seems to be naught other than the result of sheer depravity and unrestrained impulse to sexual promiscuity. It is interesting to note, however, that from the Middle Ages on many travelers, like Osborn, have commented upon the fact that the native inhabitants of Jericho and Mar Saba seem to be of a race of people quite different from the other inhabitants of Palestine, being more brown-skinned, or even almost black, and are hated and despised by both Bedouin and fellahin, who feel themselves quite distinct from and immeasurably superior to them (Mukaddasi, *Description of Syria, Including Palestine,* translated by Le Strange, p. 56; Idrîsi, in Le Strange, *Palestine under the Moslems,* p. 31; Robinson, *op. cit.;* Leary, *op. cit.;* Conder, *Tent Work in Palestine,* I, 296 f.). Not impossibly, these natives of Jericho may be direct descendants of the old, pre-Israelite inhabitants of the land, and, if so, their lewd practices may perhaps be survivals of old heathen rites.

Among some of the Bedouin tribes, too, as late as the last century, free intercourse of the women with strangers seems to have been common and proper, chiefly as an expression of hospitality, but also, in a way, as the right of the women. The practice is attested by Burckhardt (*Travels in Arabia,* II, 306, 378 ff.), after careful investigation and what seemed to him absolute confirmation, for the Beni Harb, the El Merekede, a branch of the Asyr tribe, and seemingly also for the Kelb (*ibid.,* pp. 385 f.), the beni Yam (*ibid.,* pp. 386 f.), and the Hutain (Wellsted, *Travels in Arabia,* German translation of Roediger, II, 203; Burton, *A Pilgrimage to Al Madinah and Mekka,* II, 121). A somewhat similar practice exists in Abyssinia (Dye, *Egypt and Abyssinia,* pp. 94, 385). Whether a religious origin attaches in any way to these practices it is impossible to tell, although it is by no means improbable.

Kindred practices of certain tribes of northern Africa are recorded by Doutté (*Magie et Religion dans l'Afrique du Nord,* pp. 560 f.): "The large tribe of Oulad Nâïl . . . is well known for the practice of its young women, so soon as they arrive at the age of puberty, of quitting their homes in order to go to practice commerce with their charms in the towns and thus earn a sum of money which will permit them to marry. Nowadays the natives of the tribe, who have had contact with our civilization, voluntarily relinquish this custom, and pretend that the young Oulâd Nâïl women who prostitute themselves belong to lower social strata; but it is certain that formerly this custom was almost completely general and that still today no dishonor attaches to those who follow it. Moreover, the natives, whoever they may be, marry without the least reluctance those women who have trafficked with their bodies. . . . Among the Oulâd 'Abdi de l'Aures the women frequently divorce themselves and in the intervals between their marriages deliver themselves up to prostitution. During this time they do not cease to dwell at home with their families, and their relatives regard their conduct as perfectly natural. The government, being disturbed by this, sought to regulate this prostitution, but the entire population opposed it, claiming that this practice furthered the abundance of the crops. From this it seems that a real *baraka* is attached to this prostitution." Therefore, following Frazer, Doutté associates this prostitution, in considerable part at least, with similar magical practices current in many parts of the earth, designed to promote the fertility of the soil and the consequent abundance of the crops. Accordingly, the primary relationship of such magical rites with the cult of the great Semitic mother-goddess, the deification of the earth as the great mother, is self-apparent.

Elsewhere (*Merrâkech,* pp. 149 f.), Doutté describes in detail kindred practices among various tribes of Algeria and Morocco. Of the Doukkâla tribe he says: "The coquetry, one might almost say the effrontery, of the women strikes the least suspecting travelers. They address them in the open country and about the wells extend the most cavalier invitations to them, nor do they hesitate to call them from a distance and make their proposals to them. Prostitution in the households is general, and the number of complaisant husbands is legion. The repudiation of a woman because of adultery is rare, and as for the slaying of a faithless wife by her husband, it is almost entirely unknown. The custom, widespread in some regions of Algeria, of inviting a guest to pass the night with a daughter of the house exists also among many of the tribes of the Doukkâla and almost all the

Châouia. Precisely as among certain tribes of our Kabyle-country, he who presents himself as a guest is asked if he is a *deïf el jmâ'a* or a *deïf el kheïma,* that is to say, 'a guest of the group' or 'a guest of the tent.' In the first place, he is brought under a common tent, such as is to be found in every douar, where the necessary things are furnished him and he passes the night without obligation to anyone. In the second case an inhabitant of the douar brings him to his own tent, gives him food and provides him with what he needs. Finally he is permitted to choose among the daughters of the family, but not among the married women, one who will pass the night with him. In the morning a small gift is obligatory of the value of one or two pesetas."

C[1]

Against this conclusion it might be argued that post-Biblical Hebrew employs the expression *ḳaddeš 'iššah* (literally, "to sanctify a woman") for "to betroth a woman" (Jastrow, *Dictionary,* pp. 1319f.), and also that we have the terms *ḳᵉdešah* in Hebrew and *ḳadištu* and *ḥarimtu* in Accadian for "a sacred harlot." These facts, however, occasion not the slightest difficulty. *Ḳaddeš 'iššah* certainly does not mean "to consecrate a woman to a deity," but merely "to consecrate a woman to her husband," to make her his particular property, and therefore *ḳadôš* to him and taboo and forbidden to every other man. (So *Ḳiddûšîn* 2b; cf. Levy, *Neuhebräisches und chaldäisches Wörterbuch,* IV, 250b.) In this sense it is used in precisely the same manner as Arabic employs the stem *ḥarima* in the double and related connotations "sacred" and "forbidden" or "taboo," and the noun *ḥarîm* (literally, "forbidden") in the connotations "women" and "the women's part of the home and all its inmates."

And as for the words *ḳᵉdešah* and *ḳadištu* and *ḥarimtu,* while they undoubtedly designate these women as consecrated to a deity, they do not necessarily imply that the act of copulation was in itself anything but a profane function on their part. In fact, this is indicated by the very ceremony of first giving the woman a coin, which becomes the property of the deity, before her favors may be enjoyed. The payment of this coin parallels exactly the payment of the five shekels as the redemption-money for a first-born child, prescribed in Num. 18:16. Just as the payment of the money redeems the child from the possession and power of the deity, so here the payment of this coin releases the devotee—however, in this case, of course, only temporarily—from the possession of the deity and renders her profane and free for enjoyment by the man. But with the conclusion of this act of sexual intercourse she automatically reverts to her normal condition of consecration to the deity and, very probably, even to theoretical virginity. The payment of the coin could have no purpose other than this. And this confirms our conclusion that, after the sacrifice of the hair and the virginity to the deity, sexual intercourse was regarded as a profane act performed by women in a profane state.

Against this it might be argued that, according to Herodotus, at the first act of intercourse, that with a stranger, when the virginity was sacrificed, a coin was given by him to the maiden for the goddess. But this would be only a seeming objection. On the one hand, Lucian in his parallel account makes no mention of the payment of any such coin; and, on the other hand, the principle holds good for the first and only act of sexual intercourse on the part of the virgin, as well as for repeated acts of intercourse on the part of a sacred

[1] Chapter XII, note 73.

harlot, that the payment of a coin to the deity redeems her for that one occasion from the possession of the deity. But when the maiden ceased to be a virgin, the deity's claim upon her also ceased completely, and so, unlike the sacred harlot, she did not have to be redeemed again for further intercourse.

With the evolution of religion and the gradual forgetting of the original purpose and significance of the various primitive rites, it seems that the natural tendency was for the women, whether virgins or sacred harlots, to appropriate to themselves the money received for the enjoyment of their favors, or at least a part thereof, instead of turning this over to the deity, as was originally the custom. Thus, in Gen. 38, Tamar kept for herself what she had received from Judah. And, according to Justin, as we have seen, the Cypriote maidens likewise kept for themselves what they received from the strangers who consorted with them, or at least a part thereof, for their own dowries.

From this there undoubtedly developed the custom, seemingly common among all Semitic peoples as well as in other parts of the world, that the groom had to purchase from the bride by the gift of money or some other rich present the privilege of consorting with her for the first time. From this it is but a short and easily comprehensible step to regard such payment or gift by the groom to the bride as an essential and indispensable rite of marriage. So the Mishnah (*Ḳiddûšîn* I, 1) provides that one of the three legitimate ways in which a man might acquire a woman in wedlock was by giving her a coin.

Musil tells that among the fellahin in the vicinity of Palestine, just before the groom is left alone with the bride for the first time, he gives her a *mejidi* and then cuts the ostrich feathers from her headdress (*Arabia Petraea,* III, 195). Similar customs exist among the Bedouin (*ibid.,* p. 206). Another traveler (Newman, *Babylon and Niniveh,* p. 240) relates that among the Bedouin a girl may reject a suitor if she wishes, provided that he is not her cousin, but if she accepts any gift whatsoever from him, she is bound to give herself to him.

Among the medieval Arabs the groom gave the bride a present as "the price of uncovering her face" (Lane, *Arabian Society in the Middle Ages,* p. 237), while among the Moslems of Palestine today the groom gives the bride in addition thereto a coin as advance payment for her disrobing before him (Rothstein in *PJB* [1910], 122). Another traveler (Grant, *The Peasantry of Palestine,* p. 60) relates that in Palestine "in the evening of the wedding day, when the bridegroom is allowed a glimpse of his wife's face, before he goes to join his friends in the merry-making, he presses a gold coin on her forehead. It is his gift and falls into her lap." This last is almost the very same act as that described by Herodotus, "until a stranger, casting a coin into her lap, etc." Among the Mandaeans also the bridegroom tenders the bride a gift just before they are left alone together for the first time (Petermann, *Reisen im Orient*², II, 118).

And in Algeria, we are told (Certeux and Carony, *L'Algérie Traditionelle; Contributions au Folklore des Arabes,* I, 211 f.), "The bride being seated, the bridegroom puts aside her veil and sees her for the first time. But she makes no response at all to the words which he addresses to her until he first makes her a present, bracelets, rings, or pieces of money." And in Morocco, according to Westermarck (*Marriage Ceremonies in Morocco,* pp. 237–253), the money regularly given by the bridegroom to the bride is called among the different tribes variously "the opening of the girdle" (although the bride actually wears no girdle), "the money of the hymeneal blood," "the money of greeting," "the money of the drawers," and "the opening of the belt." Westermarck (*ibid.,* pp. 262 f., 325) believes it to be a safeguard against the evil spirits which threaten the marriage, and this it undoubtedly was in origin. But in its present form it has become nothing more than a payment by the bridegroom to the bride for the privilege of cohabiting with her for the first time (cf. Doutté, *Merrâkech,* p. 336).

Unquestionably, the modern occidental custom of the bridegroom giving the bride a wedding ring as the solemnizing rite of wedlock is a development from this ancient custom of first paying a coin to the deity, then of the bride retaining the coin for herself, and, finally, of substituting for or supplementing this coin by some other object of value as a gift to her.

D[1]

Wellhausen, *Reste des altarabischen Heidentums*[2], p. 199. Today the unmarried girls let their hair hang in short curls over the forehead (Doughty, *Arabia Deserta,* I, 340), and during the marriage ceremony itself they wear a veil (Musil, *Arabia Petraea,* III, 205, 216). And in Southern Arabia from the moment the proposal of marriage is accepted the maiden may no longer go abroad unveiled (Featherman, *The Aramaeans,* p. 421). Married women, on the other hand, plait their hair into a kind of knot or horn, which hangs down in front (Doughty, *op. cit.,* I, 75, 382, 418, 467; II, 220; Palmer, *The Desert of the Exodus,* p. 79; Buckingham, *Travels in Palestine,* pp. 49, 115).

For the Assyrian custom of veiling women and its significance, cf. Jastrow, "An Assyrian Law Code," *JAOS,* XLI (1921), 34 ff. Jastrow holds that, at least among the Assyrians, the wearing of the veil by a woman signified that she belonged to a particular man—in other words, was married. Therefore the public prostitute was not required to wear a veil. This, however, can hardly be correct, for we know that among most Semitic peoples among whom the institution existed, the sacred prostitute was required to wear a veil, presumably in her capacity as the representative of the goddess Ishtar-Astarte (cf. von Oppenheim, "Der Tell Halaf und die verschleierte Göttin," *AO,* X, I, 24 ff.; cf. also Gen. 38 : 14, 19). If, therefore, Jastrow's interpretation of the somewhat fragmentary text be correct, that among the Assyrians the public prostitute was not required, or was even forbidden, to wear the veil, this probably indicated no more than that her profession and social position were regarded as shameful.

In ancient Israel, it is clear, the veil was assumed by women preliminary to, and as a part of, the marriage rite. Thus Rebecca, who had permitted herself to be seen by Eleazar without any compunction, drops her veil when she catches her first glimpse of Isaac, her future husband (Gen. 24 : 65). Obviously, it would have been improper for her to be seen by him unveiled before their marriage. Likewise, Leah is brought to Jacob veiled, so that in consequence he does not realize until the next morning that he has married her instead of Rachel (Gen. 29 : 25). But previous to this, and before contemplating marriage with her, Jacob had beheld Rachel, and had even kissed her, without the slightest implication of impropriety in so doing. This is obviously the same custom as that obtaining in Southern Arabia, that from the moment of betrothal the maiden may not be seen, at least by her future husband, unveiled. Among the fellahin of Palestine today from the betrothal until the proper moment in the marriage ceremony the groom may not look upon the face of his future wife. Should they accidentally meet, she either turns her face away or covers it with her veil, precisely as did Rebecca in the Biblical narrative (Klein, "Mitteilungen über Leben, Sitte und Gebraüche der Fellachen in Palästina," *ZDPV,* VI [1883], 92).

[1] Chapter XII, note 84.

And, as we have just seen, the practice is not unknown, that the groom must pay the bride a certain sum of money or bestow a gift upon her in order that she open or remove her veil before him.

Possibly closely related to the veil, assumed by maidens preliminary to marriage, is the Druse and Maronite *tantur,* formerly donned by women upon marriage, and never removed, not even in sleep: a metal piece, shaped something like a horn and fastened to the head, from which the veil covering the hair was suspended (cf. Petermann, *op. cit.,* I, 45, 343; Kelly, *Syria and the Holy Land,* pp. 90, 148; Porter, *The Giant Cities of Bashan,* p. 302; Buckingham, *Travels among the Arab Tribes,* pp. 394, 450 f., 467). Nowadays the wearing of the *tantur* is becoming less and less common.

Probably akin to this custom is that of the women of Bethlehem. The maidens there wear on their heads only a white veil, while the married women wear underneath this veil "an extraordinary cylinder of felt, not unlike a Greek priest's cap, generally sewn over with coins" (Conder, *Tent Work in Palestine,* I, 287, 293; II, 246). This felt hat is called *schatue* (Bauer, *Volksleben im Lande der Bibel,* p. 51; Canaan, *Aberglaube und Volksmedezin im Lande der Bibel,* p. 74, note 6).

Among the modern fellahin the maidens wear a peculiar headdress of ostrich feathers, which is cut off by the bridegroom at marriage (Musil, *op. cit.,* III, 196; Jaussen, *Coutumes des Arabes au pays de Moab,* pp. 52 f., and planche I, Fig. 3). Among some tribes of the Sinaitic peninsula the maidens "have an ornament (*shebeyka*), which they put on at the age of puberty, and which is composed of pieces of mother-of-pearl fastened to a string and hanging down over the cheeks and forehead. As no married woman is permitted to wear it, the bridegroom takes it off by force on the first night of the nuptials" (Burckhardt, *Notes on the Bedouins and Wahabys,* p. 133; Featherman, *The Aramaeans,* p. 349). This peculiar headdress of the maidens, which is removed by the bridegroom at marriage, and apparently preliminary to the first copulation, is unmistakably closely akin to the crown of cord worn by the Babylonian maidens and severed by the stranger who first cohabited with one of them. Both may well have been the substitute for the hair itself, originally cut off at marriage or at the first copulation.

E[1]

All this mass of evidence, here presented, of the significance of the sacrifice of the hair as a rite marking the conclusion of a festival and the passing of the celebrant thereby from the state of festal consecration or superprofane taboo into a state of ordinary, profane existence, probably throws light upon the hitherto inexplicable procedure of Absalom, as described in II Sam. 14 : 26. The verse tells that Absalom would cut his hair only once each year, and that at the end of the year. (This is unquestionably the meaning of the expression *mikkeṣ yamîm lᵉyamîm.* That *yamîm* or, more frequently, *yamîm lᵉyamîm* or *yamîm yamîmah* connotes "a year" is clear from I Sam. 1 : 3, 20, 21; cf. Krauss, *Talmudische Archäologie,* I, 644, note 828.) But had the author of II Sam. 14 : 26 wished to convey merely that Absalom was accustomed to cut his hair only once a year, without regard to the particular time or occasion when the operation was performed, it would have sufficed to say *miyamîm yamîmah,* as in I Sam. 1 : 3. The use of *ḳeṣ* therefore implies that this operation was per-

[1] Chapter XII, note 114.

formed not only once each year, but also at the very end of the year. (Cf. also Robertson Smith, *Religion of the Semites*³, p. 484.) As I have shown elsewhere ("The Chanukkah Festival and the Calendar of Ancient Israel," *HUCA,* XXI [1948], 374–401; "The Calendar of the Book of Jubilees," *VT,* V [1955], 34–76), until the erection by Solomon of the Temple in Jerusalem and with this the inauguration by him of a new system of time-reckoning—a solar calendar—the old, agricultural, Canaanite pentecontad calendar was in official use in Israel. Under this calendar the year came to a formal end with the celebration of the seven-day *Maṣṣôth* festival in the early spring. The day following the close of this festival was accordingly the New Year's Day, the first day of the new year. Upon it the first sheaf of the new grain crop was cut with appropriate ceremonial. It must have been in connection with the celebration of this New Year's Day that Absalom would cut his hair each year. There is cogent evidence supporting this conclusion, but its consideration would lead us too far afield to justify its presentation here. But granting that Absalom would cut his hair regularly each year upon the New Year's Day, it must have been primarily a ceremony of removal of taboo especially appropriate for the celebration of this day of supreme sanctity.

Moreover, it is clear that the purpose of the author of II Sam. 14 : 26 was not at all to tell that Absalom was accustomed to shave his head only once each year, and that, too, upon, or in anticipation of, the immediately ensuing New Year's Day, but rather that his hair was so thick and heavy that, when he did cut it upon each successive New Year's Day, it was regularly found to weigh two hundred shekels. Manifestly, the second third of the verse is a circumstantial clause giving the occasion for this rite quite incidentally. And in this section of the verse the last four words of the Hebrew text bear all the earmarks of a late, explanatory gloss which has really missed the point. And if we construe the second third of the verse as a circumstantial clause and the last four words thereof as a late gloss, it follows then that the verse seems to tell not only that Absalom was accustomed to cut off his hair only once each year, and that too at the very end of the year, but also that this was a common, or even a regular, procedure for all the males of Israel, an established New Year's Festival rite.

This suggests also, as has just been intimated, the true explanation of the otherwise inexplicable statement that Absalom would weigh his hair upon each of these occasions, and that it would weigh two hundred royal shekels. In all likelihood, the purpose of this weighing of the hair upon this annual festal occasion was in order to distribute its weight in silver as alms to the poor. We have found this practice repeatedly attested in more recent times, as, for example, when Mohammed weighed the first hair of his grandson, Hosein, with silver and gave this as alms to the poor, or when, in more modern practice, the hair of a child, consecrated by a vow and then redeemed by means of a sacrifice and the cutting off of his hair, is weighed with money, and this money is given either to the *wely* or saint to whom the child has been consecrated, or to the poor. Unquestionably Absalom, too, would give the weight of his hair in money, viz., two hundred royal shekels, either to the sanctuary or to the poor. This was in full accord with its character as a taboo-sacrifice and also as an annual festal rite.

In this connection, it is possible to explain also the statement of Lucian (*De Dea Syria,* p. 55) that "he who comes for the first time to the holy city (Hierapolis) is obliged to shave his head and his eyebrows. This done, he sacrifices a sheep; of the residue of the flesh he makes a meal; but the skin, when drawn off, he spreads upon the ground, sets one knee upon it, puts the feet and the head of the victim upon his own head, and in that attitude prays the gods that they would be graciously pleased to accept for the present his humble offering, promising to bring a better at some future time. When this is done, he crowns himself and the several persons who accompanied him on the journey, but he takes his chaplet off again when he is setting out on his return home. All the time of his pilgrimage he must use no other than cold water, either for bathing or drinking, and never sleep otherwise than on the bare ground. It would be a sin to go to bed before he has regained his home from his holy migration" (Tooke's translation, II, 464).

Here we have an unmistakable instance of the rite of cutting off the hair, not at the close of a state of consecration seemingly, but at the commencement thereof. This is apparent from the fact that the rite was performed, it seems, when the pilgrim first entered the sacred precincts, and that thereafter, during his entire sojourn in the holy city, various taboos were incumbent upon him. The peculiar sacrifice which he offered was not the regular festival sacrifice, for the manner of offering this regular sacrifice is described later by Lucian (*op. cit.,* 57), but this was a special sacrifice (cf. Robertson Smith, *op. cit.,* p. 474), offered only by those who came to the sanctuary for the first time. Nor was this rite of cutting off the hair performed by all pilgrims when they came to the great sanctuary, but only upon the occasion of their first visit there.

A moment's thought will show, however, that this sacrifice of the hair went hand in hand with the accompanying sacrifice of the sheep, and that both sacrifices were expiatory in character; in other words, both together were designed to remove a taboo, thought to rest upon the pilgrim who came to the sanctuary for the first time. With this taboo removed, he automatically became fit to participate in all the rites and ceremonies of the sanctuary. For this, quite plainly, no particular rites of consecration were necessary, for otherwise these would have had to be performed not only when a stranger came to the sanctuary for the first time, but also upon every pilgrimage thither, no matter how frequently made. From this it is clear that this instance of the rite of cutting off the hair does not constitute an exception to the general rule which we have posited, that the sacrifice of the hair marks, not the beginning of a state of consecration but rather the passing out of a previous taboo, whether of holiness or of ritual uncleanness, but instead conforms fully to it. Before his first visit to the holy city a potential pilgrim was in a state of ritual immaturity or taboo in relation thereto comparable in every way to the taboo resting upon a child before the sacrifice of his first hair. From this state of ritual immaturity and taboo the sacrifice of the hair and of an appropriate animal upon approaching the holy city redeemed him and qualified him for participation in all the ceremonies and obligations of the festival pilgrimage. It is clear, therefore, that in every way these rites parallel the *'aḳîḳah* ceremony.

F[1]

Practically the same ceremony is observed by the Reḥamna, a tribe of northern Africa. "On the morning of the celebration of the marriage the friends of the bridegroom stain his hands with henna. . . . On the evening of this same day the bride, in turn, is similarly purified with henna. She is made to sit upon a packsaddle and to stretch out her hands in front of her. Her mother stains them with henna, and when she has finished she wipes her own hands upon the bride's feet; otherwise, no henna is put upon her feet. . . .

[1] Chapter XIII, note 60.

This ceremony of the henna, for both groom and bride, is observed throughout all of northern Africa, and frequently manifests various complications. It is regarded as a purification; and actually to the natives such is the meaning of the rite, which consists in smearing oneself with mud or paint. They believe that in eventually washing off this coat or letting it gradually wear off, as is the case here, they eliminate at the same time from their bodies all the maleficent influences which might have attached themselves to them. This explains the extraordinary vogue which the henna enjoys" (Doutté, *Merrâkech,* pp. 333 f.).

However, without questioning at all the validity of this popular explanation which Doutté offers, another hypothesis may be proposed, which will account better for the use in these marriage ceremonies and on other similar occasions of the henna with its red color. As I have shown elsewhere ("Two Ancient Israelite Festivals," *JQR* [new series], VIII [1917], 49 f.), the color red seems to have been intimately associated with evil spirits and their removal, among the ancient Semites as well as among other primitive peoples (cf. von Duhn, "Rot und Tot," *ARW,* IX (1906), 22 ff.; Crooke, *Popular Religions of Northern India*[2], I, 142, 166; Frazer, *The Golden Bough*[3]; *The Scapegoat,* pp. 146, 190, 192, 205, 208, 209, 213; *Balder the Beautiful,* I, 30, 31, 50 f., 52, 54, 77, 78; Scheftelowitz, "Das stellvertretende Huhnopfer," *ARW,* XIV (1911), 30, 47). Thus, among the Jews in the Rabbinic period evil spirits were conceived of as being either red or black in color (Gollancz, *The Book of Protection,* XXXIII, LII). Probably for this reason, the Rabbis forbade the binding of a red cord around the finger, on the ground that it was a heathen rite (*Tôsefta Šabbat* VI, 117, 4 [ed. Zuckermandel]). In ancient Babylon the images which symbolized the evil spirits of winter in the complex ritual of the New Year Festival were clad in red garments (Langdon, *The Epic of Creation,* p. 22). And when the officials of Niniveh heard of the murder of Sennacherib they clothed themselves in red, the color of death (Olmstead, *History of Assyria,* p. 341). Among the Arabs today the *rola,* or ghoul, is thought to appear frequently in the form of a bird either red or black in color (Musil, *Arabia Petraea,* III, 328). We have seen (above, p. 20) that the Shiite Persians picture the demon *Al* in the form of a young woman of ruddy color and with hair the color of red tulips, and that the word *Al* literally means "scarlet." Similarly, the Moslems of northern Africa imagine that the daughters of the *ğann* are clad in red garments (Doutté, *Magie et Religion dans l'Afrique du Nord,* pp. 92, 122, 125, 148, note 2). Among the Arabs of Egypt the sight in a dream of anything red or black in color, or of fire, was considered inauspicious (Lane, *Arabian Society in the Middle Ages,* p. 88). As we have already noted (above, p. 9), in Palestine today quite frequently the newborn babe is rubbed with a mixture of oil and red earth instead of the customary salt and oil. And among the modern Bedouin a child about to be circumcised is ofttimes clad in a red garment (Musil, *op. cit.,* III, 222). Likewise among the medieval Arabs the bridegroom seems to have been clothed regularly in red garments (cf. Usama ibn Munkidh, *Memoiren,* translation of Schumann, pp. 80, 81). Among the Druses today the bride is covered completely with a red veil (Kelly, *Syria and the Holy Land,* p. 148), and the same custom obtains among the Shiite Moslems of Persia (Adams, *Darkness and Daybreak,* pp. 128, 129) and the Sunnite Moslems of Palestine (Trumbull, *Studies in Oriental Social Life,* p. 50). And among the Moslems of Constantinople "a red kerchief is bound round the mother's head, and a gauze veil of the same colour is thrown over her temples," during the period immediately following childbirth (*ibid.,* pp. 11 f.). That in ancient Israel in Biblical times sin, and therefore evil, was conceived of as red in color is attested by Isa. 1 : 18. And the role of the color red in the expulsion of evil spirits is evidenced by the ceremony of the red heifer (Num. 19 : 2 ff. [cf. below, pp. 144]) and, in addition to the color of the animal itself, by the use of cedarwood, hyssop, both red in color, and scarlet cord in both this ceremony and that of the purification of the leper from his dread disease (Lev. 14 : 4–6, 49–53; cf. also Ps. 51 : 9; Heb. 9 : 19). On the other hand, among the Yezidis red is the color of joy, and therefore the bride wears red garments (Menzel, "Ein Beitrag zur Kenntniss der Jeziden," in Grote, *Meine Vorderasienexpedition 1906 und 1907,* I, 155, note 1). The idea that red is the color of joy is undoubtedly an expression of the characteristic Yezidi reversal of the more primitive concept that red is the color of evil. Still today we of the more cultured West picture the devil as red in color.

G[1]

Op. Cit., III, 449. Dozy (*Die Israeliten zu Mekka,* p. 119) cites an interesting instance of the practice of casting stones upon a grave (cf. also Snouck Hurgronje, *Mekka,* II, 119 note). In Palestine the best-known instance of this practice is in connection with the grave of Absalom (cf. Meshullam of Voltera [15th century], in Luncz, *Jerusalem,* I, 204, and the *Doresh Zion* of R. Simcha of Solsitz [18th century], ed. Hausdorff, p. 37). Likewise at the grave of Kalonimos, also in the Kidron Valley, the same practice is performed (cf. Hanauer, *Tales Told in Palestine,* p. 26). Burckhardt (*Nubia,* p. 270) gives an interesting illustration of the practice as a general rite among the Bedouin tribes of Upper Egypt: "One of the Sheikhs produced a basket full of white pebbles, over which several prayers were read. These pebbles were destined to be strewn over the tomb of the deceased in the manner which I had often observed upon tombs freshly made. Upon my inquiries concerning this custom, which I confessed to have never before seen practiced in any Mohammedan country, the Faky answered that it was a mere meritorious action, that there was no absolute necessity for it, but that it was thought that the soul of the deceased, when hereafter visiting the tomb, might be glad to find those pebbles, in order to use them as beads in addressing its prayers to the Creator." This last is, of course, an artificial and late explanation of the custom, the true origin and meaning of which have evidently been long forgotten.

In Syria, too, until quite recently it was forbidden to bury robbers in the same manner as respectable people. Instead, the corpse was left lying where it had been executed and was covered with stones. Everyone who passed by such a grave had to cast a stone upon the heap. Whoever neglected to do this, it was believed, became subject to the curse of God. Still today along some highroads in Syria such stone-heaps are met with, made by the stones which passers-by have cast upon the graves of robbers (Eijub Abēla, "Beiträge zur Kenntniss abergläubischer Gebräuche in Syrien," *ZDPV,* VII [1884], 102). Of course, here too the "curse of God" is a modernization, in conformity with present-day theology, of the more primitive concept of the danger which threatened all who passed by such a grave. Inasmuch as the robber had during his lifetime been a source of grave danger to all who in any way contacted him, so, it was undoubtedly thought, his ghost continued to threaten all who came into proximity with his grave. The casting of the stones would therefore not only protect them against the attacks of this otherwise dangerous spirit, but it would also serve to hold the ghost imprisoned more securely by the weight of the stones resting upon the grave.

In Algeria and Morocco the custom of casting stones and erecting stone-heaps is very

[1] Chapter XIV, note 81.

widespread among the natives. It has been discussed in detail by Doutté (*Merrâkech,* pp. 57–108; *Magie et Religion dans l'Afrique du Nord,* pp. 421–434). It serves a great variety of purposes, some of which, such as to mark off the land in which it is forbidden to pasture the flocks or herds or to designate tribal boundary lines, are perfectly natural in origin and aim and have obviously no relation whatsoever to the particular purpose of creating stone-heaps which we are considering. With this last, Doutté very properly correlated the stone-heap erected by Jacob and Laban (Gen. 31 : 45 ff; *Merrâkech,* p. 60, note 3). More often, however, stone-heaps are erected for purposes more significant for this investigation. Frequently they serve as memorials of departed heroes (cf. II Sam. 18 : 17 and Lods, *La Croyance à la Vie Future dans l'Antiquité Israélite,* pp. 200 ff.), or they mark the spot where events of great importance are supposed to have happened (so also the heap of stones in Josh. 4 : 20 ff.). More particularly, they mark the graves of martyrs or saints or famous heroes of antiquity. In such case the act of casting a stone upon the grave is a token of reverence for the one there buried. Doutté has advanced the justified and very plausible hypothesis that in the majority of these cases the casting of the stone establishes a relationship between the person who casts it and the saint or *wely* upon whose tomb it is cast, whereby, on the one hand, the evil or illness or sin resident in the body of him who casts the stone is transmitted to the saint, and, on the other hand, *baraka,* or "blessing," passes from the tomb, and therefore from the person or presence of the saint, to the caster of the stone. This last effect is naturally heightened if the latter takes something, such as a rag or other worthless object—in which, however, the *baraka* is crystallized—and carries it with him upon his person. This explanation, however, justified though it is, will not account for all instances of casting stones. And Doutté himself admits that not infrequently the obvious purpose of the rite is to frighten away, or at least to ward off the attacks of, a dangerous evil spirit, and particularly the ghost of the dead person upon whose grave or tomb the stones are cast (*Merrâkech,* p. 63). Moreover, careful consideration of all the evidence leads to the conclusion that the latter purpose, viz., to ward off the evil spirits, was the more natural, original, and primitive, and that the purpose of honoring a saint or establishing a relationship of *baraka* with his tomb was a later, secondary development.

That the custom of erecting stone-heaps was well known in ancient Israel is to be inferred from the rather obscure reference thereto in Prov. 26 : 8 (cf. Wellhausen, *Reste des altarabischen Heidentums*[2], pp. 111 f.), as well as from the story of Achan (Josh. 7 : 26). Certainly this heap of stones over the grave was erected, not as a memorial to Achan and to perpetuate his memory, but rather to hold down his ghost—no doubt considered doubly dangerous to mortals just because he had been put to death under the ban—and to keep it from working mischief upon innocent passers-by. The same reason unquestionably prompted the heap of stones over the grave of the king of Ai (Josh. 8 : 29) and the heap at the entrance to the cave in which the five Canaanite kings were buried (Josh. 10 : 27). Presumably these stones blocked the entrance completely and were thought to prevent the dangerous ghosts from coming forth. In Rabbinic times it was still customary to cast stones upon the coffin of one who had died in a state of excommunication. (Cf. Bender, "Death, Burial and Mourning," *JQR* [old series], VII [1895], 268 f., and the references cited there; Doutté, *Magie et Religion dans l'Afrique du Nord,* p. 430.)

The custom of casting stones upon a grave must not be identified or confused with the custom, at first sight seemingly kindred, of erecting a stone or, in Hebrew, *maṣṣebah,* over the grave. We shall see that this had in all likelihood an altogether different origin and purpose.

H[1]

Jaussen, *Coutumes des Arabes au pays de Moab,* p. 227. As Robertson Smith has pointed out, among the primitive Semites the belief was current that blood which falls upon the ground must be avenged; whereas if a man be slain in such a way that none of his blood touches the ground, no vengeance need be exacted for his death (*Religion of the Semites*[3], p. 369, note 1; p. 417, note 5). That this belief was current in ancient Israel is clear not only from the instance which we have under consideration, as well as from Gen. 4 : 10; 37 : 26, but also from other evidence. Num. 35 : 29 ff. provides that if it be established by the testimony of witnesses that one man has murdered another willfully, the murderer may not be permitted to escape to a city of refuge, nor may his life be redeemed by the payment of money. He must be executed, but in such manner that his blood shall not defile the land, for "blood poured out upon the ground can be atoned for only by the blood of him who shed it" (v. 33). Regardless of the guilt of the man thus executed, if he was killed in such manner that his blood dropped upon the ground, vengeance for his death would have to be visited upon someone, presumably his executioner. However, if the blood thus poured out upon the ground could be covered with some earth, no matter how small the amount, this was apparently tantamount to burial; for such blood no vengeance need be exacted; presumably the ghost of the person thus dealt with was laid and at rest in the nether world, and accordingly the executioner had nothing to fear from it. (Cf. Ezek. 24 : 7 f. I cannot follow my former colleague, Professor Moses Buttenwieser, in his interpretation of I Sam. 26 : 20; Isa. 26 : 21 and Job 16 : 18 ["Blood Revenge and Burial Rites in Ancient Israel," *JAOS,* 39 {1919}, 303–321]. For this reason I refrain from citing these three customary passages in illustration of this thesis.) A most illuminating and convincing illustration of the necessity of covering blood, no matter for what purpose shed, with dust or earth is furnished by Doughty (*Arabia Deserta* I, 492) from the life of the modern Bedouin: "Thâhir felt some megrims, and would have his son Selím let him a little blood in the neck. The young man, who had inherited the witty hands of his hunter father, came with the end of a cowhorn knife which was pierced in the tine; by this Selím, who had made with his knife a few scotches, sucked up the skin, and with a stop of leather, ready on his tongue, he closed the hole. Thâhir, cupped in the head, neck, and back, felt lightened; he covered the blood with a little heap of dust, and one who came in asking, 'What is this heap?' he answered, 'Blood which I have buried.' " (Cf. also Frazer, *Folk-lore in the Old Testament,* I, 101 ff.)

Of especial interest in this connection is a ceremony recorded by Doutté (*Magie et Religion dans l'Afrique du Nord,* pp. 425 ff., quoting Trumelet, *Les Français dans le Desert*[2], p. 88), the purpose of which is to make the blood of a man who has been slain, but whose murderer is unknown, speak and disclose the name of the murderer, so that vengeance may be exacted upon him by the surviving relatives: "The nearest relatives of the victim gather at the scene of the crime. They collect the blood and the earth with which it has been mingled, and carry this to the *gourbi* or to the tent. A *tâleb* with magical powers is immediately summoned and is invited to make the blood speak. The entire family is present, watching attentively the magical operations of the *tâleb.* The blood which has been gathered is put into a vessel, which is exposed to the action of fire. The magician wanders about the entire assembly, while pronouncing some words belonging to an unknown language; then he halts and

[1] Chapter XIV, note 99.

makes some weird marks upon a leaf of paper with a special kind of ink, into the composition of which musk and saffron enter. . . . The blood is not slow in beginning to foam in the vessel. The magician then draws near to it in solemn manner and calls out to it three times, 'Tell me the name of thy murderer!' At the third call the blood never fails to reply, 'It is So-and-so, son of So-and-so.' However, since this reply is heard only by the magician, it is his duty to transmit it to the assembly. The *tâleb* withdraws immediately after having received fifteen or twenty douros, according to the means of the relatives of the dead man. When the murderer perceives that the family has enough regard for its dead to undergo the expense of the magical ceremony, and if he has nothing or is unwilling to pay the *dia* (the blood-money), he makes haste to leave the country; nor does he make his reappearance there until he believes that the victim has been forgotten and the danger is past. Each year, so long as the *dia* has not been paid or the murder has not been avenged, on the day and at the very hour when the crime had been committed, a foam of the color of blood bubbles up upon the surface of the ground at the spot where the victim is buried and calls out mournfully his last words at the moment when he was killed, 'O, my father! O, my mother!, etc.' . . . In such case every member of the family is obligated to cast a stone upon the place where the crime was committed, whenever he passes near by." Elsewhere Doutté says (*Merrâkech,* pp. 62 f.): "When one asks the Moroccans why they cast a stone upon one of these *kerkour* (a heap of stones which marks the spot where someone has met a violent death), they usually reply that it is in order to drive away the returning spirits; for the soul of the dead man is able to return in company with other spirits, the *ǧinn,* for example, who delight in spots of this kind, in order to torment those who pass by."

I[1]

The original implication and purpose of this ceremony of kindling a light for a dead person is difficult to determine, since the rite seems to have a twofold meaning in Semitic religious practice. On the one hand, the burning light symbolizes the life or soul; when the light is extinguished, the life is ended; the soul has departed from the body (cf. Prov. 20 : 27; Sir. 22 : 11, and the numerous Biblical references with related meanings cited by Grüneisen, *Der Ahnenkultus und die Urreligion Israels,* pp. 104 f. For numerous Rabbinic references to the same concept, cf. Krauss, *Talmudische Archäologie,* II, 55, and note 413a). That the belief is current in modern times in the Orient is proved by ample evidence. Sir John Maundeville relates of the monks at Mount Sinai that "when the prelate of the abbey is dead, I have been informed that his light is extinguished. And when they choose another prelate, his lamp will light by the grace of God, without being touched by any man. For every one of them has a lamp for himself, and by their lamps they know well when any one of them shall die; for then the light begins to change and wax dim" (*Early Travels in Palestine,* ed. Wright, p. 158). At Baghdad "when a person is sick, a relative fastens a lighted taper to a piece of wood, commits it to the stream of the Tigris, and prays for the recovery of his friend. Should the light be extinguished before it recedes from his sight, he concludes that all hope is past" (Loftus, *Travels in Chaldaea and Susiana,* p. 200, note). A most illuminating illustration of this superstition is found in a Palestinian folk-tale recorded by Hanauer in *Tales Told in Palestine,* pp. 163 f.

[1] Chapter XIV, note 260.

On the other hand, lighted lamps were placed not infrequently beside the corpse. (So, for example, in Mishnah *Bᵉrakôt* VIII, 6. It is probably this custom that is referred to in *Tôsefta Šabbat* VI, 6 [ed. Zuckermandel], p. 117, and is stamped as a heathen, non-Israelite rite.) For this same reason no doubt, as we have seen (above, note 79, p. 250), at el-Kerak during the first night after burial a lantern is kept burning upon the spot where the death occurred; "for it is not nice that the house (tent) should remain dark." In modern Egypt "in honor of the deceased it is customary that on three successive Fridays and on the Friday which falls on or immediately follows the fortieth day after death, lights are kindled upon the grave." (Kahle, *Die Totenklage im heutigen Aegypten* [reprint from the *Gunkel Festschrift*], p. 18, note 2; cf. Lane, *The Manners and Customs of the Modern Egyptians*[3], p. 488.) In these last rites, in all likelihood, these lights do not symbolize the soul of the dead person, but are rather designed to illumine the darkness and guard against the soul of the dead, conceived as a dangerous spirit, and particularly dangerous in the darkness of the night.

One of these two beliefs certainly lay at the bottom of the oft-evidenced practice of depositing lights in ancient Semitic tombs or of depicting lights upon the walls of tombs in the Catacombs and elsewhere. Which of these two concepts lies at the bottom of the Jewish ceremony of kindling a lamp in the former home of the deceased upon the anniversary of his death it is difficult to determine. Inasmuch as we have good reason to believe that at an early stage in Semitic religious development the soul was thought to return to its former abode upon each anniversary of death and was regarded by the living as a none too welcome visitor, it is not at all improbable that in origin these lamps may have been kindled in order to guard against the entry of this dangerous soul or spirit into his former home. Then as the religion progressed and primitive superstitions gave way to more advanced ideas, the second meaning may have come gradually to attach itself to the custom, until finally it came to be regarded as a pious and sentimental duty to kindle a light in the home upon each recurring anniversary of the death of a loved one and thus to symbolize his spiritual presence, his abiding love, and the undying memory of him within the home and family. In fact, the *Maʿabar Yabbok,* a medieval Jewish ritualistic work, accounts for the old ceremony of kindling a lamp in the presence of a dying man at the moment when the death rattle is heard in his throat by both reasons: (1) that it is to ward off the evil spirits, and (2) that this light symbolizes the human soul, which is now about to depart (Bender, "Beliefs, Rites and Customs of the Jews Connected with Death, Burial and Mourning," *JQR* [old series], VII [1894], 668; cf. also Lods, *La Croyance à la Vie Future dans l'Antiquité Israélite,* pp. 238 ff.). It is almost supererogatory to say that it is this last, spiritual interpretation of the ancient ceremony which has survived in present-day Jewish practice.

J[1]

The word *saf,* which is used in Exod. 12 : 22, has the double connotation "threshold" and "basin" (cf. Gesenius, *Handwörterbuch*[17], pp. 548 f.; Koehler-Baumgartner, *Lexicon in Veteris Testamenti Libros,* p. 663). In this particular passage it is difficult, if not impossible, to determine with certainty which is the meaning here intended by the J authors. The great majority of the versions and commentators prefer the meaning "basin," as the receptacle for the blood. The use of the preposition *bᵉ* instead of *ʿal,* as in v. 23, is an argument in favor of

[1] Chapter XIV, note 269.

this translation. It is significant, however, that both *G* and *V* interpret the word in the sense of "threshold," while *S* evades the difficulty entirely by substituting "the blood of the lamb" for "the blood which is in (or upon) the *saf*." The Rabbis too, quite naturally, were conscious of this problem. *Mekilta, Bô'*, par. 6 and 11 (ed. Weiss, 8b and 15a) records a difference of opinion on this question between Rabbi Ishmael and Rabbi Akiba, two of the leading Tannaim of the second century. According to the former, the word *saf* in Exod. 12 : 22 implies that a hollow place was made in the threshold, and the animal was sacrified in such manner that its blood flowed into this hollow; according to the latter, however, *saf* here can connote only "basin" (cf. also *Yer. P^esaḥîm* IX, 36d, 37a). The fact that already at this comparatively early date the authoritative interpreters of Biblical law differed radically as to the meaning of this word in this particular passage shows that the understanding of the origin and meaning of this ceremony had by their time been long forgotten, and that the testimony of this Rabbinic dispute, as well as that of the varying renderings of the versions, is of no significance other than to demonstrate the possibility of two different interpretations of the passage. The solution of this problem must therefore be attempted in a different way. (So far as I can see, Trumbull, *The Threshold Covenant,* pp. 205 ff., and Meyer, *Die Israeliten und Ihre Nachbarstämme,* pp. 32, 38, are the only modern Biblical scholars who interpret *saf* here as "threshold.")

Now in the folk religion of the modern Semites the sacrifice upon the threshold is very common, and plays an important role. Trumbull (*op. cit.;* see Table of Contents and Index under various headings: Sacrifice, Red Hand, Bloody Hand, etc.) gives many instances of this sacrifice and of the import of the threshold as the place of sacrifice.

Of particular significance in this connection, however, is the fact that among the Semites the threshold is commonly regarded as the place where the *ğinn,* or evil spirits, lie in wait in order to work mischief upon the inmates of the house (Baldensperger, "Peasant Folklore of Palestine," *PEF* [1893], 205; Canaan, *Aberglaube und Volksmedezin im Lande der Bibel,* p. 19; Jaussen, "Le cheikh Sa'ad Ad-Din et les *djinn* à Naplouse," *JPOS,* III [1923], 150, 155; Stephan, "Lunacy in Palestinian Folklore," *JPOS,* V [1925], 5, notes 4 and 5). Canaan has very properly correlated with this superstition the heathen custom referred to in the Bible (I Sam. 5 : 5; Zeph. 1 : 9) of stepping over, and not upon, the threshold. I Sam. 5 : 5 states that this was a rite of Dagon worship; but this does not forbid the possibility that this rite was of more primitive character, had its origin in this very superstition which we are discussing, and was eventually incorporated into the worship of Dagon (in fact, the Talmud seems to imply this very thing [*'Abodah Zarah* 41b]), just as many similar superstitions of primitive origin were incorporated into later Yahweh-worship. Likewise, as we have seen (above, p. 150), in Tlemcen, in Morocco, the ghost of the deceased is thought to sojourn for the first three days after death beneath the door, i.e., beneath the threshold, of the room in which the death occurred. Moreover, in northern Africa the following magical practice is well known: "The *tâleb* writes with a special kind of liquid upon a piece of paper the names of the *ğinn* who are thought to have power to prevent the young husband from discharging his marital duty. Then he buries this kind of amulet beneath the threshold of the house in which the marriage is to be celebrated. It is believed that the young husband becomes impotent through the simple fact of having passed over the amulet buried beneath the door of the nuptial house. He continues in this state as long as the amulet is not dug up" (Doutté, *Magie et Religion dans l'Afrique du Nord,* p. 291). Among the Moslem Albanians, in a house in which a child has been born, during the first forty days after birth a firebrand is kept burning throughout the night upon the threshold. Whoever enters the house must leap over this firebrand (above, p. 13).

This same question of the threshold as a place of worship is discussed by Curtiss (*Primitive Semitic Religion Today,* see Index in both English and German eds.), who likewise gives numerous illustrations of the threshold sacrifice which came under his observation. One in particular merits citation (English ed., p. 233; German ed. pp. 266 f.): "The following incident, related to me in Homs, with reference to the use of a threshold in sacrifice, seems most significant in this connection: 'If a man has bought a new house, and the inhabitants have been unlucky, that is, have had ill health or death, before moving into the house the owner makes some change and offers a sacrifice. The change usually consists in taking up the old stone on the threshold and laying a new one in its place. Then the sacrifice is offered on that threshold. They call it presenting a *keffareh,* in order that no evil may befall them. So when the sacrifice is made for a new house, a similar ceremony is observed." Here, very obviously, the threshold is the place where the evil spirit lurks.

This sacrifice for a new house is described in considerable detail by Jaussen (*Coutumes des Arabes au pays de Moab,* pp. 342 f.). "The sacrifice is offered to the *ǧinn* or spirit to whom the piece of ground and everything upon it or connected with it are thought to have belonged originally. The sacrifice is designed to redeem the house and its inmates from his power and so remove all possibility of evil from him. When the house is completed, the owner, surrounded by his family and relatives, brings a sacrifice, either a male sheep, a ewe, or a goat, places it upon the threshold and sacrifices it. Often the blood runs down into the interior of the house, and at other times it spreads out in the courtyard outside the house; but always it must flow towards the door. While plunging his knife into the neck of the animal the owner says in a loud voice, 'Permission, O master of this place!' . . . At the same time he takes the blood of the victim in his hand and sprinkles it inside the house upon the walls; but this last custom is not general. The victim, thus slaughtered, is cooked immediately. It is inside the house that it is eaten. The *ǧinn* ought thus to be satisfied; the house ought to be left in peace; the family ought to prosper."

Now it is significant that in this last instance the sacrifice is slain upon the threshold and the blood is sprinkled upon the door, and presumably also, even though it is not explicitly stated, upon the doorposts and lintel, and the animal is eaten only inside the house. This, too, is the ritual of the marriage sacrifice, recorded by Jaussen and cited above (p. 113): "Among some Christian Bedouin the groom takes into his house the blood, while still quite warm, and with it anoints the lintel and the doorposts of the house. In order to render this anointing more perfect the victim is frequently slaughtered upon the terrace in such manner that the blood flows down the door. . . . Beneath the tent the blood of the victim is sprinkled about the entrance." Quite obviously the purpose of this sacrifice is to protect, not merely the bride, but the entire house and all its inmates, present and future, from the attacks of the evil spirit or spirits, which threaten particularly at this moment of marriage. Beyond the charmed circle of the sacrificial blood, sprinkled upon the threshold, doorposts, and lintel and therefore completely surrounding the entrance to the house, the evil spirits may not pass.

This is precisely, in every detail, the ritual of the Paschal sacrifice according to the J Code. We need therefore not hesitate to conclude, with Rabbi Ishmael among the Rabbis, with *G* and *V* among the versions, and with Trumbull, Meyer, and Eerdmans among modern scholars, that *saf* in Exod. 12 : 22 must be translated "threshold" and not "basin." We shall see also that the same purpose underlies, in part at least, the Paschal sacrifice and ceremony as that which underlies the sacrifice described by Jaussen, viz., to protect the house and its inmates against the attacks of a powerful and threatening evil spirit.

These considerations make clear just what is the origin and basic significance of the ancient Semitic ceremony of stepping over, but not upon, the threshold, recorded in I Sam. 5 : 5 and Zeph. 1 : 9. We have seen this same ceremony illustrated by a number of instances in present-day Semitic religious practice. The evil spirits are thought to be hovering upon and about the threshold, the last line of defense, as it were, beyond which they may not pass unless opportunity is given to them in some way, or, through the sudden kindling of their wrath, they may be incited to do so. Either of these consequences might be brought about by someone, about to enter the house, stepping upon the threshold where they are congregated. On the one hand, by adhering to the sandals of the heedless person they may be carried across the threshold into the house. Probably here we have the origin of the common Oriental custom of stripping off the sandals and leaving them outside the door before entering a house. On the other hand, by stepping upon the threshold the person about to enter the house would at the same time step upon the evil spirits assembled there and thus arouse their anger, which would then be turned with greater and more active fury not only against him but also against all the inmates of the house. To step upon the threshold, therefore, particularly at a time when evil spirits were thought to be lurking there, meant to endanger critically the inmates of the house. Undoubtedly for this reason primarily it became customary to step over the threshold, and particularly certain thresholds and at certain times. Here, quite plainly, we have the origin and meaning of the quaint custom, still practiced quite frequently even in our Western lands, of the bridegroom lifting the bride over the threshold of their future home, when, following the marriage ceremony, he brings her for the first time thither.

And correspondingly the belief developed most naturally that the most fitting place in all the house for the abode of protecting household gods or spirits was the threshold or doorposts. There the ancient Assyrians and Babylonians located their *šedu* and *lamassu,* at least in their sanctuaries (cf. Zimmern, *Die Keilinschriften und das Alte Testament*[3], p. 455); and there in ancient Israel likewise was the seat of the family or clan gods (Exod. 21 : 6; cf. Lods, *La Croyance à la Vie Future dans l'Antiquité Israêlite,* pp. 236 ff.); and there still today upon the doorpost of the main entrance into his home the Orthodox Jew affixes the *m^e^zûzah* (literally, "doorpost"), the token of his faith in and loyalty to the God of his fathers and his adherence to his ancestral religion.

All this implies that these beliefs and ceremonies, which we have established for the Semitic inhabitants of Palestine and neighboring lands in historic times and, in not inconsiderable measure, even still today, were current also and originally among the peoples which preceded them in these lands, and actually were in large measure borrowed from them by their Semitic successors in these lands.

K[1]

The realization that ceremonies of removal of taboo and ritual purification had their origin in primitive spirit-worship by the earliest Semites will help to clear up some of the intricacies and complex and difficult problems of the interrelation of the states of holiness, profane existence, and taboo which we find in Semitic religions in historic times, and particularly in the religion of Israel during the Biblical period.

As we have already pointed out (above, p. 32), the religion of ancient Israel conceived

[1] Chapter XV, Note 3.

of two states of taboo, which we have designated as superprofane and subprofane. The former is usually described in Hebrew by the term *ḳadôš*, "holy," the latter by the term *ḥerem*, which may best be translated "taboo," in the more limited and specific connotation of that very elastic term. But, as every Old Testament student knows, the use of these two terms is very confused. Frequently they seem to be wholly, or at least partly, synonymous, and occasionally the one term is used where the other would be expected. Moreover, as we have seen, the practical effects of both states, superprofane and subprofane taboo, are the same in two very essential respects. Both disqualify from participation in the ordinary activities of daily life. And the ceremonies, through the performance of which one is enabled to pass from either of these two states into the condition of ordinary, profane existence, are practically identical.

This confusion is heightened by the fact that a being or object might be normally, permanently, and irrevocably unclean and so taboo in subprofane form, and might by contact communicate this taboo to other objects, or the taboo might be only temporary and be removable by the performance of the proper rites. And again, a being or object might be normally, permanently, and irrevocably holy and so taboo in superprofane form, and might by contact communicate this holiness to other objects, or the holiness might be only temporary and lapse automatically, or through contact with some unclean or tabooed object, or in some other manner. Or a third possibility: an object might be normally profane, and pass into the state of taboo through contact with some tabooed object, with resultant desecration, or into a state of holiness through contact with some holy object, with resultant consecration. And again, holiness or taboo might be either permanent and irrevocable, or temporary and removable, through the performance of the proper rites.

The problem is made still more confused and complex by the use in Biblical Hebrew of two additional terms, *ṭahôr*, "ritually clean," and *ṭame'*, "ritually unclean," which are used apparently partially synonymously and interchangeably with *ḳadôš* and *ḥerem*, respectively.

The problem becomes, however, much simpler and more explicable when we realize that the terms, *ḳadôš* and *ḥerem*, and the conditions which they describe, had their origin in primitive spirit-worship and its institutions. In this stage of religious evolution there were only two ritual states instead of the three of later Israelite religion. These two states were (1) possession by or subjection to the power of spirits, in other words, taboo, with no distinction whatever between consecration and desecration, and (2) freedom from this state, in other words, profane existence. It was immaterial whether the spirits in question were evilly or favorably disposed; the effect of possession by them was always the same in that it debarred the person or object tabooed from participation or use in daily, profane existence.

This state or condition of taboo is designated by three main words or verbal roots in Semitic languages, *ḳdš*, *ḥrm*, and *ḥmy*. The origin of these three terms lies so far back in the cultural history of the Semitic peoples that it is difficult, or even impossible, to determine what the primary meaning of each may have been, and whether these meanings may have been identical or in any way kindred, and therefore whether these three words may have had the same or parallel etymological histories.

The root *ḳdš* is the commonest of the three. It is found in practically all Semitic languages (although its somewhat limited and technical use in Arabic suggests the possibility that in that language it had no direct development from the original Semitic language, but may well have been borrowed from the Hebrew through contact of Arabs with Jews in pre-Islamic times), and with practically the same wide range of connotation in all.

The root *ḥrm*, too, is found in practically all Semitic languages, although with a somewhat less frequent use and narrower range of connotation. Apparently this root was used more commonly in those Semitic languages, such as early Aramaic and Arabic, in which the root *ḳdš* was used less frequently, while, vice versa, in those languages, such as Akkadian and Hebrew, in which the root *ḳdš* was used extensively, the root *ḥrm* was employed far less frequently and to a certain extent with a seemingly secondary connotation.

The root *ḥmy,* at least in the connotation "to be forbidden or taboo," seems to be used only in Arabic.

Now, as has been said, originally, in the early, prehistoric period of pure spirit-worship in Semitic cultural evolution, there were only these two states, that of taboo, by whatever particular word designated, and that of profane existence. But as Semitic culture evolved and the concept of great gods, as distinct from mere, more or less impersonal and nameless spirits, evolved—and particularly gods who were regarded in the main as beneficent, all-powerful beings—the old spirits themselves came gradually to be regarded for the most part as evil, demonic forces, inimical to both gods and men. The universe was now divided into three realms instead of the two of earlier days: the realm of the great, beneficent gods, the realm of the evil spirits, and, between these two, the realm of man. Gradually the concept evolved and became ever more clearly defined that man and all things within his realm might be subject to the power of either the gods or the evil spirits. In fact, to a certain extent they struggled with each other to establish their power over him. A distinction, real, even though not defined with perfect clarity, now came to be drawn between relation with or subjection to the power of a deity and possession by evil spirits. This is the condition which existed, as we see it, in the religion of Israel during the Biblical period. Thus it developed that in Hebrew the one root *ḳdš* came to designate that which was holy because of relationship to the gods, and particularly to Israel's national god, Yahweh, while the other root *ḥrm* came to designate in the main that which was in the category of subprofane taboo, usually, though by no means invariably, because of possession, at least in the original concept of this state or condition, by evil spirits.

It was probably in this stage of the evolution of the concepts of holiness and taboo that the two terms *ṭahôr* and *ṭame'* came into use in the ritual sense. *Ṭahôr* came to apply to that which was either *ḳadôš,* holy in itself, or, although profane, in such a state that by the performance of the proper rites it might be made to pass into the condition of holiness. And, correspondingly, *ṭame'* came to apply to that which was in a state of subprofane taboo, either normally or because, though naturally profane or even holy, it had, through misuse or contact with some subprofane object or in some other, equally potent manner, entered into the condition of subprofane taboo. Through the performance of the proper rites, or subjection to the appropriate conditions, such an object might be restored to the state of profane existence; and, naturally, it might well at some future time pass again from one state to another. Such an object might therefore be at various times, on the one hand, ritually "clean" or "unclean" and, on the other hand, "holy," "profane," or "taboo."

Naturally, within the broad connotation of these terms there were many and complex variations and limitations of conditions and proper ceremonial. An object which was normally "holy" might be so in one of two degrees. On the one hand, this "holiness" might be of such degree that under no condition, in theory at least, could it be forfeited or modified. An object possessing this degree of sanctity was described in Biblical Hebrew as being *ḳôdeš ḳ^{e}dašîm,* "most holy" or "of supreme holiness." Such were the altar (Exod. 29 : 37; 30 : 10; 40 : 10), the various sacrifices (Lev. 6 : 10, 18, 22, *et passim*), and the like. Such an object was normally "ritually pure"; and, in theory, this ritual purity was indestructible.

Whatever came into contact with such a holy object became holy likewise, because, as Robertson Smith has illustrated so convincingly (*Religion of the Semites*[3], pp. 446–454), the quality of "holiness" of the sacred object was thus transmitted to that which was contacted. On the other hand, an object might be "holy" normally, but its holiness might be of a lower grade, so that contact with an unclean object might defile it or terminate its condition of ritual purity and cause it to pass into a state of "ritual impurity." Nor could such an object, as a rule, impart through contact this condition or quality of "holiness" to any nonholy object.

Correspondingly, an object might be normally "taboo." Obviously, it was at the same time "ritually unclean." Theoretically at least, an object, such as a corpse, for example, which was normally and inherently "taboo," could never lose this quality and become either "profane" or "holy." Naturally, then, whatever touched it acquired the condition of "taboo" and with it, of course, "ritual impurity."

In practice, however, many objects which were normally "taboo" required frequent handling by persons in the ordinary, profane state of existence. Either the person in question was thought to become ritually impure for a brief period, and was required to purify himself by proper rites, normally by washing in pure or "living" water, as, for example, the participant in the ceremony of the red heifer (Num. 19 : 7, 10). Or the tabooed object itself might, if this were feasible, be subjected to purificatory rites of a minor character, which were doubtless thought to reduce, temporarily at least, the condition and degree of "taboo" or of "ritual impurity" and permit it to be handled, insofar as necessary, without its too greatly affecting the persons handling it. Thus, for example, in Palestine the custom of washing a corpse is observed in both Judaism and Islam. The purpose of this rite is not merely to cleanse the corpse in a physical sense, but even more to expel from it the evil spirits which were thought to dwell in it or to be hovering about it (cf. Scheftelowitz, "Die Sündentilgung durch Wasser," *ARW,* XVII [1914], pp. 399 f.). Among the Moslems in particular, for this purpose the corpse is frequently washed in salt water, and a piece of iron is laid beside it (cf. Bliss, *The Religions of Modern Syria and Palestine,* p. 292). Perhaps for the same reason the custom, which we have already noted, existed in ancient Israel (cf. Krauss, *Talmudische Archäologie,* II, 56) as well as in modern Palestine (cf. Bauer, *Volksleben im Lande der Bibel*[2], p. 244) of shaving off the hair of a corpse while preparing it for burial.

And if perchance an object which was normally and unchangeably "taboo" touched an object which was normally and unchangeably "holy," the latter did not lose its holiness nor did the former acquire this condition through the contact. Each remained "holy" or "taboo" as it was at first. But the "holiness" of the first object was rendered ritually impure; and this ritual impurity disqualified the object for use for any holy function whatsoever until it had first undergone ritual purification. Just such a theoretical condition constituted the basis for the ritual purification of the sanctuary once each year on Yom Kippur (Lev. 16).

It is in the application of these principles to objects which under ordinary conditions were profane that the greatest complexity and confusion appear. As we have seen, very few, if any, objects were normally inherently profane. Whether regarded as the creation of a deity or of spirits or the work of human hands, they were believed to be originally subject to a positive taboo. Human child, animal offspring, the crop in the field, the fruit upon the tree, the house built by human hands, the field or vineyard made ready for human use for the first time, all these, as we have seen, were regarded as being originally under the influence of spirits, and therefore required redemption for ordinary, profane life or use. But once redeemed, they were *ḥôl,* "profane," neither "holy" nor "taboo."

Ordinarily they were not only "profane" but also *ṭahôr,* "ritually clean." But the state of such persons or objects might be altered in either of two ways. While still remaining "profane" they might for one reason or another become *ṭame',* "ritually impure." Or for one reason or another they might cease to be "profane" and become "holy." Thus an object which was normally "profane" but came into contact with that which was "most holy" became "holy" through this contact. Or a person or object ordinarily "profane" might, through proper consecration—the Nazirite, for example—become "holy." Such "holiness" might be either temporary or permanent; and if temporary, this "holiness" might be terminated either automatically, through the expiration of the period for which the person or object had been consecrated, or purposely, through the performance at the proper time of the prescribed ceremonies of redemption, or accidentally, through defilement by contact with an object which was either "taboo" or temporarily "ritually impure."

Or an object or a person, ordinarily "profane," might in some way become "taboo," as, for example, Achan and the booty of Jericho (Josh. 7 : 13). And this "taboo," too, might be either permanent, in which case the person or object, forbidden for both "holy" and "profane" purposes, was ordinarily destroyed (hence the secondary connotation of *ḥrm* in the causative conjugation, "to make taboo, to destroy"), or it might be temporary and removable by the proper ceremonies.

Between the conditions of "holiness" and "ritual purity" the distinction was easily drawn, and there was in consequence very little confusion. A person or object might be "holy" and be at the same time "ritually pure" or "ritually impure." But the conditions and effects of "ritual impurity" and taboo were so strikingly similar in a practical way that it was difficult to draw a hard and fast line of demarcation between them; and consequently, in effect, *ḥerem* and *ṭame'* were almost synonymous. An object which was inherently and permanently "taboo" was per se "ritually impure." Under no condition and through no ceremony whatsoever could it be made "ritually pure" and fit for even "profane" use. And an object which was only temporarily "taboo" was during the entire period of this "taboo" likewise "ritually impure." But when the condition of "taboo" was removed by the performance of the proper ceremonies, the condition of "ritual impurity" departed with it and the object entered into the states of both "profanity" and "ritual purity."

These considerations show clearly that the terms *ṭahôr,* "ritually pure," and *ṭame'*, "ritually impure," have theological import only in relation to the concept of the great gods, as contrasted with the spirits. That is "ritually pure" which is qualified for participation or use in the worship of these deities; and, correspondingly, that is "ritually impure" which is disqualified from such participation or use. Obviously, therefore, these terms, with the conditions which they describe, are secondary developments, which could have arisen only after the concept of the great gods, as contrasted with the spirits, had evolved. In the earliest stages of the religious evolution of the Semitic peoples these concepts did not yet exist, and consequently these terms must have been unknown, at least in their technical connotation. This is borne out by the fact that, unlike the roots *ḳdš* and *ḥrm,* the roots *ṭhr* and *ṭm'* are not found in all Semitic languages; nor even in those languages in which they do exist is their use at all extensive. Neither root is found in Akkadian. *Ṭm'* is used in the Aramaic and Arabic language groups in addition to Hebrew. But in these various languages the use of both terms is so limited, both in extent and in range of connotation, that it is difficult to avoid the conclusion that in every case they have been borrowed from the

Hebrew. Naturally, the ideas which these technical terms convey in Hebrew are expressed in other Semitic languages by parallel, although etymologically unrelated, terms. This is perhaps the best proof of the late development of these terms and of the ideas which they express. Apparently the terms did not exist, nor did their underlying ideas need expression, in the original Semitic language.

On the other hand, as we have seen, the roots *ḳdš* and *ḥrm,* even though not *ḥmy,* are found in all Semitic languages. Obviously they go back to origins in original Semitic speech, and the basic idea underlying them must have had its roots in primitive Semitic religious concepts. We have seen what these primitive concepts were, and that they are explicable only from the conditions of spirit-worship, antecedent to the rise of the concept and worship of great, individual gods. Thus, this philological consideration is another pathway which leads backward along the course of evolution of Semitic religions to its origin in spirit-worship in the remote, prehistoric past.

L[1]

In this connection, the significance of one, usually overlooked or misinterpreted detail of the ritual procedure of these dances becomes clear. As we have seen above, *Mishnah Ta'anît* IV, 8, prescribes that the maidens participating in these dances must be clad in white garments, which had been borrowed especially for this occasion. The reason given for this institution, that it was to prevent any maiden who had no proper garments being put to shame, is altogether beside the mark and, like so many other Rabbinic interpretations of ancient customs, is only a characteristic attempt to offer a rationalistic, ethical explanation of an ancient rite, the true origin of which had been forgotten entirely, or which the Rabbis were no longer willing to admit (cf. Lauterbach, "The Ceremony of Breaking a Glass at Weddings," *HUCA,* II [1925], 351–380). Not only were the maidens of Jerusalem participating in these festal dances required to wear borrowed garments, but still today the Bedouin maidens, tripping lightly in the dances of the circumcision festivals, are clad in new cloaks borrowed for the occasion (Doughty, *Arabia Deserta,* I, 340). And as the Bible specifically records (Exod. 11 : 2 f.; 12 : 35 f.), the Israelites, about to leave Egypt—ostensibly to celebrate their spring, nomad festival in the desert, one of the important ceremonies of which was the dances of the maidens, as Exod. 15 : 20 f. states—borrowed garments and also ornaments of gold and silver from their Egyptian neighbors. Exod. 12 : 36 interprets this as an opportunity seized by Israel to despoil the Egyptians. However, this too can be only the explanation of a later age which no longer understood the true origin and purpose of the custom. Certainly the story implies that a plausible explanation must have been given by the Israelites to the Egyptians for wanting to borrow their garments; and this explanation could have been only that the wearing of borrowed apparel was an essential rite in the celebration of the impending festival, which, so it was represented by Moses to Pharaoh, the Israelites had been commanded by their god, Yahweh, to celebrate out in the desert (Exod. 5 : 1–3). Unquestionably we have here another, and the oldest, record of the practice of the maidens of Israel borrowing garments and ornaments to wear in the festal dances.

And only one purpose can account for this otherwise inexplicable practice. The bor-

[1] Chapter XV, note 24.

rowed garments served to disguise the maiden who wore them, and thus to protect her against the attacks of the evil spirits which threatened her at this particular moment. This practice is paralleled by the custom, current among the Jews of Egypt, of the bride and groom exchanging garments just previous to the marriage ceremony in order to deceive the threatening evil spirits and ward off their attacks (Samter, *Geburt, Hochzeit und Tod,* p. 93). Still today, as has already been noted, the superstition is widely current in Europe and America, that during the marriage ceremony the bride should wear something borrowed in order to ensure future good fortune for herself. This evidence confirms definitively our explanation of this rite, that it was designed to safeguard the maidens from the evil spirits which now threatened them as candidates for marriage. And since among the present-day Bedouin, as well as in ancient Israel, one of the occasions when the maidens celebrated these dances was the Passover-*daḥîyyeh* festival, the natural inference is that the particular evil spirits which threatened them upon this occasion were the ghosts of their dead kinsmen, returned to their former abodes at just this season of the year.

It is difficult, because of insufficient evidence, to trace these dances back to remote antiquity and determine their connection, if any, with *beena* and *mota'a* marriage. Our oldest references to these dances, with the single possible exception of the dances of Miriam and her maidens, correlate them most intimately with the conditions of agricultural life and the celebration of agricultural festivals (Judg. 21 : 19ff.; Jer. 31 : 3). Moreover, Judg. 21 : 19ff. and also *Mishnah Ta'anît* IV, 8, very definitely associate these dances with *ba'al* marriage. Nonetheless the celebration of these dances by the Bedouin maidens in connection with the circumcision festivals seems to be an institution too deeply rooted in nomadic life to warrant the hypothesis that they were adopted by the nomad Semites from their agricultural neighbors. Such a hypothesis would invert the usual and almost invariable procedure. And the fact that, according to the Biblical narrative, these dances were performed by Miriam and the other Israelite maidens with her in the celebration of the festival out in the desert corroborates further our conclusion that these dances had their origin in the early, nomadic stage of Semitic cultural evolution.

But even granting that these dances were performed in the most primitive, nomadic stage of Semitic cultural evolution, it is nonetheless difficult to conceive of any possible, immediate connection which they may have had with *beena,* and still less with *mota'a,* marriage. At the utmost, we may assume only a remote and incidental connection. In all likelihood, in the days of *beena and mota'a* marriage these dances, if then practiced, had no direct bearing upon the marriage itself, but rather were festal rites performed by the maidens, perhaps in connection with other kindred ceremonies, upon the attainment of puberty and the first menstruation. In such case these dances would, in part at least, have played a role in relation to maidens somewhat parallel to that which circumcision played with youths. As we have seen, circumcision had to be performed in all cases prior to the attainment of puberty, and therefore to have sexual intercourse with a lad still uncircumcised was regarded as tantamount to having intercourse with a child, a shameful act indeed. Similarly, to associate sexually with a maiden who had not yet participated in these dances, and whose attainment of puberty and readiness for marriage had therefore not been publicly announced and recognized, would have been regarded as shameful in the extreme. Under the conditions of *beena* and *mota'a* marriage these dances of the maidens, if practiced in that early period, could hardly have had a purpose and import other than this. In this respect they must have had an origin and primary purpose closely akin to the sacrifice by maidens of the hair and of virginity.

Abbreviations

AJSL — American Journal of Semitic Languages and Literatures
AJT — American Journal of Theology
AO — Archiv Orientálni
ARW — Archiv für Religionswissenschaft
BW — Biblical World
CT — Cuneiform Texts from Babylonian Tablets, etc., in the British Museum
ERE — Encyclopedia of Religion and Ethics
G — The Septuagint (the Greek version of the Old Testament)
GGN — Göttinger Gelehrte Nachrichten
HUCA — Hebrew Union College Annual
JAOS — Journal of the American Oriental Society
JBL — Journal of Biblical Literature and Exegesis
JE — The Jewish Encyclopedia
JPOS — Journal of the Palestine Oriental Society
JQR — Jewish Quarterly Review
KAT³ — Die Keilinschriften und das Alte Testament, H. Zimmern und H. Winckler (Berlin, 1903)
KB — Keilinschriftliche Bibliothek, ed. E. Schrader, 6 vols. (Berlin, 1889–1915)
MAOG — Mitteilungen der altorientalischen Gesellschaft
MDPV — Mitteilungen des Deutschen Palästinavereins
MGWJ — Monatschrift für Geschichte und Wissenschaft des Judentums
MT — Masoretic Text of the Old Testament
MVAG — Mitteilungen der Vorderasiatisch-ägyptischen Gesellschaft
NGM — National Geographic Magazine
NT — New Testament
OT — Old Testament
PEF — Palestine Exploration Fund
PJB — Palästinajahrbuch
RB — Revue biblique
RES — Revue des études semitiques
RHR — Revue de l'histoire des religions
S — The Peshitta' (the Syriac version of the Old Testament)
TT — Theologisch Tijdschrift

V — The Vulgate (the Latin version of the Old Testament)
VT — Vetus Testamentum
ZA — Zeitschrift für Assyriologie und verwandte Gebiete
ZAW — Zeitschrift für die alttestamentliche Wissenschaft
ZDMG — Zeitschrift der Deutschen Morgenländischen Gesellschaft
ZDPV — Zeitschrift des Deutschen Palästinavereins

Bibliography

ABELA, EIJUB. "Beiträge zur Kenntniss abergläubischer Gebräuche in Syrien," *ZDPV,* VII (1884), 79–118.

ADAMS, I. *Darkness and Daybreak.* Persia, 1901.

ALI BEY. *Travels of Ali Bey.* Philadelphia, 1816.

APTOWITZER, V. "The Rewarding and Punishing of Animals and Inanimate Objects," *HUCA,* III (1926), 117–155.

ARNOBIUS. *Oratio contra Gentes* (Eng. tr.), in *The Ante-Nicene Fathers,* ed. ROBERTS and DONALDSON, Vol. VI, 1899. Pp. 413–540.

ATHANASIUS. *Festal Letters,* in *The Nicene and Post-Nicene Fathers of the Christian Church,* ed. SCHAFF and WACE, Vol. V. New York, 1904.

BAENTSCH, BRUNO. *Exodus,* in Nowack, *Handkommentar zum Alten Testament.* Göttingen, 1903.

BAKER, S. W. *The Nile Tributaries of Abyssinia.* Philadelphia, 1867.

BALDENSPERGER, P. J. "Peasant Folklore of Palestine," *PEF* (1893), pp. 203–219.

———. "Religion of the Fellahin in Palestine," *PEF* (1893), pp. 307–320.

———. "Woman in the East," *PEF* (1901), pp. 66–90, 167–184.

———. "The Immovable East," *PEF* (1910), pp. 259–268.

BARTON, G. A. "The Semitic Ishtar Cult," *Hebraica,* X (1893).

———. *A Sketch of Semitic Origins.* New York, 1902.

BASSET, R. *Le Culte des Grottes au Maroc.* Algiers, 1920.

VON BAUDISSIN, W. W. F. *Adonis und Esmun.* Leipzig, 1911.

BAUER, L. *Volksleben im Lande der Bibel*[2]. Leipzig, 1903.

BAUMSTARK, A. *Festbrevier und Kirchenjahr der syrischen Jakobiten.* Paderborn, 1910.

BEER, B. *Las Leben Abrahams nach Auffassung der jüdischen Sage.* Leipzig, 1859.

BEHRENS, E. *Assyrisch-Babylonische Briefe kultischen Inhalts aus der Sargonidenzeit.* Leipzig, 1906.

BEL, A. "La Population Mussulman de Tlemcen." *RES,* I (1908), 200–225, 417–447.

BELL, G. M. L. *The Desert and the Sown.* New York, 1907.

BENDER, A. P. "Beliefs, Rites and Customs of the Jews, Connected with Death, Burial and Mourning," *JQR* (old series), VII (1895), 101–118, 259–269.

BENJAMIN, I. J. *Eight Years in Asia and Africa.* Hanover, 1859.

BENNETT, C. W. *Christian Archaeology.* New York, 1898.

BERTHOLET, A. *Deuteronomy,* in Marti, *Kurzer Handkommentar zum Alten Testament.* Leipzig-Tübingen, 1899.
———. *Kulturgeschichte Israels.* Göttingen, 1919.
BEWER, J. A. "The Rite of the Red Cow," *JBL,* XXIV (1905), 41–44.
BINGHAM, J. *Origines Ecclesiasticae.* London, 1843–45.
BLACKMAN, W. S. *The Fellaḥin of Upper Egypt.* London, 1927.
BLAU, L. *Das altjüdische Zauberwesen.* Budapest, 1898.
BLISS, F. J. *The Religions of Modern Syria and Palestine.* New York, 1912.
BLUNT, LADY ANNE. *The Bedouin Tribes of the Euphrates.* London, 1879.
BRANDT, W. *Mandäische Religion.* Leipzig, 1889.
———. "Die jüdischen Baptismen," Beiheft zur *ZAW,* XVIII (1941).
BROCKELMANN, K. *Lexicon Syriacum.* Berlin, 1895.
BRÜNNOW, R. E. *A Classified List of All Simple and Compound Cuneiform Ideographs.* Leiden, 1889.
BÜCKINGHAM, J. S. *Travels in Palestine.* London, 1821.
———. *Travels among the Arab Tribes.* London, 1825.
———. *Travels in Assyria, Media and Persia.* London, 1829.
BURCKHARDT, J. L. *Travels in Nubia.* London, 1819.
———. *Travels in Syria and the Holy Land.* London, 1822.
———. *Travels in Arabia.* London, 1829.
———. *Arabic Proverbs.* London, 1830.
———. *Notes on the Bedouins and Wahabys.* London, 1830.
BURTON, R. F. *Personal Narrative of a Pilgrimage to Al-Madinah and Mekka.* New York, 1856.
BURY, G. W. *The Land of Uz.* London, 1911.
BUTTENWIESER, M. "Blood Revenge and Burial Rites in Ancient Israel," *JAOS,* XXXIX (1919), 303–321.

CANAAN, T. *Aberglaube und Volksmedezin im Lande der Bibel.* Hamburg, 1914.
———. *Dämonenglaube im Lande der Bibel.* Leipzig, 1929.
———. "Folklore of the Seasons," *JPOS,* III (1923), 21–35.
———. "Mohammedan Saints and Sanctuaries in Palestine," *JPOS,* V (1925), 163–203; VI (1926), 1–88.
———. "The Child in Palestinian Arab Superstition," *JPOS,* VII (1927), 159–186.
———. "Unwritten Laws Affecting the Women of Palestine," *JPOS,* XI (1931), 195 ff.
———. "The Palestinian Arab House," *JPOS,* XIII (1933), 1–83.
———. "The Curse in Palestinian Folk-Lore," *JPOS,* XV (1935), 235–279.
CERTEUX, A., and CARONY, E. H. *L'Algérie Traditionelle; Contributions au Folk-Lore des Arabes,* Vol. I. Paris, 1884.
CHARDIN, J. *Voyages en Perse.* Paris, 1830.
CHWOLSOHN, D. A. *Die Ssabier und der Ssabismus.* St. Petersburg, 1856.
CLEMEN, K. "Miszellen zu Lukians Schrift über die syrische Göttin," in *Abhandlungen zur semitischen Volkskunde und Sprachwissenschaft Wolf Wilhelm Grafen von Baudissin . . . überreicht.* Giessen, 1918.
CLERK, A. M. *Ilam-en-Nas.* London, 1873.
CONDER, C. R. *Tent Work in Palestine.* New York, 1878.
COOK, S. A. *Glossary of Aramaic Inscriptions.* Cambridge, 1898.
CORY. *Ancient Fragments,* ed. E. R. HODGES. London, 1876.

CRICHTON, A. *History of Arabia Ancient and Modern.* New York, 1894.
CROOKE, W. *Popular Religions of Northern India*[2]. London, 1896.
CRUICKSHANK, W. "Numbers," in Hastings, *ERE,* IX, 416.
CURTISS, S. I. *Primitive Semitic Religion Today.* Chicago, 1902.
———. "The Ancient Religion of Syria in Centers of Moslem and Christian Influence," *BW,* XXIII (1904), 326–338.

DALMAN, G. H. *Palästinischer Diwan.* Leipzig, 1908.
———. "Das Samaritanische Pasah im Verhältniss zum Jüdischen," *PJB,* VIII (1913), 121–138.
DAMIRI, K. *Ḥayât al-Ḥayawân.* Translation of JAYAKAR (Cairo).
DANDINI, H. in Paulus, *Sammlung der merkwürdigsten Reisen in den Orient,* Vol. II. Jena, 1792.
DAPPER, O. *Asia.* Amsterdam, 1681.
DAUMAS, M. J. E. *La Femme Arabe.* Algiers, 1912.
DEFRÉMERY, C. F., and SANGUINETTI, B. R. *Voyages d' Ibn Batoutah.* Paris, 1853–54.
DELITZSCH, F. *Assyrisches Handwörterbuch.* Leipzig, 1896.
———. "Zu Herodots Babylonischen Nachrichten," in *Festschrift für Eduard Sachau.* Berlin, 1915.
DICKSON, H. R. P. *The Arab of the Desert.* London, 1949.
DIETERICH, A. *Mutter Erde.* Leipzig and Berlin, 1905.
DÖBEL, E. C. *Wanderungen im Morgenlande.* Berterode, 1863.
DOUGHTY, C. M. *Travels in Arabia Deserta.* Cambridge, 1888.
———. *Documents épigraphiques recueilles dans le nord de l'Arabie.* Paris, 1891.
DOUTTÉ, E. *Merrâkech.* Algiers, 1907.
———. *Magie et Religion dans l'Afrique du Nord.* Algiers, 1909.
DOZY, R. P. A. *Die Israeliten zu Mekka.*
DRIVER, S. R. *Modern Research as Illustrating the Bible; The Schweich Lectures.* London, 1909.
DU BERNAT, in Paulus, *Sammlung der merkwürdigsten Reisen in den Orient,* Vol. IV. Jena, 1792.
DUHM, H. *Die bösen Geister des Alten Testaments.* Tübingen, 1904.
VON DUHN, F. "Rot und Tot," *ARW,* IX (1906), 1–24.
DYE, W. M. *Moslem Egypt and Christian Abyssinia.* New York, 1880.

EBELING, E. "Aus dem Tagewerk eines assyrischen Zauberpriesters," *MAOG,* V (1931); reprinted under same title, Leipzig, 1931.
ELHORST, H. J. "Die israelitischen Trauerriten," in *Festschrift für Julius Wellhausen.* Giessen, 1914.
ELIEZER (Rabbi). *Pirqe de Rabbi Eliezer.* Translation of G. FRIEDLANDER. London, 1916.
EN-NADIM. *Fihrist.*
EPSTEIN, A. *Eldad ha-Dani* (*La lettre d'Eldad sur les dix Tribus*). Paris, 1892.
EUSEBIUS. *Vita Constantii.* Paris, 1844–64.
———. *De Laude Constantii,* in *Church History,* ed. HEINICHEN, Vol. III. Leipzig, 1870.
EUTING, J. *Tagebuch einer Reise in Inner-Arabien.* Leiden, 1896–1914.
EWALD, H. *Journal of Missionary Labor in the City of Jerusalem.* London, 1904.

FEATHERMAN, A. *The Aramaeans.* Boston, 1881.
FEHRLE, E. "Das Sieb im Volksglaube," *ARW,* XIX (1916–1917), 547–551.

FELDMAN, W. M. *The Jewish Child.* London, 1913.
FRAZER, SIR J. G. *Adonis, Attis and Osiris*[2]. London, 1907.
———. *The Golden Bough*[3]. London, 1911–15.
———. *The Magic Art and the Evolution of Kings.* London, 1911.
———. *The Belief in Immortality and the Worship of the Dead.* London, 1913.
———. *Folk-lore in the Old Testament.* London, 1919.
———. "The Origin of Circumcision," *IR,* IV (1904), 204–218.

GARNETT, L. M. *The Women of Turkey and Their Folk-lore.* London, 1890–91.
GAUDEFROY-DEMOMBYNES, M. *Les Cérémonies du Marriage chez les Indigènes de l'Algérie.* Paris, 1901.
GESENIUS, H. F. W.–BUHL, F. *Hebräisches und aramäisches Handwörterbuch über das Alte Testament*[17]. Leipzig, 1921.
GHOSN-EL-HOWIE. "The Evil Eye," *PEF* (1904), pp. 148–150.
GINZBERG, L. *Legends of the Jews.* Philadelphia, 1909–1938.
GOLDZIHER, I. *Muhammedanische Studien.* Halle, 1889–90.
———. "Le culte des ancêtres et le culte des morts chez les arabes," *RHR,* X (1884), 332–359.
———. "Le Sacrifice de la chevelure chez les Arabes," *RHR,* XIV (1886), 49–52.
———. "Eisen als Schutz gegen Dämonen," *ARW,* X (1907), 41–46.
———. "Wasser, als Dämonen abwehrendes Mittel," *ARW,* XIII (1910), 20–46.
GOLLANCZ, SIR H. *The Book of Protection.* London, 1912.
GOODRICH-FREER, A. *Arabs in Tent and Town.* London, 1924.
GRANQUIST, H. N. *Birth and Childhood among the Arabs.* Helsingfors, 1947.
GRANT, E. *The Peasantry of Palestine.* New York, 1907.
GRESSMANN, H. "Die Haartracht der Israeliten," in *Festschrift für Karl Budde.* Giessen, 1920. Pp. 61–68.
GRIMME, H. *Das israelitische Pfingstfest und der Pleiadenkult.* Padeborn, 1907.
GRÜNBAUM, M. "Beiträge zur vergleichenden Mythologie aus der Hagada," *ZDMG,* XXXI (1877), 359 ff.
GRÜNEISEN, K. *Der Ahnenkultus und die Urreligion Israels.* Halle a.S., 1900.
GUNKEL, H. *Genesis*[2], in Nowack, *Handkommentar zum Alten Testament.* Göttingen, 1902.
———. "Ägyptische Parallelen zum Alten Testament," *ZDMG,* LXIII (1909), 531–539.
GUYS, P. M. F. H. *Voyage en Syrie.* Paris, 1855.

HADDAD, E. N. "Die Blutrache in Palästina," *ZDPV,* XI (1917), 225–235; English translation in *JPOS,* I (1921), 103–112.
———. "Methods of Education and Correction among the Fellaḥin," *JPOS,* III (1923), 41–44.
HAEFELI, L. *Die Beduinen von Beerseba.* Lucerne, 1938.
HAMILTON, T. *Antar, A Bedoueen Romance.* London, 1820.
HANAUER, J. E. *Tales Told in Palestine.* Cincinnati and New York, 1904.
———. "Palestinian Animal Folk-Lore," *PEF* (1904), pp. 265–274.
———. *The Folk-Lore of the Holy Land.* London, 1907.
HARDY, E. J. *The Unvarying East.* New York, 1912.
HARPER, R. F. *Assyrian and Babylonian Letters Belonging to the Kouyunjik Collection of the British Museum.* Chicago and London, 1892–1914.

HARTLAND, E. S. "Concerning the Rite in the Temple of Mylitta," in *Anthropological Essays Presented to Edward Burnett Tylor.* Oxford, 1907.

———. *Primitive Paternity.* London, 1909.

HARTMANN, R. "Volksglaube und Volksbrauch in Palästina," *ARW,* XV (1912), 137–152.

HAUPT, P. "The Etymology of Mohel, 'Circumciser,'" *Hebraica,* III (1905), 249–256.

———. "Midian and Sinai," *ZDMG,* LXIII (1909), 506–530.

HEHN, J. *Siebenzahl und Sabbath bei den Babyloniern und im Alten Testament.* Leipzig, 1907.

HESS, J. J. "Beduinisches zum alten und neuen Testament," *ZAW* (1915).

HOLZINGER, H. *Genesis,* in Marti, *Kurzer Handkommentar zum Alten Testament.* Freiburg, 1898.

———. *Exodus,* in *ibid.* Tübingen, 1900.

HOSKINS, G. A. *Travels in Ethiopia.* Leiden, 1815.

HURGRONJE, C. SNOUCK. *Mekka.* The Hague, 1888–89.

HUXLEY, H. M. "Syrian Songs, Proverbs and Stories," *JAOS,* XXIII (1902), 175–288.

IRBY, C. L., and MANGLES, J. *Travels in Egypt and Nubia, Syria and the Holy Land.* London, 1847.

JACOB, G. *Altarabisches Beduinenleben.* Berlin, 1897.

JASTROW, MARCUS. *A Dictionary of the Targumim, the Talmud Babli and Yerushalmi and the Midrashic Literature.* London and New York, 1886–1903.

JASTROW, MORRIS, JR. *Die Religion Babyloniens und Assyriens.* Giessen, 1905–12.

———. "Older Elements in the Code of Hammurabi," *JAOS,* XXXVI (1916), 1–33.

———. "An Assyrian Law Code," *JAOS,* XLI (1921), 1–59.

JAUSSEN, J. A. *Coutumes des Arabes au pays de Moab.* Paris, 1908.

———. *Naplouse.* Paris, 1927.

———. "Le cheikh Saʿad Ad-Din et les djinn à Naplouse," *JPOS,* III (1923), 145–157.

JAUSSEN, J. A., and SAVIGNAC, R. *Coutumes des Fuqarâ.* Paris, 1914.

JENNINGS-BRAMLEY, W. E. "The Bedouin of the Sinaitic Peninsula," *PEF* (1907), pp. 22–33, 131–137, 279–284.

JENSEN, P. *Assyrisch-Babylonische Mythen und Epen,* in *Keilinschriftliche Bibliothek,* Vol. VI, No. 1. Berlin, 1900.

JEREMIAS, A. *Die babylonisch-assyrischen Vorstellungen von Leben nach dem Tode.* Leipzig, 1887.

JIRKU, A. *Die Dämonen und ihre Abwehr im Alten Testament.* Leipzig, 1912.

———. *Materialien zur Volksreligion Israels.* Leipzig, 1914.

JOHNSON, F. E. "Here and There in Northern Africa," *NGM,* XXV (1914), 1–132.

KAHLE, P. "Gebräuche bei den moslemischen Heiligtümern in Palästina," *PJB,* VIII (1912), 139–178.

———. "Die Totenklage im heutigen Aegypten," in *Festschrift für Hermann Gunkel.* Göttingen, 1923.

KEANE, J. F. T. *Six Months in Meccah.* London, 1881.

KELLY, W. K. *Syria and the Holy Land.* London, 1844.

KENNETT, A. *Bedouin Justice; Laws and Customs among the Egyptian Bedouin.* Cambridge, 1925.

KING, L. W. *Babylonian Magic and Sorcery.* London, 1896.

KLEIN, F. A. "Mitteilungen über Leben, Sitte und Gebräuche der Fellachen in Palästina," *ZDPV,* VI (1883), 81–101.

KLIPPEL, E. *Études sur le Folklore Bedouin de l'Egypte.* Cairo, 1911.
KLUNZINGER, E. *Upper Egypt, Its People and Products.* New York, 1878.
KOEHLER, L.–BAUMGARTNER, W. *Lexicon in Veteris Testamenti Libros.* Leiden, 1953.
KOHLER, K. "Seltsame Vorstellungen und Bräuche in der biblischen und rabbinischen Literatur," *ARW,* XIII (1910), 75–84.
———. *Jewish Theology.* New York, 1928.
KRAUSS, S. *Talmudische Archäologie.* Leipzig, 1910–12.
———. "Childbirth," *JE,* IV (1903), 28–31.

DE LAGARDE, P. A. *Übersicht über die im Aramäischen übliche Bildung der Nomina.* Göttingen, 1889.
LAGRANGE, M. J. *Études sur les Religions semitiques*[2]. Paris, 1905.
VON LANDBERG, C. *Critica Arabica.* Leiden, 1886.
LANE, E. W. *An Arabic-English Lexicon.* London and Edinburgh, 1863–1889.
———. *Arabian Society in the Middle Ages.* London, 1883.
———. *The Manners and Customs of the Modern Egyptians*[3]. London, 1890.
LANGDON, S. H. *Tammuz and Ishtar.* Oxford, 1914.
———. *The Epic of Creation.* Oxford, 1923.
LAUTERBACH, J. Z. "The Ceremony of Breaking a Glass at Weddings," *HUCA,* II (1925), 352–380.
LAYARD, A. H. *Niniveh and Its Remains.* New York, 1849.
LEARY, L. G. *The Real Palestine of Today.* New York, 1911.
LEES, ROBINSON. *The Witness of the Wilderness.*
LEO AFRICANUS. *Africae Descriptio.* Leiden, 1632.
LE STRANGE, G. *Palestine under the Moslems.* Boston and New York, 1890.
LEVY, J. *Neuhebräisches und chaldäisches Wörterbuch.* Leipzig, 1876–1889.
LEVY, L. G. *La Famille dans l'Antiquité Israélite.* Paris, 1905.
LEWY, J. and H. "The Origin of the Week and the Oldest West Asiatic Calendar," *HUCA,* XVII (1942–43), 1–152*c*.
LIDZBARSKI, M. *Handbuch der nordsemitischen Epigraphik nebst ausgewählten Inschriften.* Weimar, 1898.
LINDNER, S. "Die Passahfeier der Samaritaner auf dem Berge Garizim," *PJB,* VIII (1912), 104–120.
LITTMANN, E. "Sternensagen und Astrologisches aus Nordabessinien," *ARW,* XI (1908), 298–319.
LODS, A. *Le Culte des Ancêtres dans l'Antiquité hébraique.* Paris, 1906.
———. *La Croyance à la Vie Future et le Culte des Morts dans l'Antiquité israélite.* Paris, 1906.
LOFTUS, W. K. *Travels and Researches in Chaldaea and Susiana.* New York, 1857.
LOISY, A. *The Religion of Israel.* New York, 1910.
LUCIAN OF SAMOSATA. *De Dea Syria.* TOOKE's translation. London, 1820.
LUNCZ, A. M. *The Customs of Our Brethren in the Holy Land* (Hebrew). *Jerusalem,* I (1886).
LYALL, C. *Translations of Ancient Arabian Poetry.* London, 1885.

MAHLER, E. "Der Sabbat, seine etymologische und chronologischhistorische Bedeutung," *ZDMG,* LXII (1908), 33–79.
VON MALTZAN, H. *Meine Wallfahrt nach Mekka.* Leipzig, 1865.
———. *Reisen in Arabien.* Braunschweig, 1873.

MANN, J. "Rabbinic Studies in the Synoptic Gospels," *HUCA*, I (1924), 323–355.

MARGOLIOUTH, D. S. "Circumcision, Muhammedan," *ERE*, III, 677 f.

MARTI, KARL. *Geschichte der israelitischen Religion*[4]. Strassburg, 1903.

MASTERMAN. "Jewish Customs of Birth, Marriage and Death," *BW*, XXII (1903), 248–257.

MATTHES, J. C. "De Besnijdenis," *TT*, VI (1907), 163–191.

MEHREN, A. F. *Manuel de la Cosmographie du Moyen Age.* Copenhagen, 1874.

MEINHOLD, J. *Sabbath und Woche im Alten Testament.* Göttingen, 1905.

———. "Indogermanen in Kanaan," in *Festschrift für Wolf Wilhelm Grafen von Baudissin.* Giessen, 1918.

MEISSNER, B. *Supplement zum Assyrischen Wörterbuch.* Leiden, 1898.

MENZEL. "Ein Beitrag zur Kenntniss der Jeziden," in Grote, *Meine Vorderasienexpedition.* Leipzig, 1911.

MESHULLAM OF VOLTERRA. in Luncz, *Jerusalem*, I.

MEYER, E. *Die Israeliten und Ihre Nachbarstämme.* Halle, 1906.

MILLARD, D. *A Journal of Travels in Egypt, Arabia Petraea and the Holy Land.* New York, 1948.

MORGENSTERN, J. "The Doctrine of Sin in the Babylonian Religion," *MVAG*, III (1905).

———. "Three Hebrew Synonyms for 'to Dance,'" *JAOS*, XXXVI (1916), 321–333.

———. "The Bones of the Paschal Lamb," *JAOS*, XXXVI (1916), 146–153.

———. "Two Ancient Israelite Agricultural Festivals," *JQR* (new series), VIII (1917), 31–54.

———. "The Origin of Maṣṣoth and the Maṣṣoth Festival," *AJT*, XXI (1917), 275–293.

———. "The Three Calendars of Ancient Israel," *HUCA*, I (1924), 13–78.

———. "The Oldest Document of the Hexateuch," *HUCA*, IV (1927), 1–138.

———. "Beena Marriage (Matriarchat) in Ancient Israel," *ZAW*, VI (1929), 91–110.

———. "Supplementary Studies in the Calendars of Ancient Israel," *HUCA*, X (1935), 1–143.

———. "The Chanukkah Festival and the Calendar of Ancient Israel," *HUCA*, XXI (1948), 365–496.

———. "The Foundations of Israel's History," in *As A Mighty Stream.* Philadelphia, 1949. Pp. 3–67.

———. "The Calendar of the Book of Jubilees, Its Origin and Its Character," *VT*, V (1955), 34–76.

———. "David and Jonathan," *JBL*, LXXVIII (1959), 322–325.

———. "The 'Bloody Husband' (?) (Exod. 4:24–26) Once Again," *HUCA*, XXXIV (1963), 35–70.

MOVERS, F. C. *Die Phönizier.* Bonn, 1841–56.

MUKADDASI. *Description of Syria, including Palestine.* Translation of LE STRANGE. London, 1886.

MUSIL, A. *Arabia Petraea.* Vienna, 1907–1908.

———. *Arabia Deserta.* New York, 1927.

———. *The Manners and Customs of the Rwala Bedouins.* New York, 1928.

———. *In the Arabian Desert.* New York, 1930.

MUSTAFA NURI PASCHA. "Die Teufelanbeter," in Grote, *Meine Vorderasienexpedition.* Translation of Menzel. Leipzig, 1906–1907.

MYHRMANN, D. V. "Die Labartu Texte," *ZA*, XVI (1902), 141–200.

NEWMAN, J. P. *From Dan to Beersheba.* New York, 1864.

———. *Babylon and Niniveh.* New York, 1876.

NICHOLSON, R. A. *Studies in Islamic Poetry.* Cambridge, 1921.

NIEBUHR, C. *Reisebeschreibung nach Arabien und anderen umliegenden Ländern.* Copenhagen, 1774–1857.

NILSSON, M. *Études sur le culte d'Ishtar.*

OESTERLEY, W. O. E. *The Sacred Dance.* Cambridge, 1923.

OLIN, S. *Travels in the East.* New York, 1846.

OLIPHANT, L. *Haifa.* Edinburgh, 1887.

OLMSTEAD, A. T. E. *History of Assyria.* New York and London, 1928.

OORT, H. "De doodenvereering bij de Israeliten," *TT,* XV (1881), 350–363.

VON OPPENHEIM, M. "Der Tell Halaf und die Verschleierte Göttin," *AO,* X, I (1909), 24–28.

OSBORN, H. S. *Palestine, Past and Present.* Philadelphia, 1859.

PALMER, E. H. *The Desert of the Exodus.* New York, 1872.

PARKYNS, M. *Life in Abyssinia.* London, 1853.

PATON, L. B. *Spiritism and the Cult of the Dead in Antiquity.* New York, 1921.

PEDERSEN, J. *Der Eid bei den Semiten.* Strassburg, 1914.

PERLES, F. "Die Leichenfeierlichkeiten im nachbiblischen Judentum," *MGWJ,* X (1861), 376–394.

PERRY, C. *The Pilgrim in Jerusalem.*

PETERMANN, J. H. *Reisen im Orient*[2]. Leipzig, 1865.

PETERS, J. P. *The Religion of the Hebrews.* Boston, 1914.

PETRIE, W. M. F. *Researches in Sinai.* New York, 1906.

PIEROTTI, E. *Traditions and Beliefs of Palestine.*

———. *Customs and Traditions of Palestine.* Cambridge, 1864.

PLOSS, H. H. *Das Kind in Brauch und Sitte der Völker.* Stuttgart, 1876.

———. *Das Weib in Natur- und Völkerkunde.* Leipzig, 1902.

POCOCKE, E. *Travels,* in *A Compendium of the Most Approved Modern Travels,* Vol. II. Dublin, 1757.

POEBEL, A. *Babylonian Legal and Business Documents from the Time of the First Dynasty of Babylon, Chiefly from Nippur.* Philadelphia, 1909.

PORTER, J. L. *The Giant Cities of Bashan.* New York, 1884.

PRIME, W. C. *Tent Life in the Holy Land.* New York, 1857.

RANKIN, O. S. *The Origins of the Festival of Hanukkah: The Jewish New-Age Festival.* Edinburgh, 1930.

RASSAM, H. *Assur and the Land of Nimrod.* Cincinnati, 1907.

RASWAN, C. *The Black Tents of Arabia.* New York, 1947.

RATHJENS, K. *Die Juden in Abessinien.* Hamburg, 1921.

RICHTER. "Zwei alttestamentliche Studien: I, Der Blutbräutigam," *ZAW,* XXXIX (1922).

ROBINSON, E. *Biblical Researches in Palestine, Mt. Sinai and Arabia.* Boston, 1841.

ROTHSTEIN, G. "Moslemische Hochzeitsgebräuche," *PJB* (1910), 103–126.

RUTTER, E. *The Holy Cities of Arabia.* London, 1928.

SALE, G. *The Koran, Preliminary Discourse.* London, 1885.
SAMTER, E. *Folk-Lore in the Holy Land.*
———. *Geburt, Hochzeit und Tod.* Leipzig, 1911.
———. "Die Bedeutung des Beschneidungsritus und Verwandtes," *Philologus,* LXII.
SANCHUNIATHON, in Cory, *Ancient Fragments.* London, 1876. Pp. 1–21.
SCHAFF, P., and WACE, H. *A Select Library of Nicene and Post-Nicene Fathers of the Christian Church.* New York, 1890–1904.
SCHEFTELOWITZ, I. *Die altpersische Religion und das Judentum.* Giessen, 1920.
———. *Alt-Palästinensischer Bauernglaube.* Hanover, 1925.
———. "Das Fischsymbol in Judentum und Christentum," *ARW,* XIV (1911), 1–53, 321–392.
———. "Das Stellvertretende Huhnopfer," in *Religionsgeschichtliche Versuche und Vorarbeiten.* 1911.
———. "Die Sündentilgung durch Wasser," *ARW,* XVII (1914), 353–412.
———. "Der Seelen- und Unsterblichkeitsglaube im Alten Testament," *ARW,* XIX (1916), 210–232.
———. "Das Opfer der roten Kuh," *ZAW,* XXXIX (1921), 113–123.
SCHMIDT, H., and KAHLE, P. "Volkserzählungen aus Palästina," in *Forschuungen zur Religion und Literatur des Alten und Neuen Testaments.* Göttingen, 1918.
SCHULZ, C. G. in Paulus, *Sammlung der merkwürdigsten Reisen in den Orient.* Jena, 1794–1801.
SCHWALLY, F. *Das Leben nach dem Tode.* Giessen, 1892.
———. *Semitische Kriegsaltertümer.* Leipzig, 1901.
———. *Aegyptica* ("Orientalische Studien Th. Nöldeke zum 70ten Geburtstag gewidmet," ed. C. BEZOLD). Giessen, 1906.
SCHWARZ, J. *Das heilige Land.* Frankfurt a.M., 1852.
SELDEN, J. *De Dis Syris Syntagmata.* Leipzig, 1864.
SICARD, P. C. in Paulus, *Sammlung der merkwürdigsten Reisen in den Orient,* Vol. V. Jena, 1794–1801.
R. SIMCHA OF SOLSITZ. *Doresh Zion,* ed. HAUSDORFF. Jerusalem, 1887.
SKINNER, J. *A Critical and Exegetical Commentary on Genesis.* New York, 1910.
SMEND, R. *Lehrbuch der alttestamentlichen Religionsgeschichte*[2]. Freiburg, 1893.
SMITH, H. P. *The Religion of Israel.* New York, 1914.
———. "Notes on the Red Heifer," *JBL,* XXVII (1908), 153–156.
SMITH, W. ROBERTSON. *Kinship and Marriage in Early Arabia*[2]. London, 1903.
———. *Lectures on the Religion of the Semites*[3]. London, 1903.
SOCIN, A. *Islamischer Diwan.*
———. *Diwan aus Centralarabien.* Leipzig, 1900.
SOCRATES. *Historia Ecclesia.* New York, 1890.
SOZOMEN. *Historia Ecclesia.* New York, 1890.
SPENCER, H. *Principles of Sociology.* New York, 1896–97.
STADE, B. "Das Kainzeichen," in *Akademische Reden.* Leipzig, 1877.
STEPHEN, S. H. "The Division of the Year in Palestine," *JPOS,* II (1922), 159–170.
———. "Lunacy in Palestine," *JPOS,* V (1925), 1–16.
———. "Studies in Palestinian Customs and Folk-lore," *JPOS,* VIII (1928), 214–222.
STEVENS, MRS. E. S. *Folk-Tales of Iraq.* London, 1931.
SUMNER, W. G. *Folkways.* Boston, 1906.

Thomas, B. *Arabia Felix.* New York, 1932.
Thompson, R. C. *The Devils and Evil Spirits of Babylonia.* London, 1904.
———. *Semitic Magic.* London, 1908.
Thomson, W. M. *The Land and the Book*[1]. New York, 1859.
Thonnelier, J. *Le Livre des Dames de la Perse.* Paris, 1881.
Tobler, T. *Topographie von Jerusalem und seinen Umgebungen.* Berlin, 1853–54.
Toy, C. H. *Introduction to the History of Religions.* Boston, 1913.
Trachtenberg, J. *Jewish Magic and Superstition.* New York, 1939.
Trumbull, H. C. *The Threshold Covenant.* New York, 1896.
———. *Studies in Oriental Social Life.* Philadelphia, 1907.
Trumelet, C. *Les Francais dans le Desert*[2]. Paris, 1863.
Tylor, E. B. *Primitive Culture*[3]. London, 1891.

Ungnad, A. *Das Gilgameš-Epos.* Göttingen, 1911.
Usama ibn Munkidh. *Memoiren.* Translation of Schumann.

Valerius Maximus. in Selden, *De Dis Syris Syntagmata.* Lipsiae, 1662.
Vincent, L. H. *Canaan d'après l'Exploration récente.* Paris, 1907.
Volney, C. F. C. *Travels through Egypt and Syria.* New York, 1790.

Wad-el-Ward, G. *Palestine through the Eyes of a Native.* New York, 1907.
Wansleb, J. M. in Paulus, *Sammlung der merkwürdisten Reisen in den Orient,* Vol. III. Jena, 1794–1801.
Waser, O. "Ueber die äussere Erscheinung der Seele," *ARW,* XVI (1913), 336–388.
Webster, H. *Rest Days.* New York, 1916.
Wellhausen, J. "Die Ehe bei den Arabern," *GGN,* XI (1893), 431–481.
———. *Reste des altarabischen Heidentums*[2]. Berlin, 1897.
———. *Die Composition des Hexateuchs*[3]. Berlin, 1899.
———. *Prologomena zur Geschichte Israels*[6]. Berlin, 1905.
Wellsted, J. R. *Travels in Arabia.* German translation by Roediger. Halle, 1842.
Westermarck, E. *Marriage Ceremonies in Morocco.* London, 1914.
———. *History of Human Marriage*[5]. London, 1921.
———. *Ritual and Belief in Morocco.* London, 1926.
Wetzstein. "Sprachliches aus den Zeltlagern der syrischen Wüste," *ZDMG,* XX (1868), 69–194.
Whiting, C. T. "Village Life in the Holy Land," *NGM* (1914).
Wilson, C. T. *Peasant Life in the Holy Land.* London, 1906.
Wright, T. *Early Travels in Palestine.* London, 1848.

Zacharias of Mitylene. *Syrian Chronicle.* London, 1899.
Zimmern, H. *Ritualtafeln.*
Zimmern, H., and Winckler, H. *Die Keilinschriften und das Alte Testament*[3]. Berlin, 1903.
Zuckermandel, M. S. *Tosefta Šabbat.* Frankfurt a.M., 1908–1909.
Zwemer, S. M. *Arabia the Cradle of Islam.* New York, 1900.

Index of Biblical Passages

Index to the Book